Jewish Perspectives
on Christianity

Jewish Perspectives on Christianity

Leo Baeck, Martin Buber,
Franz Rosenzweig, Will Herberg,
and Abraham J. Heschel

Edited by FRITZ A. ROTHSCHILD

CONTINUUM • NEW YORK

1996

The Continuum Publishing Company
370 Lexington Avenue
New York, NY 10017

Printed in the United States of America

Library of Congress Cataloging-in-Publication Data

Jewish perspectives on Christianity / Fritz A. Rothschild, editor.
    p. cm.
    Includes biliographical references and index.
    ISBN 0-8264-0895-8 (pbk. : alk. paper)
    1. Judaism—Relations—Christianity. 2. Christianity and other
religions—Judaism. 3. Judaism—20th century. I. Rothschild,
Fritz A.
BM535.J465   1996
296.3'872—dc20   96-21216
                                                        CIP

Acknowledgments will be found on pages 357–359, which constitute an extension of the copyright page.

To my wife Lotte
and
to the memory of my mother
Bella Rothschild
born in Bad Homburg v.d.H.
10 May 1884
deported from Frankfurt am Main to Lodz
19 October 1941
and
murdered in Auschwitz

Contents

Preface ix

General Introduction by Fritz A. Rothschild 1

I. Leo Baeck (1873–1956)

Introduction by J. Louis Martyn 21

1 Harnack's Lectures on the Essence of Christianity (1901) 42

2 Mystery and Commandment (1921/22) 46

3 Romantic Religion (1922, 1938) 56

4 Judaism in the Church (1925) 92

II. Martin Buber (1878–1965)

Introduction by Ekkehard W. Stegemann 111

1 The Two Foci of the Jewish Soul (1930) 122

2 Church, State, Nation, Jewry (1933) 132

3 Two Types of Faith (1950) 143

4 On Concluding the Translation of the Bible (1964) 154

III. Franz Rosenzweig (1886–1929)

Introduction by Bernhard Casper 159

1 Selections from the Letters 169
 To Rudolf Ehrenberg (October 31, 1913) 169
 To Rudolf Ehrenberg (November 4, 1913) 172
 To Eugen Rosenstock (October 1916) 174

To Eugen Rosenstock (November 7–9, 1916)   179
To Gertrud Oppenheim (May 1, 1917)   185

2   The Star of Redemption (1921):   187
The Rays or the Eternal Way   187
The Star or the Eternal Truth   204

3   A Note on Anthropomorphism (1928)   227

4   The Significance of the Bible in World History (1929)   229

IV. Will Herberg (1901–1977)

Introduction by Bernhard W. Anderson   235

1   Judaism and Christianity: Their Unity and Difference (1952)   240

2   A Jew Looks at Jesus (1966)   256

V. Abraham J. Heschel (1907–1972)

Introduction by John C. Merkle   267

1   More Than Inwardness (1955)   278

2   A Hebrew Evaluation of Reinhold Niebuhr (1956)   283

3   Protestant Renewal: A Jewish View (1963)   301

4   No Religion Is an Island (1965)   309

5   The Jewish Notion of God and Christian Renewal (1967)   325

Bibliography   341

Supplementary Bibliography for the Paperback Edition   352

Sources and Acknowledgments   357

Contributors   361

Index   363

Preface

When first I embarked on the project of collecting and editing the writings on Christianity by Leo Baeck, Martin Buber, Franz Rosenzweig, Will Herberg, and Abraham J. Heschel, I intended to write the introduction to each author's selections myself. But it then occurred to me that the cause of true Jewish-Christian dialogue would best be served if each introductory essay could be written by a Christian theologian reacting to the Jewish critique of Christianity from the standpoint of a committed Christian.

This required five Christian theologians with established scholarly reputations in their own field of specialization, who also possess a thorough knowledge of the Jewish thinker whom they were to introduce. I chose four such scholars who were well known to me personally and one (Bernhard Casper of Freiburg in Germany) whom I had come to know through his writings. I invited their participation and asked them not only to write the usual expository essay, but to offer their own critical comment in a twofold manner: Where they disagreed with the Jewish author's critique of Christianity, they ought to state their disagreement without hesitation, and where they saw merit in his critique, they should indicate how this change in outlook might modify the Church's self-understanding and influence its future relationship to Judaism and the Jewish people.

I was gratified that all five theologians responded positively to my unusual request. I wish to thank Professors J. Louis Martyn, Ekkehard W. Stegemann, Bernhard Casper, Bernhard W. Anderson, and John C. Merkle for their pioneering effort in this field of Judeo-Christian "mutuality." I hope that this modest but novel enterprise will stimulate other attempts in this direction.

The five authors whose work is presented here did not always use the same method of transliteration for Hebrew words, and I have not attempted to achieve complete uniformity in this matter. Thus, for example, the reader may find the word *"halakhah"* (law) sometimes spelled *halacha, halachah,* or *halaka.*

I want to express my thanks to Frank Oveis, who not only was my editor when this book first appeared but has undertaken to see the present paperback edition with its updated bibliography through the press.

I want to thank those who translated material for this volume from the German: Dr. Elizabeth Petuchowski and my former students, Dr. Robert Schine and Bernard Barsky. My sincere thanks also go to Professor William W. Hallo of Yale University, who graciously gave permission to use his translations of Rosenzweig and Buber. I hope that where I have made revisions, I have caused no "disimprovements"!

I want to express my appreciation to Chancellor Ismar Schorsch and former Provost Raymond P. Scheindlin for the support provided for my research by the Jewish Theological Seminary. During the years 1986–1988 they facilitated summer stipends from the Seminary's Maxwell Abbell Research Fund, which I gratefully acknowledge herewith. And finally, I wish to thank my wife, Lotte, who not only assisted with the task of proofreading, but whose patience, love, and gentle but persistent prodding made possible the planning and completion of this volume.

General Introduction

by Fritz A. Rothschild

I

For Christianity, Judaism itself and the continuing existence of the Jews have both posed a theological problem. For Judaism, however, Christianity, with its claim to be the "true" Israel, has figured as a marginal theological problem at best, which could be explained away or ignored. But, as a politically empowered religion of the majority, it has been a constant challenge and frequently even a threat to the very survival of the Jewish people.

When a Catholic theologian living in Jerusalem and known for his knowledge of Judaism was asked by fellow Christians, "What do Jews think about Jesus?" his laconic answer was "Nothing at all!"[1] It was and still is not unusual for Jews to go through life, studying and practicing their own religion without ever evincing any interest in or knowledge of Christianity. But for over a millennium no European Jew could avoid the question: How can I, a member of a vulnerable and frequently despised minority, survive in a society made up of Christians and ruled by laws and principles largely derived from Christian teachings?

In 1824 young Heinrich Heine, under the shock of reading the enumeration of Jewish sufferings in Basnage's *History of the Jewish Religion from Jesus Christ to the Present* (1707) wrote his little poem, *An Edom* ("To Edom," i.e., the "Christian" brother of Jacob, the Jew):

> Have we not endured each other
> As true brothers through the ages?

---

[1] See R. J. Zwi Werblowsky, "Reflections on Martin Buber's *Two Types of Faith,*" *Journal of Jewish Studies* 39, no. 1 (Spring 1988): 94.

You endured that I kept breathing,
I endured your manic rages.[2]

Let us at this point confine our examination to the relationship between the two religions and disregard the relationship between the two communities. It is clear that Judaism and Christianity are not related to each other symmetrically. Christianity depends on and cannot be understood without the Judaism from which it emerged. Not only were Jesus and his disciples believing Jews, but the very essence of Christianity is firmly grounded in its Jewish heritage. Only where the faith of Israel and its Holy Scriptures (the "Hebrew Bible") are accepted as true and valid can the claim be made that in the life, death, and resurrection of Jesus of Nazareth, the promises of God have been fulfilled. Even doctrinal changes made — from Paul's repudiation of the "Law" to Luther's *sola fide, sola gratia* (only through faith and grace) — are understandable only as *reactions* to parts of the Jewish heritage with which Christianity stands in an ongoing adversarial relationship, and without which it would be unable to define itself. Constant accusations that the church is too "judaic" and needs to recover its true character have been made by theologians from Paul (against Peter), and Augustine (against Pelagius) to Luther (against the Roman Catholic Church). This "asymmetry" between Judaism and Christianity has been accepted by many competent students of comparative religion.[3]

To sum up: conscientious Christians cannot evade answering the question: What think you of Judaism?, but Jews can relate to their fellow Christians without having to answer the question: What think you of Christianity? Just as they can deal with Hindus, Navajos, and Buddhists whom they encounter in the course of their daily life, they can do likewise in their dealings with Christians.

Yet, having stated all this, it seems to me that at this hour in history Jews can no longer afford to treat Christianity with the benign neglect of past generations. Apart from such historical facts as the Holocaust and the crisis of religious faith in the postmodern world, we now face a situation where Christians are, perhaps for the first time, ready to listen to what Jews have to say, and are ready for a fruitful dialogue instead of turning such encounters into occasions for missionary propaganda or mere apologetics.

The first and last selections in this volume can illustrate the change

---

[2]My translation.
[3]Cf. the concise articulation of this point by R. J. Zwi Werblowsky, "Tora als Gnade," *Kairos* 15, no. 1–4 (1973): 157.

that has occurred between the beginning of this century and the decade after the Second Vatican Council.

(1) In the winter semester 1899/1900, Adolf Harnack, the prominent Protestant scholar, delivered the lectures on the Essence of Christianity (English title: *What Is Christianity?*) that became one of the most widely read theological books of the century. It elicited both enthusiastic acclaim and sharp condemnation after its appearance in 1900. But in the spirited controversy of the time hardly anyone paid attention to a critical review, written by a young and unknown rabbi, Leo Baeck, in a Jewish scholarly journal in 1901. In fact, part of it is being made available in English for the first time in the present volume.

(2) But when Abraham Heschel spoke on "the Jewish Notion of God and the Renewal of the Church" in August, 1967, it was at the invitation of the church and before the Catholic Congress on the Renewal of the Church in Toronto. He addressed an audience that included members of the hierarchy, theologians, religious, priests, and laity from many countries. Delivered two months after the Six Days' War, he made an impassioned appeal against the "desanctification of the Hebrew Bible" and the "dejudaization" of Catholicism. He urged his listeners to accept the creation of a unified Jerusalem as part of the State of Israel as "an event of high significance in the history of redemption," relating it to the disciples' question and Jesus' answer in the Book of Acts (1:6–7).

The fact that Jewish views — even of a critical nature — are now listened to and taken seriously, in a way they were not at the beginning of this century, is certainly encouraging. But the present state of affairs can be properly understood only if we remember the way in which Jewish-Christian confrontations and debates were conducted in the past. Every Jewish writer is in some way aware of what it meant to engage in a critique of Christianity or even the most circumspect attempt to defend Judaism against attacks by the dominant faith that saw the refutation of Judaism and the conversion of the Jews as an integral part of its divinely ordained mission.

I shall present only two examples of this phenomenon, one from medieval Spain and the other from Germany in the age of the Enlightenment.

(1) Beginning on July 20, 1263, there took place at the royal palace, the cathedral, and the main synagogue of Barcelona a series of debates ordered by King James of Aragon. The Jewish apostate Fra Pablo (Paul) Christiani, supported by Raymond Peñaforte, the venerable eighty-seven-year-old former general of the Dominican order, was to prove the truth of Christianity against Moses ben Naḥman (Nahmanides), rabbi of Gerona and outstanding talmudist, Bible commentator, theologian,

3

and kabbalist. Pablo undertook to demonstrate from the Jews' own Talmud that the messiah had come, that he had been God Incarnate and a member of the Trinity, and, in addition, that the Jewish ceremonial laws had been abolished.

Naḥmanides was somewhat restricted in his rebuttal by the rule that "the faith of the Lord Jesus Christ cannot, because of its certainty, be placed under dispute." When he asked that a day be set aside when *he* could ask questions, the request was refused by the King. The disputation was followed by anti-Jewish royal decrees and laws forcing Jews to listen to missionary sermons held in local synagogues. The book on "Judges" (*Shofetim*), the last part of Maimonides' Code, was to be burned because of its blasphemies.[4]

In 1265 the king ordered the banishment of Naḥmanides from Aragon for two years and the suppression of his report, and in 1266 or 1267 Pope Clement IV urged the king to punish the Jewish scholar more severely. Naḥmanides decided to leave Spain and emigrated to Palestine, where he died a few years later.[5]

(2) In 1763, five hundred years after the Disputation of Barcelona, a young Protestant preacher, Johann Caspar Lavater from Switzerland, visited Moses Mendelssohn in Berlin. Mendelssohn had made the transition from the medieval ghetto to the world of modern enlightenment when he had moved from his native town of Dessau to Berlin, where he had become the symbol of the new age of universal culture, tolerance, and human brotherhood. Without systematic training he had acquired a wide range of knowledge and had written books and essays on metaphysics, moral philosophy, aesthetics, and literary criticism in a felicitous German style that had gained him universal acclaim. He was hailed as the Socrates of his age who impressed everyone with his integrity, benevolence, and literary talent, while at the same time displaying loyalty to his ancestral religion and scrupulously observing its commandments.

In 1769 Diaconus Lavater had translated parts of a book by the Geneva professor Charles Bonnet, the *Palingénésie*, into German. This volume was an attempt to prove the truth of Christianity, and Lavater addressed the dedicatory epistle to "Herr Moses Mendelssohn in Berlin," challenging him either publicly to refute the author's proofs in support of Christianity or to accept baptism.

It is noteworthy that after many decades of anticlerical writings, at the height of European Enlightenment when Voltaire was the mentor of

---

[4]Part of the offending passage on Jesus can be found in this volume, below, pp. 187–188.
[5]See Salo W. Baron, *A Social and Religious History of the Jews*, vol. 9, 2d ed. (New York: Columbia University Press, 1965), 83–87.

Frederick the Great, and French *philosophes* as well as English Deists had been attacking the doctrines of the church, Mendelssohn was afraid to publish his critique of Christianity and his defense of Judaism as the more rational religion, lest he unleash a storm of anti-Jewish outbursts all over Germany. It was dangerous, Mendelssohn asserted, for a member of an oppressed people to dispute with the majority religion. Trying to act with dignity and tact on behalf of Judaism, without offending Christians, he had to walk a tightrope. Despite his repeated efforts to settle the dispute, the affair dragged on and led to a number of attacks by pamphleteers and rabble-rousers. Although his literary friends and admirers were pained and embarrassed, he hardly found anyone to come to his defense in public.

Mendelssohn's friend, the book dealer and author Nicolai, stated years later that the tension of the Lavater affair and its aftermath had affected his health and had led to the severe chronic illness that resulted in his premature death.[6]

About two hundred years later, Abraham Heschel (after the massacre of eleven Israeli athletes and trainers by a Palestinian terrorist team at the Munich Olympics in 1972) asked his Christian friends in the Vietnam Peace Movement to sign a declaration condemning the atrocity. Since many refused, the statement was never published, and the experience saddened the last three months of his life.

II

We ought to bear in mind that only after the horrors of the Holocaust became widely known did the Christian churches evince genuine interest in contemporary Jews and Judaism. In the past, Judaism had been widely studied as the historical background and the theological foil for primitive Christianity. Observant Jews were often regarded as an anachronism (like the Amish) by liberal Christians. To many orthodox and neo-Orthodox Christians they symbolized the ghost-like community of "the Synagogue," illustrating to the faithful the sad fate of those who had willfully rejected the Savior who had been sent for their redemption.

Let it be frankly stated that the shame felt by many Christians of good will after the murder of six million Jews in "Christian" Europe has been a powerful motive for much of the Christian-Jewish dialogue since the end of the Second World War. And the fear of another such

---

[6]See Alexander Altmann, *Moses Mendelssohn: A Biographical Study* (University of Alabama Press, 1973), 194–234.

catastrophe has been behind the worldwide determination of Jews to support the establishment and strengthening of the State of Israel, as well as the willingness to engage their Christian fellow citizens in interfaith dialogue. Guilt feelings and the need for forgiveness on the part of decent Christians and preventative therapy to be applied against the possibility of a future Holocaust on the part of many Jews have undoubtedly been important motives for dialogue between the communities during the last four decades.

But this is only part of the story. It ignores the religious dimension within which committed Jews ought to deal with the basic problem of their relationship to Christianity and Christians. It is my conviction that despite the asymmetry between the two religions a new relationship is developing which, for want of a better term, I shall call "mutuality." The five Jewish thinkers represented in this volume and the five Christian theologians who wrote the individual introductory essays have made important contributions to this stage of mutuality.

Let me point out at least three reasons, largely based on their work, that can impel thoughtful Jews to concern themselves with Christianity and to confront it in a serious manner, both critically and sympathetically. And perhaps for similar reasons thoughtful Christians may take a fresh look at Judaism.

(1) In the first place, Christianity, like Islam, but unlike Hinduism, Buddhism and other faiths, is a daughter religion of Israel. As Heschel put it: "Judaism is the mother of the Christian faith. It has a stake in the destiny of Christianity. Should a mother ignore her child, even a wayward, rebellious one?"[7]

(2) In the second place, however striking the differences between the two faiths seem to their own followers, "the essential similarity they exhibit becomes very striking when the two, taken together, are contrasted with the nonbiblical 'religions of the world.' In such a perspective they strike one as being virtually identical in their structure of faith."[8] Even if this somewhat overstates the case, Paul Tillich is surely right when he says that, despite the divergences of traditions, rites, symbols, organizations, doctrinal statements, and psychological attitudes, the "common elements in both [are] so strong that in comparison with other religions Judaism and Christianity belong to each other"[9]

(3) In the third place, Judaism is a religion that finds God's revelations and manifestations in history as it unfolds from creation to its messianic

---

[7]"No Religion Is an Island," below, p. 316.
[8]Will Herberg, "Judaism and Christianity," below, p. 240.
[9]Paul Tillich, "Is There a Judeo-Christian Tradition?" *Judaism* 1, no. 2 (1952): 106.

fulfillment. The rise of Christianity (a "Jewish heresy" as Tillich has called it) spread the Hebrew Bible and its message of faith in the One God and his teaching all over the globe. This process was one of the most revolutionary and fateful occurrences in world history.[10]

To assume that the transformation of the Greco-Roman world into Christendom (and Islam) was a mere accident, and not part of God's redemptive plan, is difficult to believe for Jews who take history seriously as the arena in which God and man are engaged in the achievement of ultimate redemption. It is no mere coincidence that both Rosenzweig and Heschel cite the views of Judah Halevi (ca. 1075–1141) and Maimonides (1135–1204) about the providential nature of the spread of Christianity and Islam.[11] Leo Baeck, despite his sometimes sharp strictures on Christianity as "romantic religion," chronicles the abiding role of the church as the transmitter and preserver of Judaic teachings throughout history, temporarily suppressed but always resurgent (*"Et inclinata resurget"*),[12] and Heschel turns the table on the usual view of the Old and the New Israel when he stated at his inaugural lecture at the Protestant Union Theological Seminary in New York that "leading Jewish authorities, such as Jehuda Halevi and Maimonides, acknowledge Christianity to be a *praeparatio messianica*, while the Church regarded ancient Judaism to have been a *praeparatio evangelica*."[13]

III

The views expressed by the writers in this volume are clearly presented and ought to be accepted by the reader at face value. Nevertheless, it may not be amiss to deal in these introductory remarks with a delicate point that as a rule is not mentioned in the literature on our subject. It may be true that in countries where freedom of expression is a guaranteed right, there is ostensibly no need to withhold criticism. But the after-effects of the one-sided debates and discussions that we have described earlier are still with us to some extent.

When we consider the pervasive anti-Jewish bias that until recently was characteristic in the academic treatment of the so-called intertestamental period in particular and Judaism in general, among many Christian scholars and theologians, notably those in German-speaking lands, it becomes clear that it will be helpful to explore beneath the surface of the published writings the moods and opinions that some of our authors

---

[10] See Rosenzweig, "The Significance of the Bible in World History," below, pp. 229–232.
[11] Cf. below, pp. 187–204, *The Star of Redemption*, "The Rays or the Eternal Way."
[12] Below, pp. 92–108, "Judaism in the Church."
[13] Below, p. 322, "No Religion Is an Island."

expressed only in private letters or conversations. In this section I shall try to recover some of these personal remarks to the extent that I have been able to track them down.[14] As J. Louis Martyn points out (below, p. 24), the review essay of the young Leo Baeck dealing with Harnack's lectures on the Essence of Christianity, published in 1901, shows a considerable amount of *anger* against the cavalier and tendentious treatment of pharisaic Judaism.[15] As late as 1986 Julius Schoeps at an international symposium on Jewish-Christian dialogue sponsored by the University of Duisburg asserted that a discussion on equal terms is possible only where both partners are equally powerful. This view of a sociologist need not be accepted literally to drive home the point that Jews as a minority in the Christian world do not always voice their negative views of certain aspects of Christianity without considering the possible consequences.

In addition, theologians, unlike physicists and mathematicians deal with matters that frequently touch upon the most profoundly felt values and existential convictions of their readers. The hesitancy to attack or dissect critically views that form the core of others' spiritual being is a natural attitude, most assuredly not only held by Jews, but equally to be found among Christian participants in interfaith exchanges. Jews sometimes feel that after the horrors of the Holocaust and the unjust treatment of rabbinic Judaism in modern times their fellow Christians are afraid to express their negative opinions concerning aspects of traditional Judaism because that might hurt or offend Jewish sensitivities.

The selections in this volume are for the most part forthright statements by forthright men. But the reader should be warned that not everything is always fully spelled out.

One cannot perhaps expect the kind of brutally frank outburst that we find in the exchange of letters between Franz Rosenzweig and Eugen Rosenstock-Huessy (1916), written in the trenches of the First World War and not intended for publication. Rosenzweig, the Jew, writing from the Eastern front to his friend Eugen, states that the true reason for the hatred of the Jews is that

we will not make common cause with the world-conquering fiction of Christian dogma, because (however much a fact) it *is* a fiction (and *"fiat veritas, pereat realitas"* . . . and putting it in a popular way: that we have crucified Christ, and

---

[14] For the case of Leo Baeck, see the remarks of Samuel Sandmel in his Leo Baeck Memorial Lecture no. 19, *Leo Baeck on Christianity* (New York: Leo Baeck Institute, 1975), 15–20. For Martin Buber see *Der Jude und sein Judentum,* 619f., 621–627, 216–220; and F. S. Marquardt, *Die Entdeckung des Judentums für die christliche Theologie* (Munich: Kaiser Verlag, 1967), esp. 335, note 54.

[15] Cf. the important article by G. F. Moore, "Christian Writers on Judaism," *Harvard Theological Review* 14, no. 3 (July 1921): 197–254.

believe me, would do it again, we alone in the whole world and *"fiat nomen Dei Unius, pereat homo,"* for *"*to whom will you liken me that I am like?*" [Isa. 40:25]).[16]

Of course, at about the same time (October 1916) his Christian correspondent stationed on the Western front had sent off a letter in which he expresses with similar ruthlessness his view of Judaism:

The Synagogue has been talking for two thousand years about what she has, because she really has nothing at all. . . . She portrays the curse of self-assurance, of aristocratic arrogance, and thoughtless indifference toward the law of growth of the united universe, the "Peace on Earth to all men in whom he is well pleased."[17]

But although such categorical opposition is rarely to be found in the pages of this volume, the reader ought to be aware that it exists and ought to be taken into account as part of the honest and principled Jewish-Christian theological discussion that I believe has now become not only possible, but desirable.

Leo Baeck wrote in a private letter to a fellow rabbi in 1925 that one has to make a clear choice between the two kingdoms — the earthly and the divine — and that this choice may lead to martyrdom for the sake of Heaven. He added a remark that proved prophetic eight years later:

It is a spiritual and moral disaster for Germany that many leading personalities have refused to acknowledge [the difference between] these two kingdoms and have made "Germanity" (*Deutschtum*) into a religion. Instead of believing in God, they believe — first and foremost Lutheran clergymen — in "Germanity."[18]

The best-known Jewish thinker whose writings, ideas, and personal friendship with Christian theologians and authors have had a worldwide impact from pre–World War I days until his death in 1965 was Martin Buber. In his 1930 address on "The Two Foci of the Jewish Soul," delivered in Stuttgart before a conference sponsored by organizations dedicated to convert Jews to Christianity, he stated right at the beginning that he was opposed to their cause. Two decades later in his book *Two Types of Faith*, written in 1948 during the Arab Legion's siege of Jerusalem, he expounded two contrasting kinds of religious faith, one of which according to him is basic to Judaism and the second was introduced by Paul

---

[16]Below, p. 176f, letter to Eugen Rosenstock (October 1916).

[17]Eugen Rosenstock-Huessy, ed., *Judaism Despite Christianity: The "Letters on Christianity and Judaism" between Eugen Rosenstock-Huessy and Franz Rosenzweig* (University, Ala.: University of Alabama Press, 1969), 125.

[18]"Brief an Rabbiner Dr. Cäsar Seligmann, September 2, 1925," in Eva G. Reichmann, ed., *Worte des Gedenkens für Leo Baeck* (1959), 245.

and became central for the church's doctrine of salvation.[19] The thesis of this work was sharply criticized not only by many Christian theologians, but by friends and colleagues of the author in Jerusalem such as Gershom Scholem and Hugo Bergman.

A short autobiographical statement in the foreword to the book created quite a stir: "Ever since my youth I have regarded (*empfunden*) Jesus as my great brother."[20] This confession not only disturbed many Jews — traditionalists as well as secularists — but Buber himself is said to have greatly regretted it.[21] Although many Christians were touched by this personal expression, there were exceptions. Eugen Rosenstock-Huessy, who by then had emigrated to America and was teaching at Dartmouth College, reacted sharply. In his *Soziologie* he wrote:

... the revealer [Jesus] is neither husband nor mortal man, father of the family nor uncle or brother — although Martin Buber calls him disparagingly his older [*sic*] brother.[22]

Buber's views on Jesus, Paul, Christianity ("primitive" and "orthodox"), as well as Judaism ("primitive" and "rabbinic"), are too involved to be treated in this essay.[23] But it may not be irrelevant for those who recognize the complexity and difficulties of understanding both Buber and the effects of his writing to juxtapose two incidents concerning his views on Christianity:

(1) In the early 1950s I attended a lecture of the late Professor David E. Roberts at Union Theological Seminary at which he expressed astonishment that a man with Buber's understanding and sympathy for Jesus had not converted to Christianity.

(2) On November 4, 1963, Buber's long-time friend, the poet and critic Werner Kraft, recorded a conversation in which Buber had remarked that even Jesus had not believed that the redemption had come. "That's where Paul overreached himself. Jesus believed that the Kingdom of Heaven would touch the earth, and Paul had taught that it was there already." Kraft reports that when he said, "In that case Christianity was really a failure," Buber confirmed that, and referred to his book *Two Types of Faith*. Kraft objected that he had not formulated it quite so bluntly in the book. Buber confirmed that, too, but added: "That would have been

---

[19]Cf. Ekkehard W. Stegemann's "Introduction," below, pp. 111–121.

[20]*Werke*, I, 657; my translation.

[21]Cf. R. J. Z. Werblowsky, "Reflections on Martin Buber's *Two Types of Faith*, *Journal of Jewish Studies* 39, no. 1 (Spring 1988): 95.

[22]Vol. 2 (Stuttgart: Kohlhammer, 1958), 265.

[23]I hope to publish a separate paper on "Buber, Jesus, Judaism and the Kingdom of God" and refer the reader to the already large number of articles and chapters in books, some of which will be found in the bibliography at the end of this volume.

too much of an imposition on the Christians!"[24] The purpose of reporting for the first time (at least in English!) Buber's personal remarks is not to suspect him of insincerity and to distrust his more irenic published statements on certain matters. My intention is rather to alert the reader to the complexity, occasional ambivalence, and social context in which a man like Buber tried to state his ideas without offending sensibilities and without distorting his own opinions, which are often as critical of traditional Judaism as they are of Paulinian Christianity. When remarking to Werner Kraft (entry dated June 11, 1961) that "we" don't believe in Jesus and that Jesus himself as a Jew had not believed in Christ, Kraft found that extremely strange.[25]

No competent Christian theologian would have been surprised by this *aperçu*, because it merely rephrases the distinction made by Reimarus and Lessing in the eighteenth century between the "religion of Christ" and the "Christian religion." In fact, in a letter of February 22, 1923, Rosenzweig had told Buber "the distinction between the 'religion of Jesus' and the 'religion about Jesus' was already made by Lessing."[26] Since many (but by no means *all*) elements of Christianity criticized by our five Jewish authors are to some extent found in various types of Judaism, it is often possible to correlate their critique of the former religion with a parallel critique of their own!

Buber had a profound understanding of Jewish faith as experienced in the encounter with the God of history who chose Israel as his covenantal partner for the realization of his redemptive goals. However, Judaism as a way of life lived in obedience to an all pervasive order of commandments eluded him. As early as 1911 he told his audience of Jewish Prague university students that what is erroneously called Original Christianity (*Ur-Christentum*) could be more correctly characterized as Original Judaism (*Ur-Judentum*). He opposed the rigidification of cult and law in rabbinic Judaism as much as he objected to the fixation of worship, ethical action, and dogma in Christianity.[27]

In the case of Will Herberg (1901–1977) we have little knowledge of the private reservations and qualifications that he did not consider appro-

---

[24] Werner Kraft, *Gespräche mit Martin Buber* (Munich: Kösel Verlag, 1966), 115–116: "Und auch Jesus habe nicht an die Erlösung gelaubt. Daran habe sich Paulus 'verhoben.' Jesus habe geglaubt, dass das Himmelreich sich mit der Erde berühren würde, und Paulus habe gelehrt, dass es schon da sei. Darauf sagte ich, dann sei doch eigentlich das Christentum gescheitert. Er bejaht es, unter Hinweis auf das Buch, das er darüber geschrieben habe: 'Zwei Glaubensweisen.' Ich wende ein, dass er es doch so schroff in dem Buch nicht ausgedrückt habe. Er bejaht es, aber das hätte er den Christen nicht zumuten können."

[25] Werner Kraft, *Gespräche mit Martin Buber*, 91.

[26] Rosenzweig, *Gesammelte Schriften*, 1/2, 895.

[27] *On Judaism*, 44–47.

11

priate to make part of his published writings.[28] A pioneer in opening up theological discourse between committed Jews and Christians in America, Herberg published an important essay on "the Christian Mythology of Socialism" as early as 1943; in 1955, long before Judaic studies became part of the American college scene, he was appointed Professor of Judaic Studies and Social Philosophy at Drew University. He lectured before Protestant, Catholic, and even Russian Orthodox audiences and was sometimes considered by his liberal Jewish critics to be more in tune with orthodox Christian doctrines than with "progressive" Jewish views. It is, therefore, especially valuable to have in this volume the testimony of Bernhard W. Anderson, the dean of Drew Theological School, who after moving to Princeton Theological Seminary in 1968 continued his regular luncheon conversations with Herberg, that he was dubious about the possibility of creative and frank Jewish-Christian dialogue at this time. "The time had not yet come, owing to the sad history behind us and the need for all three conversants — Protestants, Catholics, and Jews — to do more work in biblical theology."[29] The fact that this Jewish theologian, who was sometimes called "the Reinhold Niebuhr of Judaism" and who was religious editor of *National Review*, expressed these reservations to his good friend Barney Anderson should alert readers to the long way we still have to go before Jews can overcome some of their deep-seated fears in their discourse with Christians.

The last Jewish thinker included in this volume, Abraham J. Heschel (1907–1972), was critical of certain aspects of Christianity, such as its emphasis on the Fall or human depravity due to original sin, but expressed these matters in a manner calculated not to give offense to his Christian friends. In his essay "A Hebrew Evaluation of Reinhold Niebuhr"[30] the reader will be strongly impressed by his agreement with Niebuhr's realistic and courageous doctrine of human sin and the insight that even our best deeds are inextricably commingled with selfish and impure elements. What may escape him is the gently expressed opposition to two widely held traditional doctrines and attitudes: When Niebuhr denies the Kantian axiom "I ought, therefore I can," Heschel agrees, but offers as a Jewish rejoinder against the impossibility of doing God's will through "works" his own motto, based on halakhic thinking: "Thou art commanded, therefore thou canst." And against the striving for personal salvation he emphasizes the Jewish concern for universal redemption.

---

[28]The Herberg Collection of his papers at Drew University has been used by writers on W. H., but there may still be documents that could add to our understanding of his thought.

[29]Bernhard W. Anderson, below, p. 237.

[30]Below, pp. 283–300.

In a lecture given during the 1950s, Heschel expressed this criticism of orthodox Christian doctrine more bluntly, but never incorporated this text into any of his published works. It is here reprinted to complement his more cautious remarks on the same topic:

> Christianity begins with the basic assumption that man is essentially depraved and sinful — that left to himself he can do nothing. He has to be saved. . . . The first question of a Christian is: What do you do for the salvation of your soul? I have never thought of salvation. . . . My problem is what mitzvah can I do next. Am I going to say a blessing? Am I going to be kind to another person? Am I going to study Torah? How am I going to honor the Sabbath? These are my problems. . . . Despite all my imperfections, deficiencies, faults and sins, I remain a part of the covenant that God made with Abraham. . . . This is the preciousness of being a Jew.[31]

Heschel, like Leo Baeck, stressed the need to be constantly aware of the polar tension between mystery and commandment, spontaneity and the pattern of life lived in obedience to the *mitzvot* of the Jewish tradition. Unlike Baeck he insisted on the importance of ritual, worship, and celebration as having a unique validity that is not derivative from the value they have as means to ethical conduct. His critique of the Christian emphasis on the principle of passive grace on the one hand, and the need for correct doctrine (*orthē doxa*) on the other, is based on the biblical message of the *covenant* that is shared by both faiths. It is a message in which God addresses human beings and makes demands that require a human response of love and obedience. In the mutuality of the covenant man not only needs God and his grace, but God needs man and expects human partners to make their contribution to the ultimate goal of establishing his Kingship on earth.

IV

Before readers turn to the writings of Baeck, Buber, Rosenzweig, Herberg, and Heschel, they ought to remember that there is hardly such a thing as *the* standpoint of Judaism from which *the* views of a fixed entity called "Christianity" can be approached. Each of these five thinkers represents a particular Jewish outlook and each is concerned with what he believes to be the essential nature of Christianity as it appears to him from his own historically and existentially conditioned perspective. This does not necessarily diminish the objective validity of the author's judgment, but it ought to be taken into consideration by the discerning reader. The importance and seriousness of the Jewish critiques and

---

[31] Cited in Samuel H. Dresner, *The Jew in American Life* (New York: Crown, 1963), 243.

evaluations in this volume will gain in clarity and fairness after perusal of the introductory essays by the five outstanding Christian theologians who — each in his own way — deal with the question: Which Judaism confronts here which type of Christianity?[32] Thus it becomes clear that Buber, who did not accept the centrality of the halakhic (legal) nature of Judaism, has no reason to oppose Christianity's abrogation of the "Law." But he does represent classical Jewish tradition when denying the Christian claim that the decisive event of salvation and redemption has occurred through Jesus of Nazareth. Leo Baeck represents the liberal type of modern Judaism that takes the ethical message of the Bible as the "essence of Judaism" and accepts the ritual laws as the protecting "hedge" and the constitutional frame of Jewish existence. His opposition to those aspects of Christianity that he attributes to its "romantic" character are prompted by his perception of the dangers involved in reliance on divine grace, the salvific power of the sacraments, and passive faith as well as the crucial importance of correct belief ("orthodoxy"). In some of these criticisms of classical Christianity his views are closer to those of Adolf Harnack than Harnack's own views of the "essence of Christianity" are to the Protestant and Catholic traditionalists of his time. In his review of *The Essence of Christianity* he writes about his adversary:

What he [Harnack] has to say about general religious questions, about the relationship between religion and work, about religion and science is so true and so beautiful that one keeps wishing Herr Harnack would present his admirers with a work about "The Essence of Religion."[33]

And Abraham Heschel, whose own theological writings affirm the importance of the *mitzvot* (commandments) as an all-embracing pattern of ethical *and* ritual responses to God's demands, tried to recall Christians to the common source of both faiths, the Hebrew Bible. He did that because he believed that its desanctification and the consequent dejudaization of the churches were responsible for the spiritual emptiness and the loss of meaning that characterize the state of contemporary man and that made it possible to relegate religion to states of inwardness. "God asks for the heart but He needs the lives.... In this world music is played on physical instruments, and to the Jew the mitzvot are the instruments on which the holy is carried out."[34]

---

[32]Cf. the title of an interfaith symposium held in Aachen during June 1983 and published as *Welches Judentum steht welchem Christentum gegenüber?* Arnoldshainer Texte, vol. 36, ed. H.-H. Henrix and W. Licharz (Frankfurt am Main: Haag und Herchen, 1985).

[33]See below, p. 45.

[34]A. J. Heschel, *God in Search of Man: A Philosophy of Judaism* (New York: Farrar, Straus and Cudahy, 1955, and Philadelphia: The Jewish Publication Society of America, 1956), 296, 297.

V

The chief topics that are dealt with by the writers represented in this book can be listed under four separate (but not unconnected) headings:

(1) *The person and significance of Jesus.* Some of our authors deal with the figure of the "historical Jesus" in the environment of first-century Judaism and others with the "Christ of faith" whose acceptance as God Incarnate and Redeemer became the central doctrine of Christianity.

(2) *The polarity of law and gospel, works and faith, human righteousness and divine grace, first proclaimed by Paul and subsequently elaborated in the theology of the church.* The original split between the nascent Christian movement and the majority of Jews was mainly due to the latter's rejection of the claim that Jesus of Nazareth had been the Messiah. But as Christianity changed from a Jewish sect into a separate religion, with its own system of beliefs, the doctrine that the Christ event had abrogated the validity of the commandments and that human beings could be saved only by faith and not by "works" became the basic difference that separated the two communities. Since divine grace and forgiveness of sins were always an integral part of classic Judaism, it was the abrogation of the *mitzvot* as the way to the life of truth (to paraphrase John 14:6) that constituted the most profound disagreement between rabbinic Judaism and orthodox Christianity.

(3) *The place of the Hebrew Bible in Christianity.* Its acceptance as the word of God had been the unquestioned conviction of Jesus and his followers. The subsequent formation of the New Testament canon tended to attenuate the importance of the Hebrew Bible, now reduced to the role of the "Old" Testament serving as the *praeparatio evangelica.* Attempts were made to exclude it from the canon by Marcion as early as the second century; its desanctification was advocated by Schleiermacher, the "Church Father" of the nineteenth century, its rejection from the biblical canon was urged by Adolf von Harnack in 1921; its devaluation and avoidance by the "German Christians" after 1933; and its irrelevance by the "Death of God" theologians in the 1950s and 1960s.

(4) *The role of the church as the New Israel* (Verus Israel) *vis-à-vis the Jews as the Old Israel "according to the flesh."* Here the claim of the church to have superseded Judaism is examined. All five writers stress that Christians must decide whether they want to abolish the Jewish way or to continue it by bringing the God of Abraham and his will to the Gentiles. Thus the relationship of complementation rather than supersession becomes the focus of discussion.

Any attempt to give a detailed description of how the five writers

15

deal with these subjects would go beyond the limitations mercifully imposed on the writer of this Introduction. It would also prevent readers from gaining their own impressions, forming their own opinions, and drawing their own conclusions. Perhaps it will be helpful to point out that the personal biographies of the authors sometimes can provide hints for understanding differences in the way they approach these topics. Rosenzweig and Herberg turned to the Jewish faith only after almost converting to Christianity in the wake of their disenchantment with secularism and Marxism respectively. They are, therefore, mainly concerned with the Christ of faith as the central subject of classical Christianity.

Leo Baeck, although the only professional rabbi among our authors, not only won a doctorate in philosophy at the University of Berlin, but found time and energy to pursue the study of New Testament scholarship. The discovery of a strong anti-Jewish bias among German Protestant scholars, combined with their lack of knowledge in rabbinic sources, was an important factor in persuading him to rediscover the "Jewish Jesus" in a number of scholarly articles, produced in the course of more than half a century.

On the other hand, Martin Buber, the iconoclast who opposed any attempt to confine the immediacy of the experienced encounter with the human or eternal Thou, found rabbinic "legalism" and Christian "dogmatism" almost equally unpalatable. He considered Jesus his "great brother" (as mentioned earlier) — a man who exemplified the spontaneity and authenticity that Buber valued and expressed in his own dialogical thinking.

Heschel, who grew up in the traditional atmosphere of ḥasidic piety and intensive study of traditional rabbinic and mystical literature, acquired an academic university education in his twenties. It was mainly in the last twelve years of his life that he became closely involved with Christian theologians, especially Reinhold Niebuhr and Cardinal Bea, with whom he cooperated in preparing the schema on the Jews for the Second Vatican Council. Niebuhr's theology was rooted in biblical rather than Greek philosophical thought patterns, and they felt an elective affinity in their common approach to the Hebrew Bible. Bea, once a professor of Bible, had done scholarly work on the Old Testament and treated Heschel as a representative of the prophetic faith that had been the subject of his pioneering Berlin dissertation. This background may be a clue to Heschel's reluctance to discuss some of the doctrines that separated the two faiths. Nevertheless he declared before a Catholic audience in 1967 that "it is difficult for a Jew to understand when Christians worship Jesus as the Lord, and this Lordship takes the place of the Lordship of God the Creator . . . when theology becomes reduced to Christology."[35]

Today we live in a world that has experienced the erosion of faith and the increasing secularization of society. More than a century after Nietzsche proclaimed the death of God we experience the death of the gods that failed: Marxism, Hedonism, Success (William James's "bitch goddess"), and the deification of Man. In 1871 Swinburne had expressed this apotheosis in the words:

> Glory to man in the highest,
> the maker and master of things!

These words sound hollow after two world wars, the Holocaust, the Gulag, and so many other horrors that nobody anticipated in a "world come of age."

At this time we ought to pay heed to the words of Bernhard Casper, the Catholic theologian, that we live in a "situation for dialogue between Jews and Christians such as may perhaps not have existed since the beginnings of Christianity, . . . a time of global crisis for humanity [which is] both a challenge and an opportunity."[36] Judaism and Christianity, as Rosenzweig put it, share a hope. "For both of them this hope — the God of all time — is rooted in a common origin. This common origin is the revelation of the Old Testament [*Alte Bund*] . . . synagogue and church are mutually dependent on one another."[37]

The common origin is also behind the response of J. Louis Martyn, the Protestant theologian, to Leo Baeck's emphasis on both mystery *and* commandment: He asks for a bi-focal theology that is "a call to Christians to turn from the weak and ineffective — and ultimately de-humanizing — forms of both romantic passivity and shallow activity."[38]

In an age when the achievements of science have foisted the illusion that we are self-sufficient and that salvation will come through technology, the voices of Baeck, Buber, Rosenzweig, Herberg, and Heschel may remind Christians and Jews that life is not a problem to be solved, but a task imposed and a grace bestowed.

---

[35] Below, p. 331, in "The Jewish Notion of God and Christian Renewal."
[36] Below, p. 167.
[37] Below, p. 170, letter to Rudolf Ehrenberg, October 31, 1913.
[38] Below, p. 41.

Leo Baeck (1873–1956)

Introduction

by J. Louis Martyn

I

Shortly before the three-quarter mark of the nineteenth century Leo Baeck was born in the essentially Prussian city of Lissa. Well prepared in basic Judaica by his scholarly father, Rabbi Samuel Baeck, and in the Greek and Latin classics by his teachers in the Comenius Gymnasium,[1] he left home at the beginning of his eighteenth year in order to study at the famous Jüdisch-Theologische Seminar in Breslau. Here he encountered a tempered edition of the *Wissenschaft des Judentums* in the form of the rich heritage left by Zacharias Frankel, Jacob Bernays (student at one time of Albrecht Ritschl), and, not least, Heinrich Graetz. As it turned out, Baeck's first semester was the last one for Graetz; but the brief personal contact is a sign of considerable significance. From Baeck's youth onwards his world was populated by men who were both monumental Jewish scholars and profoundly dedicated and engaging teachers. And for our present concerns it is important to note that several of these giants paved part of Baeck's path by giving serious attention not only to the study of the Bible, Talmud, Jewish history, philosophy, and ethics, but also to the interpretation of Christian sources. In this regard one thinks primarily of Abraham Geiger (1810–1874), Graetz (1817–1891), and Hermann Cohen (1842–1918), each of whom decisively influenced Baeck's view of Christianity, not least by linking it to the category of the romantic.

In the summer of 1894, three years into a six-year curriculum, Baeck moved to Berlin, transferring his rabbinical studies to the Lehranstalt

---

[1] In his references to the Protestant reformation Baeck consistently differentiated the Calvinist tradition from the Lutheran. See "Judaism in the Church" in the present volume, and pp. 387–388 of *Wege im Judentum.*

für die Wissenschaft des Judentums, the Hochschule that embodied, to some degree, the dream of Abraham Geiger and Ludwig Philippson for a Jewish theological faculty that would serve as an integral part of a German university. It was scarcely a move to a foreign world; several of the faculty members had been educated at the Breslau Seminary.

Baeck also reached out, however, to the university itself, earning the Ph.D. under the direction of Wilhelm Dilthey.[2] And here a question of some import arises. Do Baeck's writings on Christianity reflect the influence not only of Geiger, Graetz, and Cohen, but also of Dilthey; and, if so, how?

One thinks of this question, first, in relation to Dilthey's horizon. He considered his subject to be nothing less than the whole of that which is human, the totality of what has been made, moulded, and affected by human minds. For that integrated whole Dilthey employed in an arresting way the expression *die geistige Welt*. Nothing human lay outside it.

Second, one thinks of method. Given this humanly cosmic horizon, how did Dilthey envision our efforts to study it? These efforts have to reach as broadly as the subject, thus comprehending what have been conceived as separable disciplines: history, economics, social anthropology, psychology, comparative religion, and so on (*die Geisteswissenschaften*). Reaching over such vast areas, do our efforts involve us in various methods of interpretation? No. There is a single, general hermeneutic, operative throughout the humanities when they are directed toward their true subject. In all of our study of *die geistige Welt*, what is happening in fact is that *Geist* is understanding what *Geist* has made. In the physical sciences one may seek to know. In the humanities one seeks, on the contrary, to understand, and here Dilthey was emphatic. "Understanding" is a term to be reserved for the interpretive event that takes place when by empathy — *Geist* with *Geist* — the interpreter rediscovers "the I in the thou." At that point *Geist* understands *Geist*.

It is clear that both Dilthey's broad horizon and his general hermeneutic proved fascinating to Baeck. It is equally clear that the learned young rabbi ground both in his own mill. *Die geistige Welt*, the great continuity of human life, became for Baeck nothing other than the continuity of Judaism. And the empathetic understanding of the human past could

---

[2]Dilthey, child of the parsonage, biographer of Friedrich Schleiermacher, and creative philosopher, was himself a deeply loved teacher, who, according to Hugo von Hofmannsthal, stimulated about himself an atmosphere of "impassioned conversation, impassioned listening." See especially H. P. Rickman's excellent introduction to Dilthey's *Pattern and Meaning in History*.

prove worthy of the true *geistige Welt* only by becoming a power for shaping the future (note quotation from Adolf Kober below). For our present concerns both points demand emphasis.

At first glance Baeck's explicitly Jewish perception of *die geistige Welt* may appear sectarian and thus a contradiction in terms. Not so. "One can be a Jew only if one sees the totality, only if one thinks in a universal manner. There is the person whose horizons remain confined to certain bounds, groups, parties, interests; such a person is perhaps on the way to that which is Jewish, but he is not yet completely a Jew."[3]

By no means, therefore, did Baeck understand himself to be sacrificing the totality to a particularistic narrowness. On the contrary, standing in the Jewish tradition of universalism, he found that the beacon that illuminates the totality shines through in the "universal history of Judaism."[4]

And what, specifically, does that mean for Christianity? For Baeck, it meant in the main two things: First, that Christianity is truly understood when one sees that, even though it is a strange mixture, elements of which are drawn, for example, from the mystery cults of the Hellenistic age, it is also the major locus of Jewish ideas that live outside of Judaism proper. In consequence, one studies Christianity by tracing the waxing and, unfortunately, the waning of Jewish forms of thought and life in the history of the church. Second, it is a distinctive mark of Christianity's deficiency that, because of its non-Jewish elements, it cannot fully appreciate that which is universally human. The study of Christianity helps us to understand the *geistige Welt* because (a) to study Christianity is to study an aspect of that which is truly universal, namely, Judaism, and (b) the study of Christianity highlights the elements of the universally human that Christianity has suppressed and that call, therefore, for special attention.

The issue of method, of a general hermeneutic, is no less important. We have suggested that Baeck's writings reflect a fascination with Dilthey's emphasis on empathetic understanding, on *Geist*'s empathetic perception of what *Geist* has made. For the one who had truly learned from Geiger, Graetz, and Cohen, however, such understanding is a matter of understanding Judaism, and it is, therefore, clear that to speak of *Geist* understanding what *Geist* has made is to speak in the first instance not of feelings, but rather of the unconditional commandments of God, by which God makes the recipients of those commandments responsible for the future. "No experience without tasks and no task without

---

[3]"Nachruf auf Felix Warburg," *Der Morgen*, 13 (1937–1938): 370.
[4]"Judaism in the Church," below, p. 51; cf. "Romantic Religion," below, pp. 82–86.

experience."[5] Here Dilthey's empathetic understanding takes on the aura of a power. Adolf Kober has put it in a single, memorable sentence:

Für Baeck wird das mitfühlende Verstehen alles Vergangenen zu einer Kraft, das Künftige zu gestalten.[6]

It is a sentence worthy of an expanded and paraphrastic translation:

Influenced by Schleiermacher, Dilthey had included in his general hermeneutic the matter of human feeling, the rediscovery of "the I in the thou." For Baeck the understanding of everything that is past by such empathy became a *power to shape the future* [italics added].

Thus the concern of this Jewish scholar to understand Christianity, and specifically his interest in tracing the history of Judaism in the church (rediscovery of "the I in the thou") is — at its best — neither a merely academic matter, nor, by design, an exercise in religious imperialism. What is at stake is the future. Baeck tried to understand Jesus and Christianity in order to play his part in the shaping of that truly human future that he saw as God's will for the whole of humanity. He was doing that when, as the unknown twenty-seven-year-old rabbi of the small congregation in Oppeln, he composed an altogether serious essay in response to Adolf Harnack's famous book on the essence of Christianity, closing the essay with Renan's reference to Judaism's importance for the future. He was still seeking to awaken a common responsibility for the future, when, as the widely-honored eighty-one-year-old survivor of Theresienstadt, he addressed a series of urgent questions to the Christian church. Through the whole of his fascination with Christianity, the constant concern is focused on that neighbor whom God has put at one's side, and on the shaping of the future with that neighbor, in accordance with the commandments that are accompanied by the announcement, "I am the Lord thy God."

II

The essay on Harnack's *Das Wesen des Christentums* (English translation 1901 published under the title *What Is Christianity?*) is a sober piece, written by a youthful but competent scholar, largely in control of the pertinent sources, especially the Jewish ones. To some extent it is a historical essay. Not far below the surface, however, one detects a considerable amount of anger, and the careful reader will easily sense the reasons. (a) In Baeck's opinion, the Christian professor, while claiming

---

[5] "Mystery and Commandment," below, p. 49.
[6] *Festschrift*, 1953, 25.

to be an objective historian, has proven in fact to be an apologist. (b) He is not only an apologist, but also one astonishingly ignorant of the Jewish sources pertinent to his subject. (c) His historical ignorance (partly willful?), added to his apologetic stance, has led him seriously to distort the image of the remarkable Jew named Jesus. As Baeck writes this essay, therefore, he is a Jew on an urgent mission, concerned to rescue Jesus for Judaism and to rescue Judaism for the future.

Early in *Das Wesen des Christentums*, as one step in his efforts to use historical comparisons to prove Jesus' uniqueness, Harnack had spoken of what he took to be the vast distance that separated Jesus from rabbinic Judaism:

First of all, it is very improbable that he [Jesus] went through the schools of the Rabbis; nowhere does he speak like a man who had assimilated a technical-theological education, learning the art of scholarly exegesis. Compare him in this respect with the apostle Paul; how clearly it can be seen from the latter's epistles that he had sat at the feet of theological teachers. With Jesus we find nothing of the kind; hence he caused a stir by appearing in the schools and teaching at all. He lived and had his being in the sacred scriptures, but not in the manner of a professional teacher.[7]

Baeck wastes no time with artificial politeness.

In this paragraph every sentence contains an error [not least because of woeful ignorance of *halakhah* and *haggadah*]. Mr. Harnack would have been correct, had there been among the rabbis only dialecticians, and no haggadists, no preachers, no religious thinkers and poets. Everyone who knows something about these matters recognizes immediately that Jesus' speech is of one spirit with the spirit of these preachers and poets. Every one of his utterances, every one of his parables, every one of his comforting words, shows him to be a disciple of the rabbis. . . . Whoever reaches judgments like those of Mr. Harnack knows nothing of a vast area of Jewish life as it actually existed at the time of Jesus and the early church; or he compels himself to know nothing of it.[8]

The first point of Baeck's critique is clear. Jesus the haggadic teacher has fallen into the hands of a historian ignorant of haggadah. When this ignorance is removed, Jesus stands before us as a rabbi.

The second point emerges if we inquire into the significance of Jesus' Jewishness, and here we do well to pay attention to the final clause in the quotation given immediately above. On the face of it, it may seem a gratuitous, impolite, even an *ad hominem* remark. The major thing to note, however, as we have suggested earlier, is Baeck's anger and its cause. One recalls the offensive tendency among Christian scholars

---

[7] 1st ed., 20–21; English translation, 31–32 (altered).
[8] *Monatsschrift für Geschichte und Wissenschaft des Judentums* 5 (1901): 110.

to study Judaism only in order to show both its inferiority and Jesus' non-Jewish superiority.[9] No one had to instruct Baeck that this tendency was altogether evident in Harnack's book. To be specific, Harnack had made extensive use of the ancient image of husk and kernel, holding that the typically Jewish elements in Jesus' teaching constituted the (plainly inferior) husk, while the (clearly superior) kernel lay in those elements that, lacking Jewish parallels, prove to be unique.

Against the background of Harnack's husk-and-kernel image, one might expect Baeck to express his anger by dissociating himself from the project of drawing such distinctions. Not so. The Reform movement in Judaism, no less than the liberal developments in Protestantism, depended on them. Thus Baeck is in agreement with Harnack in two important regards: (1) There is that which is essential, and there is that which is non-essential; (2) the distinction between the two can be discerned by studies in comparative religion. In light of these points of agreement, the major divergence becomes clear. It is the identity of the husk and the identity of the kernel. What Harnack considered a disposable Jewish husk is for Baeck the kernel of Jesus' teaching, and what Harnack saw as the kernel is in Baeck's judgment only Harnack's modern belief, and thus not something that can be historically traced to Jesus. For that reason, to the historian at least, Harnack's kernel has to be identified as husk. In this sharp disagreement there is for Baeck, however, much more at stake than historical accuracy. At stake is nothing less than the uniqueness of the Jewish people, and the power of this people to shape a human future.

If Harnack had claimed that God's good news came in the non-Jewish kernel of Jesus' teaching and *only there*, Baeck will rescue Jesus for Judaism by showing that the kernel of Jesus' teaching lies in its fidelity to the essence of Judaism and *only there*:

In all of his traits, Jesus is through and through *a genuinely Jewish* character. Such a man as he could grow up only on the soil of Judaism, only there and nowhere else. Jesus is a genuine Jewish personality; all of his striving and acting, his bearing and feeling, his speech and his silence, all of it bears the Jewish stamp, the imprint of . . . the best that was to be found in Judaism. Indeed at that time [prior to the gifts Judaism bestowed on the church] this best was found only in Judaism. . . . From no other people could a man such as he have arisen, and in no other people would such a man have been able to work; in no other people would he have found the apostles who believed in him.[10]

---

[9]See the admirable exposure of this tendency in G. F. Moore, "Christian Writers on Judaism," *Harvard Theological Review* 14 (1921): 197–254.

[10]*Monatsschrift für Geschichte und Wissenschaft des Judentums* 45 (1901): 118; below, p. 44.

Mistaking husk for kernel and kernel for husk, Harnack has failed in his location of that which is unique. For uniqueness is properly affirmed not of Jesus, but rather of Judaism and the Jewish people. Jesus is among the best of this unique people.

Does this claim of Jewish uniqueness invalidate the suggestion made earlier about Baeck's Jewish universalism? Scarcely. When, as we have already noted, Baeck closes the essay by citing Renan's reference to Judaism's importance for the future, he means, as his subsequent writings will show, to speak about the future of the world. From Isaiah to Ben Azzai, and beyond, the election of Israel has been coupled with various forms of universalism. For his own part, Baeck clearly held Jesus' people to be unique for the sake of all peoples.[11]

III

While still in Oppeln, Baeck published his first book, *Das Wesen des Judentums* [*The Essence of Judaism*] (1905), in part a full-dress answer to Harnack, but also an important and substantive treatise in its own right, as is shown by its wide influence, its several revised editions, and its translation into numerous languages. Service in Oppeln was followed by five years in Düsseldorf, and in 1912 by the call to Berlin, where together with his work as rabbi, he was within a year appointed to the faculty of the Lehranstalt.[12] After the war and service as a military chaplain, he returned to Berlin, where once again he turned part of his attention to the study of Christianity, writing the three essays that represent most fully and most effectively his understanding and assessment of that religion: "Mystery and Commandment" (1921), "Romantic Religion" (1922), and "Judaism in the Church" (1925).[13] In these seminal essays on Christianity, as in his writings on Judaism, Baeck spoke both of essence and of history.

---

[11]See especially *The Essence of Judaism*, 76–80.

[12]Baeck painted valuable portraits of some of the great figures of the Lehranstalt in "Heimgegangene des Krieges," 1919, reprinted in *Wege im Judentum*, 1933.

[13]The article "Romantic Religion," published in 1922, was part of a longer essay, the later sections of which did not appear until the publication of *Aus drei Jahrtausenden* (1938); even the original part doubtless played a key role, however, in the Nazis' decision to destroy that book. We should also mention three further essays of Baeck that repay careful study: "The Gospel as a Document of the History of the Jewish Faith" (1938), "The Faith of Paul" (presented by the survivor of Theresienstadt to the Society of Jewish Study in London, 1952), and "Some Questions to the Christian Church from the Jewish Point of View" (1954). Stretching over more than half a century, Baeck's studies of Christianity show some development as well as a basic consistency. See Reinhold Mayer, *Christentum und Judentum in der Schau Leo Baecks* (1961) and the critique of Mayer's book in W. Jacob, *Christianity through Jewish Eyes* (1974).

Essence (an attempt to paraphrase Baeck himself):
The key to the essence of Christianity lies in the recognition of its basic type; it belongs to the genre of romantic religion. What that signifies can be seen best if we begin, however, not with religion, but rather with the broad picture of romanticism in modern times. Friedrich Schlegel and Novalis gave clear definitions: romanticism is the longing to celebrate sheer feeling, as it gazes into the mirror of introspection, longing to drown in its own beautiful illusion. Here feeling is everything.[14]

When one considers the religious form of romanticism, one notes a basic distinction between classical and romantic religion. Indeed one finds the basic clue to the origin of Christianity, for by this distinction we see that the two original components of Christianity, Judaism and the mystery cults of Adonis, Attis, etc., are in fact polar opposites, the former being classical religion, the latter being romantic. To be sure, the founder of Christianity, Paul, produced a mixture of the two opposing types, thus bringing to that mixture the power of classical Judaism. The essence of the mixture is determined, however, by the romantic element, the weak and soft sentimentality of the mystery cults, with their other-worldly myth of a redeeming savior, who enables his followers to escape from the demands of real life into a fantastic beyond. Christianity was born as a romantic religion and through the whole of its development it has been marked by romantic characteristics:

(1) In Christianity faith is understood to be passive grace rather than active obedience, and the consequences for its view of the human being are remarkable.

(2) Human will is obliterated. As Paul put it, there can be no place for "willing and running" (Rom. 9:16). Indeed, religion becomes redemption from the will, liberation from deeds that are decisively done in accordance with God's commandment.

(3) The future is effectively denied. In this romantic faith everything is believed to be already given; there is no becoming, no growing. That person of faith is the already perfected person, who, having finished the task in the properly helpless feeling of absolute dependence, hears no "thou shalt," but only a "thou hast."[15] Because those of classical religion

---

[14]Baeck's definition of the broad movement of nineteenth-century romanticism is in need of correction, as one can see from the analysis given in M. H. Abrams, *The Mirror and the Lamp* (Oxford, 1953); but it is in fact heuristically important to his cogent critique of a strain that can be traced in the history of the church.

[15]Baeck does not cite the ancient expression *teleios anēr*, but his references to the "finished man" and to a grace that is thought to work "through the dark abysses of the blood" show an interest in the effects of (a misunderstood) Nietzsche on ominous developments in the Germany of the twenties. It is worth noting that these prophetic references to the

have an addressable will, capable of obeying the commandment, they
are always striving, always stretching forward to the freedom of the
future. Those of romantic religion, by contrast, are the ones who already
possess freedom through the grace that has severed them from their
will. They have no interest in the future.

(4) The neighbor and culture are both eclipsed because, for this already perfected person, neither has any true significance. Romantic
religion is fundamentally a form of solipsistic egoism. "All passivity is a
kind of selfishness ... in it the individual knows only himself and what
God or life is to bring him, but not the commandment, not the mutual
demands of men."[16]

(5) Political responsibility is avoided, for lacking all drive to improve
social and economic life, this romantic passivity can only say, "Let every
person be subject to the governing authorities" (Rom. 13:1). Enraptured
in sacred music, it sits silently by, while, in slavery and torture, the
neighbor suffers one form of dehumanization after another. If one points
out that the ancient mystery cults got along well enough with tyrants,
one has to add that, as a general rule, Christianity has done the same,
often worsening matters by consecrating the rule of the tyrant.

(6) The abdication of political responsibility and the effective denial
of the future cause those of romantic religion to retreat from the idea of
real, living history. For them the essence of history has become a theatrical drama, taking place between the below and the above, a drama put
on by suprahuman powers acting out their parts somewhere beyond the
human sphere. Human beings, ceasing to be active, well-endowed subjects of history, become the passive objects of a supraterrestrial struggle;
they therefore think that reality can be experienced only in the supernatural.

(7) Over time the steady sustenance of this romantic passivity proves
problematic, but solutions are ready at hand. One turns to a regularly enacted sacrament of an essentially magical sort, and one creates dogmas
in which the romantic mind can find a tangible certainty. Truth becomes
the correct dogmatic confession, rather than an infinite ethical duty. Justice suffers a similar fate, becoming correct belief; and in a truly Orphic
fashion, sin becomes an inheritance for which one is not responsible,
and in the face of which one is impotent.

(8) The elevation of romantic feeling and of its frozen twin, correct
dogma, spells the death of ethics as something intrinsic to faith. If there

---

"finished man" were present already in the 1922 form of "Romantic Religion"; as we have
noted earlier, the sections added for the 1938 publication will probably not have been in
themselves the cause of its being highly offensive to the Nazis.
[16]"Romantic Religion," 211.

is a moral law at all, it is extrinsic to faith; it can therefore find expression only in a casuistry that domesticates the absolute commandment of God.

(9) All of the foregoing observations, not least those pertaining to Christianity and culture, converge to show that Christianity, being an inherently reductionistic, romantic religion, is incapable of appreciating the magnificent whole of that which is human (again one recalls Dilthey). The unity of humankind is, in fact, sacrificed, for in Christian romanticism human virtue has to be denied wherever correct dogma is not found. This active intolerance always "returns to the self and remains at the level of a mere mood."[17] It is, thus, a clear sign of the impotence of romantic religion, for it shows that, utterly unlike classical religion, the romantic type is devoid of true power to create the universally human future.

History (again an attempt to paraphrase Baeck):

If the romantic element determines the essence of Christianity, then the key to Christianity's history emerges when one traces the waxing and waning of the classical element that it inherited from Judaism.

Because Jesus and his immediate apostles were, in the full sense of the word, Jews, the original gospel was Jewish. In that original gospel one can find the Jewish awareness of the indissoluble unity of mystery and commandment, of devoted faith and active deed, of absorption in the profundity of God and absorption in the will of God. Jesus and the original apostles knew that the Law stands guard equally against the loss of mystery and against the loss of commandment, and thus — one might say especially — against the divorcing of the one from the other. Moreover this original gospel maintained the Jewish understanding of real history, and therefore of the future. One knew that God's commandment, being spoken out of God's mystery, creates and begets an everlasting future; the commandment contains a promise, a messianic aspect, a life that continually comes to life.

The boundary of this Jewish integrity was crossed neither by Jesus nor by his own apostles, but rather by Paul, who, by crossing it, founded Christianity.[18] Christianity came into being when Paul abandoned the commandment, drove apart what cannot be truly separated, and gave his allegiance solely to the mystery that presented itself to him in a vision. Here the classical religion, Judaism, has to a large degree been abandoned, and a form of romantic religion, Christianity, has come on the scene, bringing from the pagan mystery cults a celebration of dreamy

---

[17]"Romantic Religion," 291; below, p. 91.
[18]"Judaism in the Church," 126; below, p. 93.

ecstasy for its own sake, and thus a retreat from the task of making a better future in the real world. Whereas Judaism had known that faith has its commandment and the commandment its faith, Paul separated the two, preaching faith alone (*sola fide*), turning to magical sacraments, and embracing dogma as a substitute for the unity of mystery and commandment. It is a move that was to have the most regrettable consequences.

Jewish roots, however, can never be entirely cut away; they form an indestructible foundation, and however suppressed their influence may be, they always reassert themselves. For this reason the true history of the church is the history of Judaism in the church, the history, that is, of the church's fidelity and infidelity to Judaism.

In this history five points are of paramount importance:

(1) In Paul's system there is no place for ethics. In the miraculous sacraments everything is already accomplished; what is done (or should be done) by human beings has no further significance. All of this means that Paul was a romantic enthusiast, a passive visionary, who was untrue both to legal piety (ethics) and to messianic piety (belief in the future kingdom of God and vigorous activity toward its realization). At the very depth of his being, however, he was a Jew, and the Jew in him — centered in his Jewish feelings[19] — was stronger than his misleading doctrine of *sola fide*.

(2) A significant change lies before us when we come to the author of the Epistle of Barnabas and climactically to the second-century gnostics and to Marcion. For here we encounter "logical and consistent" Paulinists who cannot call on a native Jewishness to save them from the quicksand of one-sided romanticism. Church history now enters its darkest period (prior, one supposes, to the rise of the *Deutsche Christen*), the uncompromising rejection of the Old Testament, indeed of everything Jewish, the embracing of a strict dualism, and total eclipse of ethics.

(3) The Catholic Church emerged from a successful struggle against Marcion and the anti-Jewish gnostics. It was thus able, by contrast, to establish the unity of the Old Testament with the New. The banner under which this victory was won bore the words — reminiscent of the Epistle of James — "faith and works." Catholic doctrine "was developed on the basis of this great compromise with the Jewish element," a compromise in which that element scarcely played the role it should have played, but in which, fortunately, Paulinism also was subjected to considerable limitation.[20] The result was the long period of medieval Catholicism, marked by a mixture of Paulinism and the Jewish element.

---

[19]"Judaism in the Church," 134; below, p. 99.
[20]"Judaism in the Church," 134; below, p. 100; "Of course the Church condemned . . .

(4) Except for the Jewish idea of the priesthood of all, the Lutheran Reformation brought a distinct and ominous setback. In his dogma Luther reverted to pure Paulinism, and thus to a thorough antithesis with Judaism (Baeck cites Troeltsch, Dilthey, Wundt). Faith once again eclipses works, doctrinal religion triumphs over active ethics, and grace obliterates the human will.

There is, moreover, the truly hazardous alliance with the state, an alliance in which the responsibility for morality, being viewed, at best, as an appendix to religion, is handed over to the civil authorities. Abdicating the task of creating its own system of ethics, the religion of Luther granted unlimited power to the state.

(5) With Calvin and with the Baptist movement things developed quite differently. There is a significant return from the unhealthy weakness of Paulinism to the healthy strength of Judaism; indeed one may speak here of a genuine revolution brought about by that which is Jewish in the church. Faith no longer has its purpose in itself; the Pauline, Augustinian, Lutheran passivity is left behind, as one realizes that faith is directed toward moral effectiveness. Connections with the state are refused, as legal piety is once again given a place internal to religion; and the positive role given to the Jewish heritage even sets question marks to the sacraments and to the doctrines of original sin and of Christ's divinity, thus suggesting the possibility of a return to Jewish monotheism.

This overview of twenty centuries of Christian history shows something of fundamental importance. Judaism has its indestructible life inside the church as well as outside it. True enough, Judaism can be strenuously opposed and even driven underground, but it always reemerges to find new forms of life, not only in its own proper stream, but also in that of the church.

Conclusion

Baeck's picture of Christianity, drawn by analyzing both its essence and its history, leaves us with two tones, one sharply negative, one affirmatively positive. As regards the former, the essays identify three major mistakes made by Christianity: First, it came into being when Paul mixed together things that cannot rightly be combined, the Jewish and non-Jewish elements mentioned above. Second, time and again it turned its back on Judaism, giving its primary allegiance to the non-Jewish, romantic element, thus pretending that it could have God's mystery without God's commandment. And third, it repeatedly failed to acknowledge

---

Pelagius, and yet it always came to terms or compromised with a sort of semi-Pelagianism" (see below p. 102).

the locus of its only true power: the stream of Judaism, which, in spite of all counterforces, coursed through its own history.

The positive side of the picture begins to come into view when one notes that, however fascinated Baeck may have been with the question of essence, in the end that question had to give way to the question of history.[21] Baeck could not speak finally in timeless categories. He had rather to speak of Judaism and Paulinism as two historical antagonists, warring against one another within the mind and heart of Christianity over the span of centuries. Something, moreover, kept Baeck from viewing this war as a struggle that would end in a victory for the romantic antagonist, or even in a stalemate between the two.

True enough, the realism of "Judaism in the Church" brings him to a lamentation of the numerous points in church history at which Pauline theology (as he understood it) achieved periodic victories. As the final paragraph shows, however, that essay is, in the main, one of Baeck's most confident celebrations of the indomitable power of Judaism ultimately to triumph; and it is clear that Baeck is confident of that triumph not only in Judaism's own proper stream, quite apart from Christianity (so in the closing paragraphs of "Mystery and Commandment" and "Romantic Religion"), but also in the stream of Judaism that flows and always will flow in the church. Thus, when his final word announces the victory of Judaism, it speaks not of a victory over the church but rather of a victory within it: *"Et inclinata resurget."* And it is, presumably, his confidence in this victory that made it possible for the one who, years later, had experienced the horrors of the Holocaust to change the angelic announcement from:

> . . . peace among men of good will

to:

> peace among men of bad will.[22]

IV

Baeck's sketch of the teaching of Jesus, his analysis of the essence of Christianity, and his account of its history constitute an impressive accomplishment, truly helpful to genuine communication between Jews

---

[21]See, however, the closing pages of the study H. Liebeschütz contributed to *Essays Presented to Leo Baeck* (1954).

[22]Cited in Th. Bovet, *Angst — Sicherung — Geborgenheit* (1975), Baeck's words are surely a conscious reversal of one of the traditional translations of Luke 2:14, a translation now generally replaced by "peace among men with whom he [God] is pleased."

and Christians. We will turn in a moment to speak of the challenge to Christians. Before that, however, there is need for a brief critique, offered, one may hope, in the same candid spirit in which Baeck offered his critique of the work of Harnack. We focus our attention on two major flaws, both of which, because of Baeck's obvious fascination with Paul, have primarily to do with the apostle to the Gentiles.

The first flaw arises from Baeck's tendency to credit first-century authors with views that emerged only much later in the church's history. We notice, for example, that in "Romantic Religion" he begins with an extensive definition of romanticism crafted on the basis of authors who lived in the nineteenth century. He thus allows Schleiermacher to speak of "the feeling of absolute dependence" before he brings his reader to the letters of Paul. One is not wholly surprised, then to find him shortly employing this very expression to encapsulate the faith of Paul himself and the result is his charge that Paul is the father of the romantic passivity of Christianity.[23] It is true that on occasion Paul can speak in terms that are distinctly enthusiastic (e.g., the refrain "but now … "). He also speaks, however, of a faith that is active in love, and specifically in love directed toward the neighbor, in accordance with Leviticus 19:18 (e.g., Gal. 5:6 and 5:14). Paul also knows that the Spirit, far from transporting the individual into a passive and egoistic state of romantic dreaminess, leads the community into an active and communal life of love, joy, peace, compassion, and the selfless service of one another (Gal. 5:22; Phil. 2:2–4).

That anachronistic flaw is then deepened by Baeck's consistent failure — together with most of his contemporaries who were professional New Testament scholars — to listen to Paul's voice in the context of the apostles's battles with various other teachers in his churches.[24]

Baeck does not see, therefore, that the true analogue to nineteenth century romanticism is to be found not in Paul, but rather in some of the members of his Corinthian church, who, much to Paul's dismay, said that they were already filled, had already become rich, and were already ruling as kings (1 Cor. 4:8). It is true, as we have noted above, that there is a strain of such enthusiasm in Paul's own theology, but it is always held in check by his insistence — often expressed in sharply polemical tones — that the church lived in the earthy (and earthly) cross of Christ and in the hope of Christ's parousia. Thus, when the Corinthian enthusiasts perceived the Eucharist to be a sort of medicine of guaranteed

---

[23] "Romantic Religion," 213 and passim.
[24] Baeck occasionally cites F. C. Baur, but the major insights of the Tübingen giant seem to have escaped him as readily as they escaped most of the New Testament scholars of the first half of the twentieth century.

immortality, to be consumed by individuals at their own convenience and for its own sake, Paul said: " . . . let anyone who thinks that he stands [by consuming the Eucharist as though it were magic food and drink], take heed lest he fall (1 Cor. 10:12).

For Paul the Eucharist is by no means a possession of the "perfected man." On the contrary, it stands precisely as a sign of the fact that the church lives in an incompleted interim, for in celebrating the Lord's supper, "you proclaim the Lord's death until he comes" (1 Cor. 11:26). No one in the early Christian church understood better than Paul the distinction between the *faith* that is active in love and the mystical *superstition* that longs to hug itself to sleep (*Glaube* and *Aberglaube*). And no one fought for that distinction more vigorously.

The second major flaw in Baeck's treatment of Paul is closely related to the first, and again, to a degree, it corresponds to a deficiency characteristic of the Pauline studies of Baeck's time. Just as he does not see that Paul fought one of his major battles against the emergence of magical enthusiasm in his churches, so he fails to see that Paul's own position is not at all romantic, but rather apocalyptic. Indeed, Baeck's preoccupation with nineteenth-century romanticism leads him to make three unfortunate errors with regard to Paul's apocalyptic perspective, the first pertaining to Paul's understanding of the present, the second having to do with his perception of the future, the third being focused on his view of man.[25]

(a) Given the provisional dualism of Paul's apocalyptic theology, Baeck is altogether correct to say that Paul sees history as "a theatrical drama being played out between the below and the above"; it is "a struggle."[26] One cannot say in Paul's name, however, that this historical struggle "really takes place *beyond* the human sphere."[27] On the contrary, the apocalyptic drama, having been inaugurated by the coming of Christ, has already begun, and it is occurring *in the world* into which Christ came. True enough, being a genuine apocalyptic drama, it includes suprahuman actors (it was, e.g., the *archontes*, the rulers of this present evil age, who "crucified the Lord of Glory"; 1 Cor. 2:8), but they do not at all drive the human actors off the stage. Daniel, one must recall, was sure that developments on the earthly stage — dominantly the machinations of Antiochus IV — were hopelessly enigmatic and enigmatically

---

[25] Neither Baeck's portrait of Jesus nor his sketch of Paul is truly informed by the works of J. Weiss and A. Schweitzer, although he had cordial and mutually respectful contacts with the latter; see the engaging picture of the two men on page 31 of *Worte des Gedenkens für Leo Baeck*; also "The Faith of Paul," 149, no. 14.

[26] "Romantic Religion," 220; slightly changed; see *Aus drei Jahrtausenden*, 65 ("Schauspiel").

[27] "Romantic Religion," 220; italics added.

hopeless apart from the bi-focal vision of apocalyptic, a vision in which one sees not only those earthly developments, but also and simultaneously the corresponding (and revealing) developments on the heavenly stage. In Paul we find something similar, even though the *archontes* are not pictured as beasts with horns.

What demands emphasis is that Paul's everyday vision is genuinely *bi-focal*, and therefore not otherworldly. Paul's apocalyptic is emphatically not a form of romanticism but rather the truly powerful antidote to that virus.[28] One can see what is involved if one will patiently interview Paul on the subject of history as a *struggle*; for while he does indeed speak of the involvement of suprahuman powers, he also knows that human beings are themselves genuine actors in the struggle of history. One will look in vain for a passage in which Paul tells the community of active faith to sit passively by, as the forces of evil have a field day.[29]

Precisely the opposite! The community is summoned now into the thick of the apocalyptic battle by an apostle who is himself thoroughly identified with the struggle of those who are weak and stumbling (2 Cor. 11:29), and who, for that reason, bears the marks of battle "through great endurance, in afflictions, hardships, calamities, beatings, imprisonments ... hunger ... " (2 Cor. 6:4–5). The present is not a timeless time in which one is encouraged to run away from real life into a dreamy romanticism. It is, on the contrary, the time of the most vigorous struggle (*agōn*) for the extension of God's rectifying justice to the whole of the world.

This understanding of the present as the time of apocalyptic war is derived, in Paul's case, from the event of Christ's crucifixion, the head-on collision between the powers of evil and the power of God (see again 1 Cor. 2:8). It involves, therefore, a profoundly serious view of evil. One notes, by contrast, that Baeck's view of evil was fundamentally influenced by the easy optimism characteristic of the European scene at the turn of the century rather than by the apocalyptic Ḥasidim whose understanding of evil is enshrined in the book of Daniel. As a result, Baeck did not grasp Paul's apocalyptically realistic portrait of evil and sin.[30]

---

[28]It is misleadingly partial and thus quite incorrect to say that Paul's vision "disclosed the 'above,' the celestial" ("The Faith of Paul," 151).

[29]Baeck rightly points to the disastrous effects of the dominant interpretation accorded to Rom. 13:1 in the history of the church ("Let every person be subject to the governing authorities . . ."): Paul's own intention was probably to combat a tendency of the enthusiasts to withdraw into a kind of privitistic individualism. See E. Käsemann, "Principles of the Interpretation of Romans 13," in *New Testament Questions of Today*.

[30]Baeck's view of evil and his understanding of the human will are, of course, inextricably intertwined. One notes with some degree of astonishment that the rightly venerated

The *centrum Paulinum* is not Paul's own vision of the resurrected Christ, in the sense Baeck accords to that expression, but rather what Paul himself calls "the word of the cross."[31] Paul sees simultaneously, as it were, the crucified Christ and the resurrected one, and it is this simultaneity that causes his apocalyptic vision of life to be truly *bi*-focal and thus altogether antithetical to romantic religion. The *real* world emerges in the cross/resurrection, the world of God's final battle for the rectification of the world, the battle into which human beings are called by being "crucified *with* Christ" (Gal. 2:20).

(b) For Paul the nature of this present battle is determined, however, not only by the past event of Christ's death/resurrection, but also by the future event of his parousia. The apocalyptic drama encompasses, therefore, not only the real and present warfare, but also the confidently hoped-for consummation of that warfare in the future. Here we have simply to say that Baeck allowed his own view of Paul to determine which texts received his attention. Knowing ahead of time, so to speak, that Paul was a consistent romantic, Baeck also knew that the structure of Paul's faith can scarcely have been characterized by genuine hope. One notes that Baeck ignores the lengthy apocalyptic discourse Paul gave to the Thessalonian church on the sure hope of the victorious parousia (1 Thess. 4:13–5:11). Disquiet at this instance of procrustean interpretations grows into amazed disbelief when one sees that in "The Faith of Paul" Baeck excises the apocalyptic paragraph of 1 Cor. 15:23–28, confidently declaring it to be a post-Pauline interpolation. although there is no manuscript of the letter that lacks it.[32] The net result is that Baeck does not give due attention to either focus of Paul's apocalyptic christology: Christ's death and Christ's future parousia!

The better route is to recognize that one of Paul's most important concerns was focused on his struggle in behalf of the not-yet-realized hope of the parousia, and thus of the view that Christian life is essentially oriented to the future, being determined by Christ's future no less than by his past.[33]

---

survivor of Theresienstadt — having come face to face with one of evil's most massive attacks in the Holocaust — maintained his earlier views essentially intact. Human beings are able to decide to be obedient. Contemplating the Nazi madness, one might rather think of Hosea's picture of an enslaved will for which a mere call to repentance (*teshuvah*) is impotent: "Their deeds do not allow them to return (*lashuv*) to their God" (Hos. 5:4). See Dorothy W. Martyn, "A Child and Adam: A Parable of the Two Ages," in Joel Marcus and Marion L. Soards, eds., *Apocalyptic and the New Testament* (Sheffield, 1989), 317–333.

[31] Baeck is not speaking for Paul when he says, "the resurrection is the gospel and nothing else. . . . This [the resurrection] is the sole theme" ("The Faith of Paul," 151).

[32] "The Faith of Paul," 152, note 26.

[33] See J. Moltmann, *Theology of Hope* (1967); Christopher Morse, *The Logic of Promise*

(c) How, then, is this hope-filled view of the future related to Paul's understanding of the human being? We recall that Baeck's Paul is one who believes that the Christian vision severs human beings from their will, making them the object of a predetermined (and thus non-genuine) history, rather than the will-endowed subjects of history, responsible for the future.

Again, Baeck goes astray because he does not see Paul's particular form of apocalyptic. It is true that for Paul there is no general freedom of the will, but the apocalyptic drama of Jesus Christ is in no way responsible for that state of affairs. On the contrary, it is in that drama that God is actively freeing the will, thus creating among the Gentiles a liberated community that is able to be addressed by the commandment (1 Cor. 7:19). And it is this newly addressable community that is called by God into the apocalyptic warfare for the glorious future of the whole of humanity. The members of this community are scarcely will-less romantics, hopeless subjects of history with no task and no genuine future; they are newly enrolled soldiers called into the obedience of faith and sent into the warfare in which God is regrasping the world for himself.

V

Does this critique tell us that the strong link Baeck discerns between Christianity and romanticism (as he defined the latter; see note 14) is entirely beside the point? Hardly! Baeck's perception and analysis of that link yield one of the major challenges put to Christianity in the twentieth century: the full hearing of that challenge is essential to a genuine dialogue between Jews and Christians and, for that reason, to the health and integrity of Christianity itself.

There is, first, the striking question Baeck has directed to the professional church historians. Is there one major key to the highly complex history of the church, and if so, what is it? Especially since the Reformation one can easily find numerous works in which that key is identified (however implicitly) as the relation of Christianity to Judaism. Thus the grand sweep of the history of Christianity has been presented as an alternation between, first, noble and healthy surges into ground that is new and distinctively Christian, and, second, timid and unhealthy relapses into modified forms of Judaism.[34] Baeck, agreeing that the key to church

---

in Moltmann's Theology (1979); J. C. Beker, *Paul the Apostle* (1984). We will have occasion below to applaud Baeck's challenge that modern Christians learn to speak of the future. In issuing that challenge, Baeck was far closer to Paul than he realized.

[34] To some degree this pattern is found, one scarcely needs to say, in the work of Baeck's early antagonist, Harnack.

history lies in the relations of Christianity to Judaism, turns this historical sketch precisely on its head. For him the periods of health and strength have been the Jewish ones; the periods of unhealth and weakness have been those marked by relapses into non-Jewish romanticism.

This is a sketch of church history that can and must alert the church to the ever-present danger presented by the ghost of Marcion. One of the current forms of the Marcionite danger can be seen in the call of some third-world theologians for the building of Christianity on the basis of various native religions rather than on the basis of the Old Testament. It is precisely at such a juncture as this that Christians need to hear the voice of Baeck as a man concerned about the future of the entire human race. For severance from the Old Testament has always thrown the church into some form of ethical chaos, dangerous both to itself and to others.

Baeck's ethical challenge is extraordinarily perceptive. He sees that ethics has had a very hard time finding a recognized and stable home in Christianity. Indeed, over the span of centuries, the dominant picture — and the one to which Baeck gives repeated attention — is the one in which ethics is excluded from the sphere considered proper to Christianity, either by being banned to live in a sort of shabby lean-to, having no organic relation to the main house of faith, or by being handed over entirely to the state. Not infrequently ethics has thus become, at worst, the sanctification of a tyrannical government and, at best, "a message that is perceived dimly, as if from a vast distance, a message that can mean everything while demanding nothing. . . ."[35] From such ethics one learns to be prudent, to find the modus vivendi; and thus, in the end, one falls into the kind of casuistry that can be comfortable with the neighbor's suffering.[36] About this part of Baeck's charge there can be no argument. Christian history provides more examples than one wishes to enumerate.

The full profundity of Baeck's analysis of Christian ethics ensues, however, from his recognition that the organic relationship between faith and ethics is equally compromised when ethics moves in from the lean-to and takes over the house, pretending to be the whole of Christianity,

---

[35]"Romantic Religion," 265; below, p. 81, slightly changed; *Aus drei Jahrtausenden*, 101.

[36]The vast distance separating casuistry from an ethics that, with integrity, permeates every corner of daily life is powerfully presented in "Mystery and Commandment," 182, below, p. 53, a passage containing a much-needed corrective to Christian caricatures of "Jewish legalism." One will find it an instructive exercise to compare that passage with some remarkably similar comments of E. Käsemann, as the latter interprets Rom. 12 under "Worship in Everyday Life," 188–195 in *New Testament Questions of Today*.

thus rendering unnecessary and, in fact, useless, everything having to do with the mystery of God's transcendence. Here we have the pattern Baeck identifies as "the commandment without the mystery." In making this point, Baeck speaks, to be sure, of Judaism, but the implications for Christianity are altogether clear, perhaps indeed clearer to us than they were to Baeck. First, recapitulating the earlier warning about the eclipse of the activity of ethics by the passivity of faith, Baeck says:

This religion of mere passivity, devoid of commandments, is no longer Judaism [In his opinion, it is, of course, Christianity].

Then he adds:

Nor is Judaism to be found where the commandment is content with itself and is nothing but commandment; where the whole sphere of life is supposed to be embraced by commandments, and only that which lies under the rays of their cold light is presumed to be the meaning of life. . . . The very ground on which [Judaism] rests is abandoned when . . . it is assumed to be merely an ethic or the support for an ethic; when it becomes a mere edifice of ideas . . . ; or when that which the mystery intimates is no longer supposed to be the foundation of Man's life. . . . There is no such thing as a Judaism . . . in which the idea of God is merely a decorative embellishment or a crowning pinnacle.[37]

Again, from the Christian side, a genuine response has to involve basic agreement. It is, as we have said, precisely the integrity of devotion and deed, of theology and ethics, that has been so often absent in the history of the church. There are, however, two groups who have lost that integrity: those thinking it possible to have the roots without the branches, and those thinking they can have the branches without the roots. To both groups Baeck's voice comes as that of the physician who is truly concerned with the patient's recovery:

The world of Judaism [and thus of health] is to be found only where faith has its commandment, and the commandment its faith.[38]

Read together with the essays on romantic religion and Judaism in the church, "Mystery and Commandment" is one of the most important words spoken to the church in the twentieth century. The future of humanity demands that Christians pay very close attention to the witness of Judaism, and specifically to the Jewish prescription offered by Leo Baeck.

For many Christians, however, the medicine cannot be swallowed precisely in the form prescribed, as though a return to Judaism, as such,

---

[37]"Mystery and Commandment," 176–178; below, p. 49f.
[38]Ibid., 177; below, p. 50.

were the effective answer to the probing challenge.[39] We must, rather, honor the integrity of Leo Baeck by taking our bearings both from his challenge and from the Christian critique of it; in this way, at least the beginning of a creditable response may be possible. The periods in the history of the church at which romanticism (again as defined by Baeck) has raised its head are indeed periods of abysmal failure; and exactly the same is to be said of the periods marked by what Baeck called the ethics of the surface.

None of these periods, however, is accurately identified as a re-emergence of Paulinism. On the contrary, each is characterized by the domestication of the bi-focal theology that emerged in early Christianity, especially in Paul. The romantics have repeatedly domesticated that apocalyptic theology by turning it into a uni-focal form of other-worldliness; enraptured, they have gazed into heaven, with no concern for this world (Acts 1:11). The surface ethicists, equally uni-focal, have carried out their domestication by eclipsing (from their own eyes!) the mystery of God's activity, turning their attention only to the earth (Col. 2:23). The antidote to both of these retreats presents itself in the bi-focal theology of Christ's cross and Christ's parousia, a theology derived from the bi-focal nature of Jewish apocalyptic, but also reformed by being focused on the past, present, and future of Jesus Christ, the one who frees the human will for obedience.

Taken in this way, Baeck's challenge is a call to Christians to turn from the weak and ineffective — and ultimately dehumanizing — forms of both romantic passivity and shallow activity. It is also a call to return to the God of Abraham, Isaac, and Jacob by means of the Christian *Shemaᶜ*, that is to say, by an active hearing of the original gospel preached by Jesus of Nazareth (so Baeck) as part of the fully apocalyptic gospel of Jesus Christ.

---

[39] The question whether the church is to be perceived as a sect within Judaism was posed very clearly in the first century. The dominant answer — and ultimately the victorious one — was in the negative, a fact partially eclipsed in some of the recent attempts on the part of Christian bodies to formulate post-Holocaust statements on the relations between Jews and Christians. No issue facing the church is more crucial to its own health than that of a theologically mature relationship with Judaism. As R. J. Zwi Werblowsky has reminded Christians, however, "Es handelt sich nicht darum — wovor uns Gott bewahre — dass Christen je sich bei Juden ihre christliche Theologie holen sollten" (p. 35 in "Trennendes und Gemeinsames," a lecture given to the Synod of the Rheinische Landeskirche in 1980 and published by the Synod in *Zur Erneuerung des Verhältnisses von Christen und Juden* [Mülheim (Ruhr), 1980].

1

Harnack's Lectures on the Essence of Christianity

1901

Anyone with enough scholarship to respect scholarship will pick up a book by Adolf Harnack with respect....

As one reads the book, however — and with repeated readings increasingly so — one is overcome by regret because one is confronted with something unusual, a contradiction between title and content. The purposeful plan and the methodical execution stand in sharp contrast to one another: a work of a purely apologetic kind comes before us claiming to be pure history. Indeed, its apologetic trend is being expressly denied and its historical character stressed. The preface and first lecture decidedly emphasize: "What is Christianity? It is solely in its historical sense that we shall try to answer this question here; that is to say, we shall employ the methods of historical science, and the experience of life gained by studying the actual course of history. This excludes the view of the question taken by the apologist and the religious philosopher" [English translation, 6]. This however, remains a mere ideal, in the glow of which the reader may rejoice.

For Harnack the historian, too, Christianity is nothing but three intersecting circles: the kingdom of God, the infinite worth of the human soul and that "higher" righteousness manifested in love. Whatever else is found in the Gospel is not, in truth, contained in it. Asceticism has no place in the Gospel. The Gospel does not preach renunciation of property, it is socialistic only to the extent that "solidarity" and "helping of others" are its essential contents. It does not forbid fighting for justice, and does not view cultural work with hostility. The phrase "Jesus, the son of God" is alien to the Gospel, but whoever accepts the Gospel, must testify that in its preacher "the divine appeared in the utmost purity possible on earth." There is only one confession, and that is "the practical demonstration of faith." Moreover, it is Paul's merit to have interpreted the Gospel as the fulfillment of salvation, as redemption which has taken place, as something new, as it were, through which the old is being abolished; to have recognized that this which is new belongs to everyone; and finally to have connected it with the spiritual "capital gained by working in history." "The knowledge and recognition of God as the Father, the certainty of redemption, humility and joy in God, works and love of one's brother"; all this brought into connection with the one who proclaimed this message is the final result in which Harnack sees the essence of Christianity expressed.

Harnack himself appears to have been aware of this apologetic trait — which other examples will illustrate further — because it seems as if he were trying to justify it by declaring repeatedly that it is the duty of the historian to discover the essential. Indeed, the writer of history should focus on the essential if he seeks to describe the spiritual current of an era. However, two things need to be carefully kept apart, especially by the historian of religion: that which was significant in *that* time, and that which he himself, from the vantage point of an achieved height, regards as significant for *his day*. Harnack has not always distinguished rigorously....

It is also lack of historical clarity when Harnack pays little attention to the influence which the course of political events leading to the destruction of the Temple and the fall of Betar, had on the history of the apostolic era — that is: on the time when the difference between Jews and Christians consisted in those saying the Messiah would come and the others saying he would come again. Similarly, the whole climate of the century in which Jesus lived has not been sufficiently regarded, which would have been necessary for grasping the fervor of the messianic hopes, for understanding that Jesus believed in himself because his disciples believed in him. In order to comprehend Jesus and his disciples and that whole epoch, one must feel in what air Jews lived then, particularly in Palestine. One has to know what kind of people had been formed through historical events. The Babylonian exile resembled a sieve in which the chaff of Israel was being shaken, the forced selection by Ezra and Nehemiah of all those who hesitated, the great separation of minds in the battles of the Maccabeans: all this was a continued natural selection and the result the "survival of the fittest." There remained a congregation of "heroes of religion." There may have been "virtuosi of religion" at that time, but the majority were heroes. The Jews of that time were — to use an expression of Spurgeon's — the "great nonconformists of the world," people, almost every one of whom was able and prepared to sacrifice himself for the idea — not merely, as happened elsewhere, for purposes: weariness of life or to make a noble exit, force of necessity or because the law decreed it.

The ability to become a martyr, to be able to act the fool for the sake of heaven before the clever ones on earth — this ability has been cultivated in the ancient world only by the Jews, and it is their bequest wherever it crops up later. One need only read the Roman authors to see how the Jews struck the whole heathen world as strange and incomprehensible, how they were perceived now as ridiculous and now as uncanny, almost spooky. One has to know the Jews in order to understand the Gospels.

And this leads to still another matter. Most writers about the life of Jesus fail to point out that Jesus, in every one of his traits, was a *thoroughly Jewish character*, that a man such as he could arise only from the soil of Judaism, only there and nowhere else. Jesus is a genuinely Jewish personality, all his striving and doing, his bearing and feeling, his speech and his silence all mark him as of the Jewish kind, the kind of Jewish idealism, the best that could and can be found in Judaism, but at that time could be found only in Judaism. He was a Jew among Jews. A man such as he could not have emerged out of any other people, and among no other people could he have been active. Among no other people would he have found the apostles who believed in him. — This matrix of the personality of Jesus has not been regarded by Harnack.

These are the basic mistakes of Harnack's work[1]: the apologetic purposefulness and then the disregard of Jewish literature and Jewish scholarship. Decades ago, Abraham Geiger wrote accusingly: "One would consider and reconsider before disparaging matters which one does not explore independently for lack of the necessary preconditions and abilities. Only vis-à-vis Judaism does one believe that one can set about with sovereign arbitrariness." Unfortunately, Geiger's words have not lost any of their timeliness, and they are to be repeated with respect to Harnack. That his book contains much that is excellent, that each page stimulates the reader, that the art of description arouses admiration again

---

[1] The chapters dealing with Catholicism and Protestantism have not been included in this review. — In the *History of Dogma*, the judgment about the Pharisees is not so harsh. To be sure, they can be found here "in the thesis," not, as here, "in the antithesis."

and again is such a matter of course in a work by Harnack that one almost hesitates to stress it. Particularly what he has to say about general religious questions, about the relationship between religion and work, about religion and science is so true and so beautiful that one keeps wishing Herr Harnack would present his admirers with a work about "The Essence of Religion."

In conclusion: If Herr H. were to ask what, after all that has been said against his presentation, would remain that is of significance, and was brought and created by Jesus so that a world religion was named after him with pride, then the following might briefly he said in reply. One could obviously say, with a banal aperçu in the manner of Wellhausen: America, as is well known, was not named after Columbus, either. Such a retort, however, would be a snide joke, not an answer. The only answer is that at that moment the time was ripe, and that ripe time needed a God-sent personality. For the pagans, the day had come when they could begin to absorb Israel's teaching, and God let his own people rise to the occasion. And if only for that reason, Judaism has nothing but love and respect for the founder of Christianity. Tales are often told about Judaism's hatred of Christianity. This has never existed. A mother never hates her child, but the child has ofttimes forgotten and denied its mother. Very often, Christianity has manifested precious little of the spirit of its founder. A deep meaning lies in the parable of the New Testament: "A man had two sons and went to the one and said: My son, go and work today in my vineyard. He replied: Yes, Master, and did not go. . . . " In the course of Christian history, this has often come true. But far be it, especially from a Jewish theologian, not to recognize or even to offend or disparage a religion which has blessed, comforted and lifted the hearts of millions. Also the Jewish theologian will regard it as a good and noble deed when a Christian pens apologetics, a writ of glorification on behalf of his religion. What he objects to is solely that these apologetics seek to pass as history and that it believes it could wield historical injustice as a weapon. The defense and shield of even an apologete should be clean and without fault. Perhaps such a true apologete may harbor some of the spiritual independence and freedom of a Renan[2] who said openly: "Judaism which in the past rendered such great services, will yet render more of them in the future."

---

[2] Attention should, above all, be drawn to the courageous words which Friedrich Alb. Berner spoke in his lecture about "Judaism and Christianity."

2

Mystery and Commandment

1921/22

There are two experiences of the human soul in which the meaning of his life takes on for a man a vital significance: the experience of mystery and the experience of commandment; or, as we may also put it, the knowledge of what is real and the knowledge of what is to be realized.

When man wants to be certain of his existence, when he therefore listens intently for the meaning of his life and life in general, and when he thus feels the presence of something lasting, of some reality beneath the surface, then he experiences the mystery: he becomes conscious that he was created, brought into being — conscious of an undetectable and, at the same time, protective power. He experiences that which embraces him and all else. He experiences, in the words of the ancient metaphor in the Blessing of Moses, "the arms of eternity."

And when man looks beyond the present day, when he wishes to give his life direction and lead it toward a goal, when he thus grasps that which defines his life and is clear about it, then he is always confronted with the commandment, the task, that which he is to realize. The foundation of life is the mystery; the way of life is the revealed. The one is from God; the other to be achieved by man. To cite another thought from the Bible: "That which is concealed belongs unto the Lord our God, but that which is revealed belongs unto us and unto our children forever, that we may do all the words of this Torah." And both, mystery as well as commandment, represent certainty — the certainty of life, the certainty of the self.

This twofold experience could also be called humility and reverence. The humility of man is the recognition that his life is framed by infinity and eternity, by that which transcends all human knowledge and apprehension, and surpasses all that is natural and existent; that his life is absolutely dependent; that the unknowable and unnameable, the unfathomable and unthinkable enters into his life. Humility is the feeling for that deep and mysterious sphere in which man is rooted; the feeling, in other words, for that which remains in being and is real — the great quiet, the great devotion in all philosophy and all wisdom. And reverence is man's feeling that something higher confronts him; and whatever is higher is ethically superior and therefore makes demands and directs, speaks to man and requires his reply, his decision. It can reveal itself in the small and weak no less than in the sublime; it can manifest itself in the other as well as in oneself. Reverence is thus the recognition of the holy, that which is infinitely and eternally commanding, that which man is to accept into his life and realize through his life — the great impelling force, the active aspect of wisdom.

This twofold experience can also be intimated in this way: the consciousness that we have been created versus the consciousness that we are expected to create. The former is our certainty of that through which all that lives has life; our certainty that, at heart and in truth, we are related to the oneness of all life; our certainty of that which is omnipresent and enduring. It is the capacity of the soul for grasping the invisible in the visible, the lasting in the momentary, the eternal in the transitory, and the infinite in the earthly and limited. It is this faith which ever and again grasps that which has reality and which is the principle and source of life. The latter, on the other hand, is the capacity to be aware of the demand and determination of the hour; it is the certainty of the task, of that which admonishes, points ahead, and directs our life; the certainty that every man's life can do its share and accomplish its function; that man has some quality that lifts him out of the universe which has been created even as he himself has been created — a quality which gives man a quite personal aspect, a quite individual place and a unique direction and freedom, a capacity for decision by virtue of which man comprehends again and again what he is supposed to fulfill.

These are the two experiences of the meaning of life. And what is peculiar to Judaism is that these two experiences have here become one, and are experienced as one, in a perfect unity. And it is thus that the soul becomes conscious of its own unity and totality; it is thus that piety springs up in the soul. From the one God come both mystery and commandment, as one from the One, and the soul experiences both as one. Every mystery means and suggests also a commandment; and every commandment means and suggests also a mystery. All humility also means and suggests reverence, and all reverence, humility; all faith, the law, and all law, faith. All consciousness that we have been created means and suggests the demand to create, and every demand to create means and suggests the consciousness that we have been created. What is evident is here rooted in that which is concealed, and what is concealed always has its evident aspect for man. The profundity of life cannot be grasped without its also speaking to us of duty in life; and not a single duty of life is perceived truly without at the same time proclaiming the profundity of life. We cannot have knowledge of the foundation of our life without at the same time beholding our way, and we cannot understand this way without penetrating to the foundation of our life. We cannot fully take to heart that we are the creatures of God without apprehending also that we ought to be the creators of our own lives; and we cannot be in full possession of this commandment to create unless we remain aware that we ourselves have been created — created by God that we ourselves may create, and creating because we have been created by God. This unity of both experiences in the human soul constitutes Jewish piety and Jewish wisdom; the meaning of life reveals itself here in this form.

Therefore Judaism is not marred by the split which is introduced by other conceptions of God. Judaism lacks any foundation for the conflict between transcendence and immanence. Jewish piety lives in the paradox, in the polarity with all its tension and compactness. That which is a contradiction in the abstract world of mere theory is made of unity and a whole in the religious consciousness. For this consciousness there is no such thing as this world without any beyond, nor a beyond without this world; no world to come without the present world, and no human world without that which transcends it. Whatever is on this side is rooted in the beyond, and whatever is beyond demands completion on this side by man. The infinite appears in the finite, and whatever is finite bears witness to the infinite. The life of man leads from God to man and from man to God. God is He in whom is all being, and God is also He that is positively different. God gives man life, and God demands man's life from him. Our soul is what is divine in us, it is our mystery and shares the mystery of all souls; and yet it shows also our individual stamp, that which is unique within us, our very self, that which belongs to it alone. The human dwells in the divine, and the divine demands of every man his humanity. This unity of both, the meaning which emerges from this opposition, alone is truth and pregnant with thoroughgoing certainty.

Hence any opposition between mysticism and ethics has no place here either. The religious consciousness here is never without its immediacy, its experience — nor without that which has been commanded and still is to be realized in life. No experience without tasks and no tasks without experience; life dwells only where both are present. In Judaism, all ethics has its mysticism and all mysticism its ethics. This applies to the whole far-flung history of its ideas. For Jewish mysticism the energies welling up out of God are energies of the will. Floods of mystery full of commandments and floods of commandment full of mystery issue from God. And the deed which fulfills God's commandment opens up a gate through which these floods surge into man's day. All absorption in the profundity of God is always also an absorption in the will of God and His commandment. And all Jewish ethics is distinguished by being an ethic of revelation or, one might almost say, an ethic of experience of the divine: it is the tidings of the divine. Every "thou shalt" is confronted with another word which introduces it and simultaneously replies to it — another word which is at the same time the word of mystery: "Thus saith the Lord." And it is followed by this same word both as a conclusion and a new beginning: "I am the Lord thy God." Ethics is here rooted in the profundity of living experience, and it is significant that in the Hebrew language of the Middle Ages the same word is used to designate an ethical disposition and a mystical absorption.[1] The history of Judaism from ancient times to the present could be written as a history of mysticism; and the history of Judaism from its origins until now could also be written as a history. And for the most part it would be the history of the very same men. Many of the most influential and decisive teachers of the law have been mystics; for example, the author of the oft-cited *Shulḥan Arukh.*

Of course, mystery and commandment were not always emphasized equally in Judaism. Now the one was stressed more, now the other; and this distinguished different spheres and epochs. Only where one or the other was supposed to constitute the whole of religion, only where the whole of piety was exclusively identified with one or the other, did the religion cease to be Judaism. Judaism ceases where the mood of devotion, that which is at rest and restful, would mean everything; where faith is content with itself, content with mystery; where this mere faith finally extends its darkling glimmer to the point where it drowns the world and dreams become the stuff of life. The religion of mere passivity, devoid of commandments, is no longer Judaism. Nor is Judaism to be found where the commandment is content with itself and is nothing but commandment; where the whole sphere of life is supposed to be embraced by commandments and only that which lies under the rays of their cold

---

[1] *Kavvanah* = "direction, intention"; see Leo Baeck, "Ursprung der jüdischen Mystik," in *Aus drei Jahrtausenden* (1958), 248f. —F. A. R.

light is presumed to be the meaning of life; where man thinks that he has seen everything when he sees the way on which he is to proceed. The religion of mere activity without devotion — this religion which becomes an ethic of the surface, or no more than the custom of the day — is not Judaism. The world of Judaism is to be found only where faith has its commandment, and the commandment its faith.

That is why Paul left Judaism when he preached *sola fide* (by faith alone) and thereby wound up with sacrament and dogma. Mystery became everything to him, not only that which is concealed but also that which is manifest. Hence mystery finally had to become for him something tangible, namely, sacraments, and something that can be molded, namely, dogma. For it is always thus: sacraments are a mystery into which man enters, a mystery of which man can take hold; and dogma, like myth, is a mystery which man can build up and shape. The gospel — that old gospel which had not yet been adapted for the use of the Church and made to oppose Judaism — was still wholly a part of Judaism and conformed to the Old Testament. It is relatively less important that it was written in the language of the Jewish land and thus was a piece of Jewish literature. A full understanding of Jesus and his gospel is possible only in the perspective of Jewish thought and feeling and therefore perhaps only for a Jew. And his words can be heard with their full content and import only when they are led back into the language he spoke. The boundary of Judaism was crossed only by Paul at the point where mystery wanted to prevail without commandment, and faith without the law.

Judaism, however, can be abandoned no less on the other side. The very ground on which it rests is abandoned when these other developments take place: when it is assumed to be merely an ethic or the support for an ethic; when it becomes a mere edifice of ideas, a doctrine; or when that which the mystery intimates is no longer supposed to be the foundation of man's life but merely some postulate of his thought — when Judaism is taken to be a Judaism without paradox. There is no such thing as a Judaism which is nothing but Kantian philosophy or ethical culture, nor a Judaism in which the idea of God is merely a decorative embellishment or a crowning pinnacle. And the distinctive essence of Judaism is lost, too, where the abundance of its laws may still prevail, but merely as something that is performed, severed from its roots in mystery, void of devotion.

Jewish piety and Jewish wisdom are found only where the soul is in possession of the unity of that which is concealed and that which is evident, of the profound and the task — the unity of devotion and deed. What matters is the unity experienced in the soul, a unity which is born of a reality and points toward a truth — not a mere synthesis, and least of all syncretism. A synthesis merely puts two things alongside each other or at best into each other; but however closely it connects them, it merely connects one thing with another. A unity, on the other hand, involves no mere connection but a revelation: one thing is grasped and experienced through the other and each receives its meaning only from the other. Mystery and commandment are not merely connected and interwoven but proclaim each other and give each other their distinctive essences. The commandment is a true commandment only because it is rooted in mystery, and the mystery is a true mystery because the commandment always speaks out of it. Because it is rooted in mystery, the commandment is unconditional and absolute, independent of the ephemeral and useful, urgent and triumphant. It has the force of unconditional unity, of the unity of morality, or — and this is merely another way of putting it — it has the capacity for taking itself absolutely seriously, to think itself through; and this gives it its entire meaning. And because mystery here cannot be without commandment, it has its own blessing and creative power, and remains fertile; it has the power to demand real life and to give real life; it can let the well of profundity rise into the light of day and introduce the eternal into the present hour; it has the gift of being in everything and giving unity to everything or — and this is just another way of putting it — the gift of being real instead of merely existent. And it is this alone that gives mystery its full meaning. This totality and unity — this peculiar way in which each is grasped by way of the other — this is Judaism.

Not only the individual's life but history, too, receives its meaning from this. There is history because there is a unity of creation and future. Creation is unthinkable apart from a future, and the idea of the future is inseparable from the certainty of the divine creation. Every commandment that issues from God, every commandment through which God speaks to man whom He has created, has its own infinity, its everlasting future. It creates and begets, it commands on and on, it transcends itself; every duty begets another duty. This endlessness of the law impressed Paul particularly; and it was his opposition to this, his rebellion against that which could not be fulfilled once and for all, that troubled his soul and eventually gave birth to his faith in a redemption that was fulfilled, in a salvation that had been accomplished. For Judaism, however, this endlessness is something positive, it gives man something. A commandment that can be fulfilled completely is merely a human law. The commandment of God is a commandment which leads into the future and involves a mission which, in the words of the Bible, continues "from generation unto generation." It contains a promise, it has a life that continually comes to life, it has a messianic aspect. All creation has its future; in the words of an ancient Jewish parable: "The creation of the world contained the idea of the Messiah." Thus the future is not merely something historical or a mere result, not merely a synthesis of theses and antitheses of the past, but it signifies the certainty that God has created. All future issues from creation; it is the reply to the question of man's nature; it is that which man must expect — not miracle, nor myth, nor fate, but the future of the way, life begotten by Life. Creation and future, mission and confidence depend on each other and reveal each other. And all ages, too, have their unity. God has made a lasting covenant with man.

Therefore religion is not, in our case, a faith in redemption from the world and its demands, but rather — and this has often been called the realism of Judaism — trust in the world or, to be more precise, the assurance of reconciliation. All reconciliation is the reconciliation of the day with eternity, of the limited with infinity, of that which is near with that which is distant, of existence with being, with that which is real and therefore shall be realized. Reconciliation is the liberating assurance that even now, during our life on earth, while we are coping with what is given and assigned, we are related to God. When we speak of the meaning of life, we have in mind such reconciliation. Wherever we find both mystery and commandment, we also encounter the possibility of such reconciliation; for there it is possible for man to become certain of his origin as well as of his way, and so turn back to devotion and to the task of his life — he can always return to himself. Reconciliation and redemption are correlative here. Redemption here is not redemption from the world, but in the world, consecration of the world, realization of the kingdom of God. Mere redemption means that the spheres of mystery and commandment, of this world and the beyond, are separated as two realms which are in a sense opposed to each other. Reconciliation, however, means that they belong together and that everything is unified in the one God. Whatever is beyond enters into this world, and this world bears witness to the beyond. A sentence in the Talmud exhibits the paradox which characterizes Judaism: "One hour of returning to God and good deeds in this world is more than all the life of the world to come; one hour of peace in the world to come is more than all the life of this world." The kingdom of God comprehends everything: mystery and commandment, the beyond and this world; it is the kingdom of reconciliation. "The whole world is full of His glory."

Thus religion is everything here. It permeates the whole of life, carries the meaning of all days, and comprehends the meaning of all ways. There is nothing left that could be called mere "world," and nothing set aside as basically merely "everyday"; there is no mere prose of existence. That which is seemingly commonplace speaks, too, with a voice that comes from the depths; and all prose is also a parable and speaks of that which is concealed. Religion here is nothing isolated, nothing that is shut off; it does not exist only alongside our life or only under or above our life. There is no mystery outside of life and no life outside the commandment. Even all solitude is the solitude of life and has its place in the social sphere. Again there is a unity even in opposition. The depth of life always leads to solitude because it leads us away from the merely human to God; and the task of life leads us into the social realm because it is to be fulfilled by man among men. Yet every commandment should issue from the depths of the self, from that solitude in which the human is surrounded by the divine and in which man perceives the voice of God; and all depth, all solitude is here meant to be the beginning of the way on which the commandment guides us and where we hear the voice of our fellow men. And all thinking of God and searching for God, too, places us in the midst of life. Knowledge of God is not the conclusion of some speculation or the end of some ecstasy, but the ethical, the commandment, something demanded and demanding, a challenge to man's personality. The prophetic dictum places it alongside faithfulness and love. It is owned by piety, by humble reverence for the Lord, by the fear of God. "Behold, the fear of God is wisdom."

As soon as we understand these traits and trends of Jewish religion, we can also comprehend that which many would consider its only aspect: the profusion of rules and customs with which the community surrounds itself, its so-called Law. In Judaism the attempt has been made to give life its style by causing religion to invade every day and penetrate the whole of everyday. Everything is in a sense divine service and has its mood and its dignity. In the view of the earthly, the spirit is to be safeguarded; and in the view of the desire, the freedom is to be kept. Judaism cannot do without this ascetic trait unless it wants to forego all that is inward and religious. It does not lead man out of his everyday world, but relates him to God within it. Every partition of life into the profane and the sacred is to be avoided, and the sanctuary dare not possess merely one day beside all the other days. The word "remember" is inscribed above this law: "That you may remember and do all my commandments and be holy unto your God." Thoughtlessness is the true Godlessness; it is the homelessness of the soul. And the Law would guard man against this state in which he is without mystery and commandment; it would give every surface its symbolic function and every bit of prose its parable. Every man is to be made the priest of his own life. Therefore are we confronted with such an abundance of customs, arrangements, and order which surround everything, "when thou sittest in thy house, and when thou walkest by the way, and when thou liest down, and when thou risest up" — all the way to the ample prose of eating and drinking. All this has helped to consecrate the day and especially also the evening; and it is in his evenings perhaps even more than in his days that man really lives, and it is in his evenings that he dies. A form of life has been fashioned here, though it is, of course, not entirely free from the danger which confronts every style of life: it may cease to be something personal and alive and degenerate into something purely external, into mere tradition. The "Law," too, has sometimes been degraded in this way: that which was meant to be consecration has at times become a mere routine, the fulfillment of something handed down. But even then it was preferable to pure lack of style. And it contains the power of always coming to life again and retrieving its soul.

The whole love of the "Law" has been lavished on and has cherished the Sabbath. As the day of rest, it gives life its balance and rhythm; it sustains the week. Rest is something entirely different from a mere recess, from a mere interruption of work, from not working. A recess is something essentially physical, part of the earthly everyday sphere. Rest, on the other hand, is essentially religious, part of the atmosphere of the divine; it leads us to the mystery, to the depth from which all commandments come, too. It is that which re-creates and reconciles, the recreation in which the soul, as it were, creates itself again and catches its breath of life — that in life which is sabbatical. The Sabbath is the image of the messianic; it proclaims the creation and the future; it is the great symbol. In the words of the Bible, it is "a sign between God and Israel"; or, in the words of the Talmud, it is "the parable of eternity." In the Sabbath, life possesses the great contradiction of any end, a perpetual renaissance. A life without Sabbath would lack the spring of renewal, that which opens the well of the depth again and again. An essential and fruitful aspect of Judaism would dry up in such a life; it could still be an ethical life, but it would lack that which defines the Jewish life. Therefore the Jewish community clings to the Sabbath as its possession in spite of all civic difficulties and troubles. The care for the Sabbath is one of the fundamental cares of Judaism.

The Law, and quite especially the sabbatical element in it, has educated that capacity in man which is born only of the depth of life — the capacity to be different. Without this, life cannot be unique. Whoever experiences mystery and commandment becomes unique among men, different, an individual within the world. Whoever knows only mystery becomes merely unique and knows only the day of silence. Whoever knows only the tasks is only among men and knows only the days of work and times of recess. But whoever experiences both, both in unity, lives in the world and yet is different, is different and yet is in the world, lives for other men and with other men and yet within himself, within himself and yet also for other men and hence also with them. This is the gift and possession of Judaism. And it may well be its historic task to offer this image of the dissenter, who dissents for humanity's sake.

It is one of the capacities of religion to sustain, to conserve; and the old spirit of China created a religion in this sense — but only in this sense. Elsewhere we find that it is also one of the capacities of religion to assuage and to still, to teach denying and diverting; and the soul of India was able to do this — and this alone. The distinctive feature of Judaism — and its history also lives on in those religions which issued from it either immediately or mediately — is the power to liberate and renew, this messianic energy. Wherever Jewish piety is found, we encounter this strong drive to create, to fashion for the sake of God, to build the kingdom of God. We encounter this urge to exhibit the strength which is derived from the source of all things, from that which is beyond all strength; we encounter this decision which grows only in the man who knows mystery, not to bow and not to yield, to speak out and contradict. This demanding faith, this demand prompted by faith, is encountered where the soul experiences its depth and its task, that which is concealed and that which is evident, each in the other and each through the other. It is found in the religion of paradox and reconciliation, that religion which lives on the strength of the unity of mystery and commandment in the soul of man.

3

Romantic Religion

1922, 1938

Romanticism

If we classify types of piety in accordance with the manner in which they have historically become types of religion, then we encounter two forms above all: classical and romantic religiousness, classical and romantic religion. The distinction and opposition between these two types is exemplified especially by two phenomena of world history. One of these, to be sure, is connected with the other by its origin and hence remains determined by it within certain limits; and yet the significant dividing line separates them clearly. These two religions are Judaism and Christianity. In essential respects they confront each other as the classical religion and the romantic religion.

What is the meaning of romantic? Friedrich Schlegel has characterized the romantic book in these words: "It is one which treats sentimental material in a phantastic form." In almost exactly the same words one might also characterize romantic religion. Tense feelings supply its content, and it seeks its goals in the now mythical, now mystical visions of the imagination. Its world is the realm in which all rules are suspended; it is the world of the irregular, the extraordinary and the miraculous, that world which lies beyond all reality, the remote which transcends all things.

We can observe this disposition of the soul in relative historical proximity when we consider the German romantic of the last century. For him, everything dissolves into feeling; everything becomes mere mood; everything becomes subjective; "thinking is only a dream of feeling." Feeling is considered valid as such; it represents the value of life which

56

the enthusiastic disposition wants to affirm. The romantic becomes enraptured and ecstatic for the sake of ecstasy and rapture; this state becomes for him an end in itself and has its meaning within itself. His whole existence is transformed into longing — not into the longing for God, in which man, raising himself above the earth, overcomes his earthly solitude; nor into the powerful longing of the will which thirsts for deeds; but into that sweet wavelike longing which pours itself out into feelings and becomes intoxicated with itself. Suffering and grief, too, become a good to him, if only the soul is submerged in them. He revels in his agonies as much as in his raptures.

Thus something agitated and excited, something overheated or intoxicated easily enters the feelings and not only the feelings, but the language, too. Every expression seeks to excel in this direction; voluptuousness becomes a much sought-after word. The feelings talk in terms of superlatives; everything has to be made ecstatic. Fervently, the romantic enjoys the highest delight and the deepest pain almost day after day; he enjoys the most enchanting and the most sublime; he enjoys his wounds and the streaming blood of his heart. Everything becomes for him an occasion of enraptured shuddering, even his faith, even his devotion. Thus Novalis praises his Christianity for being "truly the religion of voluptuousness."

These souls can always be so full of feeling because their abundant suffering is, for the most part, only reverie and dream; almost all of it is merely sentimental suffering. They like so much to dream; the dim distances, twilight and moonlit night, the quiet, flickering hours in which the magic flower lowers its blossoming head, represent the time for which they are wearily waiting. They love the soft, the sweet illusion, the beautiful semblance; and whereas, Lessing had said to God, "Give me the wrestling for the truth," the romantics implore, "Accord me lovely illusions." They want to dream, not see; they shun the distinctness of what is clearly beheld in the light, to the very point of antipathy against fact. Disgruntled they confront reality; and in its stead they seek the less clear attraction of fluctuating feelings to the point of outright delight in confusion. What is within and without becomes for them a semblance and a glimmer, resounding and ringing, a mere mythical game; and the world becomes a sadly beautiful novel, an experience to be felt. As Hegel once put it: "The sense for content and substance contracts into a formless weaving of the spirit within itself."

The desire to yield to illusion, justifiable in art, here characterizes the entire relation to the world. In the deliberately sought-out twilight of longing and dream, the border lines of poetry and life are effaced. Reality becomes mere mood; and moods, eventually, the only reality.

Everything, thinking and poetry, knowledge and illusion, all here and all above, flows together into a foaming poem, into a sacred music, into a great transfiguration, an apotheosis. In the end, the floods should close over the soul, while all and nothing become one, as the grandson of the romantics celebrates it:

> In the sea-like rapture's billowy swell,
> In the roaring waves of a drowsy smell,
> In the world-breath's flowing all —
> To drown —
> To sink down —
> Unconsciousness —
> Highest bliss.[1]

In this ecstatic abandonment, which wants so much to be seized and embraced and would like to pass away in the roaring ocean of the world, the distinctive character of romantic religion stands revealed — the feminine trait that marks it. There is something passive about its piety; it feels so touchingly helpless and weary; it wants to be seized and inspired from above, embraced by a flood of grace which should descend upon it to consecrate it and possess it — a will-less instrument of the wondrous ways of God. When Schleiermacher defined religion as "the feeling of absolute dependence," he condensed this attitude into a formula.

Romanticism therefore lacks any strong ethical impulse, any will to conquer life ethically. It has an antipathy against any practical idea which might dominate life, demanding free, creative obedience for its commandments and showing a clearly determined way to the goals of action. Romanticism would like to "recover from purpose." All law, all that legislates, all morality with its commandments is repugnant to it; it would rather stay outside the sphere of good and evil; the highest ideal may be anything at all, except the distinct demands of ethical action. From all that urges and admonishes, the romantic turns away. He wants to dream, enjoy, immerse himself, instead of clearing his way by striving and wrestling. That which has been and rises out of what is past occupies him far more than what is to become and also more than what wants to become; for the word of the future would always command. Experiences with their many echoes and their billows stand higher in his estimation than life with its tasks; for tasks always establish a bond with harsh reality. And from this he is in flight. He does not want to struggle against fate, but rather to receive it with an ardent and devout soul; he does not want to wrestle for his blessing, but to experience it, abandoning himself, devoid of will, to what spells salvation and bliss. He wants no way

---

[1] Richard Wagner, *Tristan and Isolde*, end of Act 3 (*Liebestod*). —F. A. R.

of his own choosing. For the romantic the living deed is supplanted by the grace whose vessel he would be; the law of existence, by mere faith; reality, by the miracle of salvation. He wants to exist, without having an existence of his own; he want less to live than to experience — or, to use the German, he prefers *erleben* to *leben*.

Therefore the romantic "personality" is also something totally different from, say, the Kantian personality who confronts us as the bearer of the moral law and who finds himself, and thus his freedom, in being faithful to the commandment. The romantic, too, loves his own being; but he seeks this individuality in the fluid world of his feelings which, capable of the quasi miraculous, can enter into everything and mean everything. Only out of this emotional experience, which becomes for him the measure of all things, does he derive what is good and evil for him. It is not through ethical action and not through clear knowledge that he expects to find the way to himself. He believes that he can become certain of himself only in self-contained feeling, in emotional self-contemplation which does not give expression to the emotions but dwells on them and all-too-easily becomes sheer virtuosity of feeling, admiring itself in the mirror of introspection and preening its own beautiful soul. There is, therefore, no more unromantic remark than Goethe's when he says that man comes to know himself by doing his duty and living up to the demands of the day. The romantics say instead: experience yourself and revel in yourself.

It is for these reasons that romanticism is usually oriented backwards, that it has its ideal in bygone ages, in the paradise of the past. It does not want to create but to find again and restore. After all, whoever prefers to feel and dream soon sees himself surrounded by ancient images; and only those who direct their will toward fixed tasks know themselves to be standing in a living relationship to the future. Therefore it is also given to romanticism to hearken to the voices from former times. Romanticism is especially qualified for this because, with its abundance of emotion, it is capable of reflecting all the recesses and mysteries of the human soul and to feel its way into different individualities. It has discovered the poetry of transitions, also the poetry of the divisions and clefts of the soul; it has known how to comprehend the radiation that emanates from the individual phenomenon and has cultivated the devotion to what is minute. Man with his contradictions is its subject. Hence romanticism has produced the artists of biography and cultivated the kind of history which demands empathy. But only this kind; it has not shown much vision regarding over-all connections or the ideas of the centuries. Romanticism remains lyrical even when it contemplates the seriousness of great events, and history becomes for it a game in which one becomes absorbed. One will here look in vain for the great message of the past. The strength and weakness of emotion determines the power and the impotence of romanticism.

It is the same everywhere. It is always feeling that is supposed to mean everything. Hence the capacity for feeling defines the dimensions and the limits of romanticism. We see this at close range in its representatives of the last century with their merits and their weaknesses. In opposition to the exclusive rule of the sober understanding, romanticism had legitimately demanded another right and another value. But romanticism itself soon fell victim to the same fundamental mistake which it had arisen to combat; for almost immediately it, too, claimed exclusive validity. It elevated pure feeling above everything else, above all conceptual and all obligatory truth — and eventually not only above everything else but in place of everything else. It strove to drown in beautiful illusion more and more of reality with its commandment, and to let the profound seriousness of the tasks of our life fade into a mere musical mood, to let them evaporate into the floating spheres of existence.

It gave its name to a whole generation in the last century; and yet romanticism is not applicable merely to a particular epoch, to a mere period of history. Romanticism means much more: it designates one of the characteristic forms which have emerged again and again in the development of mankind — a certain type in which, from time immemorial, religious life in particular has manifested itself. To be sure, historical types, just like human types, never appear quite pure. Whatever exists is a mixture; nowhere does life know sharp boundaries and distinctions; it is never an equation without any remainder. There are certain romantic elements in every religion, no less than in every human soul. Every religion has its dream of faith in which appearance and reality seek to mingle; each has its own twilight valley; each knows of world-weariness and contempt for the factual. But in one religion this is merely a quiet path alongside the road, a sound which accompanies, a tone which also vibrates. In another religion it fixes the direction; it is the dominant basic chord which determines the religious melody and gives it its character. Thus, depending on whether this or a wholly different motif is the decisive one, the romantic religion distinguishes itself quite clearly from the classical. And in this sense it may be said: Judaism is the classical religion and Christianity, compared with it, the romantic religion.

Paul

Christianity accepted the inheritance of ancient — Greek and oriental — romanticism. At an early date, the traditional national religion in the Hellenic lands had been joined by a victorious intruder, probably from the north: another religion — darker, phantastic and sentimental — the Dionysian or Orphic cult of which much might be said, but certainly not: "What distinguished the Greeks? Reason and measure and clarity." It had all the traits of romanticism: the exuberance of emotion, the enthusiastic flight from reality, the longing for an experience. Holy consecrations and atonements were taught and ecstatically tested with reeling senses. They aimed to relate man to the beyond; they aimed to make him one with the god and thus grant him redemption from primordial sin and original guilt. For this, it was said, could not be attained by mortal man with his own power, but must be a gift of grace which had to descend from hidden regions and to which a mediator and savior, a god, who once had walked on earth had shown the way. Marvelous traditions told of this and handed on the stories of the redeeming events and their mysteries, that they might be renewed again and again in the believers. Mystical music dramas, showy, phantastic presentations, seemingly removed into mysterious distances by the twilight, granted the weary, drowsy soul the beautiful dream, and the sentimental longing its fulfillment: the faith that it belonged to the elect.

In the official religion, this wish of the individual to be chosen and to stand before the god, this individual desire to be important and attain eternal life and bliss, had not found satisfaction. Now all this was offered to him by this enthusiastic religion of moods. And thus it was that this religion found its way more and more into the souls; it became the new religion which gradually decomposed the old naïve faith and the classical spirit of the Greeks, and eventually destroyed it.

Moreover, it had received further strength from all sides, wherever religious romanticism had a home: from the oriental and Egyptian mysteries, from the cults of Mithras and Adonis, of Attis and Serapis. In essentials they were all alike: they shared the sentimental attitude which seeks escape from life into living experience and turns the attention towards a phantastic and marvelous beyond. What they proclaimed, too, was at bottom always the same. It was the faith in a heavenly being that had become man, died, and been resurrected, and whose divine life a mortal could share through mysterious rites; the faith in a force of grace, entering the believer from above through a sacrament, to redeem him from the bonds of earthly guilt and earthly death and to awaken him to a new life which would mean eternal existence and blessedness. The roving yearning of a weary age was only too ready to become absorbed in these conceptions of resurrection and apotheosis, of instruments of grace and consecrations; and it even sought them out everywhere. From all lands the mysteries could flow together in mighty waves.

The tide moved along a free and wide course. The region from the Euphrates to the Atlantic Ocean had under Roman rule become the place of a matchless mixture of peoples fused into a cultural unity. Just like the ancient states, the old pagan religions, too, had more and more lost their boundaries and their former definiteness. A cosmopolitan yearning and hope gripped and united all of them. The way was prepared for a new faith without limits or boundaries. In the worldwide empire it could become the world religion and the world philosophy. Whatever it was that a human being might seek, it promised everything to everybody — mystery and knowledge, ecstasy and vision, living experience and eternity. It was everything and took the place of everything and therefore finally overcame everything. The great romantic tide thus swept over the Roman empire, and the ancient world drowned in it. Even as the old naïve poetry of the gods perished in the sentimental myth of the redeeming savior, so what was classical vanished, along with its sure sense of law and determination, and gave way to the mere feeling of a faith which was sufficient unto itself.

What is called the victory of Christianity was in reality this victory of romanticism. Before Christianity took its course, that through which it eventually became Christianity — or, to put it differently, whatever in it is non-Jewish — had already become powerful enough to be reckoned as a world faith, as a new piety which united the nations. The man with whose name this victory is connected, Paul, was, like all romantics, not so much a creator of ideas as a connector of ideas; the genius of seeing and establishing such connections was characteristic of him. He must be credited with one achievement — and this single achievement was of world-historical significance and truly something great — that he carried living Jewish ideas into the mysteries which even then commanded the allegiance of a whole world. He knew how to fuse the magic of the universal mysteries with the tradition of revelation of the secrecy-wrapt Jewish wisdom. Thus he gave the ancient romanticism a new and superior power — a power taken from Judaism. It was this blend, compounded by him, that the world of the dying Roman empire — Orient and Occident, which had become one world — accepted.

In Paul's own soul, this union in which romantic and Jewish elements were to be combined, had prevailed after a period of transition. Subjectively, this union represented the story of his struggles which became the story of his life. The images of his homeland, Asia Minor, had early revealed to him the one element, romanticism; the parental home and the years of his studies had presented him with the other, the Jewish one. Then, in the land of his people, he had found those who longingly awaited the helper and liberator of whom the prophets had spoken — some hoping that he might come, others waiting that he might return.

Eventually he discovered himself among those who were thus waiting —
those whose eyes were fixed on the image of their messiah, their Christ,
who had died young and would return when his day came — an image
similar in many of its features to that offered by his pagan homeland
in its mysteries. The pagans in those days were aware of Judaism; and
Jews, too, paid attention to the thinking and seeking of paganism. Thus
the promises and wisdom from here and there, from paganism and from
Judaism, entered into his unrest and doubts which pulled him hither
and thither, looking and listening far and wide, in his craving for the
certainty of truth. He did not want merely to wait and hope; he wished
it might be given him to have and to believe.

Finally he had perceived an answer. It was a victorious and liberating
answer to his mind because it did not merely grant a coming, a promised, day, something yet to be, but a redemption which was fulfilled even
then — as it were, a Now. This answer became for him the end which
meant everything because it contained everything: both that of which
the mysteries of the nations had told him and that which the proclamations of his own Jewish people had said to him. Alongside the one God
before whom the gods of the pagans were to vanish, it now placed the
one redeemer, the one savior before whom the saviors of the nations
could sink out of sight: it placed the oneness of the savior alongside
the oneness of God. Thus he experienced it: paganism, with its deepest aspirations and thoughts, was led to Judaism; and Judaism, with its
revelation and truth, was bestowed on the pagans, too.

Now everything seemed to fall into place. What his Judaism had let
him find in the circle of those waiting, in the proclamation of the messianic faith, as the fulfillment and goal of all prophecy, this faith in the
final answer, in the final certainty, in him who had come and would
come — all this he discovered now in the quest of the pagans; all this he
perceived when he contemplated the myth which the marvelous mysteries everywhere presented to the world. And where confused strains
out of the pagan world had spoken to him of the mysterious tidings of
grace, in which a whole world had created for itself the satisfaction of
its yearnings, his own people's faith in a messiah now permitted him
to comprehend quite clearly all that had till then seemed so dark. Now
he grasped it: not Attis or Adonis, not Mithras or Serapis was the name
of the resurrected, the savior, who became man and had been god, but
his name was Jesus Christ. And the significance of Jesus, who had become the Christ of his people, could not be that he had become king of
the Jews, their king by the grace of God, their admonisher, comforter,
and helper; but his life and his power signified the one, the greatest,
thing, that he was the resurrected, miracle-working, redeeming God, he

that had been from eternity. And for all who owned him, who had faith in him and possessed him in sacrament and mystery, the day that was promised had become today, had been fulfilled. In him Jew and pagan were the new man, the true Israel, the true present.

The last veil now seemed to Paul to have been taken from his eyes, and he saw the hitherto divided world unified. In the messianic certainty of Judaism he now recognized the goal toward which the seeking and erring of the pagans had, in the depths of truth, always aspired; and in that which the pagans had wanted but not known, he now grasped the content and the answer which was spoken, which was promised to Judaism. Judaism and paganism had now become one for him; the one world had arrived which comprehended everything, the one body and the one spirit of all life. That Jewish and pagan wisdom meant, at bottom, the same thing, was one of the ideas of the age. Now it seemed to have become the truth. Now the Jews need no longer merely wait, as the community of the expectant, for the last day, which would then in turn become the first day, when the messiah would come or come again; in a mysterious sacrament, the fulfilled time in which everything has been accomplished, the goal of the longed-for redemption, was given to them even now, given in every hour. And now the pagans really could come to know him for whom they had from time immemorial looked, the named but unknown; and now they could comprehend the mystery which had since ancient times been present among them as their precious possession. Judaism and paganism were now reconciled, brought together in romanticism, in the world of the mystery, of myth, and of sacrament.

Precisely how this net of ideas took shape in the mind of Paul, how the different threads found each other and crossed each other, which idea came first and which one it then attracted — to ask about this would merely lead to vain and useless speculation. Beginning with his childhood, Paul had been confronted both with the possession of Judaism in the parental home and with the sight of the mystery cults in his homeland. In his consciousness both had their place, and they were woven together and became one. This union which was fashioned in him then emerged out of him into the world. And it became victorious in a world which had become weary and sentimental; it became the religion for all those whose faint, anxious minds had darted hither and thither to seek strength. It represented the completion of a long development.

For what had been most essential in the ancient mysteries is preserved in this Pauline religion. It, too, believed in the romantic fate of a god which reflects the inexorable lot of man and is the content of all life. What everything represents is not a creation of God and not an eternal moral order, but a process of salvation. In a heavenly-earthly drama, in the miraculous mystery that took shape between the here and the above, the meaning of world history and of the individual human life stands revealed. There is no other word but the definite word "myth," romantic myth, to characterize this form of faith. With this, Paul left Judaism; for there was no place in it for any myth that would be more than a parable — no more for the new sentimental one than for the old naïve myths of former times. This myth was the bridge on which Paul went over to romanticism. To be sure, this man had lived within Judaism deep down in his soul; and psychically he never quite got away from it. Even after his conversion to mystery and sacrament, he only too often found himself again on the old Jewish ways of thought, as though unconsciously and involuntarily; and the manifold contradictions between his sentences derive from this above all. The Jew that he remained in spite of everything, at the bottom of his soul, again and again fought with the romantic in him, whose moods and ideas were ever present to him. But in spite of this, if we are to label him as he stands before us, the apostle of a new outlook, then we can only call him a romantic. Trait for trait we recognize in his psychic type the features that distinguish the romantic.

The Experience of Faith

Paul, too, sees everything — to use Schlegel's term — in the "phantastic form" in which the border lines of appearance and reality, of twilight and event, are lost; in which he sees images which the eye never saw and hears words which the ear never perceived; in which he can feel redeemed from this world and its harshness, from what is earthly in him and from what desires to cling to the soil of this earth. Thus he lives in the beyond which transcends all things, beyond the struggle between upward drive and gravity, beyond becoming and perishing, where only faith can reach and only miracles can take place. Therefore faith is everything to him. Faith is grace, faith is salvation, faith is life, faith is truth; faith is being, the ground and the goal, the beginning and the end; commencement and vocation meet in it. Faith is valid for faith's sake. One feels reminded of the modern slogan, *l'art pour l'art*; Pauline romanticism might be labeled correspondingly, *la foi pour la foi*.

This faith is so completely everything that down here nothing can be done for it and nothing may be done for it; all "willing or running" is nonsensical and useless. The salvation that comes through faith is in no sense earned, but wholly received; and it comes only to those for whom it was destined from the beginning. God effects it, as Luther later explained the words of Paul, "in us and without us."[2] Man is no more than the mere object of God's activity, of grace or of damnation; he does not recognize God, God merely recognizes him; he *becomes* a child of redemption or of destruction, "forced into disobedience" or raised up to salvation. He is the object of virtue and of sin — not its producer, it subject. One feels like saying: man does not live but is lived, and what remains to him is merely, to speak with Schleiermacher, "the taste of infinity," that is, the living experience; the mood and the emotional relation of one who knows himself to be wholly an object; the feeling of faith in which grace is present or the feeling of unbelief in which sin prevails.

The theory of original sin and election, which Paul formulated after the manner of the ancient mystery doctrine and then shrouded in a biblical-talmudic dress, serves only to demonstrate the completeness of that power which makes passivity — or, to say it again in the words of German romanticism, pure "helplessness" and "absolute dependence" — the lot of man. A supernatural destiny which, whether it be grace or damnation, is always a *fatum*, determines according to an inexorable law that a man should be thus or thus. He is pure object; fate alone is subject. In this way, religion becomes redemption from the will, liberation from the deed.

Later on, the Catholicism of the Middle Ages softened this conception and granted a certain amount of human participation. But Luther then returned to the purer romanticism of Paul with its motto, *sola fide*, through faith alone; "it must come from heaven and solely through grace."[3] The image which he supplies to illustrate this point is, quite in keeping with Luther's style, harsh in tone, and yet thoroughly Pauline in its meaning: *velut paralyticum*, "as one paralyzed,"[4] man should wait for salvation and faith. The heteronomy of life is thus formulated: the life of man has its law and its content only outside itself.

This faith is therefore decidedly not the expression of a conviction obtained through struggle, or of a certainty grown out of search and inquiry. Seeking and inquiring is only "wisdom of the flesh" and the manner of "philosophers and rabbis." True knowledge is not worked out by man but worked in him; man cannot clear a way toward it; only the flood of grace brings it to him and gives him the quintessence of knowledge, the totality of insight. Knowledge here is not what instructs but what redeems, and it is not gained by thinking but given in faith; it

---

[2] *In nobis et sine nobis.* Weimar edition, VI, 530 (*De capt. Babyl.*).

[3] Weimar edition, XIV, 244.

[4] Ibid., II, 420: *oportet ergo hominem de suis operibus diffidere et velut paralyticum remissis manibus et pedibus gratiam operum artificem implorare.*

goes with the consciousness of absolute dependence. "Do not seek, for to him who has faith all is given!" This is the new principle, the axiom of romantic truth; and all wrestling and striving for knowledge has thus lost its value and, what is more, its very meaning. There is no longer any place for the approximation of truth, step for step; there is no longer any middle ground between those who see everything and those who see nothing. Grace now gives complete light where up to now only darkness held the spirit in its embrace. Grace places man at the goal, and he is the perfect, the finished man.

The conception of the finished man which appears here — truly the brain child of romanticism for which truth is only a living experience — became one of the most effective ideas in the entire Pauline doctrine. It has again and again attracted and even permanently captivated those minds who would like so much to believe in their entire possession of the truth and who long for the rest which such complete possession would afford. Since the end of the ancient world, the intellectual life of the Occident has in many ways been determined by this notion. It has established that orientation in which the answer precedes every question, and every result comes before the task, and those appear who quite simply have what is wanted and who never want to become and grow.

The philosophy appropriate to this conception of the finished man is that doctrine which considers truth as given from the outset, that scholasticism which possesses and knows the whole truth, down to its ultimate ramifications, from the start and merely needs to proclaim it or to demonstrate it *ex post facto*. Most of the thought produced by the Catholic Middle Ages shows the influence of this conception. And Luther's world of thought is completely dominated by it; for Luther clings to the rigid faith in such possession and, in that sense, to the Middle Ages.

Only the age of the Enlightenment began to push the conception back, but it really made a beginning only. For when romanticism re-awakened in the last century, the conception returned with it, and it has survived together with romanticism. It has, indeed, created what might be called racial scholasticism, with its doctrine of salvation, with its system of grace, and with its faith that this grace works through the dark abysses of the blood — this modernized *pneuma* — and gives the chosen everything, so that the finished man is once again the goal of the creation. Wherever romanticism is found, this conception appears by its side.

The much quoted *credo quia absurdum* — "I believe because it is absurd" — is nothing but the ultimate formulation which results from this conception, almost as a matter of course. What confronts the inquiring spirit and his thinking as something opposed to reason, and unacceptable, may be the truth for the finished mind of the completed man, whether he owes his completion to grace or another source. To this faith knowledge must submit. Sooner or later, every romanticism demands the *sacrificium intellectus*, the sacrifice of the intellect. Here, too, the best commentary for Paul is found in Luther's words: "In all who have faith in Christ," he says, "reason shall be killed; else faith does not govern them; for reason fights against faith."[5]

Unquestionably, the romantic certainty which Paul proclaims is derived from an original psychic experience. When a strong idea emerges out of the hidden darkness of the unconscious, where it had slowly and silently taken shape, and all at once enters consciousness, it is always at first distinguished by the suddenness of the unexpected and seems to possess the power of a revelation. As if it had been fashioned by a miracle, as if the path of thought had not in this case been covered step by step, truth seems to confront the mind finished and completed; it appears to speak to him, and he feels that he does not have to do anything but listen; and the person who has this experience may have the feeling that grace has descended upon him and elected him. This is, after all, also one of the forms in which the seeking genius may find his solution; it is, in the words of a modern thinker, the romantic type of invention. And it is the same which confronts us in Goethe's epigram: "In very small matters, much depends on choice and will; the highest that we encounter comes who knows from where." Something universally human is expressed here. . . .

One might characterize the Pauline religion in sharp juxtapositions: absolute dependence as opposed to the commandment, the task, of achieving freedom; leaning as opposed to self-affirmation and self-development; quietism as opposed to dynamism. There the human being is the subject; here, in romantic religion, the object. The freedom of which it likes so much to speak is merely a freedom received as a gift, the granting of salvation as a fact, not a goal to be fought for. It is the faith that does not go beyond itself, that is not the task of life; only a "thou hast" and not a "thou shalt." In classical religion, man is to become free through the commandment; in romantic religion he has become free through grace. . . .

Culture and History

. . . In the religious activity demanded by classical religion, man finds himself directed toward others; in mere religious experience, in this devotion devoid of any commandment, he seeks everything in himself. He

---

[5]Erlangen edition, 44, 156f.

is concerned only with himself, satisfied with himself, concentrated on himself to the point of religious vanity, of a coquettishness of faith. Thus Nietzsche, in his superlative manner, once described this type: "He is terribly preoccupied with himself; he has no time to think of others." Nothing could be more opposed to the aspirations of a social conscience than this romantic piety which always seeks only itself and its salvation.

Romantic religion is completely opposed to the whole sphere of existence with which the social conscience is concerned. Every romanticism depreciates the life devoted to work and culture, that context of life which the active human being creates for himself and in which he knows himself in relation to others. Where life disintegrates into momentary moods, as in romanticism, and where living experience alone — the instant, in other words — is recognized as essential, while everything else appears merely as "the void between the instants," work will always be counted only as something lowly, or at least as something subordinate. Mere living experience, the instant, is the contradiction of work. Hence romanticism cannot gain any clear and positive relation to work. It is not a mere poetic whim but representative of the very flesh and blood of romanticism when Friedrich Schlegel sings the praise of leisure, of romantic sloth, and "sleep is the highest degree of genius" for him. All this is nothing else than that passivity of romanticism which would rather dream than work.

This defect has become most calamitous for romantic *religion*. As soon as it entered an area of cultural activity and was to be *inside* it and not just alongside, it had to find itself divided against itself: work was depreciated and yet had to be demanded. The history of medieval Catholic ethics with all its dualism, with its distinction between earthly and heavenly vocation, with the "commandments" and "counsels" it offered, manifests this contradiction. Nor was Luther able to overcome it. To be sure, he raised the estimation of worldly work. But to begin with, he got to this point only by the way of negation, through his opposition to an idle monkhood. And as soon as he looked for a positive appreciation of work, he was unable, here, too, to get beyond the Pauline conception of absolute dependence. For him the earthly sphere of existence and work, in which man is placed after all, is a decree from above, to which man must resign himself in humility and obedience; caste and guild represent a firm barrier which must not be tampered with, because it has been erected by God. For any upward social drive Luther lacked any sense or sympathy whatever: the conception of a God-given dependency and of the subordination of social classes as a divine institution is thoroughly Lutheran. Only Calvinism — in this respect, too, returning closer to Judaism — began to recognize more clearly that there is a liberating, ethical power in worldly work and that the rights and aims of civilian occupations manifest an upward drive. . . .

Much as was demanded of the state ecclesiastically, little was asked from it morally. One did not have to ask anything. The romantic principle of the finished and completed was in any case opposed to any upward drive, and the romantic mood came to terms with everything that was low. One can have a strong faith and pious experiences without being disturbed by slavery, torture, and public horrors. The feeling of absolute dependence which is sensitive to sacred music is not disturbed by any of this. Already the ancient mystery religion got along very well with tyrants, and these in turn were very well disposed toward it, because they could easily see that the devotee of supernatural events is an obedient subject on the earth below. It has been ever thus, and episodes of Jewish romanticism attest it, too. The alliance between ruler and believer has been readily formed wherever romantic religion has held sway; every reaction has been consecrated and every forward drive been damned. . . .

. . . It becomes the quintessence of religion, that one becomes absorbed in the incomparable event which once occurred and tries to re-experience it. The past is turned into dogma.

This essentially unhistorical attitude toward history is particularly evident in modern Protestantism; indeed, here above all, because a completed story is almost all that remains to it. After it has given up most dogmas, a completed story remains almost its only axiom of faith. The question of the "unique" personality of Jesus becomes for it the question of the very existence of religion. All its exertions and aspirations must be directed again and again toward some kind of historical evidence for this one particular life, to counter the ever new objections. All its striving and efforts are thus a perpetual restoration, an ever renewed attempt to present the one event of the past in a fitting style; restoration is, after all, a romantic enterprise. The relation to religion becomes a relation to a story. . . .

The Sacrament

But it is not only the position here conceded to subjective experience, it is rather this very experience itself which threatens romanticism as a dangerous cliff. The experience which "comes out of faith and becomes faith" is supposed to mean everything; it becomes the cornerstone of religion. Yet it is found in the soul only in rare festive hours. Man does not live on moods alone. And here we find the critical point of Pauline, as indeed of every romantic, religion: it can never do without the living experience, yet this experience does not want to and cannot come continuously, nor can it be brought to everybody; it "bloweth where it listeth." It is supposed to be the one and all of religion, that power without which religion cannot do; but the gates to it do not open every day, nor to everybody. Only one solution is possible: a way must be found for making the extraordinary constant; and the gift of the festive hour a gift of the weekday, too. The experience must be brought down to earth. . . .

That romanticism, on the other hand, on which Paul drew, had followed higher paths. It had taught the sacraments — that is, the means of grace and blessedness, the sacred objects and rites, baptisms, anointments, meals which always produce a union of the deity with the human being — so that the miracle of the experience can, by means of them, be made objectively effective day after day. In them the phantastic form of this religion becomes palpable and plain; they furnish the ever-ready miracle, the *miraculum ex machina*; they open the door through which the miracle enters time and again, through which the spirit blows repeatedly: the living experience is to be made a guaranteed possession. Paul accepted these means of grace almost unchanged from ancient romanticism, and there is nothing which connects his religion more obviously with the ancient mystery cults than his doctrine of the sacraments. For him, too, they are indispensable, the firm ground of existence in the faith, the necessary condensation of the living experience; without them, his religion would float in the air.

This physical image from the natural sphere is no mere metaphor here. No less than in the mystery cults, the sacraments are for Paul, too, something entirely material and objective. Any attempt to see mere symbols in them, he would have vigorously repudiated as profane and shallow. They are something completely real, tangible; the miraculous divine energy dwells in them, and hence they are valid as such and productive as magical and sacred things through which the vital power of God is transmitted to man. Man himself is here, too, as indeed in the whole Pauline doctrine, an object only; he does not consecrate the action nor work it, but it infuses itself into him and works a miracle in him; and it is, in the words of an ancient Christian document, "the medicine of eternal life, the antidote against death."[6] The human conscience does not add anything to this action and does not subtract anything from it, at least nothing essential; it possesses its full and indestructible power within itself. Its significance is that of an objective event, of an actual process in man. Hence it is only consistent that the sacrament is said to work, too, quite independently of the human will and of anything a person might contribute — working simply by happening, *ex opere operato*. Without in the least impairing the miracle or diminishing it, the miracle can be

---

[6]Ignatius, Ephes. 20, 2.

obtained and carried out for a human being and in him by others — even for one who has died exactly as for those into whom the life of thought has not yet entered, such as newborn children. The human being in whom the miracle takes place need not participate either through action or through knowledge. That complete passivity, that absolute dependence in terms of which Paul conceives of human nature, and the heteronomy of existence which he teaches find unequivocal expression in these ideas.

But not only this; another essential point also finds expression here: the religion which began so spiritually becomes condensed and materialized. The sacraments accomplish the miracle and create the state of salvation; they join one to God precisely as the experience of faith did. But the salvation they bring is no longer something that relates purely to the soul, no longer something that works in the psychic realm and can be understood psychologically; it is something supernaturally material, something that works magic. Salvation here becomes a substance which enters man; a substance, to be sure, of a supernatural kind, and yet a substance. It is a heavenly water of baptism and a heavenly bread of communion that save from death for life.

The form in which the sacrament has prevailed is one in which it has retained its significance as a real thing: the Roman Catholic as well as the Greek Orthodox Church cling to this, and Luther, too, accepted it as a matter of principle. And gradually it pushed back the original state of faith more and more. Very understandably, for it offered no less: it gave everything and accomplished everything, it saved and redeemed, and was at the same time the ever ready gift of every day. Thus it gradually had to occupy an ample area in this religion.

To be sure, the Catholic Church has tried to remain faithful to its romantic origin and principle and has sought to preserve the experience itself, too, in all its extraordinary, immediate spiritual power. It has assigned a high status to those who turn their backs on this life so that they might have the full and immediate experience, and in consequence the Church has released other people from this obligation: in its monks and hermits it has created vicars of romanticism. For this was after all the meaning and idea of monasticism, namely, that there should be human beings whose existence would not merely be interrupted now and then by religion, people to whom the sacrament would not be the only thing to bring the moment in which the divine confronts and enters man — those, in other words, to whom the stream of the hours would again and again bring the experience as a whole so that it might arch over their existence and provide its dominant mood. To these persons religion is given in its romantic fullness, as the *vita religiosa*.

Some later movements in the Church, too, are best understood as efforts to restore its all-important place to the living impression of God. Luther's original striving and aspiration, the period of his "Methodist" piety, also aimed at this as did the enthusiastic Baptist movement and Pietism. In the same way, the Catholic Church has, as a matter of principle, clung to the original, extraordinary "miracle"; it has found the quintessence of sanctity only in those who perform this miracle, or in whom it is performed; and it has also time and again known how to discover such saints. . . .

Romantic Truth

In the Church, authorities were created quite early: personal ones in the hierarchy of a miracle-working priesthood and objective ones in the propositions of the *dogma*, the profession of the miracles. These belong together and complete each other. The dogma comprehends and grants the knowledge of faith, even as the priesthood with its sacraments possesses and dispenses the experiences of faith. Both of them embody, and transform into a body, an originally spiritual content of faith. If romanticism began by finding knowledge in such seizure and transport as come over man through meditation and ecstasy and let their waves close over him, now all this floating and flowing became condensed. Dogma is frozen feeling; clotted, petrified mood. Billowing knowledge becomes firm, tangible acknowledgment. Just as in the sacrament, the process of materialization also reveals itself in the dogma. Sooner or later, this process takes place in all romanticism.

The desire for dogma appeared quite early. The miracle of the mysteries in which faith seeks knowledge is, by its very nature, something fluctuating and unstable and therefore calls for a standard determination which can always be pointed to and handed on: its symbol, its "mark of recognition" which discloses its true significance and effect. The Greek mysteries already had their sentences which were to proffer the saving truth, their passwords which opened the gate of redemption. What such formulations grant to faith is that it need no longer be ecstatic or seek transfiguration. The faith which had wanted to drown, to sink down in the infinite, amorphous, now has its firm complex of ideas, determined once and for all, which can simply be accepted. Now the believer finds it still easier to be a finished man in his own eyes and to remain assured of the fulfillment of his knowledge. This calm conviction will be even stronger in him insofar as it is a wide-spread conviction. It may be nourished as a catholic, all-embracing conviction, with the powerful consciousness that one possesses what is valid without exception "always, everywhere, and for all." Though this dogmatic certainty is created by the Church, it in turn fortifies the idea of the Church.

But this power of certainty still has to be paid for dearly in the end; for in this universal faith which the individual merely shares, any individual or personal faith is easily lost, as has been shown. The faith now is no longer that which has been revealed and experienced, but what is formulated and published. It becomes faithfulness; the experienced becomes something learned and spoken, a systematic doctrine of faith whose propositions have to be accepted. Since it is no longer the individual as such who believes but the Church, the individual merely stands within the faith of the Church. And the Church, in turn, confronts everything personal with mistrust and must repudiate it and reject it as raving enthusiasm and addiction to innovations. . . .

Along with dogma appeared also its corollary, orthodoxy — that bent of mind which would cultivate respect for the answer but, in the process, often loses respect for the problem. The history of classical religion also tells of this; but here it appears only as the claim of a party, not as the manifestation of an original, native tendency. In romantic faith, on the other hand it is an essential quality, something grounded in this faith from the beginning. There is, therefore, no Christianity without it. However protestant a movement may here be at the start, in the end, if it would remain Christian, it must assume the form of orthodoxy. Precisely in Lutheranism, the religion of the Word To Be Preached, orthodoxy appears as a dominant concept, as the condition of all piety; the profession of the creed occupies here also the place which the cult occupies in Catholicism. Orthodoxy here gains what the sacrament has lost — lost, to be sure, not in miraculous significance, but in breadth — it gains, above all, in voice and pathos. It had to become more pronounced, more emphatic, because it could not base itself on the popular conception of infallibility, that Catholic consciousness of what is valid "always, everywhere, and for all"; it became a professing orthodoxy, *fides explicita*. But whether it is this orthodoxy or the quieter one of Catholicism, its *fides implicita*, it always amounts almost to stripping the individual believer of the rights of majority; he now appears only as the lowly subject who accepts, whose first virtue is obedience, and who has done enough for himself when he believes the authority and resigns himself to the finished propositions of the dogma. The heteronomy of this kind of religion manifests itself in this, too. . . .

Here dogma received its full, all-embracing significance; for here knowledge, *gnosis*, does not merely instruct — it redeems. The salvation of man, his eternal bliss, depends on it. Thus the dogma becomes the one and all to which a man "must hold fast"; in the dogma we have the very essence of the religion. Dogmatic exactitude becomes the guarantee of the possession of the eternal good. Deviation from the confession is the road to damnation; error becomes abyss. . . .

The Commandment and the Deed

. . . For the believer there is no command to do anything. "Christ is the end of the law"[7]; the new justice annuls the old: thus Paul formulated it. But the idea is older than Paul: it is that romantic notion which recognizes man only as an object and considers valid only what happens to man, what he experiences. Paul merely gave this notion its most exaggerated formulation by finding justice altogether in *not* willing, in passivity; he not only measured the value of activity by the standard of romantic aimlessness, but placed it in the category of unbelief, of godlessness. Justice is for him exclusively something that happens to man: man therefore need not exercise it; he only must believe in it. Thus it presupposes as its very condition that the will to be just, and indeed any active striving and willing, is negated. The whole theology of Paul revolves around this negation.

That this became the pivot of his romanticism is connected with the climate of thought in which he lived. An old Jewish saying has it that in the ideal days of the future, when the spirit of God will dwell in the hearts of men, every commandment, every "ought" will cease. One felt that all fulfillment of duty was based upon a tension; the tension between will and obligation, between inclination and duty. The ideal is for this antagonism to give way to a higher unity: duty should become one with our inmost nature; what we ought to be should become one with what we are; or in the words of a saying current in those days, God's will should become our will, and thus our will would become one with the divine will. The idea here is precisely the same as in Schiller's remark: "Accept the deity into your will and it will descend from the throne of the world." The language of Paul's time had also expressed this idea by saying that in the messianic days there would be no more guilt or merit, neither commandment nor law. Seeing that the community founded by John had considered Jesus the messiah and had waited for his return, it might well have been said here already that the Law would come to an end as soon as he appeared again, and with him the expected time in which "all has been fulfilled."

For Paul, this time had come already. In the sacrament all was "fulfilled," and salvation, the life of eternity, was given. Hence the Law had to be finished and annulled. If it continued to be valid, then the redemp-

---

[7]Romans 10:4. —*Tr.*

tive mystery could not be what it should be. That the Law should cease for the baptized was therefore for Paul the crucial question on which the very existence of his religion depended, from his Jewish messianic point of view, too. Any recognition of the Law meant the denial that salvation had come and that the redemption had occurred. Sacrament or Law —- the decision between these two had to be made. Paul could not get away from this. Thus the old ideal was romanticized: the wish begotten by longing was transformed into the secure possession granted by grace. For the finished man the Law is annulled. . . .

The strictness of this romanticism was admittedly attenuated before long; the human desire for deeds made its demands. Even in the scriptures of the New Testament we encounter the word of James of "faith *and* works," and the Catholic Church was glad to follow him; here, too, as elsewhere, it granted human aspiration a legitimate sphere. Through the sacrament of penance the Church made a place for it; and, for its sake, the Church even adopted a certain ambivalence and the danger of an ambiguity for which it was to be reproached frequently. Luther, however, later returned to decided and uncompromising romanticism, and "solely through faith" became for him what it had been for Paul: the sole meaning of justice. Again, justice becomes nothing but the consciousness of absolute dependence on the grace of God in Christ; all spontaneous willing is again identified with sin. Luther says this expressly: "The Gospel is a doctrine which admits no Law."[8] "The Law has been fulfilled — by Christ; one need not fulfill it, but only adhere with faith to him who has fulfilled it and be made like him."[9] "We are called just, not when we do what is just, but when we believe and trust in God."[10] "Christian justice is faith in the son of God."[11] "All that you begin is sin and remains sin, however prettily it may glisten. You can do nothing but sin. . . . All is sin that you do alone from free will."[12] . . .

Ethics

The Pauline dogma removes the very ground from under man's rights as a moral subject, as an ethical individual. That which could and should unfold into a personality, that which is unique and individual, must give way to the concept of the species. Man appears merely as one of the

---

[8] Ibid., I, 113: *Est ergo Evangelium doctrina talis, quae nullam legem admittit.*

[9] Weimar edition, I, 106: *quod lex est impleta, scil. per Christum, quod non sit necesse eam implere, sed tantummodo implenti per fidem adhaerere et conformari.*

[10] Ibid., I, 84: *Non enim qui justa operatur, justus est, ut Aristoteles ait, neque operando justi et dicimur justi, sed credendo et sperando in Deum.*

[11] *Ep. ad Gal.*, ed. Irmischer, I, 334: *Justitia christiana est fiducia in Filium Dei.*

[12] Erlangen edition, 10 (2), 11.

manifestations of sin or grace; in Spinoza's terminology one might say: he is merely a mode of one or the other. It is clear why Schleiermacher could suppose that he was somehow close to Spinoza. Moral freedom — the freedom revealed in the fact that the good is possible for man and should become actual through his agency — is rejected. There is only a freedom that has been granted, predestined, "lotted" — a freedom which consists in being free from the devil and the demons.

The point must be stated still more comprehensively. The Pauline faith deprives ethics itself of its basis. The sacrament had already rendered ethics all but superfluous: the mystery alone meant something and the moral sphere lagged behind. Moreover, baptism has become decisive, and the great work of grace is finished: what could any human achievement mean after that? The Church, especially the early Church, always found it difficult to say what could happen to and through man after the sacrament. Ethics was from now on reduced to a subordinate, if not altogether superfluous, position. The new justice seemed to annul it altogether. Where the will that decides for itself is considered the path of destruction, no place is left for ethics; indeed, it is expressly repudiated. Religion now becomes the opposite, the contradiction of ethics; each excludes the other in principle. Either faith or ethics! That is the innermost meaning of the fight which Paul and Luther waged against the "Law." They did not merely oppose something ceremonial; "Law" is for them any valuation of human activity, even the most moral. Man becomes good only through the miracle which has been accomplished. Whoever expects the good from the fulfillment of the commandments and duties, still lives under the yoke of the Law. Law and miracle cannot be reconciled. Either the one or the other; either will or grace, deed or mystery, ethics or religion. However one chooses to put it, it is always the same opposition that defines the essence of religion, first for the apostle and then for the reformer.

What we have here is a unique approach to religion that has not only historical significance but also some psychological justification. It is justifiable as something peculiar that should not be obliterated. The romantic experience in which man is purely receptive is indeed the contradiction of the deed. The deed confronts it as something strange, almost as a disturbance and an obstacle which must be removed. If religion is to be exhausted by the miraculous experience, as Paul would have it, then no place can be conceded to this strange element, for activity and this receptivity preclude each other. Where the Pauline doctrine is ethicized, as happens at times today as a concession to what is felt to be modern, the doctrine is deprived of its very essence, loses its own character, and ceases to have its own path. The demands of ethics have a place only outside the sphere of this faith; at best, alongside it. The commandments of ethics can at most constitute a supplement to the doctrine of salvation, an appendix to that which alone is of vital significance. Ethical religion is in this context a contradiction in terms, *contradictio in adjecto*. Romantic religion says in effect: religion must supplant ethics.

The anarchical principle of Gnosticism, "everything is permitted," is therefore only the new justice carried to its logical conclusion. In principle and theoretically, it is a matter of indifference for the Pauline doctrine how man behaves in action, whether he does good or evil. For deeds are deeds and have nothing to do with religion; they always involve a valuation of the human subject and a denial that only faith in grace remains. Already the Epistle of Barnabas proclaimed: the tablets of Moses are broken.

Paul himself was still too deeply rooted in Judaism and hence made moral demands time and again. These demands are genuine insofar as they proceeded from his honest and deeply ethical personality and from his living past from which he could never disentangle himself entirely. But they are not genuine insofar as they did not proceed from his romantic religion which he proclaimed as that which was most truly his own: they are merely mounted on it as something extraneous and essentially different. They proceed from his personality but not from his faith, and they constitute the contradiction of his character; the human being here was stronger than the form of his faith. The Gnostics, however, were no longer rooted in Jewish soil nor disturbed by "fruitless remembrances" or "futile struggles"; so they took up the idea of romantic anarchy in earnest. Paul and many of his followers soon shrank from this development in horror; but this was merely the horror they felt at seeing their own ideas carried to their logical conclusion. Gnosticism is Christianity without Judaism and, in that sense, pure Christianity. Whenever Christianity wanted to become pure in this way, it became Gnostic. . . .

The Sentimental

. . . It has been Paul's work to substitute faith in Jesus for the faith of Jesus. He had implanted the savior of the mystery religions who redeems by grace into the person of the Jewish messiah: the latter had furnished the name and the future, the former the content. Now the Gospel, the tidings of the messiah — of his life, his preaching, and his death — was romanticized and transformed into the tidings of the god-man. In this form, the Gospel could be placed alongside the Pauline epistles, the book proclaiming the victory of the redeemer over original sin. A certain unity had been achieved, even if in spite of everything, it remained artificial.

There was one factor which facilitated this union: the sentimental mood which pervades the Gospel. This mood is not confined to the Gospel: a large portion of the Jewish literature of that time is characterized by this tone of world-weariness and *Weltschmerz*. But it is most fervent in the Gospel. And it is notable how we perceive it here even in the words about nature. There is nothing left here of the ancient biblical naiveté which had simply listened to the songs and sounds outdoors and looked out into the green and the blossoms, now gay, now sorrowful. The simplicity which saw and heard quite without affectation had developed into a sentimentality which seeks and desires only itself in everything that is outside — that melancholic poetry of the city-dweller who can grasp nature only with the yearning which impels him toward that which is distant and different. Only the mind and thought of a sentimentalist could have found expression in such emotion-laden expressions as those about the fowl of the air which neither sow nor reap nor gather into barns, and of the lilies of the field, how they grow and neither toil nor spin. That would hardly be the song of the unsentimental peasant.

But in spite of this sentimentality, in spite of all the points of contact with romanticism, the Gospels constitute, at least as far as their original content is concerned, a thoroughly unromantic book — or, as we might say just as well, a book in the spirit of the Old Testament, a thoroughly Jewish book. For the determinate commandment has its place in them; the demands of the Gospels do not lack the ancient prophetic decisiveness; and the Law they put up is unconditional. This is what is most essential and most genuine in them, and by virtue of this they stand, to be precise, outside the Christian sphere, if we use the word "Christian" exclusively in the sense which its whole history has given it. Christianity is, ever since Paul created it, a doctrine of salvation, the doctrine of grace which redeems through Christ; and of this, which alone is truly Christian, the old, the real, Gospel has nothing at all. Whatever of all this is to be found in the Gospels, in the form which they eventually assumed, has merely been added to them to fit them for the New Testament; but for the original Gospels this is an accretion, something alien and opposed.

History proves it by experience. The real Gospel has always been something of an embarrassing reproach in the Church, as long as it could not be reduced to a mere image for romantic exuberance. In a literary sense, one possessed it and praised it loudly; but in any other sense, in practice, one did not take it seriously. The Christian attitude toward it was nothing but a continual attempt to get rid of its essential core and to interpret away its power to command. One often spoke and wrote of the imitation of Christ; but one guarded against understanding it in its original sense as a demand made upon all men.

The Catholic Church, to be sure, has in this case, too, as elsewhere, contrived a way out. In much the same way in which it dealt with pure romanticism, it took the Gospel also off the shoulders of the community of believers and handed it over to a few chosen persons. It was removed from the sphere of duty, and faithfulness to it was declared to be a supererogatory accomplishment, *opus supererogationis*. Thus it was circumvented and still left intact. Catholicism never lacked men and women of such evangelical piety. It had its Francis of Assisi, this most moving figure of the Middle Ages — moving in its cheerful purity and infinite longing — and though he had no peers, there have been a number who were of his kind. But the decisive influence he had within the world of the Church was really due less to his fulfillment of the ideal, than to his ready obedience to the authority of the Church. Essentially, he himself belongs to the group that had followed John the Baptist and then found their messiah in Jesus. But those who followed him and called themselves after his name were men of the Church for which Paul had laid the foundation. In spite of everything, however, a place had been left for the Gospel within Catholicism, even if such a place was purchased at the price of a division between ordinary and extraordinary religion.

Protestantism, on the other hand, became utterly helpless at this point. Apart from occasional possibilities in Pietism, it had no room at all for the real Gospel. Here it has always been pure literature. It offered a beautiful text for sermons; but the sermon which followed the text generally said something completely different. People were not told that to be a disciple of Jesus and a Christian one had to live up to the commandments of Jesus. Instead, the sermon generally proclaimed clearly and loudly that a Christian need not fulfil them, or at least not always, or not entirely, and could still be a good Christian. All eloquence was devoted to this theme. The determinate demand is interpreted away, the commanding force is annulled by some demonstration, and the essential message and the enduring significance of the Gospel has again and again been summarized in this way: its value remains great and exalted, but it is not meant so precisely and seriously that one should also fulfill it. This was called the interpretation of the Gospel.

Modern liberal Protestantism, finally, has turned this romantic irony into a romantic play — one might almost say, a romantic comedy. It wanted to make room again for the evangelical ideals. The ancient Church had assigned them a place in the sacrifice entailed in pure monasticism, but modern liberal Protestantism grants them a more comfortable and eloquent place — in the wide and windy expositions of the New Testament handbooks. Here alone this evangelic piety has its field: here it sows and reaps. It brings in abundant sheaves of words and thus satisfies itself. In the commentaries to the New Testament, poverty, for example, and self-denial, and renunciation of all earthly aspiration and cares are exalted, though very soon thereafter, in the theory and practice of the Christian life, the very opposite of all this is taught and demanded. In the commentaries, any invoking of God in an oath is repudiated as a typically inferior show of faith; but in life oaths are defended and even demanded. There it is considered pious and noble not to resist evil, while here it is accepted as a duty for a man to fight all injustice. There one speaks of moralism with the scorn of those who are elevated far above it, while here the blessings of sober civic morality are praised and inculcated. This commentary idealism, this textbook holiness — what else can one call it but romantic comedy? That those performing it do not at all experience it as such, can perhaps be explained only by remembering that the real Gospel could not at any time be taken seriously in Protestantism.

But at bottom, this is true of the Church altogether: it has scarcely got around this difficulty. What confronts us is not a contradiction between ideal and reality — that is essentially human — but the romantic discord of text and sermon, of word and will, the triumph of romantic irony over the ideal. From Joachim da Fiore and Savonarola down to Kierkegaard and Tolstoi, men have frequently protested with agony and scorn against this condition, but always in vain. It was bound to be in vain, because all this is of the very essence of romanticism which is, after all, the essence of the Christian Church; and the Church therefore could endure this condition so easily, in spite of everything. . . .

Casuistry

The piety which abounds in maxims and lives on interpretation shows how closely romantic enthusiasm and casuistry are connected. The opposition between speech and action, between teaching everything and fulfilling nothing, easily leads to the result that everything ethical becomes ambiguous; and then ethics becomes a mere matter of words, a matter of interpretation. The very pitch of feeling, just because it lacks all solid ground, can be like something conjured up out of the void: there can be something captiously contrived about it, as if it were a game played with oneself. Even Augustine shows this when, for all his fervor, he cannot resist plays on words. And we encounter the same witty ecstasy in Novalis and those surrounding him. Where religion confronts the soul as a dream that has come to us and as a vision that is enjoyed, the religious actuality with its commandments is no more than an image that is beheld. It is a message that is perceived dimly, as if from a vast distance, and can mean everything without demanding anything: one can play with it and subtilize it.

81

There is another point that belongs here. Romantic enthusiasm, this feeling that feeds on itself, often finds expression in sentimental flaccidity: emotion blurs all outlines and lets everything human coalesce. Such gentle melancholy can be pure and noble: it can take the form of that graciousness which comprehends and forgives all. But much more often it means forbearance of a different sort: forgiving and transfiguring all our own faults and responding with silence toward our own guilt. The result is a calm, an almost serene, consciousness of sin — the lovely melancholy of religion. At this point it is again accompanied by the danger of irony, the danger of casuistry. . . .

Humanity

We may deem it further proof of these considerations that the universally human, the humane, cannot be freely appreciated either. It is encroached upon from all sides. The value of the right act, created by the human will and hence possible for everybody, is blotted out or overshadowed by the significance of that supernatural providence which elects one man and rejects another. The ideal of the baptized believer, which goes hand in hand with the sacraments, interferes with the growth of the ethical ideal of the good man. In addition, there is the feeling of contentment and self-righteousness. This feeling that one has been redeemed without having done anything to merit it generally rules out any feeling for those who are merely human but who live in a different world, without salvation. They are considered men set apart, and no connecting link establishes a bridge to them.

What is thus taken away from humanity is at the same time a loss for universalism. It had already been narrowed down considerably by the conception of the Church, which had done away with the unity of mankind and all but reduced the God of all men to a God of the Church. To be sure, within the Church the equality of all believers was claimed at least in principle. But the price for this is that all who stand outside the circle of the elect are placed immediately and absolutely in the realm of depravation and become *massa perditionis* — the multitude that is destined to perish. When the Epistle to the Galatians, and similarly also that to the Romans, exults, "here is neither Jew nor Greek, here is neither bond nor free," the full emphasis falls on the word "here"; and Luther's translation brings this out very well.[13] Between "here" and "there" lies a deep cleft, and the unity of mankind is thus destroyed.

What romantic religion takes away from the worth of man and his freedom is not compensated for by the fact that the ideal and command-

---

[13]Galatians 3:28; Romans 10:12. —*Tr.*

ment had their place in the original preaching of the Gospel. In this case, too, the essence of the Gospel has been without lasting effect in the development of the Church doctrine. This is understandable enough when we consider that the Gospel is in this respect at one with the Old Testament, which is also attested by the fact that the commandment to love one's neighbor appears in the Gospel as a quotation from the Old Covenant. Hence this humane word generally required interpretation in the Church; and theoretical and practical intolerance had an opportunity to test their skill on it.

But for all the triumphs that this particularism won in the Church, it did not owe its existence to the Church: it always attends romanticism. Diogenes the Cynic already had been able to mock that "an Agesilaus and an Epaminondas, because they were not initiated in the mysteries, are supposed to be among the reprobates in the underworld, while the most insignificant wretch is granted an abode on the isle of the blessed if only he was one of the initiated."

It is no more than a consequence of such narrowness when a man like Augustine claims that any supposed excellence in a pagan or unbeliever has merely borrowed the semblance of goodness and is, in reality, "sooner a vice."[14] And it is another such consequence when the literature of the Church asserts for centuries, whenever the question of human virtue is brought up, that virtue does not exist where the right faith is lacking. This, of course, is quite consistent: where the strength of moral action is gained only through the miracle of grace, and the non-Christian stands outside and has no part in this gift, he must also be lacking in any true moral capacity. A capacity for good in a pagan or a heretic is, in this context, almost a self-contradiction.

In the self-assured consciousness of its strength, the Catholic Church has often built bridges. Even as it was always inclined to make some concessions to the sphere of human activity and its value, it did not hesitate at times, especially in the age of the Renaissance, to circumvent this principle of narrowness. Later, when a day came that demanded it, the Church even repudiated the principle expressly: Jansenism seems to have risen against the Church in the name of Augustine and was proclaiming this ethical particularism in his name. The Church had to fight this position. At the same time, it also wanted to define its position as against Protestantism. For in the Protestant doctrine, too, this principle of exclusiveness had again become more prominent — not simply as something more or less accidental or occasional, but as a clear conse-

---

[14]*De civitate Dei*, XIX, 25: *Proinde virtutes, quas sibi habere videtur — sc. mens veri Dei nescia — nisi ad Deum retulerit, etiam ipsae vitia sunt potius quam virtutes.*

quence of the central and decisive phrase "by faith alone." It is part of the new romanticism that morality, too, can be born only of that faith which is received as a gift. Melanchthon merely gave this doctrine the characteristic imprint of his dry, cold manner. In the *Loci Communes*, in the chapter on "The Power and the Fruits of Sin," we find the soberly and rigidly stated proposition: the excellencies of a Socrates or a Zeno are the attributes of pagan, hence of "unclean," souls, and as such mere "shadows of virtue"; they "must not be considered true virtues, but are to be regarded as vices."[15] These harsh words are aimed, above all, at humanism; for this movement had sought piety outside the Church, too. Nor was this the only point at which humanism, after preparing the way for Lutheranism, was dispossessed and displaced by the latter.

Assuming the presuppositions of Paulinism, the repudiation of the merely human was entirely consistent. Augustine and Luther were merely the faithful disciples of the apostle; they took seriously the word of the Epistle to the Romans: "Whatsoever does not issue from faith is sin."[16] Or, to cite Melanchthon again: "By virtue of the forces of nature, all men are truly and always sinners."[17] This principle was certainly helpful for the missions. Their success could be assured if the unbeliever was denied everything and the convert could thus be promised everything. It strengthened the missionary tidings that all those who were addressed could be considered as lacking in everything. The affirmation of the dignity of man certainly brings men together and teaches them to understand and respect one another; but for this very reason, any missions based on this idea cannot equal the compelling effect of the threat of damnation. Where the dignity of man is affirmed, heaven is not set off by the frightening image of hell in the foreground. The conception of a Church "which alone makes blessed," completely excluding all outsiders, seems to offer the potential convert a greater bargain.

The next step to active intolerance is small indeed. Where everything is denied to those outside the Church, while everything is given to those who are within it, it is easy to see how the Church would soon claim the right to drive out whatever remains outside it as being void of value.

---

[15] *Loci Communes*, ed. Plitt-Kolde, 86: *Esto, fuerit quaedam in Socrate constantia, in Xenocrate castitas, in Zenone temperantia, tamen quia in animis impuris fuerunt, immo quod amore sui ex philautia oriebantur istae virtutum umbrae, non debent pro veris virtutibus, sed pro vitiis haberi.* [Both here and in the quotation from Augustine in the preceding footnote, Dr. Baeck translates *vitium* as *Fehler*: fault, error. But the word also often means "vice" — particularly when coupled with *virtus* in discussions of moral matters. —*Tr.*]

[16] This quotation, from Romans 14:23, is reiterated time and again in Kierkegaard's *The Sickness unto Death* and represents one of the central tenets of that book. —*Tr.*

[17] Ibid., 87: *Et ut rem omnem velut in compendium cogam, omnes homines per vires naturae vere semperque peccatores sunt et peccant.*

Gradually, such a Church becomes convinced of its competence, even its duty, to annihilate that which it cannot acknowledge. Whatever is apart from and without it is null and void and hence should be annulled. The Church possesses salvation and has been gifted with perfect justice which, to be complete, must include this office of passing judgment by virtue of which it abolishes whatever contradicts it. In the desire for such full judicial power, there has been little difference between the Papacy and Lutheranism.

Another development has been no less calamitous and no less frequent. This finished perfected justice, this self-assurance of the possessing, has also often found expression in a tranquil, comfortable, almost smug indifference. Being satisfied with itself, the Church was capable of beholding a great deal without being at all upset. Since it considered itself a world apart, it could leave many matters in this world to take care of themselves. Having issued from divine grace, the pious faith was superior to everything impermanent and human; hence it could regard earthly deeds, of whatever character, as something inferior and indifferent, as beneath it. So one was prepared to overlook and discount and indulge anything: the correct faith was easily satisfied with itself; for "whoever believes in him is just."

A good deal of Church history is the history of all the things which neither hurt nor encroached upon this piety, all the outrages and all the baseness which this piety was able to tolerate with an assured and undisturbed soul and an untroubled faith. And a spirit is characterized not only by what it does but, no less, by what it permits, what it forgives, and what it beholds in silence. The Christian religion, very much including Protestantism, has been able to maintain silence about so much that it is difficult to say what has been more pernicious in the course of time: the intolerance which committed the wrongs or the indifference which beheld them unperturbed. Perhaps such indifference is even more romantic than intolerance, for it is more passive. It is wholly fitting for the faith which does not want to wrestle and act, but is content to wait and experience; it is entirely commensurate with the repudiation of the Law. The moral duty of justice and the fight for justice are associated with the phase that lies in the past and has been overcome.

Redemption

... This was not the only decisive trait within the Church. As has been pointed out a number of times already, the Pauline faith contained, from the very beginning, some elements of legalism which had been derived from the Old Testament without having been overcome. In the course of the history of the Pauline faith these elements came to the surface time and again and were responsible for the other major tendency — that which is opposed to all egoism. This is most evident in the history of monasticism, in the development that leads from the solitary and self-seeking anchorites, who lived in the desert and desired only their own salvation, to the brothers and sisters of mercy and love who knew how to sacrifice themselves for their fellow men. They became the pride and glory primarily of the Catholic Church, but also of some of the other Churches.

It was not in vain that the Church possessed the Old Testament and the old Gospel which belonged with it. But whenever the romantic faith reflected on itself and tried to recover an awareness of its distinctive essence, it experienced and manifested itself again as the religion of pure egoism. The higher it ascended and the more tender and ecstatic it became, the more egoistic it became. Its distinctive character has always shown itself in this manner. . . .

The Messianic Idea
The romantic faith in salvation also furnishes us with the very opposite of the ancient messianic idea which was still the idea of Jesus, too: the idea of the days to come, the idea of the promised kingdom. Such confidence in the meaning of man's exertions is clearly the opposite of the desire for the possession of the promise as a gift. In Paul these two ideas had still contended against each other: the Old Testament on the one side, romanticism on the other. He was full of his new faith and yet also still full of his Jewish heritage; and this inner conflict had introduced a split into the world of his ideas. The contradiction here was the same as that which the question of the Law had introduced into his thought. Those who later went beyond him, the Gnostics, lacked in this respect, too, the experience of that which had still checked and determined his course; hence they were able to give the pure romantic answer void of the tension of the "time to come."

Even then, however, this pressing thought of the future could not be completely silenced. That which had confronted Paul as his Jewish legacy, the old Bible, had been accepted as part of the Holy Scriptures of the new faith; and once this had been done, the messianic heritage could never disappear entirely. Again and again, and often quite suddenly, it emerged, especially as the doctrine of the "eternal gospel" of which John had spoken in his Apocalypse. But in the end, it never came to more than a heroic episode. The whole spirit of the Church was altogether too deeply opposed to this heritage and always rejected it as soon as possible, disposing of it as the voice of phantastic visionaries. Luther in particular, as a decided romantic, bade it be silent; in the Augsburg

Confession[18] it is specifically condemned as a "Jewish doctrine."[19] It has had a certain effect only among the Calvinists and Baptists who stood outside the main stream of strict romanticism. In all the other Churches the pure doctrine of salvation remained predominant. This has been one of the most significant or, if one prefers to put it that way, one of the most fateful spiritual consequences of the triumph of romanticism in the Church: the messianic idea out of which Christianity had developed and from which it has received its name was now pushed back more and more and eventually annulled historically. The place of the kingdom of God on earth, the ancient biblical ideal, was taken over by the kingdom of the Church, the romantic *civitas Dei*.

The tremendous missionary activity developed by the Church may seem to contradict these assertions. For it is after all the meaning of missionary work that one goes out for the sake of one's fellow men to save them and to show them the way of salvation in order that all men may eventually be as one in a single kingdom of salvation — *ut omnes unum*. Yet this desire to convert grew originally, no less than all other messianic hopes, out of strong roots in the Old Testament which remained part of the new Christian community. It was taken over from Judaism almost as a matter of course and continued to be active, and was further strengthened by the feeling that one was proclaiming a new truth. The form of Christian missionary preaching, especially insofar as it was addressed to the educated, was, to begin with, in no way essentially different from the manner of the old Jewish apostles (*Sendboten*) who had proclaimed the one God, His commandment, and His judgment. A change set in only during the second and third century, the decisive period in the development of the Church when dogma and authority prevailed: then the distinctive character of the Church which set it off from Judaism asserted itself in its propaganda. And here it may be mentioned in passing that this is what happened quite generally: as the Church developed, the changeful history of its faith consisted quite often in this — that one contended and wrestled, consciously or unconsciously, about the space to be left to the ideas of the Old Testament. Consider the issues which, after changing fortunes, eventually were decided formally at the

---

[18] The confession of the faith of the Lutheran church, written by Melanchthon to be read at the Diet of Augsburg in 1530. —*Tr.*

[19] XVII, 5, ed. Tschackert, 14: *Damnant et alios, qui nunc spargunt judaicas opiniones, quod ante resurrectionem mortuorum pii regnum mundi occupaturi sint, ubique oppressis impiis.* The German version reads: *Item, hie werden verworfen auch etliche jüdische Lehren, die sich jetzt auch eräugen, dass vor der Auferstehung der Toten eitel Heilige, Fromme ein weltlich Reich haben und alle Gottlosen vertilgen werden.* In English: "Here we also repudiate various Jewish doctrines which are now being spread to the effect that the pious will have a worldly kingdom before the resurrection of the dead and destroy the impious."

Council of Nicaea[20] not a few of them were, at bottom, not fights for or against Jewish Christianity, as was supposed at one time — for this Jewish Christianity had had a very brief history which scarcely extended beyond the destruction of the temple — but for or against the Jewish elements in Paulinism itself. For these elements still drew strength from their ancient tradition and still aspired to be effective. In later centuries, too, this dispute was renewed not infrequently.

The missions developed in their own way once the edifice of the Church had been built. Not only the preaching changed, but the whole character of the missions, their motivation and the nature of their successes became something completely different. The Church was not a powerful kingdom of this world, and it began to follow the pressures and the laws of its power. To be sure, the Church did not at any time lack men who wanted to convert others out of promptings of deep love; but any such heartfelt wish to save souls was bound to recede considerably before the domineering aspiration to extend and expand the sphere of dominion. The power of the sword and the art of politics spoke more frequently and urgently than the language of the heart. It was combat and conquest that issued in the great triumphs. It was the decisive age of the egoistic and really vigorous missions that really created the world-wide church.

The "Catholic" motive, to be sure, did its share and contributed to this development; that is, the now evident and then again unconscious desire to see one's own faith confirmed by the agreement or the subjection of others and to see the principle demonstrated as far as possible: "everywhere and by everybody." This strong Catholic tendency and the God-fearing desire to lead men into the light were easily fused in the mind of the believers. Both are inspired by the image of the one herd led by the One Shepherd, and this is only too easily transmuted into the compelling idea of the world-wide empire wanted by God, the "city of God" to which all must belong who wish to claim any right to existence on earth. *Coge intrare!*[21] Thus in the end everything culminates in the striving for ecclesiastical power. When romanticism turns toward this world, it always arrives eventually at the idea of dominion and authority which, in turn, wants subordinates. The missions, too, are in the end a demand for universal obedience; here, too, the concept of man is discarded in favor of the concept of the obedient subordinate.

That the pious desire to convert men is altogether derived from the

---

[20]The first oecumenical council, held in 325, at which the position of Arius was condemned and the so-called Nicene Creed adopted. —*Tr.*

[21]Luke 14:23: "compel (them) to enter" — often interpreted as here. —*Tr.*

sphere of the Old Testament is shown time and again by history. And the course of its further development amply illustrates this origin. The purely religious missions continued where the Jewish heritage was preserved at least within limits. The fate of this Jewish heritage has always been the same as the fate of the purely religious missions. Hence there is no place for such missions in the Greek Orthodox Church which has, for the most part, preserved very little of the Old Testament legacy, while the wish for redemption and deification is most prominent in it. The opposite is true of Roman Catholicism. Here there has always been a tendency to agree with the ancient Jewish demand which extolled the value of man's task and man's work. In spite of all purely ecclesiastical aspirations, the heartfelt and unselfish desire to convert has never lost its place entirely in the Catholic Church, but remained as a way of martyrdom. And it emerged still more freely in the Baptist sects, that is, in those churches which accepted more than any of the others the legal tradition and Old Testament elements. Among these the call to seek and save souls for God's sake was heard often.

Lutheranism as such, on the other hand, knows little or nothing of religious missions; it is something that has been grafted onto it only relatively late. Its characteristic and original fire spends itself in the interior affairs of the Church, in the care for the authority of the word, for the pure doctrine in preaching and instruction. Nor does Pietism refute this, though it did indeed feel the urge to send out apostles of its faith. For while it is certainly part of Protestantism, it took over the motif of the missions, and the decision and feeling associated with it, not from Lutheranism but entirely from the Calvinistic, Baptist churches. The forms in which this desire to make conversions has manifested itself are manifold indeed, but throughout an inner connection with the survival of Jewish elements is quite evident. The romantic idea of salvation could only produce the demand for unlimited ecclesiastic power and the missions that relied on coercion. What we find in the end are once again external authority, instituted power, and obedient subordinates with their dazzling poetry and their gloomy prose.

Thus the circle is closed. Feeling is supposed to mean everything: this is the quintessence of romanticism. It can be the strength of romanticism that it is capable of immersing itself and of drawing on powerful feeling; and it is the tenderness of romanticism that it knows the experience of that which flows and floats. The romantic may indeed have the gift of which Schleiermacher spoke in his eulogy on the deceased Novalis: "everything which his spirit touched became art, and his whole world view immediately became a great poem." Romanticism is the contradiction and the opposition, often so necessary, against that shallow reasonableness which would dispose of everything, against that enlightenment which has knowledge of and answers to everything, and against that activism which would take care of and execute everything.

Its danger, however, which it cannot escape is this: the all-important feeling culminates eventually in vacuity or in substitutes, or it freezes and becomes rigid. And before this happens, it always follows a course which takes it either into sentimentality or into the phantastic; it dodges all reality, particularly that of the commandment, and takes refuge in passivity when confronted with the ethical task of the day. Empathy makes up for much and gives a freedom which is really freedom from decision and independence from any inner obligation. All the aesthetic airs and all the irony that give romanticism its attractive appearance merely secure for the few pre-eminent that presumption which reduces religion to the religion of the *beaux-esprits* or the skeptics. And for the many who either do not belong or are not supposed to belong to this élite, strong and strict authority, coercive statutes have been erected and serve at the same time as a great bulwark against that anarchy in which the few are wallowing. Nothing remains unaffected by this development which seizes, in turn, faith and symbol, history and culture, truth and justice, commandment and ideal.

It is not by any means true that romanticism is characterized by some subtle apprehension and knowledge of the irrational. On the contrary, this is no less characteristic of classicism, and above all classical religion which is something altogether different from rationalism or "enlightenment." But for classical religion the irrational is not an ocean in which the ego, swelled with feeling, drowns. Classical religion finds in the irrational the revelation of the existent which summons the self; the revelation of that which is actual and commanding; of that in which everything is rooted that is and shall be; of that in which creature and creator meet. In classical religion, the irrational is the profound truth of life and therefore also the profound source of the Law, the profound guarantee of certainty, the "arm of eternity" which embraces everything. In classical religion, the irrational appears as the holy, the covenant between the Eternal and man.

The longing which surpasses all mere reason is probably also one of the ingredients of romanticism and its religion. One of its representatives, Augustine, spoke the moving words of the heart that is restless until it rests in God. But there is yet a decisive difference: in romanticism, longing always in the end returns to the self and remains at the level of a mere mood. In classical religion, longing strives ever again for the goal which is to unify all men and impels them to follow the commandment of God: after all, these two things really mean one and the same thing. For all future is here the future of the commandment, the future in which it is realized and fulfilled. Perhaps it is in this that we find the most clear-cut difference between romantic and classical religion.

4

Judaism in the Church

1925

In a two-fold sense there is such a thing as a history of Jewish ideas. These ideas have in Judaism itself their life and their development, their periods of fruitfulness and their days of drought and barrenness. But in an entirely similar manner likewise they have their existence outside of the province of Judaism in the great world of ideas; there, too, and not to a lesser extent either, they are active as a living force, as a leaven, and there, too, they create and produce changing epochs. Hence there is both a Jewish and a universal history of Judaism.

We can recognize this factor in the history of the social movement, to give an example which the present brings near unto us. This movement has a two-fold origin. On the one side, it is derived from Plato, from his idea of the mathematical state. The state, with its perfect law, in the infallible power and effect of which Plato firmly believes, is to create the man and impel him to virtue and to happiness. The state alone can achieve this, and therefore it must be the absolute state, the state which determines and decides everything, the state of dictatorship. This right of absolute power must be given to it, and over against it there must not be left to the individual any right of what is his own, any right of his own choice and longing. Plato is the founder of every system of state omnipotence and of all hierarchy. Every secular, every ecclesiastical, as

---

This essay was first published in English in 1925. In 1938 Baeck published his original German text with additional footnotes in the volume *Aus drei Jahrtausenden* (reprint, Tübingen, 1958). The more important of those notes are included here and are marked with an *a*.

92

well as every ideological dictatorship, even up to the Bolshevism of our own days, derived its ideas from Plato's state philosophy and from his sociology, and nourished them thereon.[1] Another altogether different tendency, which has only the name of socialism in common with the first one, has its origin in the Bible, in Judaism. It does not proceed from the state, but from man, from the idea of the fellow human being, of the human brother. Judaism, unlike Plato, who is pessimistic in his attitude toward man, does not believe in the state, but it has an optimistic belief in man. For Judaism man is the strongest reality upon earth, and the state and its law become good only through the agency of the good human being. When human beings are brought up with this purpose in view, that of exercising justice and love towards each other, when each one conceives of the human being who is next to him as his brother, as the one who belongs to him and who is bound up with him, when each one recognizes the rights which his fellow human being possesses, then men will have realized the true, social law, and will have created the true state, the social state. "Thy brother shall live with thee," in this maxim is contained the social idea.[2] These two tendencies the Platonic and the Jewish, can be followed out in the social movements of the last century, and it is very interesting that, for example, the Jew, Karl Marx, goes back to Plato in his socialism, while Christians, for example, like Saint-Simon or Kingsley, proceed from the basis of Jewish ideas. Thus Jewish life lives in universal socialism.

But it is in the Church that the Jewish ideas have their own particular history outside of Judaism. The man who founded Christianity, Paul, regarded Judaism and its Bible, with conflicting emotions. On the one side, he regarded the period of Judaism, and in conjunction therewith likewise the period of the Bible, as ended. At that time the view was prevalent that there were three epochs of world history: first that of chaos, of Tohu-wabohu; then that of the Torah, which began with the revelation on Mount Sinai, and finally, that of the Messiah.[3] If this last epoch has begun, it followed therefore that the one of Judaism and of its Bible must have come to its termination. There was a word which was announced in the Gospel, to the effect that until everything had been fulfilled, not one jot or title should pass from the law.[4] But when every-thing had been fulfilled, when the Messiah had come, then the period of

---

[1] Eduard Zeller, *Vorträge und Abhandlungen*, I, 62ff.; cf. Hatch, *The Influence of Greek Ideas and Usages upon the Christian Church.*
[2] Baeck, *Wesen des Judentums*, 6th ed., 213ff.; *Wege im Judentum*, 236ff.
[3] Sanhedrin 97a; cf. Jer. Meg. 70d.
[4] Matthew 5:18. Cf. Baeck, *Das Evangelium*, 92f.

the law had come to its conclusion.[5] The law — and for Paul the word "law," just as in the Talmudic literature frequently the word "Torah," is the designation for the entire Bible — is for him only the teacher of minors, the "schoolmaster (to bring us) unto Christ";[6] with Christ the time of those who were in their majority began. If the redeemer had come, then the Bible and Judaism as well could have no further significance; at least they could have no meaning other than that of a completed period of past time. If, however, they were still valid, then the redeemer could not have come. Hence it is explicable why Paul fought against the law with all the determination of his belief, just as though he were waging a struggle for his very existence. And, to repeat our previous statement, for him the law meant all commandments in the Bible, that is to say, the entire Bible, and not merely the so-called ceremonial law. Hence this question for him became one around which everything revolved, the problem upon which his religious existence and the certainty of his belief depended. If the redemption were at hand, manifestly present through faith and baptism, then the law must have ceased; if the law were still in force, it was thereby proved that the hoped-for time, the time of the fulfillment, was not yet at hand. Either the law or redemption: either the former had come to its termination or else the latter had not yet made its appearance. Whoever maintained that the law was still binding stood therefore in unbelief, for he denied the redemption. Hence, for Paul Judaism had to cease to be religion, the religion of the present and of the future, and the Bible had to cease to be the Bible, i.e., the Book of the present and of the future.[6a]

However, on the other hand, everything which Paul thought and announced, everything which was the proof for his belief, still depended upon this self-same Bible. It was for him the divine revelation, the announcement of Christ, and it is therefore "holy" and "just and good" in his eyes.[7] It provided him with all his arguments. From this self-same Book, the present validity of which he strongly opposed, he took that which supported his teaching; the necessity of the death of the Messiah — he could explain this fundamental feature of his doctrine only with the help of this Book. For him too the formula which decides everything is: "It is written."[7a] His entire process of thinking has its life in the Bible. It was this self-same contradiction which lay in his very being,

---

[5] Nidda 61b; Pes. 50a; Sabb. 151b; Yalkut to Isaiah 26:2.

[6] Galatians 3:24

[6a] Colossians 2:14f.; Ephesians 2:15.

[7] Romans 7:12, 14.

[7a] The same "dialectic" exists in the contemporary dialectical theology, which also has its psychological source in Paul.

in his entire personality. His personality too indicates this discord, this discrepancy, that on the one side he announces his freedom and independence from Judaism, and on the other side he keeps on searching for Judaism, for the Jewish mode of thinking and for the Jewish teachings. He had lived so deeply within Judaism that spiritually he could never become altogether free from it. Whether he willed it or not, he always found his way back into the Jewish paths of thought. The Jew, which he still remained at the very depth of his being throughout his entire life, constantly kept up in his soul a struggle with the man of the new faith which he had become. The discord, which is to be found in his teaching as well as in his personality is to be explained on the ground of this fact.[8]

Among those who came after Paul and who became the disciples of his teaching, there were many who, quite differently from him, possessed the possibility of pure consistency, of unlimited opposition to Judaism. They no longer had any bond whatsoever, whether of the blood or of the soul, with Judaism, and they felt it to be their task to free the new religion from everything Jewish and thus to establish the pure Paulinism. There were several ways in which this could be done. The first method had been adopted by the author of the Barnabas epistle, who lived about 100 C.E. and who probably came from Egypt.[9] He sought to save the Old Testament as the foundation of Paul's theology for Christianity by denying it entirely to Judaism, and by claiming it entirely for Christianity. The means for carrying out the purpose was provided by allegorical explanation. He applies this system generally to the entire Old Testament. By its help everything objectionable in the Old Testament, i.e., everything which is at all Jewish, is removed, and every real, actual relation with Judaism is eliminated. Every word in the Old Testament is filled with a Christian meaning, with the result that the book in its true sense is made to belong to Christianity alone, just as the Church should be indeed the true Israel, the true seed of Abraham.[10] All literal and verbal understanding of the Old Testament is, in his eyes, a detestable Jewish misunderstanding, the work of Satan. Thus the entire Old Testament became an exclusively Paulinian book; only that which is purely Christian is Biblical. As the result of this method the additional advantage was obtained, that Christianity received its early history, and that its beginnings were traced back to the time of the creation of the world. The Jewish people with its history was exposed as a people which had been led astray

---

[8]Baeck, *Romantische Religion*, 11 and 37 [1st ed., 1922].

[9]G. Hoennicke, *Das Judenchristentum*, 284ff.; M. Guedemann, *Religionsgeschichtliche Studien*, 99ff.; E. Hennecke, *Handbuch zu den neutestamentlichen Apokryphen*; Geffcken, *Christliche Apokryphen*, 52f.

[10]Harnack, *Mission u. Ausbreitung des Christentums*, 41f., 49, 289f.

by the devil, which had never possessed a covenant with God and which had never had any understanding at all of the divine revelation.

And yet this method had its dangers as well as its advantages. If the right of interpretation were once granted, then at the same time each and every possibility of interpretation was granted. If the book was recognized under this one allegorical form, then it could lay claim to be recognized under any other allegorical form whatsoever. Freedom from this book was to be secured only by rejecting it altogether, without any limitation. This conclusion was drawn by Gnosticism, and especially by Marcion.[11] They were actually theological and consistent Paulinians. They rejected Judaism and its Bible absolutely and completely. Indeed, Marcion himself, in order to preserve the absolute force of this rejection, explains and therefore rejects everything in the Pauline epistles which appeared to him to be Jewish, everything in which there was claimed to exist a linking of Jesus or of Paul with Judaism, as a forgery, as a Jewish interpolation. For him only that which is absolutely hostile to Judaism is true and genuine. For the sake of establishing pure Paulinism, he revised and corrected the text of the Gospels and of the Epistles. And in order to guard against any possibility that something which was Jewish should find its way into his religion by way of allegory, he demanded the literal interpretation of the Old Testament — just the same as did the man who was his contemporary and who, according to an old report, came from the same city, from Sinope, and whose bitterest opponent Marcion was, i.e., Aquila, the translator of the Bible, the proselyte, the pupil of Akiba.[12]

The essential fundamental of the theology of this tendency likewise consists in its rejection of Judaism. In order to separate Judaism altogether from their Christianity, in order to have an unambiguous Christianity and a God who belongs only to them, the adherents of this tendency teach dualism. There were to be no combinations and no alliances, but only an absolute separation. In their opinion there existed a two-fold God, the wicked, dark, cruel God who was bound up with the world, the God of Judaism, and the good, pure, spiritual, kind God who was exalted above all and above the whole world, the God of Christianity, who manifested Himself for the first time in Christ, and who had never revealed Himself in any other person previous to that time. When the Gospels speak of the two trees, of the bad tree, which bears only bad fruits, and of the good tree, which bears only good fruits,[13] there are

---

[11]Bousset, *Hauptprobleme des Gnosis*, 109ff.; Harnack, *Lehrbuch der Dogmengeschichte*, I[4], 243ff.; De Faye, *Introduction a l'étude du gnosticisme*; Harnack, *Marcion*.

[12]Schürer, *Geschichte des jüdischen Volkes*, III[3], 313f.

[13]Matthew 12:33.

meant by these nothing else than these two Gods, first, the inferior, Old Testament God, who creates evil exclusively and who possesses no higher value than does the world itself, whose creator and ruler He is and who will pass away at the same time as His heaven and His earth, and second, the sublime Christian God, who brings forth good exclusively and who is without any contact with the world. There is no deeper antithesis than that which exists between these two. For Paul, the God of the Old Testament was the God of Christ and his own God; but here, in this doctrine of the Gnostics, the two Gods stand in hostile opposition to each other. The God of the Jews and His Book, these constitute the proper adversary; they are the evil principle; all redemption signifies redemption from this world of Judaism. And for this reason the Jews themselves are the real enemies of Christ and of the true God. They are the ones who, all of them together, with their patriarchs, their prophets and their teachers, can never be redeemed.

But due to this very concept a great difficulty manifested itself. Since the Old Testament had been given up, and every thing which was of an Old Testament character had been removed from the Gospels and the Epistles, there was left only the doctrine of the redemption and of the sacraments, and everything which was ethical, everything which represented a commandment and an obligation, had been done away with. Hence there remained only two alternatives, either complete libertinism or absolute asceticism.[13a] Both of them actually made their appearance within a very short time. At first there became prevalent the practical nullification of all the commandments, and the principle was proclaimed: for the redeemed man, the man of pure Paulinism, "everything is allowed."[14] People felt themselves to be pneumatical, to be free men of the spirit, and as such they believed that they were beyond good and evil, exalted above chastity and morality, and free, and bound by no law, by no commandment. Whoever is exalted above the law must be able to recognize not only God, but likewise "the depths of Satan";[15] for the man of the spirit[16] it is altogether immaterial what his body does.

This is the first method of getting away from the law. Marcion pointed out the second method. For him all earthly existence had been cast off at the same time as the law; for him the corporeal life was "caro stercoribus infersa."[17] There was only one kind of piety here on earth, i.e.,

---

[13a] Cf. Baur, *Das Christentum und die christliche Kirche der ersten drei Jahrhunderte*, I⁴, 487ff.
[14] 1 Corinthians 6:12.
[15] Apocalypse (Revelation) 2:24.
[16] Koehler, *Gnosis*, 28.
[17] Tertullian, *Adversus Marcionem*, I, 29 ("Flesh stuffed into filth").

asceticism and the annihilation of self. He forbade the enjoyment of the flesh and demanded most painful fasting. He forbade all sexual intercourse even in marriage, and he admitted to the rites of baptism and communion only those who were willing to take the vow of celibacy or who, in case they were already married, would vow to preserve absolute sexual separation. In his opinion marriage was tantamount to dying; real life was the annihilation of everything corporeal. The struggle against the corporeal is the struggle "ad destruenda et contemnenda et abominanda opera creatoris."[18] Whoso has conquered everything corporeal has conquered the God of the Jews. Religion exists for the purpose of bringing the human race to extinction. When this is accomplished it will then have triumphed over the Jewish, the wicked creative God. This was the final consequence of the purging of Christianity from Judaism.

It is self-understood that a Christianity which had been freed from Judaism in such a manner rendered all living in the world and all connection with culture impossible. If the Church wished to exist in the world, then it had to conduct the struggle against Gnosticism for the sake of its very existence, and this struggle in behalf of its existence, whether it willed it or not, became for the Church a struggle in behalf of the place of the Old Testament in Christianity. To the original historical reasons for which the Church had adhered to the Old Testament, there now were added these decisively essential ones. The Catholic Church became formed and consolidated in the struggle against Gnosticism and in the conflict in behalf of the Old Testament, and it had finally succeeded in establishing its Bible, the unity of the Old and of the New Testament, and thereby the unity of the Jewish and of the Christian God.[19] It was then the period in which the Church was beginning to be connected with the state, at first, for the purpose of existing jointly with it, and then for the purpose of being above the state, as its ruler. The Church was able to accomplish this end because of a two-fold reason: first, because of this canonization of the Old Testament, and then secondly, and in connection therewith, because of its adoption of the Stoic principle of natural law. These two, natural law and Old Testament law, were identified the one with the other by the Catholic Church, a process which is, at the same time, interesting and likewise characteristic of the Church. The entire medieval period is characterized by this equalization of the decalogue and of natural law, by this unity between the natural and the

---

[18] Tertullian, *Adversus Marcionem*, I, 14 ("for the purpose of destroying, despising, and rejecting the works of the creative God").

[19] Harnack, *Lehrbuch der Dogmengeschichte*, I[4], 550ff.

divine law.[20] As the result thereof the Church was now in a position to establish, in addition to the pure individualism of its doctrine of salvation and of redemption, likewise a social feature, to develop a state and social doctrine. In this manner a co-existence of the Church and the state, a recognition and a utilization of the state, was rendered possible for the first time.

As the result of this joining together of the Old and of the New Testament, as the result of this confession and admission to Judaism, Catholicism was now able to obtain likewise its system of ethics. Gnosticism, and especially the doctrine of Marcion, had been a religion entirely devoid of ethics, as has already been indicated. And as a matter of fact, this was actually the logical Christian standpoint, because as far as principles were concerned, there was no place for ethics in Paul's system: ethics had been done away with, because it was considered to be the Law which had been abrogated by the new righteousness of faith. Everything actually took place through the miracle of baptism, through mysteries; everything was accomplished in faith alone; and therefore by comparison that which was done by man could have no further significance. In this doctrine faith forms the antithesis to ethics. Any evaluation of conduct, even of the most moral conduct, of the Ten Commandments, for example, belongs to the province of the Law which had been overcome by Christ.[21] It was a choice either of faith or of ethics, either of the savior or of the Law.

This is the fundamental alternative which Paul places before the individual. With reference to Paul himself, his Jewishness was still too strong in this respect likewise. His ethics, the same as his attitude towards the Old Testament in general is the result of this inconsistency, i.e., that with his ideas he had stepped out of Judaism, and that he still lived in Judaism, as far as his ethical feelings, his feelings towards the commandments, were concerned. In this respect likewise the Jew in him was stronger than the doctrine. And in this respect, too, his disciples, drawn as they were from paganism, had no such connection with Judaism. The epistle of Barnabas had been in a position to announce the following principle: "The tablets of Moses are broken into pieces."[21a] Among the Nicolaites in Ephesus and Pergamum, and the Baleamites, the consciousness that they had already been redeemed had led to lack of restraint, to that libertinism of which mention has already been made;[22]

---

[20] Troeltsch, *Soziallehren der christlichen Kirchen u. Sekten,* 52f.; 156ff., 171ff.
[21] Baeck, *Romantische Religion,* 36f.
[21a] Epistle of Barnabas, IV:8.
[22] Apocalypse (Revelation) 2:6 and 2:14ff.; 1 Corinthians 6:12f.; 8:7ff.; 1 Peter 2:16; Clemens, *Stromata,* 2:20; 3:5.

among the Cainites the Biblical malefactors had served as patterns of the one who was redeemed.[23] The ceremonial and the ethical had been placed upon the same plane by Paul; both were the Law; whoso felt himself elevated above the former could therefore believe himself to be exalted above the latter likewise.

In order to be able to oppose this principle likewise, the Church was in need of having the Old Testament and its moral code. Hence the Church established the principle of "faith and work," in order to assign both to the Old Testament as well as to the New Testament its rights. How strong the necessity of compromise was in this instance is shown by the fact that the epistle of James was adopted into the New Testament and placed at the head of the Catholic epistles, this epistle which is nothing else but a most violent polemic against Paul, and which, in opposition to Paul's principle that man is justified through faith without works of the law, expressly declares that man is justified on the ground of works, and not through faith alone.[24] The Catholic doctrine was developed on the basis of this great compromise with the Jewish element. It was a compromise, and the Jewish element in it lost its own character. The one God, Whom the prophets had taught, was reinterpreted into the trinitarian concept of God which the Church Fathers held. The sense of the Old Testament was interpreted in a christological manner; the Biblical law was identified partly with the natural law and was accordingly relegated to the plane of that which was purely natural in contrast with that which was intrinsically religious, and partly its work (the practice of the law) was placed alongside of the service of the sacramental cult, in juxtaposition with the ceremonial practices of the Church, the one as well as the other being regarded as "good works," both having the same name and the same value. But just so Paulinism had suffered harm as the result of this compromise, and its principle of "faith alone," for sake of the compromise, had experienced restriction and limitation.

Thus it is comprehensible that within the church, in the same manner as previously, contradictions made themselves manifest anew, either for the purpose of reestablishing the pure Paulinism, or for the purpose of securing a greater place for the Jewish element. From this time forth the inner development of the Church, its internal life and activity, is now conditioned by this two-fold struggle. Of course it must be stated first of all that there was no contradiction as far as the doctrine of the trinity was concerned. Here the Church doctrine was firmly established, even

---

[23] Epiphanius, *Haer*, 39.
[24] James 1:14–16.

though the so-called doctrine of tritheism, in accordance with which the three persons of the God-head are to be separated from each other,[25] was in evidence at the time in addition to the official Church tenet. But there soon commenced explanations and counterexplanations with reference to the question of faith and works. The teachers and the tendencies of the Church were divided in their attitude towards this problem. One may say that the history of the dogmas of the Church is actually a history of Judaism within the Church, that it has its various phases, according as the active ethical-psychological element of Judaism, with its emphasis on the personal, or the passive, magically sacramental element of faith of Paulinism, with its dissolution of that which is individual into the metaphysical, is brought more strongly into prominence. And the task which the Papacy performed, the purpose which it executed again and again with great diplomatic art, and, above all, with great spiritual strength, in all conflicts and antitheses, is the maintenance of that compromise.

The retention of this compromise was rendered necessary at a very early date, since the principle of works as well as the principle of faith each found a champion very soon in a strong personality, the one in Pelagius, the other in Augustine. In the opinion of Pelagius the concept of mercy has an entirely ethical character, and for this reason he reckons the Law as forming a part of it, and in general he assumes no essential difference between the Old and the New Testament. He teaches the free will of man, before whom God has placed both the good and the evil. He teaches the doctrine that every man, even the non-Christian, can do what is good, and therefore there is such a thing as salvation even for him who is not baptized.[26] But with the same determination with which Pelagius emphasizes this doctrine of "liberum arbitrium," and this "possibilitas boni et mali," Augustine opposed them. He stresses the fact that ever since Adam's fall there is no such thing as free-will, that man ever since has been evil by nature, under the ban of the original sin. In Augustine's opinion the attribute of grace has a purely supernatural character. It grants everything and man contributes nothing; it selects some few people without any reason, and equally without reason it allows the greater number of other persons to become the "massa perditionis," the great mass doomed to perdition, and this supernatural mercy has its place only in the Church; only the Church's baptism brings with it salvation; and even an infant which dies without having been baptized is damned.

---

[25] Harnack, *Lehrbuch der Dogmengeschichte*, II[4], 300ff.
[26] Baur, *Geschichte der christlichen Kirche*, II[2], 132ff., 143ff.; Bruckner, *Quellen zur Geschichte des pelagianishen Streites*.

Although, according to the principle of Pelagius, in agreement with ancient Jewish teachers, the virtue of those of other faiths or of unbelievers is recognized, because virtue itself is of decisive importance and faith means belief in the good, none the less according to the point of view of Augustine there can be no virtue on the part of a pagan, and all virtue has no significance whatsoever in comparison with the sacrament; all salvation is dependent upon the belief in sin.[27]

Opinion and thought fluctuated between these two poles during the Catholic medieval period, thus, for example, between Thomas and Duns — it is interesting in this connection to note that Pelagius and Duns were both Englishmen; and compromises were continually being made between these two poles. Of course the Church condemned and proscribed Pelagius, and yet it always came to terms or compromised with a sort of semi-Pelagianism. The Church, it is true, declared Augustine a saint, but it nevertheless resolutely continued to reject pure Augustinism, even at the time when it was revived by such significant personages as Jansen and the circle of Port-Royal. It remained the Church of compromise and of combination between Paulinism and the Jewish element, even though it allowed the former to preponderate.

Luther's reformation then proceeded from the opposition to the compromise. In one point Luther reverted to Judaism, i.e., in the doctrine of the priesthood of all. Even in this teaching the Catholic Church had created its own intermediatory doctrine; it had made a distinction between an inner priesthood, which was to be regarded as held out for all those who were baptized, and the external priesthood, which belonged only to the class of the consecrated.[28] In this respect Luther had adopted in its entirety the Jewish idea, which had likewise been very active elsewhere in medieval Catholicism; at least he did so during his early, revolutionary years. Hence the Jewish idea here, too, conquered in Christianity. On the contrary, however, Luther in his dogma entered into a thorough antithesis with Judaism, into pure Paulinism.[29] His doctrine is that of the absolute original sin, of the unlimited effectiveness of grace, towards which the believer is able to be merely and completely motionless in a purely passive manner. Luther had arrived at this point of view by reason of his quest for the complete certainty of salvation. Inasmuch as Catholicism had demanded works on the part of man, and man was never able to perform all these works, so the believer, no matter to what

---

[27] Harnack, *Lehrbuch der Dogmengeschichte*, III⁴, 68ff., 90ff., 166ff.; Troeltsch, *Augustin*, 98ff.; Sell, *Christentum u. Weltgeschichte*, I, 3, 363ff.

[28] *Catechismus Romanus*, VII, 23.

[29] Troeltsch in *Kultur der Gegenwart*, I, 4, 276ff.; Dilthey, *Archiv für Geschichte der Philosophie*, V, 330ff.; Wundt, *Ethik*, I, 3, 363ff.

extent grace has been granted to him, can forever possess only the hope of salvation, but never the complete certainty and security of salvation. In order to make this certainty one's own peculiar possession, Luther, just like Paul and Augustine in previous times, had therefore completely eliminated the value of human action and had made everything dependent upon grace exclusively, and upon unlimited faith therein, upon "sola gratia," upon "sola fide." In order to preserve his belief he had to reduce the deed to complete insignificance, and represent the belief in the importance of the act as real unbelief, as a sin against the Holy Ghost. In place of the Catholic principle of faith and works, there now reappears the old antithesis: either faith or works, and for this there may be substituted likewise the following mode of expression: either religion or ethics, either grace or intention! According to this principle each and every will, even if it be the best and the noblest, every will whose object is to be good and righteous, is only the way of destruction. Salvation can come from faith alone, which for Luther means faith without the action. Herewith everything Jewish had been eliminated in his dogma, and war had actually been declared against whatever was Jewish.

But it went the same with Luther as it had formerly gone with the generation of Paul. The same results followed in both cases. Just as formerly asceticism and libertinism followed as the result of the principle that everything depended upon faith alone, so now again, among Luther's following, there resulted partly the tendency towards asceticism,[30] and partly the so-called tendency of antinomism, which set about the task in all seriousness of rejecting the law.[31] And just as, at that time, the Church was forced to concede a place to works in order to be able to live and exist in the state, so Luther found that he had to do the same thing, when he founded his church with the help of the state. Indeed, Luther found a way out of his difficulty as the result of his adoption of the fatal expedient whereby he removed the moral commandments from the province of religion proper and relegated them to the province of that which was purely civil, and handed them over and subordinated them to the power of the police, to the civil authorities. Morality is here only that which the authorities demand. It has nothing whatsoever to do with religion proper, and at best it is only an appendix to religion. In this manner man is to a certain extent divided into two separate and distinct divisions, into the class of the spiritual man of faith, and into

---

[30] Troeltsch in *Kultur der Gegenwart*, I^4, 407ff.

[31] Hunzinger, *Lutherstudien*, II, 1; cf. Amsdorf (a contemporary and assistant of Luther) "bona opera ad salutem esse perniciosa" (that good works are destructive to salvation) in Hase, *Hutterus Redivivus*^{2}, 308.

that of the civil man who keeps the commandments. Herein consisted the un-Jewish feature of the religion of Luther, and herein likewise consists its intrinsic weakness, its religious as well as its cultural weakness. It was never able to create a real system of ethics on the ground of and proceeding from religion, and on the other hand it had established the state, which it moreover recognized as the supreme lord of the Church, likewise as the lord and master over morality, and had thereby given the state its unlimited power.

In contrast with the religion of Luther, the great historical contribution of Calvinism[32] consists in the fact that it once again restored to the actions of men their ample place, just as is demanded by Judaism. Of course Calvinism deviated from Judaism by reason of its dogma of predestination, but it actually had reverted to Judaism in a decided manner in its doctrine of the significance of man's actions, in its emphasizing of the commanding law and of the Divine Will. And even this idea of predestination in Calvinism finally becomes ethicized more and more. The conduct of man is here the sign that God has chosen him. Man is chosen if he conceives it to be his task to adopt the Will of God as his own will, to ameliorate the world, to devote his life and labor and that of the human beings near him to the service of that which is moral, to labor for that which is good on earth for the sake of the glory and honor of God. In Calvinism, unlike the religion of Luther, faith does not have its purpose in itself, but its goal is the determination of moral effectiveness and activity. The old Jewish idea of the covenant which God makes with man and, together therewith, the idea of the Law and of its social demands such as was announced by Judaism, everything which is called the legal feature of Judaism, all this becomes more and more active within Calvinism. Here religion is to be manifested in life, and religion is to be given a serious place in life. In opposition to the Lutheran religion of passivity, Calvinism stands out as the religion of activity and of heroism; and the Old Testament gains in place and significance in its Bible. Furthermore with this legal idea there is thoroughly associated in Calvinism likewise, just as in Judaism, the Messianic idea. Wherever the demand for the commandment is made, the demand that there be prepared a proper place for that which is good upon the earth and that the kingdom of God be founded in life, here there is awakened likewise the Messianic idea, this belief in the progressive realization of the good, this belief in the true kingdom of God of the future. The Puritans of England were inspired by this Jewish idea when they struggled against ungodliness and despotism; the Presbyterians were guided by

---

[32]Max Weber, *Die protestantische Ethik u. der Geist des Kapitalismus.*

this self-same Jewish idea when they journeyed westward and created the New England states. Here, as well as in Judaism, there is indicated to what a great extent legal piety always becomes Messianic and to what a great extent Messianic piety is legal piety.

This Messianic expectation had been done away with by Paul in its essential features. Since for him the coming of the Messiah and the redemption was something which had already been fulfilled, was already an actual possession of the present, the idea of the great future hope had consequently lost its significance. Occasionally, however, this Messianic idea became revived ever and anew, not only in the old Church but likewise in the Middle Ages. In days of oppression especially this Jewish longing for a coming period of the rulership of God and of eternal peace became an active force in the doctrine of the so-called "evangelium aeternum" and of the millennium. The Church had constantly perceived therein something of a revolutionary nature and had fought against it with all the means at its disposal. This idea did not become an ecclesiastical movement until the time of so-called Baptism,[33] this religious movement from which, together with Calvinism, there was derived and from which there proceeded the strongest religious force, indeed, almost everything which transformed and reorganized religion and religious thought in England and the United States. This movement had a free pathway, because it refused, fundamentally and on principle, each and every connection with the state and each and every structure on the part of the state, such as those into which Catholicism and Protestantism had entered. In place thereof the new movement established the free community in which the religious ideal was to be realized. And this freedom did not lead to libertinism and antinomism because it did not proceed from the contradiction and opposition to the Law. On the contrary, it led to the resuscitation of Biblical socialism and of the Biblical ideal of holiness, because it directed its attention to the commanding Jewish idea. The Baptists could be Independents and Congregationalists, because they placed ethics above the forgiving of sins, and the commandment above the doctrine of justification. With this stressing of the ethical there was closely associated a suppression of the sacramental and a tendency to strip it of some of its importance; hence in this case, too, there is manifest a turning away from Paulinism to Judaism. The Baptist movement represents a real revolution of that which was Jewish within the Church. It strove for and gained its world-historical successes at the time of Cromwell in

---

[33] Troeltsch, *Die Soziallehren der christlichen Kirchen u. Sekten*, 797ff.

England, and in the states of the Pilgrim fathers. Although, or perhaps because, it did not become a church, it was one of the most effective and fruitful ecclesiastical movements of comparatively modern times.

All these reformation tendencies have the following feature in common, i.e., that for them the question of grace and Law, of faith and works, was the decisive one; all other questions occupied a position in the background. But already in Baptism the opposition to the dogma of the trinity likewise had manifested itself occasionally. Ludwig Haetzer[34] had opposed the divinity of Christ. This question, in which Judaism and Christianity are deeply divided, came to occupy a position in the foreground for the first time in Socinianism,[35] which was the first Unitarian tendency, and therefore, with reference to the doctrine of God, the first Jewish tendency in Christianity. It, too, had proceeded on the ground of the Pelagian idea; this idea had been reawakened at the period of Humanism. The right of the human being and of human freedom and action, the ethical and the Messianic stress is laid upon these, and in order to grant the individual human being his full right, the doctrine of the original sin and of justification through Christ is opposed. On the ground of these views, therefore, there developed the shunting aside of that which was dogmatical and the simple explanation of the word of the Bible, the rejection of Christology and of the trinity, and the conception and comprehension of the unity of God, therefore a return to Judaism. Socinianism is the attempt to create a humanistic renaissance of Christianity in place of the dogmatical reformation. As far as its external history is concerned, Socinianism had only a very brief term of life. It established its own church in Poland, but this church only too soon succumbed to the Polish reaction, and in such a thorough-going manner that no trace of it was left in Poland. It was only in Transylvania that a group of communities managed to maintain its existence throughout all the persecutions of the centuries to which it was subjected, even after some few of its believers had there become converted to Judaism as Sabbatarians. And despite the fact that at first dogma and reaction were triumphant throughout almost the whole of Europe, none the less the ideas of Socinianism became widely disseminated. In conjunction with the ideas of Baptism they became seed grains, from which there sprouted forth in subsequent years a full measure of fruit. Especially in the Netherlands, and then, above all, in England, where they gained a Milton, and then

---

[34] Hege, *Die Täufer in der Kurpfalz.*
[35] Harnack, *Lehrbuch der Dogmengeschichte,* III[4], 765ff.

in America, these ideas became a powerful and important ferment of theological progress and of human and undogmatical religiousness. They were the means whereby fruitful Jewish thoughts were carried over into the life of the Church. The Unitarianism of a Priestley, a Channing, a Parker, and of a Martineau goes back to these Socinian germs, which blossomed forth and reared themselves aloft in modern Protestantism.

Throughout Protestantism this definite inclination towards Judaism is everywhere apparent. What has remained of the old ecclesiastical dogma in modern Protestantism? The trinity has more and more become a mere word: the Holy Ghost is no longer the actual divine personage, the paraclete, but it now represents nothing more than an ethical concept; it has assumed a Jewish character. The ecclesiastical doctrine of the divinity of Jesus, it is true, is regarded as a dogma in wide circles even of present-day Protestantism, and yet even as such it is, for the most part, only a theological concept, which is pushed and twisted hither and thither dialectically, in order to rid oneself more or less of its content and thereby to get back to Jewish monotheism. In quite a similar manner there has disappeared the old ecclesiastical doctrine of dualism, which divides the world into two great divisions, that of the son of God and of Grace, and that of the devil and of original sin. When do people still speak of this dogma? On the contrary, how much the more do they speak of that universalism which comprehends all human beings, of this prophetical doctrine. And finally, the doctrine of faith, that faith which was considered to be all-important and all-significant, it too more and more comes to occupy a place behind the Jewish teaching of the actions and disposition of man, both of which lead him to God. Faith now is to be ethical belief, and this in turn means Jewish belief. Every change in modern Protestantism had received its tendency from the Church's realm of thought and goes back ultimately to the sphere of ideas of Judaism; and it is to be regarded as having only the significance of something bizarre, that occasionally in German Protestantism there became active, as the result of a feeling of anti-Semitism, ideas like those of Marcion in previous times, for example, among men like Lagarde and Houston Stewart Chamberlain, who wish to have everything Jewish removed from Christianity. The history of the Church has already shown what will be left of Christianity if it is to be cleansed and purged of everything Jewish.

When we cast a retrospect over the centuries of the Church's existence, we see in the Church, too, in such a manner, a history of Jewish ideas. Every change which took place in the spiritual and religious life of the Church represents a coming to grips with these ideas, with a turning

107

away from them or a renewed inclination in the direction towards which they tended. There is thus such a thing as a history of Judaism within the Church. Judaism has an indestructible life by reason of its ideas; it can be fought against, and it can be forced to give ground, and yet it always becomes reanimated. "Et inclinata resurget." Even when it is bowed down, it only rises again to still loftier heights.

Martin Buber (1878–1965)

Courtesy of the Leo Baeck Institute, New York

Introduction

by Ekkehard W. Stegemann

I

Martin Buber is rightly reckoned, in the words of Hans Urs von Balthasar, among the "great founder figures of our time." Like many such outstanding men Martin Buber and what he was is not easily characterized in terms of the usual categories. He is generally counted among philosophers of religion, for he was indeed a philosopher as well as a theologian. But he was more than that and something else also, namely a poet and a scholar, educator and publicist.

Martin Buber was born on February 8, 1878, in Vienna. Because his parents separated, he grew up, after 1881, with his grandparents in Lemberg, in the Austrian section of Galicia. His grandfather Salomon Buber (1827–1906) was a well-known Midrash expert. He transmitted to his grandson a solid Jewish education and, above all, philological ambition, that is: a love for words. Furthermore, he had contact with traditions of most varied kinds and provenances, a matter of course in multilingual Lemberg. Buber spoke German at home, Polish at school, Yiddish and Hebrew in the synagogue. He spent his vacations with his father in the Bukovina where he first encountered the living reality of East European Hasidism, in particular, that of Sadagora. All of this makes clear why Buber always thought of himself as a Polish, not a German Jew.

Buber's university studies brought him back to Vienna in 1896, and then to Leipzig, Zürich, and Berlin. The philosophers Wilhelm Dilthey and Georg Simmel were his teachers here. He received his Doctor of Philosophy degree in 1904 in Vienna. His university years alienated Buber temporarily from Judaism, although he became rooted in it again through his encounter with Zionism.

But in contrast to Theodor Herzl, Buber stressed the cultural self-

111

reflection and renaissance of Judaism. Already at the Third Zionist Congress in 1899 he declared that Zionism was a *Weltanschauung* whose spread among Jews should be fostered "through promotion of Jewish culture and education for the people." Buber writes in 1918: "That Zionism got hold of me and newly dedicated me to Judaism was only the first step. Confession of nationality alone does not change the Jewish person."[1] Instead he hoped that "Jewish religiosity, too, would undergo renewal in Zion."[2]

Zionism as renewal of the Jewish community, also in a religious and cultural sense, now became the task of Buber and some friends, and they published on the subject. They founded the publishing house Jüdischer Verlag in 1902, and finally published the monthly *Der Jude* from 1916 to 1924. Buber's cultural Zionism excited much interest among a Jewish student group in Prague, of which Hugo Bergmann and Max Brod also were members. Before this group, Buber gave his famous three *Reden über das Judentum* (Addresses on Judaism) in 1909 and 1911.

In those years, Buber found his own religious renewal by steeping himself in the legends and stories of the disciples of Rabbi Israel Baal Shem Tov and other Hasidic writings. He creatively recast parts of this tradition, and thus transmitted it to a public completely unacquainted with this this-worldly *mysticism*. It is true that Buber's particular interpretation of Hasidism has been severely criticized, especially by Gershom Scholem.[3] However, it reflected Buber's personal view and was not meant as historical reconstruction or interpretation. His aim was to make the *original Jewish* tradition, which, in his view, had nourished Hasidism, fruitful also for the present.

This turning towards Hasidism already indicated what Buber, at that time, discovered philosophically, namely the *"dialogical principle,"* the "Realization" (*Verwirklichung*). Thus he was still writing in 1952: "The great deed of Israel is not to have taught the real God, . . . but to have shown the addressability of this God as a reality, the ability to address him as Thou."[4] Starting out from the fundamental position that there is "no I-in-itself" (*an sich*), but only a Being-in-the-World and thus a Being-in-a-Relationship of a human being, Buber characterizes human existence as "having part" or "taking part." Here, he distinguishes be-

---

[1] M. Buber, *Mein Weg zum Chassidismus* [My way to Hasidism], now in *Hinweise: Gesammelte Essays* (1953), 187.

[2] M. Buber, "Der Jude und sein Judentum" (The Jew and his Judaism), *Gesammelte Aufsätze und Reden* (1963), 707.

[3] G. Scholem, "Martin Bubers Deutung des Chassidismus," *Judaica* 1 (1968): 165–202.

[4] "Die chassidische Botschaft" (The Hasidic message), *Werke III: Schriften zum Chassidismus* (1963), 739–894.

tween two kinds of "having part," namely the mode of "I-Thou," the *encounter*, and the mode "I-It," the *experience*. Buber develops this starting point in different directions in a series of writings, the most famous of which is "I and Thou" (1923). It was to lead to further paedagogical work, and specifically to the cooperation with Franz Rosenzweig, in particular to the great task of translating the Bible. But in both instances it is the word, speech and dialogue through which experience and encounter take place and become communicable. Even about his own work Buber would, therefore, say: "I have no doctrine, but carry on a conversation."[5]

Buber became active as teacher and *educator* in several ways. Together with Franz Rosenzweig and others, he founded the Freie Jüdische Lehrhaus (Free Jewish House of Study) in Frankfurt on the Main in 1920. He took the place of the ailing Rosenzweig as adjunct at the University of Frankfurt in 1924, and, beginning in 1930, continued as "Honorarprofessor" for Religious History and Ethics. Ousted from this position by the National Socialists in 1933, Buber concentrated on adult education. He was highly successful in this area in Germany, as well as in Holland and Switzerland until he emigrated to Palestine in 1938. And in Palestine, he devoted himself to similar tasks immediately by cofounding the Seminary for Adult Education, which trained teachers for new immigrants. Buber also became Professor for Social Philosophy at the Hebrew University in Jerusalem in 1938.

If there is anything that characterizes Buber's *Hebrew Humanism*, then it must be his translation of the Hebrew Bible into German. He induced Rosenzweig to collaborate with him in 1925. After Rosenzweig's early death, Buber had to continue alone from 1929 on. The National Socialist State forced an interruption in 1938. In 1950, Buber resumed the work and completed it in 1961. Its author's intentions became concentrated here as in a lens. A supplementary series of interpretation of the Bible bore the thematic fruits of an intense occupation with its "words" and with its "Word." In the last analysis, but not in last place, it is also out of the Bible that Buber sought dialogue with Christianity, desiring its renewal from its Jewish roots.

When Buber died in Jerusalem on June 13, 1965, he, the one who continually stressed the renaissance and renewal of the "Community" of Israel, had remained unable to find "the way of praying together with the Community which was already in existence."[6]

---

[5] "Antwort" (Reply) in P. A. Schilpp and M. Friedman, eds., *Martin Buber* (Stuttgart, 1963), 593; English translation: La Salle, Ill., 1967, 693.
[6] E. L. Ehrlich, "Martin Buber — ein unexemplarischer Jude," *Wer Tora vermehrt —mehrt Leben: Festgabe für Heinz Kremers*, E. Borcke, ed. (Neukirchen, 1987), 211.

II

Ever since the Enlightenment, Jews have participated in shaping the intellectual and cultural life in all places which permitted them to do so, and essential progress in the sciences would not have been made without them. Undoubtedly, political expertise and economic development in many lands owe much to contributions by Jews whose Jewishness in all this, however, rarely played a part. If it became public knowledge at all, it did so mostly through those who were envious or in opposition, that is: out of hatred and with defamatory intent.

One has to be aware of those facts in order to understand how differently his environment judged Martin Buber. For he is surely "the first Jew since and like Moses Mendelssohn who had an effect on the spiritual life of his non-Jewish surroundings *qua* Jew. They accepted him not only as a human being but as a Jew who opened Judaism to them, who made it important and accessible to the educated among its detractors."[7] To be sure, there remained many, far too many detractors — also, incidentally, among the educated.

Nonetheless, it is remarkable that Buber's acceptance was positive and genuine, that it came very early, not only among Protestant and Catholic theologians, but equally in philosophical discussion, for instance.[8] Of course, as thinker of the faith and as interpreter and translator of the Bible, Buber was noted primarily by Christians and theologians. James Muilenburg has described this in almost hymnic terms, though surely without exaggeration: "Buber is not only the greatest Jewish thinker of our generation, not only a profoundly authentic exponent and representative of the Hebrew way of thinking, speaking and acting, not only a celebrated teacher 'both to Jew and to Greek,' but also the foremost Jewish speaker to the Christian community."[9]

Of course, this was said of Buber more than two decades ago while he was still living and at the then high point of his spiritual impact, and the spiritual confrontation with him has in no wise diminished. However, some Christians and theologians have, in the meantime, also come to know other significant Jewish philosophers and thinkers of the faith. They have, moreover, begun to discover the vitally colorful variety of the religious and cultural world of Jewish history and tradition. Still, it was usually Buber who first drew their attention

---

[7]H. Gollwitzer, "Martin Bubers Bedeutung für die protestantische Theologie," *Leben als Begegnung: Ein Jahrhundert Martin Buber*, P. von der Osten-Sacken, ed. (Berlin, 1978), 63.

[8]Cf. P. A. Schilpp and M. Friedman, eds., *The Philosophy of Martin Buber* (La Salle, Ill., 1967).

[9]J. Muilenburg, in Schilpp-Friedman, 383; German ed., 365.

to these. Through him, a path to the wealth of Jewish wisdom and teaching was opened up for Christians. Through him, they learned that he himself represented only a part of this spiritual and religious cosmos.

If one were to ask why it was Buber, of all people, who could become such a recognized Jewish teacher for Christendom, one would most likely hear many different answers, some colored by personal impressions. But finally the reason might be that Buber really did not convey teaching in a doctrinal sense. However, one must add at once that he formulated well and impressively whatever he had to say. It is possible that today his language no longer captivates everyone to the same degree because its expressiveness may seem outmoded. Its elemental quality, however, and sometimes its undisguised subjectivity explain why, to this day, Buber's texts are capable of establishing a most personal relationship with their reader — "an encounter," as he would say.

Buber's attraction for Christians rests, to be sure, also on a certain affinity between his thinking about belief and their own. However, I would consider it wrong, or at any rate misguided if, for that reason, one were to attribute an unconscious Christian tendency to Buber. It is true, however, that he has emphasized certain aspects of the Jewish tradition and neglected others. He has thus stressed the vital religiosity of Hasidism, but screened out the halakhic tradition of rabbinic Judaism. Correspondingly, he concentrates his view of the Bible mainly on the historical books, the Prophets and Psalms, while hardly noticing its legal tradition, except for its moral-ethical component which, at any rate, has entered Christian-occidental ethics. In this fashion, Buber undoubtedly stands close to Christianity, especially its liberal Protestant theology at the beginning of our century. But this does not mean that his mode of thought was at bottom perhaps, after all, Christian. The correspondence is rather due to the fact that, like some forms of Christianity, Buber, too, in his effort to make biblical religion intelligible to modern European thought, utilized the norms of that thought. That is why Buber shares some convictions of Protestant theology, but also some of its idiosyncrasies.

This is quite apparent from his three *Reden über das Judentum* (Addresses on Judaism), which also reflect Buber's own path towards Jewish self-understanding and self-awareness. Very much like Protestant theology, Buber here describes post-biblical Judaism as an entity coming more and more under the definitional sway of the "ceremonial law." As the latter became "ever more rigid and estranged from life" and degenerated at last into a "heap of petty formulas" and "hairsplitting casuistry," true

Judaism with its vibrant inner religiosity was buried alive.[10] This view corresponds entirely to the prejudice that originated in the Enlightenment and was pursued by the theological Enlightenment, albeit with a decisive difference: for what Christians regarded as the essence of Judaism, Buber saw as its distortion. Accordingly, he declares the founder of Christianity, Jesus of Nazareth, to be precisely a witness of the original Judaism. He describes Jesus as the reformer who taught return to "what the prophets taught: the absoluteness of the deed." Because of that, Buber, like, Protestant theology, would see Paul as marking a decisive caesura in primitive Christianity. But whereas Protestant theology celebrated the Apostle to the Gentiles as the liberator of Christianity from the shackles of Judaism, Buber saw him as the one who transformed the teaching of Jesus into "Ideology": "This man sums up the vast disappointment dealt to that inclination within Judaism which made for realization, up to his own time. Adding up the national as well as the human total, he declares that we can accomplish nothing of our own accord, but only through the grace of God." In this transformed configuration, Paul transmits "the teaching of Jesus to the nations and hands them the sweet poison of faith which is to scorn works, to exempt the faithful from realization and to stabilize dualism in the world."[11]

It is this constellation between Jesus and Paul which exemplifies the difference between Judaism and Christianity for Buber up to his last remarks on the subject. He thus turns the tables, as it were. If Christians have commended Christianity to the Jews as fulfilling and thereby overcoming and abolishing Judaism, then Buber countered: "Whatever is creative in Christianity is not Christianity, but Judaism, and this we *need* not reapproach, we need only to recognize it within ourselves and take possession of it, because we carry it within us without possibility of loss; but that, in Christianity, which is not Judaism, is uncreative, mixed together out of a thousand rites and dogmas, and with this — so we say as Jews and as human beings — we do not *want* to establish a rapprochement."[12] This it is which determines the self-consciousness which Buber, as Jew, can muster vis-à-vis Christians on the one hand. On the other, it also determines his respect for Christianity which, through its founder, Jesus of Nazareth, carries the original Judaism within its heart. And finally the beginning of Buber's criticism of Christianity lies here also.

---

[10]Martin Buber, *Der Jude und sein Judentum: Gesammelte Aufsätze und Reden* (Cologne, 1963), 76; English translation, *On Judaism*, 91f. *Reden über das Judentum* (1932), 120. For its genesis, see R. Weltsch, Introduction to the volume, xxi–xxii.
[11]*Der Jude und sein Judentum*, 105; *On Judaism*, 127f.
[12]*Der Jude und sein Judentum*, 38f.; *On Judaism*, 47.

But before proceeding to the detailed content of and reason for this criticism, an area needs to be stressed that lies outside of it but where Buber, in my view, will always remain exemplary and pointing the direction. I mean his incomparable faculty for dialogue, his ability to hold converse without a sense of domination, where the partners may come forward with their own concerns. This includes, absolutely, a discourse that may lead to critical self-knowledge. But it always excludes that the one has to, or would even be allowed to, convert the other to his conviction. Because one person's truth is not the other man's untruth. In God's house, the world, there exists only partnership in matters of truth and fellowship among contemporaries, and there can be no head start with a view to eternity. This totally "unmissionary" presupposition, this fundamental equality of belief — Buber's point of departure even when it is expressly not that of his partners among the Christians — this charisma of brotherliness is possibly the most precious thing he had and has to teach.

III

The first of the texts reproduced below is a lecture given by Buber in Stuttgart in March 1930 before a Conference of Societies for German Language Missions to the Jews. It is a beautiful instance of Buber's power of articulation as well as of his just mentioned capacity for dialogue, that is: for its unshakability. The opening is rhetorically brilliant. But when Buber here characterizes the mission to the Jews as an activity positively blocking the way to the kingdom of God, "the kingdom of unification," then this is more than an expert opening gambit. Rather, it contains already his whole criticism of that Christianity which has here challenged him to provide a justification for the Jewish soul. For behind the Christian inability to become a partner of Judaism — an inability institutionalized as the Mission to the Jews — Buber detects a certain Christian eccentricity. Namely, the mission to the Jews is a manifestation of a displacement of those two foci about which the soul of Judaism moves elliptically. The first is the tensive unity of distance and closeness between God and man, creator and creature. For Buber, Christianity has resolved this tension by teaching incarnation, that is: by positing in place of God's unity God's unification with man. The second focus is the tension between God's omnipresent redemptive power and the unredeemed state of the world. According to Buber, Christianity has resolved this tension by maintaining that Jesus Christ is a caesura in history, namely, the change from absence of redemption to redemption, even if it is only proleptic and partial. One can clearly feel that for Buber

117

the Christians, with both these foci, cross a sanctified, inviolable border. And yet, he seeks what is held in common, transcending the difference.

Buber says something similar in this matter also in the second text, his contribution to a conversation organized by the Jüdische Lehrhaus in Stuttgart on January 14, 1933, that is a few days before Hitler seized power. Already, the dark shadow of the National Socialist terror can be noticed over this dialogue. Buber's partner was the Professor for New Testament in Bonn, Karl Ludwig Schmidt (1891–1956). Schmidt was at that time one of the most brilliant minds of German Protestantism and, as a Social Democrat, a decided and noted opponent of the Nazis. He provided a forum for the opposition to Hitler and his theological and ecclesiastical aiders and abetters in the theological journal *Theologische Blätter*, which he published. He himself would soon pay a price for his political conviction and his human decency. He was banished from the university in September 1933 and dismissed from state employment. Shortly thereafter he fled to Switzerland and so escaped the threat of being taken into custody. In 1935, he received a call to a professorship in New Testament at the Theological University of Basel, where he lived until his early death in 1956, his latter years gravely ill.

Schmidt's contribution to the dialogue, while maintaining high regard for Buber's person, and with all respect for the biblical dignity of Israel, is yet characterized by the classical Christian attitude, that is to say: the claim of absolutism and the mission to the Jews.[13] Correspondingly, Buber repeats in his response what, basically, he had said in the first text. However, the question of the Messiah is added as concretization, but this is only a variant of the conflict over redemption, or as the case may be, lack of redemption. Buber goes remarkably far in his tolerance of the Christian theologoumenon about the rejection of Israel, which he respects as an untouchable certainty of faith. But one feels in every single sentence how sure, on his side, Buber is of Israel's "self-knowledge," that is: the knowledge concerning the election which, in spite of all humiliation, has not been abrogated. His statements, rhetorically culminating in the confrontation of the *ecclesia triumphans,* as embodied in the marvelously powerful cathedral of Worms and its Jewish cemetery, become valid, absolutely. And Buber adds another important criticism when he measures the Christian nations with the biblical yardstick and thus uncovers the discrepancy between the claim to be the true people of God and their actual deeds. For now he raises the question of how Christian

---

[13]Cf. P. von der Osten-Sacken, "Begegnung im Widerspruch: Text und Deutung des Zwiegesprächs zwischen K. L. Schmidt und M. Buber im Jüdischen Lehrhaus in Stuttgart am 14. Januar 1933," *Leben als Begegnung,* 116–144.

nations could possibly act in accordance with the Bible which, in the Torah, makes very concrete demands with regard to conduct vis-à-vis strangers.

The ethical paralysis, for which Buber brings examples, makes apparent, for the first time, the weight of his critical theological enquiries addressed to the Christians. For he thus brings home that the contradiction between Christian talk about the accomplished redemption and the actual unredeemed character of the world has been projected and visited upon the Jews. Jews remind Christians of the impotence of their messianic belief and call upon them to face the truth about the unredeemed reality of the world. After the Holocaust, this has become an altogether unavoidable enquiry addressed to Christians. Only if they succeed in overcoming their blindness, their obstinacy, if they succeed in ceasing to hide from the evidently total absence of redemption — only then need their messianic belief no longer fear the reproach that it is a false perception. And only then can the suspicion be laid to rest that anti-Judaism is the left hand of Christology.

The third text reprinted here is an excerpt from Buber's monograph "Two Types of Faith." This book was written "in Jerusalem during the days of its so-called siege" (Foreword) by the Arab Legion in 1948, a classical setting (*Sitz im Leben*) for the concept "Faith," as Isaiah 7:9 shows. The theologian Emil Brunner, a friend of Buber's who also comes in for criticism in the book, has characterized it as "a major attack on Christianity." That is perhaps exaggerated. But it is certainly true that in this work Buber has most critically formulated his dispute with Paulinian Christianity. For that, he met little approval among Christians. In one respect for good reason, because the contrast between Hebrew and Greek understanding of faith as applied to the difference between Judaism and Christianity may yet correctly characterize something regarding the respective historical phenotype. And with respect to many an age in Christianity, quite apart from any differentiated theological reflection, Buber might very well have been right in saying that the vulgar Christian principle of faith was represented as the recognition and acceptance, and thus also as the truth claim of certain propositions that had hitherto not been considered as true, but rather as absurd. But particularly to deny Paul and to ascribe only to Jesus the quite different principle of faith — namely maintaining faith in God's guidance even contrary to appearances — is probably incorrect. Here Buber misunderstands not only the Paulinian concept of faith, as could be evidenced by the fact that in texts by Paul Abraham's belief in God's promise of descendants — that is, Abraham's hope against hope — serves as paradigm for faith altogether (cf. Rom. 4). Furthermore, Buber misunderstands that the Greek word *pistis* (or its verbal derivatives) always evokes for Paul, as for Greek-speaking Judaism in general, the meaning of the equivalent Hebrew *emunah* (or its verbal derivatives). For the Greek word served as translation of the word *emunah* in the Septuagint and thus assumed the meaning of a semantic borrowing.[14] And it kept this "hebraized" meaning also in primitive Christianity, as long as it kept up its relationship with Greek-speaking diaspora Judaism and its social and religious minority status in the Roman Empire. The Christian faith-concept did not change until the Christian tradition was transformed into the Latin language and culture, especially in the fourth century, with the concomitant transformation of its social status, that is to say, with its rise as a majority and state religion.

Of course, one should regard Buber's interpretation of the Paulinian concept of faith also against the background of New Testament scholarship of his time. In doing so, one will become aware of the fact that, for example, Rudolf Bultmann's article, which appeared in the renowned *Theologisches Wörterbuch zum Neuen Testament* in 1965, stresses something about Paul that is quite similar to what was said about him by Buber. To be sure, Bultmann, too, sees that the factor of trust and hope is contained in the Paulinian understanding of faith. However, he speaks in addition and at the same time about a "specifically Christian usage," contained precisely in the formula *pisteuein eis*, that is, "to believe in." It is this which refers to "the acceptance of the 'kerygma' of Christ." Therefore Bultmann sees the "factor of trusting hope in the specifically Christian" understanding of faith receding in favor of the recognition that God has worked eschatologically in Jesus.[15]

A great deal of what Buber would detect in Paul might, upon closer view, prove to be a retrojection of a later history of Paul's reception in Christianity. Some of what Buber recognizes in Jesus also pertains to Paul. But not to be dismissed is the notion that Christianity forfeited its "Jewish" contour initially not from the inside, but outwardly, namely as it achieved social and political domination. For the development of Christianity, the turn taken under Constantine is of greater significance than the transition from Jesus to Paul. Yet Buber has surely seen correctly that Christianity has to think anew about its origin.

The last text is a concluding note pertaining to the Bible translation. It altogether speaks for itself. But it reveals a tragic side of Buber's lifework, as Shemaryahu Talmon has rightly said. For "as translator, he [Buber]

---

[14]Cf. D. Lührmann, *Glaube im frühen Christentum* (Gütersloh, 1976).

[15]Cf. R. Bultmann, s.v. *pisteuō*, in *Theologisches Wörterbuch zum Neuen Testament* (Stuttgart, 1965), 6:209.

primarily addressed the German Jew for whom the Bible in the Hebrew original was a sealed book." But because of German mass murder, this translation can no longer reach its addressees. In some way, Buber's translation therefore experienced "the fate of the Septuagint," which, originally meant for Greek-speaking Jewry, "ultimately became the authorized version of the Church."[16] May Buber's version help make those whose language it speaks mindful of the "original truth" of its word, and of the humanity of its command.

What the life work of Buber means for a Christianity that reflects upon itself cannot today be stated conclusively or exhaustively. I see Buber's contribution primarily in this: that he invited Christians to reflect upon the Jewish roots of their faith and the biblical imprint of their hope. This will, first of all, lead to a recognition of Judaism as equal partner in God's house, the world, indeed, to the recognition that Israel is the irreplaceable people of God, without a substitute. But today, this has to be followed up with reflections upon the foundations of responsible living in the world. Standing before us Christians is the discovery of the Torah, the biblical signature of the deed.

---

[16]Sh. Talmon, "Buber als Bibel-Interpret," *Leben als Begegnung*, 53.

1

The Two Foci of the Jewish Soul

1930

You have asked me to speak to you about the soul of Judaism. I have complied with this request, although I am against the cause for which you hold your conference, and I am against it not "just as a Jew," but also truly as a Jew, that is, as one who waits for the Kingdom of God, the Kingdom of Unification, and who regards all such "missions" as yours as springing from a misunderstanding of the nature of that kingdom, and as a hindrance to its coming. If in spite of this I have accepted your invitation, it is because I believe that when one is invited to share one's knowledge, one should not ask, "Why have you invited me?" but should share what one knows as well as one can — and that is my intention.

There is however one essential branch of Judaism about which I do not feel myself called upon to speak before you, and that is "the Law." My point of view with regard to this subject diverges from the traditional one; it is not a-nomistic, but neither is it entirely nomistic. For that reason I ought attempt neither to represent tradition, nor to substitute my own personal standpoint for the information you have desired of me. Besides, the problem of the Law does not seem to me to belong at all to the subject with which I have to deal. It would be a different matter were it my duty to present the teaching of Judaism. For the teaching of Judaism comes from Sinai; it is Moses' teaching. But the *soul* of Judaism is pre-Sinaitic; it is the soul which approached Sinai, and there received what it did receive; it is older than Moses; it is patriarchal, Abraham's soul, or more truly, since it concerns the *product* of a primordial age, it is Jacob's soul. The Law put on the soul and the soul can never again be understood outside of the Law; yet the soul itself is not of the Law. If one wishes to speak of the soul of Judaism, one must consider all the transformation it underwent through the ages till this very day; but one must never forget that in every one of its stages the soul has remained the same, and gone on in the same way.

This qualification, however, only makes the task more difficult. "I should wish to show you Judaism from the inside," wrote Franz Rosenzweig in 1916 to a Christian friend of Jewish descent, "in the same 'hymnal' way as you can show Christianity to me, the outsider; but the very reasons which make it possible for you to do so make it impossible for me. The soul of Christianity may be found in its outward expressions; Judaism wears a hard protective outer shell and one can speak about its soul only if one is within Judaism."[1] If, therefore, I still venture here to speak about the soul of Judaism from the outside, it is only because I do not intend to give an account of that soul, but only some indication of its fundamental attitude.

It is not necessary for me to labor the point that this fundamental attitude is nothing else than the attitude of faith, viewed from its human side. "Faith," however, should not be taken in the sense given to it in the Epistle to the Hebrews, as faith that God exists. That has never been doubted by Jacob's soul. In proclaiming its faith, its *emunah*, the soul only proclaimed that it put its trust in the everlasting God, *That he would be present* to the soul, as had been the experience of the patriarchs, and that is was entrusting itself to him, who was present. The German romantic philosopher Franz Baader did justice to the depth of Israel's faith relationship when he defined faith as "a pledge of faith,[2] that is, as a tying of oneself, a betrothing of oneself, an entering into a covenant."

The fealty of the Jew is the substance of his soul. The living God to whom he has pledged himself appears in infinite manifestations in the infinite variety of things and events; and this acts both as an incentive and as a steadying influence upon those who owe him allegiance. In the abundance of his manifestations they can ever and again recognize the One to whom they have entrusted themselves and pledged their faith. The crucial word which God himself spoke of this rediscovery of his presence was spoken to Moses from the midst of the burning bush:

---

[1] Franz Rosenzweig, "Judentum und Christentum," appendix to *Briefe* (Berlin, 1935). See below, p. 181.
[2] Baader assumes that the German *Glaube* (faith) is derived from *geloben* (to pledge).

"I shall be there as I there shall be" (Exod. 3:14). He is ever present to his creature, but always in the form peculiar to that moment, so that the spirit of man cannot foretell in the garment of what existence and what situation God will manifest himself. It is for man to recognize him in each of his garments. I cannot straightaway call any man a pagan; I know only of the pagan in man. But insofar as there is any paganism, it does not consist in not discerning God, but in not recognizing him as ever the same; the Jewish in man, on the contrary, seems to me to be the ever renewed rediscernment of God.

I shall therefore speak to you about the Jewish soul by making a few references to its fundamental attitude; I shall regard it as being the concretion of this human element in a national form, and consider it as the nation-shaped instrument of such a fealty and rediscernment.

I see the soul of Judaism as elliptically turning round two centers.

One center of the Jewish soul is the primeval experience that God is wholly raised above men, that he is beyond the grasp of man, and yet that he is present in an immediate relationship with these human beings who are absolutely incommensurable with him, and that he faces them. To know both these things at the same time, so that they cannot be separated, constitutes the living core of every believing Jewish soul; to know both, "God in heaven," that is, in complete hiddenness, and man "on earth," that is, in the fragmentation of the world of his senses and his understanding; God in the perfection and incomprehensibility of his being, and man in the abysmal contradiction of this strange existence from birth to death — and between both, immediacy!

The pious Jews of pre-Christian times called their God "Father"; and when the naively pious Jew in Eastern Europe uses that name today, he does not repeat something which he has learned, but he expresses a realization which he has come upon himself of the fatherhood of God and the sonship of man. It is not as though these men did not know that God is also utterly distant; it is rather that they know at the same time that however far away God is, he is never unrelated to them, and that even the man who is farthest away from God cannot cut himself off from the mutual relationship. In spite of the complete distance between God and man, they know that when God created man he set the mark of his image upon man's brow, and embedded it in man's nature, and that however faint God's mark may become, it can never be entirely wiped out.

According to hasidic legend, when the Baal Shem conjured up the demon Sammael, he showed him this mark on the forehead of his disciples, and when the master bade the conquered demon begone, the latter prayed, "Sons of the living God, permit me to remain a little while to look at the mark of the image of God on your faces." God's real commandment to men is to realize this image.

"Fear of God," accordingly, never means to the Jews that they ought to be afraid of God, but that, trembling, they ought to be aware of his incomprehensibility. The fear of God is the creaturely knowledge of the darkness to which none of our spiritual powers can reach, and out of which God reveals himself. Therefore, "the fear of God" is rightly called "the beginning of knowledge" (Prov. 1:7). It is the dark gate through which man must pass if he is to enter into the love of God. He who wishes to avoid passing through this gate, he who begins to provide himself with a comprehensible God, constructed thus and not otherwise, runs the risk of having to despair of God in view of the actualities of history and life, or of falling into inner falsehood. Only through the fear of God does man enter so deep into the love of God that he cannot again be cast out of it.

But fear of God is just a gate; it is not a house in which one can comfortably settle down — he who should want to live in it in adoration would neglect the performance of the essential commandment. God is incomprehensible, but he can be known through a bond of mutual relationship. God cannot be fathomed by knowledge, but he can be imitated. The life of man who is unlike God can yet be an *imitatio Dei*. "The likeness" is not closed to the "unlike." This is exactly what is meant when the Scripture instructs man to walk in God's way and in his footsteps. Man cannot by his own strength complete any way or any piece of the way, but he can enter on the path, he can take that first step, and again and again that first step. Man cannot "be like unto God," but with all the inadequacy of each of his days, he can follow God at all times, using the capacity he has on that particular day — and if he has used the capacity of that day to the full, he has done enough. This is not a mere act of faith; it is an entering into the life that has to be lived on that day with all the active fulness of a created person. This activity is within man's capacity: uncurtailed and not to be curtailed, the capacity is present through all the generations. God concedes the might to abridge this central property of decision to no primordial "Fall," however far-reaching in its effects, for the intention of God the Creator is mightier than the sin of man. The Jew knows from his knowledge of creation and of creatureliness that there may be burdens inherited from prehistoric and historic times, but that there is no overpowering original sin which could prevent the late-comer from deciding as freely as did Adam; as freely as Adam let God's hand go the late-comer can clasp it. We are dependent on grace; but we do not do God's will when we take it upon ourselves to begin with grace instead of beginning with ourselves. Only our beginning, our having begun, poor as it is, leads us to grace. God made no tools for himself, he needs none; he created for himself a partner in the dialogue of time and one who is capable of holding converse.

In this dialogue God speaks to every man through the life which he gives him again and again. Therefore man can only answer God with the whole of life — with the way in which he lives this given life. The Jewish teaching of the wholeness of life is the other side of the Jewish teaching of the unity of God. Because God bestows not only spirit on man, but the whole of his existence, from its "lowest" to its "highest" levels as well, man can fulfil the obligations of his partnership with God by no spiritual attitude, by no worship, on no sacred upper storey; the whole of life is required, every one of its areas and every one of its circumstances. There is no true human share of holiness without the hallowing of the everyday. Whilst Judaism unfolds itself through the history of its faith, and so long as it does unfold itself through that history, it holds out against that "religion" which is an attempt to assign a circumscribed part to God, in order to satisfy him who bespeaks and lays claim to the whole. But this unfolding of Judaism is really an unfolding, and not a metamorphosis.

To clarify our meaning we take the sacrificial cultus as an example. One of the two fundamental elements in biblical animal sacrifice is the sacralization of the natural life: he who slaughters an animal consecrates a part of it to God, and so doing hallows his eating of it. The second fundamental element is the sacramentalization of the complete surrender of life; to this element belong those types of sacrifice in which the person who offers the sacrifice puts his hands on the head of the animal in order to identify himself with it; in doing so he gives physical expression to the thought that he is bringing himself to be sacrificed in the person of the animal. He who performs these sacrifices without having this intention in his soul makes the cult meaningless, yes, absurd; it was against him that the prophets directed their fight against the sacrificial service which had been emptied of its core. In the Judaism of the Diaspora prayer takes the place of sacrifice; but prayer is also offered for the reinstatement of the cult, that is for the return of the holy unity of body and spirit. And in that consummation of Diaspora Judaism which we call hasidic piety, both fundamental elements unite into a new conception which fulfils the original meaning of the cult. When the purified and sanctified man in purity and holiness takes food into himself, eating becomes a sacrifice, the table an altar, and man consecrates himself to the Deity. At that point there is no longer a gulf between the natural and the sacral; at that point there is no longer the need for a substitute; at that point the natural event itself becomes a sacrament.

The Holy strives to include within itself the whole of life. The Law differentiates between the holy and the profane, but the Law desires to lead the way toward the messianic removal of the differentiation, to the all-sanctification. Hasidic piety no longer recognizes anything as simply and irreparably profane: "the profane" is for hasidism only a designation for the not yet sanctified, for that which is to be sanctified. Everything physical, all drives and urges and desires, everything creaturely, is material for sanctification. From the very same passionate powers which, undirected, give rise to evil, when they are turned toward God, the good arises. One does not serve God with the spirit only, but with the whole of his nature, without any subtractions. There is not one realm of the spirit and another of nature; there is only the growing realm of God. God is not spirit, but what we call spirit and what we call nature hail equally from the God who is beyond and equally conditioned by both, and whose kingdom reaches its fulness in the complete unity of spirit and nature.

The second focus of the Jewish soul is the basic consciousness that God's redeeming power is at work everywhere and at all times, but that a state of redemption exists nowhere and never. The Jew experiences as a person what every openhearted human being experiences as a person: the experience, in the hour when he is most utterly forsaken, of a breath from above, the nearness, the touch, the mysterious intimacy of light out of darkness; and the Jew, as part of the world, experiences, perhaps more intensely than any other part, the world's lack of redemption. He feels this lack of redemption against his skin, he tastes it on his tongue, the burden of the unredeemed world lies on him. Because of this almost physical knowledge of this, he *cannot* concede that the redemption has taken place; he knows that it has not. It is true that he can discover prefigurations of redemption in past history, but he always discovers only that mysterious intimacy of light out of darkness which is at work everywhere and at all times; no redemption which is different in kind, none which by its nature would be unique, which would be conclusive for future ages, and which had but to be consummated. Most of all, only through a denial of his own meaning and his own mission would it be possible for him to acknowledge that in a world which still remains unredeemed an anticipation of the redemption had been effected by which the human soul — or rather merely the souls of men who in a specific sense are believers — had been redeemed.

With a strength which original grace has given him, and which none of his historic trials has ever wrested from him, the Jew resists the radical division of soul and world which forms the basis of this conception; he resists the conception of a divine splitting of existence; he resists most passionately the awful notion of a *massa perditionis*. The God in whom he believes has not created the totality in order to let it split apart into one blessed and one damned half. God's eternity is not to be conceived by man; but — and this we Jews know until the moment of our death — there can be no eternity in which *everything* will not be accepted into God's atonement, when God has drawn time back into eternity. Should there however be a stage in the redemption of the world in which redemption is first fulfilled in one *part* of the world, we would derive no claim to redemption from our faith, much less from any other source. "If You do not yet wish to redeem Israel, at any rate redeem the goyim," the rabbi of Koznitz used to pray.

It is possible to argue against me, that there has been after all another eschatology in Judaism than that which I have indicated, that the apocalyptic stands beside the prophetic eschatology, It is actually important to make clear to oneself where the difference between the two lies. The prophetic belief about the end of time is in all essentials autochthonous; the apocalyptic belief is in all essentials built up of elements from Iranian dualism. Accordingly, the prophetic promises a consummation of creation, the apocalyptic its abrogation and supersession by another world, completely different in nature; the prophetic allows "the evil" to find the direction that leads toward God, and to enter into the good; the apocalyptic sees good and evil severed forever at the end of days, the good redeemed, the evil unredeemable for all eternity; the prophetic believes that the earth shall be hallowed, the apocalyptic despairs of an earth which it considers to be hopelessly doomed; the prophetic allows God's creative original will to be fulfilled completely; the apocalyptic allows the unfaithful creature power over the Creator, in that the creatures' actions force God to abandon nature. There was a time when it must have seemed uncertain whether the current apocalyptic teaching might not be victorious over the traditional prophetic messianism; if that had happened, it is to be assumed that Judaism would not have outlived its central faith — explicitly or imperceptibly it would have merged with Christianity, which is so strongly influenced by that dualism. During an epoch in which the prophetic was lacking, the Tannaites, early talmudic masters, helped prophetic messianism to triumph over the apocalyptic conception, and in doing so saved Judaism.

Still another important difference separates the two forms of Jewish belief about the end of days. The apocalyptists wished to predict an unalterable immovable future event; they were following Iranian conceptions in this point as well. For, according to the Iranians, history is divided into equal cycles of thousands of years, and the end of the world, the final victory of good over evil, can be predetermined with mathematical accuracy.

Not so the prophets of Israel: They prophesy "for the sake of those who turn."[3] That is, they do not warn against something which will happen in any case, but against that which will happen if those who are called upon to turn do not.

The Book of Jonah is a clear example of what is meant by prophecy. After Jonah has tried in vain to flee from the task God has given him, he is sent to Nineveh to prophesy its downfall. But Nineveh turns — and God changes its destiny. Jonah is vexed that the word for whose sake the Lord had broken his resistance had been rendered void; if one is forced to prophesy, one's prophecy must stand. But God is of a different opinion; he will employ no soothsayers, but messengers to the souls of men — the souls that are able to decide which way to go, and whose decision is allowed to contribute to the forging of the world's fate. Those who turn co-operate in the redemption of the world.

Man's partnership in the great dialogue finds its highest form of reality at this point. It is not as though any definite act of man could draw grace down from heaven; yet grace answers deed in unpredictable ways, grace unattainable, yet not self-withholding. It is not as though man has to do this or that "to hasten" the redemption of the world — "he that believeth shall not make haste" (Isa. 28:16); yet those who turn co-operate in the redemption of the world. The extent and nature of the participation assigned to the creature remains secret. "Does that mean that God cannot redeem his world without the help of his creatures?" "It means that God does not will to be able to do it." "Has God need of man for his work?" "He wills to have need of man."

He who speaks of activism in this connection misunderstands the mystery. The act is no outward gesture. "The ram's horn," runs an haggadic saying, "which God will blow on that day will have been made from the right horn of the ram which once took Isaac's place as a sacrifice." The "servant" whom God made "a polished shaft" to hide apparently unused in his quiver (Isa. 49:2), the man who is condemned to live in hiding — or rather, not one man, but the type of men to whom this happens generation after generation — the man who is hidden in the shadow of God's hand, who does not "cause his voice to be heard in the street" (Isa. 42:2), he who in darkness suffers for God's sake (ibid.) — he it is who has been given as a light for the tribes of the world, that God's "salvation may be unto the end of the earth" (Isa. 49:6).

The mystery of the act, of the human part in preparing the redemption, passes through the darkness of the ages as a mystery of concealment, as a concealment within the person's relation to himself as well, until one day it will come into the open. To the question why according to tradition

---

[3] Talmud, Berakhot 34b.

the Messiah was born on the anniversary of the day of the destruction of Jerusalem, a hasidic rabbi answered: "The power cannot rise, unless it has dwelt in the great concealment. . . . In the shell of oblivion grows the power of remembrance. That is the power of redemption. On the day of the Destruction the power will be lying at the bottom of the depths and growing. That is why on this day we sit on the ground; that is why on this day we visit the graves; that is why on this day was born the Messiah."

Though robbed of their real names, these two foci of the Jewish soul continue to exist for the "secularized" Jew too, insofar as he has not lost his soul. They are, first, the immediate relationship to the Existent One, and second, the power of atonement at work in an unatoned world. In other words, first, the *non-incarnation* of God who reveals himself to the "flesh" and is present to it in a mutual relationship, and second, the unbroken continuity of human history, which turns toward fulfillment and decision. These two centers constitute the ultimate division between Judaism and Christianity.

We "unify" God, when living and dying we profess his unity; we do not unite ourselves with him. The God in whom we believe, to whom we are pledged, does not unite with human substance on earth. But the very fact that we do not imagine that we can unite with him enables us the more ardently to demand "that the world shall be perfected under the kingship of the Mighty One."

We feel salvation happening; and we feel the unsaved world. No savior with whom a new redeemed history began has appeared to us at any definite point in history. Because we have not been stilled by anything which has happened, we are wholly directed toward the coming of that which is to come.

Thus, though divided from you, we have been attached to you. As Franz Rosenzweig wrote in the letter which I have already quoted: "You who live in an *ecclesia triumphans* need a silent servant to cry to you whenever you believe you *have partaken* of God in bread and wine, 'Lord, remember the last things.' "[4]

What have you and we in common? If we take the question literally, a book and an expectation.

To you the book is a forecourt; to us it is the sanctuary. But in this place we can dwell together, and together listen to the voice that speaks here. That means that we can work together to evoke the buried speech of that voice; together we can redeem the imprisoned living word.

Your expectation is directed toward a second coming, ours to a coming which has not been anticipated by a first. To you the phrasing of world

---

[4]See below, p. 182.

history is determined by one absolute midpoint, the year nought; to us it is an unbroken flow of tones following each other without a pause from their origin to their consummation. But we can wait for the advent of the One together, and there are moments when we may prepare the way before him together.

Pre-messianically our destinies are divided. Now to the Christian the Jew is the incomprehensibly obdurate man, who declines to see what has happened; and to the Jew the Christian is the incomprehensibly daring man, who affirms in an unredeemed world that its redemption has been accomplished. This is a gulf which no human power can bridge. But it does not prevent the common watch for a unity to come to us from God, which, soaring above all of your imagination and all of ours, affirms and denies, denies and affirms what you hold and what we hold, and which replaces all the creedal truths of earth by the ontological truth of heaven which is one.

It behooves both you and us to hold inviolably fast to our own true faith, that is to our own deepest relationship to truth. It behooves both of us to show a religious respect for the true faith of the other. This is not what is called "tolerance," our task is not to tolerate each other's waywardness but to acknowledge the real relationship in which both stand to the truth. Whenever we both, Christian and Jew, care more for God himself than for our images of God, we are united in the feeling that our Father's house is differently constructed than our human models take it to be.

2

Church, State, Nation, Jewry [1]

1933

First Response: When Karl Ludwig Schmidt and I exchanged letters in preparation for this dialogue, we were first of all obliged to come to an understanding about the formulation of the topic. He proposed "Church, State, Nationhood, Synagogue." I declined this, in the first place because I did not feel myself empowered to speak for a "synagogue," but more than this because I consider "synagogue" to be an unauthentic designation and not one with which to address a Jew in a manner enabling him to answer. Instead I accepted the designation "Jewry," although I do not consider this entirely correct either. Rather, I regard that designation as correct which Schmidt himself used with emphasis — so that we have already gained common ground by virtue of this word — this name, the name "Israel."

Israel is not something about which we possess only a Biblical report, something with which thanks to this report, we Jews feel a history-laden connection. Rather Israel is something existing — something once and for all, unique, unclassifiable by either category or concept. Every pigeonhole of world history defies attempts at subsuming it. Israel is that which, to this day, amidst various distortions, dissimulations, destructions, still hides within this "Judaism" something peculiarly its own,

---

[1] German *Volk*. Buber seems to use this term in the sense of "people" as well as "nation." I have tried to translate by "people" when it clearly applied to Israel, by "nation" when clearly applied to political entities. I have used "Jewry" rather than "Judaism" in the light of what follows; both meanings are contained in the word *Judentum*. —*Tr.*

something which continues to live within it as a concealed reality. Only from within this reality can we Jews address Christians; only from there have we the existential possibility of a response. And the more truly we are addressed as Israel, the more legitimate is the dialogue.

Karl Ludwig Schmidt has acknowledged that Israel is something unique, something unclassifiable. Israel exists for the Church in the Church's legitimate existence, and Israel exists for us in *our* legitimate existence. Both of us, Church and Israel, know "concerning" Israel. But we know one another in fundamentally different ways — a fundamental difference which is radically other than a mere difference of opinions such as one may express in order to try to harmonize them with each other. That is impossible here; for we are dealing here with a fundamental difference of perception or intellection. For like Israel, the Church too claims to know. This knowledge of the Church concerning Israel confronts Israel's knowledge concerning itself in a manner more strictly irreconcilable than a mere logical contradiction. The Church perceives Israel as a reality *rejected* by God. This condition of rejection necessarily follows from the claim of the Church to be the true Israel. Those of Israel have, according to this view, forfeited *their* claim because they did not recognize Jesus as the Messiah.

Christians believe that they have received this "being Israel" — the office, dignity, and election of Israel — from God. The certitude of their belief on this point is unassailable. We have no means of opposing this knowledge of the Church concerning Israel which could serve as more than an argument. We, however, who know concerning Israel from within, in the darkness of a knowing from within, in the light of a knowing from within, know otherwise concerning Israel. (I cannot even speak of "perceiving" here any more, for we know it from within, and we know it, not with the "eye of the spirit," but with our very lives.) We who have sinned against God a thousand times, who have turned our backs on God a thousand times, who have experienced throughout these millennia a divine dispensation which it would be too simple to call punishment (for it is greater than punishment) — we know that nonetheless we have not been repudiated. We know that this dispensation is an event, not in the conditionality of the world, but in the reality of the space between God and ourselves. And we know that precisely there, in this reality, we have not been repudiated by God, that in this discipline and chastisement, God's hand holds on to us and does not let go, holds us into this fire and does not let us fall.

Such knowledge is fundamentally and irreconcilably different. I would not dare to call ours a "claim." That is too human, too arrogant a term for our situation. We do not have a claim at all. We have only our poor but

133

exceedingly factual knowledge concerning our existence in the hands of God. However, this fundamental difference cannot be resolved from the side of men, by human undertaking, by human speech, by human willingness to come to terms, no matter how comradely. But if we "wait patiently," it is for what cannot come to us from man but only from God; we await a unification which cannot be constructed by men, which, indeed, contemporary man is utterly incapable of conceiving in concrete terms.

Paul's dictum regarding the resolution of differences in the world of the Christian event has already been noted; however, we are incapable of sensing this resolution. We feel ourselves, in fact find ourselves, in a world where differences are unresolved and appear by their nature to be irresolvable. To be sure, however, we also feel something else. We feel that the "Spirit" — a term of belief which we have in common with Christians, although they call it *pneuma hagion* (holy spirit) and we *ruah ha-qodesh* (spirit of sanctification or of holiness) — is itself not bound by this differentiation. We feel that the Spirit alone wafts over our irresolvable differences, that though it does not bridge them, it nevertheless gives assurance of unity, assurance in the experienced moment of unity for the communality of even Christians and Jews.

In this sense I would like to understand that Jewish dictum which I set opposite that of Paul.[2] True, it is more reserved, but it radiates a factuality which can be experienced, it seems to me, by every man. It is a dictum from an ancient book dealing with matters taught in the "School of Elijah" after his assumption: "I invoke heaven and earth as witness: whether one be of the Gentiles or of Israel, whether man or woman, man-servant or maid-servant — only according to the deed which he does will the Spirit of Sanctification descend upon him" [Seder Eliyahu, Friedmann, ed., 48]. This is no resolution of differences, but rather a distribution of the Spirit to humanity as it is, in the fragmentation in which it stands, in such a way, however, that humanity as a whole, from whatever side, can look upon that which descends on men, no matter how different their point of departure or their very certitude of belief may be.

We, Israel, confront the Church's rejection of our knowledge concerning ourselves. The Church can perhaps say to us: "You who feel yourselves sustained by God, not abandoned, not spurned, still existing in the Presence — what you call actually experienced self-knowledge is an illusion prompted by your instinct for self-preservation." What then

---

[2]Schmidt quoted Galatians 3:28: "Here is neither Jew nor Greek, here is neither slave nor free, here is neither male nor female."

if the certitude of one side is thus rejected by the other, as final eschatological reality?[3] I believe that this is one of those decisive points at which we human beings have to acknowledge the genuine teaching of what human existence means, that hard and salutary teaching. We have to deal with each other in the diversity of the human, and we see how deep such diversity can go, even to the ultimate roots of belief. What then shall we do?

We can try to do something extremely difficult, something which is extremely difficult for the religiously oriented person, something which runs counter to his orientation and relationships or, rather, seems to run counter to them, something which seems to run counter to his relationship with God. We can acknowledge as a mystery that which, notwithstanding our existence and self-knowledge, others confess as their reality of belief. We are not in a position to appraise the meaning of their confession because we do not know it from within as we know *ourselves* from within.

Karl Ludwig Schmidt justifiably put the question of the Messiah, the Christological question, at the center of his observations.

If we wish to reduce the schism between Jews and Christians, between Israel and the Church, to a formula, we can say: "The Church stands on the belief in the 'having come' of Christ as the God-given redemption of man. We, Israel, are *incapable* of believing this."

The Church views our declaration either as a case of not wanting to believe, as a very grave sort of obduracy, or else as a kind of curse, as a basic limitation on the ability to recognize reality, as the blinding of Israel which prevents it from seeing the light.

We, Israel, understand in another fashion our inability to accept that gospel. We understand the Christology of Christianity quite definitely as a substantive occurrence between the Above and the Below. We view Christianity as something whose spread over the world of nations we are in no position to penetrate. But we also know that universal history has not been rent to its foundations, that the world has not yet been redeemed. We know it as surely as we know that the air which we breathe exists, that the space in which we move exists. We know it more deeply, more authentically. We apprehend the unredeemedness of the world.

The Church may or must understand precisely this sensation of ours as the consciousness of *our* unredeemedness. But we know it otherwise.

For us, the redemption of the world is indivisibly equated with the

---

[3] A difficult passage to render in English. The German is *von einem Letzten her, als Letztes.* [The *ultimate* conviction of Israel denies the claim of the *ultimate* character of realized eschatology made by Christianity. —F. A. R.]

135

completion of creation, with the erection of a unity no longer hindered by anything, no longer suffering any contradiction, realized in all the multiplicity of the world, equated, in short, with the fulfillment of the Kingdom of God. We are incapable of comprehending anticipation of the *consummate* redemption of the world in any partial respect, such as the soul's already being redeemed, however much redeeming and becoming redeemed manifest themselves to us too in our mortal hours.

We are not aware of a caesura in history. We know no midpoint of history, only a goal, the goal of the way of God who does not pause on his way.

We are incapable of holding God to any one manner of revelation. We are prevented from regarding any unique event as a definitive revelation of God, prevented by that word from the burning bush: "I will be what I will be" (Exod. 4:14), i.e., I will exist as I will exist at any given time. It is not as though we were able to declare anything about God's ability or inability to reveal himself. I am referring precisely to the fact that we are incapable of affirming anything absolute about all the revelations concerning which we know. We do not say: "God cannot reveal himself this way." It is only that we do not attribute unsurpassability, the character of an incarnation, to any revelations. That futuristic dictum of the Lord points unconditionally beyond each and every moment of occurred time. God is utterly superior to every one of his manifestations.

I have already stated: what joins Jews and Christians together is their knowledge concerning one uniqueness. And we can also confront this most profoundly divisive factor from the same vantage point. Every authentic sanctuary can acknowledge the mystery of every other authentic sanctuary. The mystery of the other one is internal to the latter and cannot be perceived from without. No one outside Israel knows concerning the mystery of Israel. And no one outside Christendom knows concerning the mystery of Christendom. But for all this ignorance, they can acknowledge each other in the mystery. How is it possible for the mysteries to exist side by side? That is God's mystery. How is it possible for a world to exist as a house in which these mysteries dwell together? That is God's affair, for the world is a house of God. We serve, separately and yet all together, not by each one of us shirking his reality of belief nor by surreptitiously seeking a togetherness despite our difference, but rather when, acknowledging our fundamental difference, we impart to each other in unreserved confidence what we know of the unity of this house, a unity which we hope one day to feel surrounding us without partitions. We serve thus, till one day we may be united in the common service, till we shall all become, as the Jewish prayer on the festival of the New Year puts it: "a single fellowship for doing his will."

I repeat: that Israel exists is something unique, outside all categories. This name, bestowed by God, not by father and mother, marks the community as one which cannot be comprehended by the categories of ethnology and sociology. We fail to do Israel justice whenever we apply such a category to it. What this uniqueness of Israel is based on is declared in the Bible. It makes the origin of this community identical, historically and episodically, with the religious experience and the religious behavior of a human multitude in its decisive hour.

The human multitude of Israel experiences something which happens to it as a believing multitude, as a multitude united by belief, not as so many believing individuals but rather as a believing community. As such it hears and it responds. In this process of being addressed and answering, it is constituted in that very hour into what we call a people. It becomes something which endures henceforth in a closed circle of generations and births. This differentiates Israel for all time from nation-states and religions.

We deal here with a unity of belief and people which is unique. To regard its uniqueness as incidental implies incredulity vis-à-vis history as it has occurred. Its origin is designated as a covenant between the divine and the human.

This is a unique royal covenant: God says to a people (Exod. 19:6) that he takes it to himself as his immediate royal realm, and a people says of God (Exod. 15:18) that he will remain its king "forever and ever." To understand such a covenant as a privilege, however, is fundamentally mistaken. To be sure, the popular side of this people again and again succumbs to the temptation to do this.

Against such misconstruction there stands the great phenomenon of prophecy, which repeatedly reminds the people that it is nothing more than, so to speak, an experiment of God. Genesis recounts how God first attempted such an experiment with a mankind which failed. Only then did he attempt to cultivate a people for himself as the beginning of a mankind, the beginning of the realization of his Kingdom. God calls it the "beginning of his harvest" (Jer. 2:3).

This Israel, which is at once nation and religion and yet neither of these, is exposed to all the temptations of nations and religions. It would like to rest within itself; it would like to feel itself, by God's grace, as an end unto itself. But its leaders censure it for any sense of security: it exists as a people only because "people-hood" is the presupposition of the *whole* human response to God.

There must be a people in order for the human response to fulfill itself

137

in the whole of life, to which public life belongs. The whole life-response of man cannot be given to God by the individual person but only by the community in its plurality and unity, in the joint labors and the joint realization of its variously endowed and variously commissioned members. That is why there must be a people, why there must be an Israel. The community must endure as a presupposition of the fulfillment. If it wants to be otherwise, it must be sundered and renewed.

The knowledge concerning Israel can degenerate into the superstition that God is a purveyor of power. To counter this, the prophets point ever more clearly to the historical mystery. The way of God through history will not be represented schematically. God manifests himself as master of history, but not through bestowal of power and success. There is a covenant of God with suffering, with darkness, with concealment. In the prophetic dictum, the sinful people confronts God as one whom it can rejoin in darkness and suffering, not in power.

Ever since that time we have believed in this. It is again and again a contemporary concern that a people can sin by calling its obedience to self an obedience to God. Not until the Exile did Israel learn to disabuse itself of this sin.

With the Babylonian Exile, the conception of the "Servant of God" matures. It is a conception of the human type which ever and again appears on earth and effects what it has to effect, in suffering and in darkness, in the quiver of God; "He made me a polished arrow, in his quiver he hid me away" (Isa. 49:2).

A suffering for God's sake, the concealed history of the arrows which God does not dispatch, which do his work in the darkness of the quiver: it is for this that we, as Israel, endure. Every struggle of ours can be understood only on this account.

According to our tradition, the destruction of Jerusalem took place because the community was not fulfilled, because there was a conflict in Israel which prevented the "beginning" from growing into a harvest. And not only do the Jews hence come among the nations: Israel too comes over the nations. That is, Jesus' gospel of the coming age as the triumphant revelation of the concealed universal history, which grew up in Israel, comes over the nations.

The concealed universal history seeks to ascend from the quiver and to manifest itself as the history — the way — of God. From a late, spiritualized form of theocracy, Jesus points back to the original certitude of the Kingdom of God and its fulfillment; he proclaims it by renewing and transforming the conception of the Servant. His gospel, however, reached the nations not in its authentic form but rather in a dichotomy which is alien to Jesus' gospel. We know this dichotomy most forcefully through Augustine, who surrendered the realms of the national community, of the state, who cut off this presupposition of the *whole* life-response of man from the domain of God. The dichotomy leads consequently to a separation of "religion" and "politics." Again and again some imperial concept attempts to surmount this duality, only to fail again and again.

The nations erected their concepts of empire as Christian nations. They accepted the Kingdom of God as their assigned task; they took it up and enunciated it as Christians. The nations' great imperial concepts all derive from the mission of Israel, but in such a way that, empowered by the Church, they declare Israel dismissed from its function, as no longer appointed to help build the godly community of mankind.

Thus the nations oppose Jewry in their concepts of empire. Jewry, however, confronts the nations in this way: it knows a Yea opposed to this Nay, a Yea which is neither light nor self-willed, but rather imposed and terribly hard to bear. It knows this precisely, in its pitiful way, but also immensely and inextinguishably.

The failure of the world of the nations truly to admit Jewry is connected with its opposition to Israel. Motivated by peasant traditions in the reality of its belief, Israel was excluded from agricultural production as early as the Middle Ages. It was denied participation in the creative life of the nations in whose midst it lived. The nations did not understand that what was addressed to them — indeed, enjoined upon them in their relationship to the resident alien, Israel — also is said of Israel's relationship to the resident alien: "So you shall divide this land among you according to the tribes of Israel. You shall allot it as an inheritance for yourselves and for the aliens who reside among you and have begotten children among you. They shall be to you as native-born sons of Israel; with you they shall be allotted an inheritance among the tribes of Israel" (Ezek. 47:21ff.). The nations made it impossible, thereby, for Israel to realize Jeremiah's principle for life in the Exile: "Build houses and live in them; plant gardens and eat their produce" (Jer. 29:5).

The nations of the Occident have from the first denied Israel participation in creative life. Even when they finally "emancipated" it, they did not admit it as Israel but rather as a plurality of individual Jews. Israel was not accepted as Israel by the Christians.

Some say that this is impossible. A believing person must not speak thus. He must not evade the fact that there is this Israel in the midst of the nations, that it has been dispatched into the midst of the nations. This prohibition applies to Israel as well as to the others. The uniqueness of Israel's situation corresponds to the uniqueness of Israel. But is it also properly a part of this uniqueness that that injunction to all nations with resident aliens in their midst still awaits its fulfillment; and that Israel still waits to be able to fulfill that dictum directed to it by Jeremiah?

Karl Ludwig Schmidt has asked me about Zionism. Certainly the concept of "peoplehood" has been emphasized and overemphasized in this. This has happened because, within an indissoluble union of peoplehood and belief, peoplehood had frequently been neglected in the period after the Emancipation. The attempt was made to allot Israel its place among the religions. Against this the caveat had to be expressed that Israel has no reality without its peoplehood. But today the time has come to replace national and religious concepts once more with the Israel properly so called, Israel in its unity and uniqueness. It is for the sake of this Israel that Zion must be built. And Zion cannot be solely a territorial concept, any more than Israel can be solely a national one.

Is an authentic acceptance of Israel possible?

This question seems to me to be connected in its very essence with that other question: Is it possible for the Christian nations to behave according to the Bible?

I do not know what the situation is in this regard. Whether an authentic dialogue can exist between the Church, which does not know of the mission of Israel, and Israel, which knows of its mission, seems to me, however, to depend on what this situation is. In such a dialogue one will hardly come to an understanding with another, but one can understand the other for the sake of the one Existence which the several realities of belief imply.

My Christian partner in this conversation has applied the passage about the Servant of God to Israel's understanding of itself. This speaks for the possibility of such a dialogue. It touches the depths of Israel's self-knowledge concerning its mission. We are entitled, therefore, to hope that the possibility for an authentic acceptance of Israel exists in a common struggle, hard but blessed.

Finally, the question of the relationship of Israel to the state is determined by Israel's Messianic belief. This is the belief in a human community as the royal realm of God. Therefore, the question of the social and political structure of the effort to build the human community can never and nowhere be a matter of indifference to Israel. It is a matter of innermost moment to Israel, a part of its eternal mission, to take an interest in the striving of every political structure toward the Kingdom.

Seen from the perspective of Messianic belief, every political structure, no matter what its configuration, anticipates the Kingdom of God for Israel; it is a problematic model of that Kingdom which, however, points to its true form.

But at the same time, Israel knows, precisely in its Messianic belief, just how questionable are the realizations. Therefore, it senses unendingly the other side of the state. It senses that what we call a state is ever and again an index of how much willingness is available for community and, on the other hand, how much coercion is required to maintain here and now a minimum of honest human coexistence.

This twofold viewpoint of Israel's results in its twofold relationship to the state. Israel can never turn its back on the state; it can never disavow it. It must accept it, and it must long for that fulfillment of the state which is so inadequately intimated each time by its various manifestations.

The conservative and the revolutionary Jewish attitudes are both based on the same fundamental outlook.

Second Response: I live a short distance from the city of Worms, to which I am also tied by ancestral tradition; and from time to time I visit there. When I do so, I always go first to the cathedral. It is a visible harmony of members, a whole in which no part deviates from the norm of perfection. I walk around the cathedral, gazing at it in perfect joy. Then I go to the Jewish cemetery. It consists of cracked and crooked stones without shape or direction. I enter the cemetery and look up from this disorder to the marvelous harmony of the cathedral, and it seems to me as if I were looking from Israel up to the Church. Here below there is no suggestion of form, only the stones and the ashes beneath the stones. The ashes are there, no matter how they have been scattered. The corporeality of human beings who have become ashes is there. It is there. It is there for me. It is there for me, not as corporeality within the space of this planet, but as corporeality deep in my own memories, back into the depths of history, back as far as Sinai.

I have stood there; I have been united with the ashes and through them with the patriarchs. That is a remembrance of the divine-human encounter which is granted to all Jews. The perfection of the Christian God-space cannot divert me from this; nothing can divert me from the God-time of Israel.

I have stood there and I have experienced everything myself. I have experienced all the death that was before me; all the ashes, all the desolation, and all the noiseless wailings become mine. But the covenant has not been withdrawn for me. I lie on the ground, prostrate like these stones. But it has not been withdrawn for me.

The cathedral is as it is. The cemetery is as it is. But nothing has been withdrawn for us.

If the Church were more Christian, if Christians were more fulfilled, if they did not have to dispute with each other as much as they do, Karl

Ludwig Schmidt holds that there would be a keener debate between Christians and ourselves.

Were Jewry once more to become Israel, were the sacred countenance to appear once more from behind the mask, then, I would counter, the separation would remain unbridged, but there would not be a more bitter argument between us and the Church, but rather something wholly different, which today is still inexpressible.

In conclusion I ask you to listen to two quotations which appear to contradict each other but do not contradict each other.

The Talmud (Yebamot 47a) teaches:

> If in this day and age a convert comes in order to be received into Judaism let him be told: "what have you seen in us, that you wish to be converted? Do you know that the people of Israel are at this time tortured, battered, buffeted, driven about, that suffering has overtaken them?" If he says: "I know, and I am not worthy," then let him at once be received.

This might seem to be Jewish arrogance. It is not. It is nothing other than the public declaration of that which cannot be dismissed. The distress is a real distress, and the disgrace is real disgrace. But there is a divine meaning in it which assures us that as God had promised us (Isa. 54:10), he will never let us fall from his hands.

And the Midrash says (Exodus Rabba 19.4, Sifra on Lev. 18:5, Weiss, ed. 86b):

> The Holy One, blessed be he, declares no creature unworthy, rather he receives every one. The gates are opened at every hour, and whoever seeks to enter, will enter. And thus He says (Isa. 26:2): "Open ye the gates, that the righteous nation (*goy zaddiq*) that keepeth faithfulness may enter in." It is not written: That priests may enter in, that Levites may enter in, that Israelites may enter in. Rather is written: that a *goy zaddiq* may enter in.

The first quotation dealt with converts, but not this quotation: it deals with all mankind. The gates of God are open to all. The Christian need not go via Judaism, nor the Jew via Christianity, in order to enter in to God.

3

Two Types of Faith

1950

VI

The faith, which Paul indicates in his distinction between it and the law, is not one which could have been held in the pre-Christian era. "The righteousness of God," by which he means His declaration of man as righteous, is that which is through faith in Christ (Rom. 3:22, Gal. 2:16), which means faith in one who has come, died on the cross and risen.

In the matter of "faith" against "works," which Paul pursues, he does not therefore in fact intend a thing which might have existed before the coming of Christ. He charges Israel (Rom. 9:31) with having pursued the "law of righteousness" and not having attained it, because it strove after it "not by faith but by work." Is this to mean that ancient Israel did not fulfil the law because it did not strive to fulfil it by faith? Surely not, for it is immediately explained that they had stumbled on the stone of stumbling, and that cannot apply to the former Israel and a possible insufficiency of its faith in the future coming of the Messiah, but only to the Jews of that time, those whom Paul sought for Christ and whom he had not won for him because they did not recognize in him the promised Messiah of belief. In Isaiah's word (8:14), which Paul quotes here in a strange amalgamation with another (that discussed above,*28:16), the "stone of stumbling" refers to none other than God himself: the fact that

---

*Chap. 1, *Werke* I:664; English translation, 21f.

His message of salvation is misunderstood and misused as a guarantee of security means that His own word brings the people to stumbling. Paul interprets the saying as referring to Christ. "For Christ is the end of the law, so that righteousness may come to everyone that believes." The Jews, who refuse for themselves this faith, refuse to submit to the righteousness of God. Paul prays that they may be saved, but they do not desire it, for they have a zeal for God, but they lack the knowledge.

Again Paul refers to a sentence from the Old Testament, but this time he takes it neither from the history of the time before the law nor from the prophets, but from the "law" itself. It is the sentence (Deut. 30:14): "For the word is very nigh thee, in thy mouth and in thy heart." "That is," Paul continues (Rom. 10:8ff.), "the word of faith which we preach. For if thou confess with thy mouth Jesus as Lord and believe in thy heart that God has raised him from the dead, thou shalt be saved." Paul refers to the verse of Isaiah we have already discussed, "he who trusts will not hasten," but in the incorrect translation of the Septuagint, which is perplexed by the difficult text and has chosen a different version; hence the sentence which Paul quotes has become: "Whosoever believeth on Him shall not be ashamed." This is the Pauline counterpart of the Johannine reply of the apostle to Jesus, "We have believed and known that thou are the Holy One of God"; both statements supplement each other as only the report of a declaration by disciples who have been apprehended by the living Jesus and the authentic evidence of one apprehended by the dead can supplement each other. But with that sentence from Deuteronomy, where, as he says (v. 6), "the righteousness which is of faith" speaks, Paul deals very curiously. In the text itself the word which is not in heaven but in the mouth and heart means none other than "this commandment, which I this day command thee" (v. 11), thus not a word of faith but simply the word of the "law," of which it is declared here that it does not come from far above man, but in such a manner that it is felt to rise in his own heart and to force its way from there on to his lips. But in the sentence which Paul quotes he has omitted a word, the last word of the sentence. The text runs: "For the word is very nigh thee, in thy mouth and in thy heart, *to do it.*" The word which God commands man speaks to him in such a way that he feels it rising in his heart and forcing its way to his lips as a word which desires to be done by him. As in the case of the "commandment" so Paul has also left the "doing" unnoticed. Elsewhere however (2:14ff.) this "doing" appears in him precisely in conjunction with this "in the heart": where he speaks *of the heathen*, who "do by nature the things of the law" because "the work of the law is written in their hearts." One may compare with this God's word in Jeremiah (31:33) that some day the Torah of God shall be written in *Israel's* heart. Strange are the ways of the Pauline hour and its solicitation! "No flesh" (Rom. 3:20, Gal. 2:16), says Paul, becomes righteous before God by the works of the law. This thesis, of which it has been rightly said[1] that for Paul it is "the principle which requires no proof and is exempted from every conflict of opinions," means above all (Rom. 3:28) that "by faith alone," faith in Jesus (v. 26) "without the works of the law," the individual, heathen or Jew, is declared righteous, so that therefore — and this is the special concern of the apostle to the Gentiles — the Gentiles do not have to come through Judaism to Christ, but have their own immediate approach to him. It means further, as we have seen, that the Jews who refuse to believe in Jesus, have no prop in their possession of the law, but by their refusal reject the only possibility of being declared righteous by God. But the law did not come into the world at the same time as Jesus; how is it with the generations between the two? Unlike Paul's contemporaries, they were not faced with the question as to whether they believed in Christ; but of course they have "believed," or rather the "believers" amongst them have trusted God and looked for the coming of His kingship. In this "faith" of theirs they have truly fulfilled the "law." As men of faith, even if, which could not be, they did not believe in the Christ who had come, they have nevertheless, so we may assume, been declared righteous like their father Abraham; did the God who justified them detach their faith from their fulfilling of the law, and heed only the former and not the latter also which was done in faith? Paul expressly says (Rom. 2:12) that the doers of the law, its true doers in faith, were, as such, declared righteous. Or are we to understand by the futile "works of the Law" merely a performance without faith? It is however quite obviously Paul's view that the law is not capable of being fulfilled; for he bases (Gal. 3:10) his statement about the curse under which those are "who are of the works of the Law" upon the alleged verse of Scripture that everyone is accursed who "does not continue in all things which are written in the Book of the Law to do them" (the decisive word "all things" is missing in the Masoretic Text,[2] as stated), therefore the former are identical with the latter: nobody can in fact do everything which the law demands of him under the threat of the curse.

---

[1] Lohmeyer, *Probleme paulinischer Theologie, Zeitschrift für die neutestamentliche Wissenschaft* 28 (1929): 210.

[2] Even in the version which contained the word and which was followed by the Septuagint and also by the Samaritan, it undoubtedly did not have the emphatic meaning, as we can see from its use in similar passages in Deuteronomy. To be sure elsewhere (Deut. 28:58) the non-observance of "all words of this Torah" is threatened with the most severe penalties, but Scripture carefully adds straightway what is meant by this total claim: "to fear this glorious and fearful Name."

The indivisible law which allows of no selection, the "whole" law (Gal. 5:3), demands therefore according to Paul the impossible, without his differentiating between an external fulfillment which is possible and an impossible fulfillment in the complete intention of faith; evidently he already regards the outward fulfillment as impossible, without of course his indicating what makes it so.

Here not merely the Old Testament belief and the living faith of post-Biblical Judaism are opposed to Paul, but also the Jesus of the Sermon on the Mount, although from a different motive and with a different purpose.

XVI

The periods of Christian history can be classified according to the degree in which they are dominated by Paulinism, by which we mean of course not just a system of thought, but a mode of seeing and being which dwells in the life itself. In this sense our era is a Pauline one to a particular degree. In the human life of our day, compared with earlier epochs, Christianity is receding, but the Pauline view and attitude is gaining the mastery in many circles outside that of Christianity. There is a Paulinism of the unredeemed, one, that is, from which the abode of grace is eliminated: like Paul man experiences the world as one given into the hands of inevitable forces, and only the manifest will to redemption from above, only Christ is missing. The Christian Paulinism of our time is a result of the same fundamental view, although it softens down or removes that aspect of the demonocracy of the world: it sees nevertheless existence divided into an unrestricted rule of wrath and a sphere of reconciliation, from which point indeed the claim for the establishment of a Christian order of life is raised clearly and energetically enough, but *de facto* the redeemed Christian souls stand over against an unredeemed world of men in lofty impotence. Neither this picture of the abyss spanned only by the halo of the saviour nor that of the same abyss covered now by nothing but impenetrable darkness is to be understood as brought about by changes in subjectivity: in order to paint them the retina of those now living must have been affected by an actual fact, by the situation now existing.

I will illustrate my position from two books, which are very different from each other; I choose them because the view of which I am speaking comes to light clearly in them. For this reason I have chosen one from the literature of modern Christian theology, because I do not know of any other in which the Pauline view of God is expressed so directly; it is *The Mediator* by Emil Brunner. The other, one of the few authentic similes which our age has produced, is the work of a non-Christian poet, a Jew, Franz Kafka's novel *The Castle*.

I am only concerned in Brunner's book with what he has to say about God, and not about Christ; that is, with the dark foil and not the image of glory which stands out against it. We read: "God cannot allow His honour to be impugned"; "the law itself demands from God the reaction"; "God would cease to be God if He allowed His honour to be impugned." This is said of the Father of Christ; therefore it does not refer to one of the gods and rulers, but to Him of Whom the "Old Testament" witnesses. But neither in this itself nor in any Jewish interpretation is God spoken of in this way; and such a word is unimaginable from the lips of Jesus as I believe I know him. For here in fact "with God all things are possible"; there is nothing which he "could not." Of course the rulers of this world cannot allow their honour to be impugned; what would remain to them if they did! But God — to be sure prophets and psalmists show how He "glorifies His Name" to the world, and Scripture is full of His "zeal," but He Himself does not assume any of these attitudes otherwise than remaining superior to them; in the language of the interpretation: He proceeds from one *middah* to the other, and none is adequate to Him. If the whole world should tear the garment of His honour into rags nothing would be done to Him. Which law could presume to demand anything from Him? — surely the highest conceivable law is that which is given by Him to the world, not to Himself:[3] He does not bind Himself and therefore nothing binds Him. And that He would cease to be God — "God" is a stammering of the world, the world of men, He himself is immeasurably more than "God" only, and if the world should cease to stammer or cease to exist, He would remain. In the immediacy we experience His anger and His tenderness in one; no assertion can detach one from the other and make Him into a God of wrath Who requires a mediator.

In the Book of Wisdom, scarcely later than a hundred years before Christ, God is addressed in this fashion: "But Thou hast compassion upon all, since Thou canst do all things" — He is able to have compassion even upon us, as we are! — "and Thou dost overlook the sins of men up to their turning" — He overlooks them, not that we should

---

[3] Brunner explains: "The law of His being God, on which all the lawfulness of the world is based, the fundamental order of the world, the consistent and reliable character of all that happens, the validity of all standards. . . . " Precisely this seems to me to be an inadmissible derivation of the nature of the world from the nature of God, or rather the reverse. Order and standards are derived from the act of God, which sets the world in being and gives it the law, and not from a law which would determine His being. Cf. E. Brunner, *The Mediator* (1934), 444.

perish, but turn to Him; He does not wait until we have turned (this is significantly the opposite of the Synoptic characterization of the Baptist's preaching: not repentance for the remission of sins, but the remission of sins for repentance) — " . . . for Thou lovest all creatures and abhorrest nothing that Thou hast made" — here the creation is obviously taken more seriously than the Fall — " . . . Thou sparest all things because they are Thine, O Lord, Who willest good to the living. For Thine incorruptible Spirit is in all." It is as if the author wished to oppose a doctrine current in Alexandria about the Jewish God of wrath.

Kafka's contribution to the metaphysics of the "door" is known: the parable of the man who squanders his life before a certain open gateway which leads to the world of meaning, and who vainly begs admission until just before his death it is communicated to him that it had been intended for him, but is now being shut. So "the door" is still open; indeed, every person has his own door and it is open to him; but he does not know this and apparently is not in a condition to know it. Kafka's two main works are elaborations of the theme of the parable, the one, *The Trial*, in the dimension of time, the other, *The Castle*, in that of space; accordingly the first is concerned with the hopelessness of man in his dealings with his soul, the second with the same in his dealings with the world. The parable itself is not Pauline but its elaborations are, only as we have said with salvation removed. The one is concerned with the judgment under which the soul stands and under which it places itself willingly; but the guilt, on account of which it has to be judged, is unformulated, the proceedings are labyrinthian and the courts of judicature themselves questionable — without all this seeming to prejudice the legality of the administration of justice. The other book, which especially concerns us here, describes a district delivered over to the authority of a slovenly bureaucracy without the possibility of appeal, and it describes this district as being our world. What is at the top of the government, or rather above it, remains hidden in a darkness, of the nature of which one never once gets a presentiment; the administrative hierarchy, who exercises power, received it from above, but apparently without any commission or instruction. A broad meaninglessness governs without restraint, every notice, every transaction is shot through with meaninglessness, and yet the legality of the government is unquestioned. Man is called into this world, he is appointed in it, but wherever he turns to fulfil his calling he comes up against the thick vapours of a mist of absurdity. This world is handed over to a maze of intermediate beings — it is a Pauline world, except that God is removed into the impenetrable darkness and that there is no place for a mediator. We are reminded of the Haggadic account (Aggadat Bereshit IX) of the sinful David, who prays

God that He Himself may judge him and not give him into the hands of the seraphim and cherubim, for "they are all cruel." Cruel also are the intermediate beings of Kafka, but in addition they are disorderly and stupid. They are extremely powerful bunglers, which drive the human creature through the nonsense of life — and they do it with the full authority of their master. Certain features remind us of the licentious demons into which the archons of Paul's conception of the world have been changed in some Gnostic schools.

The strength of Pauline tendencies in present-day Christian theology is to be explained by the characteristic stamp of the time, just as that of earlier periods can explain that at one time the purely spiritual, the Johannine tendency was emphasized, and at another the so-called Petrine one, in which the somewhat undefined conception "Peter" represents the unforgettable recollection of the conversations of Jesus with the disciples in Galilee. Those periods are Pauline in which the contradictions of human life, especially of man's social life, so mount up that they increasingly assume in man's consciousness of existence the character of a fate. Then the light of God appears to be darkened, and the redeemed Christian soul becomes aware, as the unredeemed soul of the Jew has continually done, of the still unredeemed concreteness of the world of men in all its horror. Then to be sure, as we know indeed from Paul too, the genuine Christian struggles for a juster order of his community, but he understands the impenetrable root of the contradiction in the view of the threatening clouds of wrath, and clings with Pauline tenacity to the abundant grace of the mediator. He indeed opposes the ever-approaching Marcionite danger, the severing not only of the Old and New Testaments, but that of creation and salvation, of Creator and Saviour, for he sees how near men are, as Kierkegaard says of the Gnosis, "to identifying creation with the Fall," and he knows that a victory for Marcion can lead to the destruction of Christianity; but — this seems to me to be more strongly recognized again in Christendom today — Marcion is not to be overcome by Paul.

Even Kierkegaard, a century ago, gave expression to the fact that there is a non-Pauline outlook, that is, one superior to the stamp of the age, when he wrote in his Journal a prayer, in which he says: "Father in heaven, it is indeed only the moment of silence in the inwardness of speaking with one another." That to be sure is said from the point of view of personal existence ("When a man languishes in the desert, not hearing Thy voice there"), but in this respect we are not to distinguish between the situation of the person and that of man or mankind. Kierkegaard's prayer, in spite of his great belief in Christ, is not from Paul or from John, but from Jesus.

A superficial Christian, considering Kafka's problem, can easily get rid of him by treating him simply as the unredeemed Jew who does not reach after salvation. But only he who proceeds thus has now got rid of him; Kafka has remained untouched by this treatment. For the Jew, in so far as he is not detached from the origin, even the most exposed Jew like Kafka, is safe. All things happen to him, but they cannot affect him. He is not to be sure able any longer to conceal himself "in the covert of Thy wings" (Ps. 61:4), for God is hiding Himself from the time in which he lives, and so from him, its most exposed son; but in the fact of God's being only hidden, which he knows, he is safe. "Better the living dove on the roof than the half-dead, convulsively resisting sparrow in the hand." He describes, from innermost awareness, the actual course of the world, he describes most exactly the rule of the foul devilry which fills the foreground; and on the edge of the description he scratches the sentence: "Test yourself on humanity. It makes the doubter doubt, the man of belief believe." His unexpressed, ever-present theme is the remoteness of the judge, the remoteness of the lord of the castle, the hiddenness, the eclipse, the darkness; and therefore he observes: "He who believes can experience no miracle. During the day one does not see any stars." This is the nature of the Jew's security in the dark, one which is essentially different from that of the Christian. It allows no rest, for as long as you live, you must live with the sparrow and not with the dove, who avoids your hand; but, being without illusion, it is consistent with the foreground course of the world, and so nothing can harm you. For from beyond, from the darkness of heaven the dark ray comes actively into the heart, without any appearance of immediacy. "We were created to live in Paradise, Paradise was appointed to serve us. Our destiny has been changed; that this also happened with the appointment of Paradise is not said." So gently and shyly anti-Paulinism speaks from the heart of this Pauline painter of the foreground-hell: Paradise is still there and it benefits us. It is there, and that means it is also here where the dark ray meets the tormented heart. Are the unredeemed in need of salvation? They suffer from the unredeemed state of the world. "Every misery around us we too must suffer" — there it is again, the word from the shoot of Israel. The unredeemed soul refuses to give up the evidence of the unredeemed world from which it suffers, to exchange it for the soul's own salvation. It is able to refuse, for it is safe.

This is the appearance of Paulinism without Christ which at this time when God is most hidden has penetrated into Judaism, a Paulinism therefore opposed to Paul. The course of the world is depicted in more gloomy colours than ever before, and yet Emunah is proclaimed anew, with a still deepened "in spite of all this," quite soft and shy, but unambiguous, Here, in the midst of the Pauline domain, it has taken the place of Pistis. In all its reserve, the late-born, wandering around in the darkened world, confesses in face of the suffering peoples of the world with those messengers of Deutero-Isaiah (Isa. 45:15): "Truly Thou art a God Who hides Himself, O God of Israel, Saviour!" So must Emunah change in a time of God's eclipse in order to persevere steadfast to God, without disowning reality. That He hides Himself does not diminish the immediacy; in the immediacy He remains the Saviour and the contradiction of existence becomes for us a theophany.

XVII

The crisis of our time is also the crisis of the two types of faith, Emunah and Pistis.

They are as fundamentally different in nature as in their origin, and accordingly their crisis is different.

The origin of the Jewish Emunah is in the history of a nation, that of Christian Pistis in that of individuals.

Emunah originated in the actual experiences of Israel, which were to it experiences of faith. Small, then great numbers of people, first in search of open pasture-land, then of land for a free settlement, make their journey as being led by God. This fact, that Israel experienced its way to Canaan, which was its way into history, already in the days of the "Fathers" as guidance, sensually as guidance through wilderness and dangers — this fact which took place historically once only is the birth of Emunah. Emunah is the state of "persevering" — also to be called trust in the existential sense — of man in an invisible guidance which yet gives itself to be seen, in a hidden but self-revealing guidance; but the personal Emunah of every individual remains embodied in that of the nation and draws its strength from the living memory of generations in the great leadings of early times. In the historical process of becoming individual the form of this embodiment changes, but not its essence. Even when a hasidic rabbi sees the *Shekhinah,* the "indwelling" of God, approach him at a crossing of the road, something of the former guidance is present. In our day for the first time the connection is increasingly becoming loose. In the generations of the period of emancipation the People of Faith is being broken up increasingly into a religious community and a nation which are no longer organically bound together, but only structurally. In the secular nation Emunah has no longer a psychical foundation nor in the isolated religion a vital one. Therefore the danger which threatens personal faith is to become impoverished in its essential spontaneity in the time of eclipse and in its place to be succeeded by elements of Pistis, in part of a logical and in part of a mystical character. But the crisis of the People of Faith extends further. For the purpose of the guidance, which was expressed at the beginning of the revelation, was actually (Exod. 19:6) that Israel might become "a royal sphere of direct attendants (this is the original meaning of the word *kohanim*, usually: priests, preserved in this and a few other places) and a holy nation" (that is, consecrated to God as its Lord). When the breaking-up is completed this purpose is repudiated. Then only a great renewal of national faith would be able to provide the remedy. In this the ever-existent inner dialectic of Israel between those giving up themselves to guidance and those "letting themselves go" must come to a decision in the souls themselves, so that the task of becoming a holy nation may set itself in a new situation and a new form suitable to it. The individuals, regenerated in the crisis, who maintain themselves in Emunah, would have fulfilled the function, when it comes about, of sustaining the living substance of faith through the darkness.

Christian Pistis was born outside the historical experiences of nations, so to say in retirement from history, in the souls of individuals, to whom the challenge came to believe that a man crucified in Jerusalem was their saviour. Although this faith, in its very essence, was able to raise itself to a piety of utter devotedness and to a mysticism of union with him in whom they believed, and although it did so, yet it rests upon a foundation which, in spite of its "irrationality," must be described as logical or noetic: the accepting and recognizing as true of a proposition pronounced about the object of faith. All the fervour or ecstasy of feeling, all the devotion of life, grew out of the acceptance of the claim and of the confession made both in the soul and to the world: "I believe that it is so." This position, in its origins arising from a Greek attitude, a thorough acknowledgement of a fact which is beyond the current circle of conceptions, yet an acknowledgement accomplished in a noetic form, came into being (in distinction from the major part of the later history of conversion) as the action of the person who was sharply separated thereby from the community of his nation, and the demand was directed just to such an attitude. To be sure Jesus also addresses himself to the individual, or, when he speaks to a number of people, to the individuals amongst them; but one has only to listen how (Matt.15:24) he speaks about the "lost sheep[4] of the house of Israel"; he sees even them still in the frame of the "house." The like is not heard after him. Paul often speaks about Jews and Greeks, but never in connection with the reality

---

[4] The expression (see Jer. 50:6; Ezek. 34:4, 16; Ps. 119:176) is to be understood of animals which have strayed from the herd.

of their nationalities: he is only concerned with the newly-e tablished community, which by its nature is not a nation. The concep n of the "holy nation" in its strict sense has faded altogether, it does no nter into the consciousness of Christendom, and soon that of the Churcͱ takes its place. The consequence of all this is that even in the mass-baptisms of the West — occurrences which were far removed, both phenomenologically and psychologically, from the individual act of Hellenistic Pistis — the individuals as individuals, not the nations, became Christian, that is, subject to Christ: the "People of God" was Christendom, which in its nature differed from the nations, and these remain in their own nature and their own law as they were. Therefore those who believed in Christ possessed at every period a twofold being: as individuals in the realm of the person and as participants in the public life of their nations. This state of existence remained, preserved from the crisis so long as the sphere of the person was able to assert itself against the determining power of public affairs. The crisis grows according to the degree in which the sphere of the person has been penetrated, in our era, by this. The blessing of Christian salvation, the true consistency of the redeemed soul, is imperilled. A hundred years ago Kierkegaard recognized this severely and clearly, but without estimating adequately the causes or showing the seat of the malady. It is a question of the disparity between the sanctification of the individual and the accepted unholiness of his community as such, and the disparity is necessarily transferred to the inner dialectic of the human soul. The problem which rises here points to the task inherited by Israel — and to its problematic nature.

But in connection with this we are allowed to anticipate in our thought that here also there is a way which leads from rigid Paulinism to another form of Pistis nearer to Emunah. The faith of Judaism and the faith of Christendom are by nature different in kind, each in conformity with its human basis, and they will indeed remain different, until mankind is gathered in from the exiles of the "religions" into the Kingship of God. But an Israel striving after the renewal of its faith through the rebirth of the person and a Christianity striving for the renewal of its faith through the rebirth of nations would have something as yet unsaid to say to each other and a help to give to one another — hardly to be conceived at the present time.

4

On Concluding the
Translation of the Bible

1964

...But now I hear it said that the undertaking of this rendition into German had meanwhile become "utopian," because (I express this in my own words) after the antihistorical self-abasement of the German people, an authentic and hence an authentically receptive life of the German language no longer exists.

In matters of the spirit, all prognoses have to consider the question mark attached to their end. But a different kind of answer can be found with Rosenzweig.

He did not, indeed, reckon with the possibility of the dimensions which the Hitler business assumed, but he clearly recognized the vulgarization of the spiritual process, which was to find an albeit rather problematic expression in the activities of the "German Christians" and the continuing "German Faith Movement." At stake here is the repudiation of the Creator God, always open to his Creation, who is perceived as merely a God of strict justice and not of love. This, in turn, leads to the repudiation of the "Old Testament" — a tendency that originated in the Christian Gnostic Marcion [c. 85–c. 159] and which can, therefore, in its modern manifestations, be called Neo-Marcionism. Rosenzweig writes to me even while working on the Genesis volume (July 29, 1925): "Are you aware that the condition theoretically desired by the new Marcionists has in fact already arrived? The Christian thinks of only the New

Testament when he thinks of the Bible, perhaps including the Psalms which he then mostly assumes to be part of the New Testament. So we shall missionize." And half a year later his idea has achieved unsurpassable precision. He writes (to his friend Eugen Meyer, December 30, 1925): "Sometimes I am afraid the Germans won't stomach this all too unchristian Bible, and it will become the translation of the expulsion of the Bible from German civilization, so greatly desired by new Marcionites, just as Luther's was the Bible of Germany's conquest. But even such a *golus bovel* [Babylonian exile] might, seventy years later, be followed by a new entry, and at any rate — the end is not our concern, only the beginning, and making a beginning."

It does not look to me as if the Scriptures would have to wait seventy years. But "missionize" — yes, in any event! I am usually a radical opponent of all missionizing and I thoroughly contradicted Rosenzweig when he pleaded for a Jewish mission. But this kind of mission I agree to, where not Judaism or Christianity are the issue, but the shared primal truth, on the revitalizing of which depends the future of both. Scripture does the missionizing. And already there are signs that it is destined to prevail.*

---

*These remarks were made by Martin Buber at a festive gathering at his home in Jerusalem in February, 1961, to celebrate the conclusion of his translation of the Bible into German, which he had begun (with Rosenzweig) in 1925. —F. A. R.

Franz Rosenzweig (1886 –1929)

Courtesy of the Leo Baeck Institute, New York

Introduction

by Bernhard Casper

I

Franz Rosenzweig was presumably the first German Jew who foresaw the catastrophic end to the Jewish-German symbiosis with complete clarity and as a concrete possibility of German history. For on the very day when the American President Wilson announced the armistice conditions which concluded the First World War, we read in a letter to Magrit Rosenstock: "Pogrom — and what can a revolution in Germany ultimately lead to, if not to the persecution of Jews."[*][1]

Franz Rosenzweig was in Freiburg when he wrote this letter. Born on Christmas Day, 1886, in Kassel as the only son of a well-to-do family of manufacturers, he was highly talented and embarked on the study of Medicine, and later History and Philosophy. Upon completing his dissertation "Hegel and the State," which even today is still regarded as a fundamental work, he served during all four years of the war, first with the Red Cross and then with the army at the front. When he was demobilized from the German army, he returned to Freiburg where he had studied, in order to write, at long last, his great work *The Star of Redemption* (1921), which he had started to sketch in the trenches of Macedonia. In it he not only articulated in a rigorously structured form and an exacting style his approach to Judaism on which he had gained clarity since the end of 1913, but also responded to the major philosophical trends of his time.

---

[*]Franz Rosenzweig's writings are cited from *Franz Rosenzweig: Der Mensch und sein Werk: Gesammelte Schriften* (The Hague and Dordrecht, Netherlands, 1976–1984). Abbreviated as *GS*.
[1]Unpublished letter November 11, 1918. For permission to publish an extract from this letter and other unpublished letters I thank Rafael Rosenzweig, Tel Aviv.

159

Rosenzweig had first considered becoming a Christian. His two baptized cousins, Rudolf and Hans Ehrenberg, the former a biologist, the latter a philosopher and Protestant theologian, played as significant a role in this, with their understanding of Christianity, as did the urging of Eugen Rosenstock, who, during a conversation lasting through the night of July 7, 1913, sought to convince Rosenzweig, once and for all, of the truth of Christianity: universal and therefore compelling for all people. But Franz Rosenzweig insisted at the time that according to his understanding of Christianity he himself could become a Christian only as a Jew, not as a pagan.[2] And this led him back into the depths of his own Jewish sources and to the insight that he "already was with the Father," so that the sentence from the Gospel of John (14:6), "no one comes to the Father but by the Son," did not apply to him.[3] And thus he felt obliged to bear witness to Judaism in his own life and in his thinking.

A traditionally trained Christian theologian at that time would presumably have described this position as unacceptable. Because of Vatican II and its clear statement, based on Romans 11, "Nevertheless, according to the testimony of the apostle, the Jews still remain most dear to God because of their fathers; for He does not repent of the gifts He makes nor of the calls He issues,"[4] this position is accepted today even by Christianity itself. Therefore Rosenzweig's *Star of Redemption*, unique in the twentieth century, assumes a significance that is all the greater. For in it he formulates his own Jewish existence in such a way that not only his Christian relatives and friends gain an insight into something Other which stands justified, but also so that through it their understanding of their own Christian way is enhanced.

II

The selection of texts in this volume starts with passages from letters written between 1913 and 1917. Here, the irrevocable distinction between what is Jewish and what is Christian is formulated with the intimacy, acuity and clarity possible in a letter. They are followed by important passages from Rosenzweig's main work, and conclude with two pieces authored shortly before his death in 1929, at a time when Rosenzweig had been paralyzed and bereft of speech for seven years and constructed

---

[2] See below, p. 169; *GS* 1:134.

[3] See below, p. 170; *GS* 1:135.

[4] "Nostra Aetate," *The Documents of Vatican II*, with notes and comments by Catholic, Protestant, and Orthodox Authorities, ed. Walter M. Abbott, S.J. (New York: Guild Press 1966), 664.

words with the help of his wife by pointing to individual letters on a board.

I, as a Christian, will try to stress what is decisive for me in these texts, and will not evade questions that they raise for me.

What impresses me particularly in the famous letter of October 31, 1913, to Rudolf Ehrenberg is the brief assertion: "Church and Synagogue are dependent upon one another." Now it is true on the Christian side — after the condemnation of Marcion (at least in principle) — that no one denies the dependence of the New Testament on the "Old." But cannot the question of the significance of the two testaments for one another be a matter of indifference to Judaism? Of what interest is the New Testament to Judaism?

However Rosenzweig speaks here precisely from the Jewish side about a completely serious affirmation of *mutual* interdependence. And he justifies this with an "identical final hope" that places Jews and Christians into suffering in an equal degree.[5]

Here, it seems to me, one is presented with the whole context in which Rosenzweig thinks. This context is that of *world history*, which was not only, from the beginning, the academic topic of the historian Rosenzweig, but also the existential theme of the man and Jew Rosenzweig who took part for four years in that war that deserves the name First *World War*. Only peripheral mention needs to be made of the facts that Rosenzweig had scientific training through his study of medicine. Through his relative, the physicist Nobel Prize winner Max Born, and through short, everyday meetings with Einstein (1919–1920), Rosenzweig had dipped into those aspects of world history that makes this word so important for us today.

Jews and Christians find themselves together and dependent upon one another in their responsibility for world history — a responsibility that inflicts *suffering* upon them. Such suffering arises for the Jews out of their "negation of the world," for the Christians, by contrast, out of their "affirmation of the world." This formula for the differentiation, which is kept from 1913 into *The Star of Redemption*, requires elucidation because, taken in the abstract and purely as contrast, it can be misunderstood and misleading. Understood abstractly, it would hardly meet with the approval of a Jew today. Moreover, it is at variance with Rosenzweig's own magnificent sentence from *The New Thinking*: "For God has not created religion, but the world."[6] So Judaism cannot be a world-denying religion.

---

[5]See below, p. 170; *GS* 1:135.
[6]*GS* 3:153.

What, then, is the meaning of the sentence that suffering for the sake of redemption arises for the Jew out of negation of the world, but for the Christian out of affirmation of the world? In order to understand it, it may first be necessary to point out Rosenzweig's incredible ability to think in pairs of opposites, polar tensions, and differentiations, the corresponding members of which cannot be reduced to one another and yet require each other. The core sentence in *The New Thinking*, which Rosenzweig admittedly cannot formulate with such clarity until 1925, namely that the decisive element of this thinking lies in "the need of the Other one and, what is the same thing, in taking time seriously,"[7] emerges from the start as the soul of that apprehension of reality which occurs in Rosenzweig's thinking. And this soul which determines Rosenzweig's style and conceptualizations, cannot be explained satisfactorily through his intensive study of Hegel — which, to be sure, taught him constantly to think in terms of dialectical opposites, in thesis and antithesis. Rather, it emerges in all of Rosenzweig's thinking as a constant act of revering God. For precisely: the person who takes experience seriously in its temporality *cannot*, of himself, create the synthesis so obvious for Hegel. We are creatures "because of the fact that we cannot see the whole truth."[8]

It seems to me that for Rosenzweig's manner of thinking, the first chapter of Genesis with its fundamental teaching about the "separations" has therefore played an important role from the beginning.[9] Creation was wrought in pairs of opposites, in which one component cannot be reduced to the other: night and day, sea and dry land, woman and man. Consequently, to a mode of thinking which foremost deserves to be called "Absolute Empiricism,"[10] truth never appears simply as *one* — which humankind would have found and exhausted. Instead, truth is one only with God. For mortals set in history, truth is reached only "in the need of the Other."

This grand fundamental principle of his thought which, in his own understanding, leads him beyond the total tradition of Western philosophy from Parmenides to Hegel, he applies with apparent obviousness also to the answer that human beings give to the word that awakens and chooses them through revelation, the word of the ONE. Humankind's answer to the *Shema[c] Yisrael:* Hear, Israel! HE, ONE... thus you shall love HIM... and your fellow man[11] can occur Jewishly and in a Christian way. According to Rosenzweig's understanding, speaking about the

---

[7]*GS* 3:151–152.
[8]Cf. below, p. 225; *GS* 2:463.
[9]Cf. now *GS* 3:661 and also *GS* 3:611.
[10]*GS* 3:161. [The term "absoluter Empirismus" was adopted from Schelling —F. A. R.]
[11]Deuteronomy 6:5 combined with Leviticus 19:18.

"two ultimate commitments to truth"[12] in the face of "messianic expectations irreconcilable in time" does not mean relativism or betrayal of Judaism, that is to say: he grants that Christianity is an ultimate commitment to the same truth that is also Judaism's concern. It is rather an expression of the fear of God, a recognition that only before the ONE is truth ONE.[13]

It seems to me that, with this, an insight has been given, also acceptable to Christians, which places the relationship between Jews and Christians on a new footing. Neither absolutism in the claim of the Torah nor absolutism in the claim put forth in Jesus Christ is being doubted through this insight. But a rivalry has been set in motion through the voice of the ONE, heard by Jews and Christians. The rivalry is set in motion by that which concerns both Jews and Christians: redemption. The question who, in this rivalry about the event of redemption, is more with the Father, is wrongly put from the start, for it cannot be decided by human beings. "The proof lies with God himself, only before Him is truth ONE."[14]

Of course, on the basis of this insight and at the same time as a committed Jew — for his own existence can no longer be bracketed out — Rosenzweig must now address the "younger brother" and thus deal with his otherness. And here the profound knowledge of Christianity and Christian theology that Rosenzweig demonstrates again and again should be noted. In the trenches of World War I he read, of all things, the Church Fathers. The seriousness and the refreshing keenness in the correspondence with Eugen Rosenstock are unthinkable without Rosenzweig's intimate knowledge of the essence of what is Christian. And a Christian theologian could hardly give a brief introduction to the essence of the church better than does Rosenzweig on pp. 343ff. of *The Star of Redemption* (English translation). Indeed, the understanding of the accompanying Other makes apparent aspects of Christianity which, in this form, would not as a matter of course be realized by Christian self-awareness.

On the other hand it is only fair to say that Rosenzweig's understanding of what is Christian also mirrors aspects of Christian theology, contemporary with him, that have since then been recognized as onesided and have become outdated. So, for instance, Rosenzweig deals with a Christology that rather tended to overemphasize the divinity of Jesus and to forget his humanity. Rosenzweig himself knew about both sides

[12]*GS* 3:159. Eng. transl. in N. Glatzer, ed., *Franz Rosenzweig: His Life and Thought*, 206f.
[13]Cf. *GS* 3:159.
[14]*GS* 3:159.

of the Christian dogma. But he reacts against an *ecclesia triumphans* that no longer allows for a historical difference between Jesus, the son of man, and the returning Messiah.[15] Altogether Rosenzweig visualizes a static Christian theology that thought in unhistorical terms. On the Protestant side, it still relied on the thinking methods of Kant[16] incidentally leading to Pelagianism, or it relied on German Idealism, which considered history as complete. Catholic theologians used the means of rationalist neo-scholasticism. I consider it possible that Rosenzweig's critique, to which some individual Christian theologians were alerted early, contributed to that rethinking which, taking seriously that redemption is still to come, newly introduced into Christian theology the radical commitment of oneself into the petition of the Lord's Prayer, "Thy kingdom come." Christian theology in the second half of the twentieth century is generally no longer a triumphalistic theology. Moreover, it is understood that the Crucified One has not overcome the world in a way signifying "completion already presumed."[17]

But what, then, is the meaning of Jesus' saying: "In the world you have tribulation; but be of good cheer, I have overcome the world" (John 16:33)? Today's Christians are newly confronted with the task of replying to the Jew Franz Rosenzweig — at least with their own lives. In my view, a whole series of questions that Rosenzweig raises, especially in his correspondence with Eugen Rosenstock, should be taken up anew today for consideration among Jews and Christians. The aim is not to incorporate the other one, but, while maintaining the otherness of the other one, and even clearing some misunderstandings out of the way, to provide the opportunity of learning from the other's lived reply to revelation and promise. Among these items is, e.g., Rosenzweig's rejection of the doctrine of Original Sin.[18] But how is this possible if one puts this rejection by Rosenzweig next to his often expressed teaching about the unredeemed nature of the world?[19] The *Star* explains how this will cast humankind into an unsolvable *aporia*.[20] Perhaps the Christian doctrine about the corruption of the world could be considered anew in the light of Rosenzweig's view. And possibly a sotereological doctrine about the one who called himself the *way* (John 14:6) might no longer so offend Jews that it would be said: "We would crucify him again,"[21] even

---

[15]Cf. below, p. 182; *GS* 1:285.
[16]Cf. below, p. 185; *GS* 1:402.
[17]Cf. below, p. 186; *GS* 1:402.
[18]Cf. below, p. 173; *GS* 1:142.
[19]Cf. below, p. 182; *GS* 1:402.
[20]*GS* 2:254–255.
[21]Cf. below, p. 177; *GS* 1:252.

though they could not, in the last analysis, identify themselves with the doctrine. I believe I see that the axis of Rosenzweig's thinking assumed the shape of the ᶜEved YHWH — literally up to Rosenzweig's last hours of life.[22] And here, I think, the conversation between Jews and Christians ought to begin, even while it is granted that the participants will maintain their different ways.

But what is important about Rosenzweig's distinction between absence of the world in Judaism and presence of the world in Christianity, which we have shown forth in our texts? And about the sufferings that arise therefrom in the light of the promise of redemption? And while on the subject of this central question, I want to touch upon the issue once more that, according to the whole design of Rosenzweig's thinking, neither of the constituent parts of this duality should be thought of by itself, but that "they need one another." The duality of "absence of the world/presence of the world" supplies Rosenzweig, first of all, with a heuristic means for interpreting, culture-morphologically, a wealth of phenomena in Jewish and Christian life: the intimacy of Jewish life, the missionary nature of Christianity and its connection with world order and the state as they had manifested themselves most clearly in the medieval and pre-modern church. Rosenzweig remained aware of this connection in, for instance, *Kulturprotestantismus* (Culture Protestantism).

In principle, Rosenzweig here goes back to Tertullian's famous dictum that one is born as a Jew, i.e., God's orienting revelation is experienced through birth, the family, and blood affiliation, but that one could become a Christian solely through conversion. The church is essentially missionary — a sentence expressed in this way also by the Second Vatican Council.[23] The church is sustained by the conversion of the world, i.e., of *all peoples*. In this sense, therefore, it is from the very beginning related to "world" in a quite different way.

Such a description of the Jewish and Christian particularities, respectively, enables Rosenzweig to grasp the relationship between Judaism and Christianity in the image of the fire of the "Star" and the rays of the "Star," and thus to make their need of one another vivid. The heuristic value of this image is incontestable.

However, if one wants to investigate these matters thoroughly one

---

[22]Cf. here *GS* 1:1237: "The last thought the expression of which he attempted . . . was devoted to the meaning of some pieces in this book, the songs about the servant of God" (M. Buber about three lines of a letter that Rosenzweig started on December 9, 1929, in the evening. He died during the night between December 9 and 10, 1929).

[23]*The Documents of Vatican II*, Constitution "Lumen Gentium," chap. 2 (24–37) and "Ad Gentes," chap. 1, art. 2 (585–586).

would, first of all, have to say that Rosenzweig's usage of the word "world" in this context is not simply the same as his usage of the word "world" in the context of the phenomenology of primitive phenomena in *Star*, Part I. At the end of *Star*, Part II, 2, Rosenzweig rails against false mysticism, which loftily ignores the world and seeks to accommodate itself without world in the revelation of God. These attacks show clearly that Rosenzweig posits presence of world also for Judaism in a most fundamental sense. And Rosenzweig's dispute with the early Buber shows this, too.[24] Orientation towards the world in the sense of turning towards creation on the part of human beings touched by revelation cannot be questioned for the Jew. The whole concept of the Free Jewish Lehrhaus, which Rosenzweig founded in Frankfurt in 1922, cannot be grasped without this orientation towards world as creation. And although Rosenzweig had reservations vis-à-vis the Zionism of his time, he would presumably not have objected in principle to the bond with the world that Judaism entered into with the establishment of the State of Israel.

However, in Part III of the *Star*, "world," in the context of explications of what is Christian, means rather the world in the sense of the fullness of the Gentiles. Furthermore, their conversion indeed introduces the worldly, in the sense of fullness of creation, in a special way, into the discussion of orientation through revelation.

What, then, remains of the duality of "absence of world/presence of world," which in Rosenzweig's *oeuvre* appears to be the formula for the duality of "Judaism/Christianity"? The sentences in the letter of October 31, 1913, to Rudolf Ehrenberg should be read carefully. It does not there speak simply of absence of world and presence of world, but rather of the sufferings of denial of the world and the sufferings of the affirmation of the world. Judaism testifies to its bond to the ONE and to the redemption promised by him through the sufferings of separation, meaning election. And this separation does not in any way mean enmity towards creation. But it does bring with it the apartness of the witness. If Emmanuel Lévinas states today that the responsibility for all people constitutes the essentially human, and that the election for such a responsibility constitutes the proprium of the Jewish destiny,[25] then the suffering of the Jews arises from the knowledge that this universality of redemption, promised by the ONE, constitutes *witnessing separatively* here and now.

---

[24]See my essay "Franz Rosenzweig's Criticism of Buber's 'I and Thou.'" *Martin Buber: A Centenary Volume*, Haim Gordon and Jochanan Bloch, eds. (Bersheva: Ben-Gurion University of the Negev, 1984) 139–156.

[25]Cf., e.g., Emmanuel Lévinas, *Éthique et infini* (Paris, 1982), 106–108.

But have Christians not been called to witness separatively also? They have without doubt received the same call as Jews. And as a Christian, I have learned much here from Rosenzweig and from my Jewish friends. I find the message of the cross easier to express by looking at Jewish separateness.[26] Furthermore, one needs only to read the Gospels carefully, in particular the Gospel of John, to recognize — as a necessary trait of Christianity — this relation of "being in the world" and at the same time to be separate from it for the sake of its redemption (a stance that, in Christianity also, does in any case not mean enmity towards creation). But Rosenzweig thinks that the church, as a missionary movement that converts the nations as a whole, should deal differently from the way the synagogue deals with the civilizations of the nations, with their respective historical world order, their "flesh and blood." And he thinks that this will bring suffering with it for the church, suffering for the sake of redemption. Rosenzweig has very well grasped the incarnation element here, as the secret of Christianity: the secret of Christ within the secret of Christianity. This way did not become his, for good reasons. But he acknowledged the otherness of the other, and he formulated it with the methods of his thinking that was exceptionally dynamic, trained along Hegelian lines but was, in the final analysis, not dialectical, but dialogical.

It seems to me that Rosenzweig thus created a situation for dialogue between Jews and Christians such as may perhaps not have existed since the beginnings of Christianity. Moreover, such a situation for dialogue is today, at a time of global crisis for humanity, both a challenge and an opportunity. At stake is creation. And creation can "remain" only if people, in the light of revelation, see it remaining in the movement towards promised redemption. And in this situation, Rosenzweig's grand utterance about the meaning of Jewish and Christian existence is appropriate: "Before God, both Jew and Christian are laborers at the same task."[27]

---

[26]Cf. below, p. 171; *GS* 1:136.
[27]Cf. below, p. 224; *GS* 2:462.

Church and Synagogue, Strasbourg Cathedral. Bildarchiv Foto Marburg

1

Selections from the Letters

To Rudolf Ehrenberg

[Berlin] October 31, 1913

I considered the year 313 to be the beginning of the decline from true Christianity[1] because that was when Christianity set out on a path through the world which led in an opposite direction from that on which Judaism set out in the year 70. I faulted the church for its scepter, because I saw that the synagogue's staff was broken. You witnessed how I began, based on this insight, to construct my world anew. In this world — and I did not acknowledge (and do not now acknowledge) any realm beyond this immanent one which is unrelated to it — in this world, then, there appeared to be no place for Judaism. I drew the consequences from that, and, in so doing, imposed a condition on myself, a condition whose importance to me you know well. I declared that I could only become a Christian as a *Jew*, not by way of the intermediate status of paganism. I considered this condition entirely personal; you approved of it. In your view it was reminiscent of early Christianity. You were not mistaken. For this is, in

---

[1]Rosenzweig refers to the view expounded by the classical philologist Eduard Schwartz (1858–1940) and shared by most liberal Protestants, that Constantine's victory at the Ponte Molle in 313, which led to Christianity becoming the religion of the Roman Empire, changed it from the faith of the lowly and oppressed to that of the Establishment and thus destroyed its pristine purity. This was seen as the beginning of its decline and corruption. Cf. Rosenzweig's reference to Schwartz in *Gesammelte Schriften*, 1/1:293, n. 1, and Schwartz's book, *Kaiser Constantin und die christliche Kirche* (Leipzig and Berlin: G. G. Teubner, 1913), especially 148f. and 169–171. —F. A. R.

169

fact, the position that was taken by the mission to the Jews. A position which I considered to be a personal matter. It holds that the Jew who observes the laws should continue to lead an observant life, during his catechumenate and up to the moment of baptism. Nonetheless, it was at this point where our ways parted again. . . .

November 1, 1913

Christianity recognizes the God of Judaism, not as God, but as the "Father of Jesus Christ." It embraces the "Lord," but only because it knows that he alone is the way to the Father. He will remain with his church as the Lord forever, until the end of the world. Then, however, he will cease to be the Lord and he too will come under the domain of the Father, and the Father will be "all in all" (1 Cor. 15:28). What Christ and his church mean in the world — on that we agree: no one comes to the Father save through him (John 14:6).

No one *comes* to the Father — but it is different when one no longer needs to come to the Father, because he *is* already with him. And this is the case with the people of Israel (not with the individual Jew). The people of Israel, chosen by its Father, fixes its glance on that ultimate, most distant point, beyond world and history, of where its Father, the Father himself, will be the One and the Only — will be "All in All!" At that point, when Christ will cease to be the Lord, Israel will cease to be chosen; on that day God will lose the name by which only Israel calls on him; God will then no longer be "their" God. Until that day, however, Israel will live to anticipate it in belief and deed, to stand tall as a living harbinger of that day, a nation of priests, following the law which requires that one make the name of God holy by being holy oneself. We are in agreement, however, on the status of this people of God in the world, and on the suffering which it has borne on account of its seclusion, both from without (persecution) and from within (rigidity).

And yet, both the synagogue and the church have borne their sufferings in the same ultimate hope, the synagogue the sufferings of world-negation, and the church the sufferings of world-affirmation. This hope is not merely a hope for some unconscious and coincidental rendezvous in *eternity* (as would be the case, for instance, between the believer and the "universal-humanistic" pacifist). For both of them this hope — the God of all *time* — is rooted in a common origin. This common origin is the revelation of the Old Testament. For all these reasons, synagogue and church are mutually dependent on one another.

The synagogue, immortal, but with broken staff and a blindfold over her eyes, has to renounce all work in the world and concentrate all its energy on sustaining its own life, while maintaining its purity in the face

of life. Thus, it relegates work in the world to the church and acknowledges that the church brings salvation for all heathens, for all time. It
knows that what is accomplished within Judaism by works of ritual is
accomplished for the world outside of Israel by works of love. But it refuses to concede to the church that the power which enables the church
to do works of love is more than divine in *quality*, to concede that it is
itself a power of God. Here its glance is fixed on that future yet to *come*.

And the church, with its unbreakable staff, and its eyes open to the
world, a warrior confident of victory, always runs the risk that the van-
quished might impose its own law on the victor. Although the church
reaches out to all, it still must not lose itself in universality. For all time
its teaching is to remain a folly and a stumbling block (1 Cor. 1:23). That
it remain a folly is assured by the Greeks, then and now and in the future. Again and again they will be asking: why is *this* supposed to be a
divine power and not just as well some other teaching or yet another —
why Jesus and not (or not also) Goethe. And the voice of the Greeks will
resound until the last day, only it will grow ever softer, softer with every
external or internal victory by the church. For when wisdom is aware
that it is wise, it is dumbstruck whenever confronted with the obvious;
and when the last Greek has been dumbstruck by the workings of the
church in time, the word of the cross[2] at the *end* of time, but still *in* time —
will no longer be a folly to anyone. Yet it will remain, all the same, as a
stumbling block, even then. It was not a stumbling block for any Greek
to acknowledge a divine power in the world: after all, he saw the world
full of gods; what was incomprehensible to him was that he was to worship only this one savior on the cross; so it is today and so it will be in the
future. The synagogue, however, was blind-folded; it saw no world at
all — how was it to see gods in it? It saw only out of its inner prophetic
eye, and saw, therefore, only that which is last and most distant. The
demand that the synagogue view that which is closest, something in the
present, in the same way that it viewed the most distant thus became a
stumbling block; that is how it is now and so it shall be in the future.
For this reason, whenever the church forgets that it is a stumbling block,
when it tries to reconcile itself with what is "universally human" — a
reconciliation which would be welcomed by the Greeks, who would,
like the Roman emperor,[3] erect a statue of the Christ in their temple of
gods — then the church finds in the synagogue a silent admonisher who

---

[2]"For the word of the cross is folly to those who are perishing, but to us who are being
saved it is the power of God" (1 Cor. 1:18; all biblical citations from *The New Oxford
Annotated Bible* [New York: Oxford University Press, 1977]).
[3]Refers to Alexander Severus (222–235). Among the images he kept in his palace chapel
were statues of Apollonius, Abraham, Socrates, and Jesus. —F. A. R.

is not tempted by the "universally human" and knows only of the stumbling block; and then the church feels positive about itself once again, and recites its word of the cross. And thus the church knows that Israel will be preserved until the day when the last Greek vanishes, the work of love is finished, and until that later day when the harvest day of hope arrives. However, what the church concedes to Israel as a whole, it refuses to the individual Jew; it is on the individual Jew that it will and ought to test its power and see whether it can win him over. For to the church, to look to the future is not the same as it is to the synagogue. The future is not the power source of its faith, but only an image of the goal of its hopes. The power of its faith requires it to be aware of its own surroundings and to do the work of its love in the *present*.

With that I have said the essentials, at least with regard to dialogue and confrontation with Christianity....

As I said before, I have been trying of late to clarify for myself the whole system of Jewish doctrine, developing it on its own Jewish foundation. I am no longer the heretic of your eighteenth sermon,[4] who takes from faith and not from love; I now deal with other names and teach other doctrines. And nevertheless, I know that I am a thing of the past only before the will of your *Lord*, but have not been forgotten by *God* — by that God to whom someday even your Lord will be subject. That is the connection between community and non-community (community which is necessary, because it is nourished by the same root, a community based on the eternal goal, involving mutual interdependence and, therefore, differentiation for all time) — which I present to you, so that you might see and recognize it objectively. What is at issue is not that the Church recognize that each individual Jew belongs to the people of Israel, (for the church, this status of belonging has always been a problem, and, when in doubt, considered to be non-existent); what is at issue is that it recognize the people of Israel itself, from the standpoint of Christian *theology*.

To Rudolf Ehrenberg

Berlin, November 4, 1913

... *Our* recognition of Christianity actually is based on Christianity itself, that is, on its recognition of *us*. It is, after all, the *Torah* which the Bible

---

[4]In Ehrenberg's collection of sermons: *Ebr. 10:25, Ein Schicksal in Predigten* (Würzburg: Patmos Verlag, 1920).

Societies distribute even to the remotest "isles." Any Jew will grant me that. However, Jewish consciousness is not *grounded* in the relationship of the Christian church to the world; it only recognizes its own reflection in it. In and of itself, Jewish consciousness takes no note of it: Isaiah 55:5.[1] For this reason, it has no need, in time, of a new mandate; its mission did not change as a result of the events of the first century, only its destiny. Since then conditions have changed, and, I believe, they have taken on their final temporal form; but only the conditions changed. The *Mishnah*, the work through which Judaism laid a new foundation after the destruction of the Temple, claims to be *only* a "repetition" of the *Torah* (that is the meaning of "mishnah"). The purpose of the entire Talmud is to demonstrate that this is, in fact, the case. From a purely theoretical standpoint, in the letter[2] I showed you what the significance of the existence of Israel is for the church; that is also the standpoint of the church, only with a certain practical emphasis. The synagogue can only see itself; it has no consciousness of the *world*. Thus, to the church it can only say: we have already arrived at the destination, you are still enroute. The church answers: certainly, at the destination — you are the last ones, because you are the most stubborn, *absolutely* stubborn. It does not see that there is a purpose in the existence of this point of stubbornness which gets in its way (to the church, the "purpose" is a *mystērion* [mystery]); it only knows *that* it is so. And yet, from the church's standpoint, then, the position of Judaism is not a position *within* the church; on the contrary, it is absolutely outside it, a position which in the course of time will never be overcome. That is the reason why the church interprets what seems "stubbornness" as rejection, by God. From our standpoint, things look quite different. To us, our "stubbornness" is fidelity, and our "infidelity towards God" is remedied — just because it is infidelity, and not an original, primeval estrangement ("Adam's" fall into sin!) — only by repentance and return, not by a transformation or conversion. The concept of repentance, the Hebrew word for which, *teshuvah*, means "return," was rendered as *metanoia* [change of mind] in the New Testament. This is one of those cases where world history is chronicled in the pages of a dictionary. About all this, too, on Friday. We interpret the "wrath" of God in an entirely different way. For us, it did not begin with the Exile. Divine wrath has been with us since the election of Israel, and followed as a result of it (Amos 3:2).[3] We see

---

[1] "Behold you shall call nations that know you not, and nations that knew you not shall run to you, because of the Lord your God, the Holy One of Israel, for he has glorified you."

[2] The previous letter.

[3] "You only have I known of all the families of the earth; therefore I will punish you for all your iniquities."

perfect piety realized not in the history of our people, but in the age of the patriarchs; that is the age to which we "appeal" before God. To be sure, the year 70 marks a line of demarcation, but a line like one which separates the time of church history from the end-time.[4] Since then, after each particular instance of infidelity, we have no longer been compelled to hope, to hope for particular reconciliation. Now we hope only for the great reconciliation on the very last day. Before the year 70, certain prophets appeared at certain times, since then we have expected no more prophets, but only the one prophet on that last day.

To Eugen Rosenstock

[October 1916]

. . . Yes, the stubbornness of the Jews is a Christian dogma. So much so that the Church, after she had built up the substantial part of her particular dogma — the part having to do with God and Man — in the first century, during the whole of the second century turned aside to lay down the "second dogma" (the formal part of her dogma, i.e., her historical consciousness of herself). And in its aftereffects this process continued through the third and fourth centuries and beyond; and Augustine applied himself to it personally, though the Church had already for some time been moving away from it. That is, it had been becoming a Church of writings or rather of tradition, instead of spirit; in other words, it was becoming exactly the Church that history knows. Paul's theory concerning the relation of the Gospels to the Law could have remained a "personal opinion"; the Hellenizing "spiritual" Church (of John's Gospel) of the first century, in the marvelous naïveté of her "spiritual believers," had scarcely worried about it. Then came gnosticism, which laid its finger on Paul and sought to weed out the personal element from his theory and to develop its objective aspects in distinction from the personal in it. (Paul said: "The Jews are spurned, but Christ came from them." Marcion said: "Therefore the Jews belong to the devil, Christ to God.") Then the Church, which hitherto had been quite naïve in its own gnosticism (in St. John we read that salvation comes from the Jews), suddenly seeing this, pushed the spirit [pneuma] to one side in favor of tradition, and

---

[4]Rosenzweig believes that the time for partial redemptive acts in history is past, and that Jew and Christian are now awaiting the complete eschatological redemption for all mankind. —F. A. R.

through a great *ritornar al segno* fixed this tradition by returning to its cardinal point, to its founder Paul; that is, she deliberately established as dogma what previously had been considered Paul's personal opinion. The Church established the identity of the Creator (and the God revealed at Sinai) with the Father of Jesus Christ on the one hand, and the perfect manhood of Christ on the other hand, as a definite, correlated Shibboleth against all heresy — and thereby the Church established herself as a power in human history. You know the rest better than I do. (N.B. I have just read all this in Tertullian, of whom I bought a complete edition. . . . I prefer his rhetoric, as that of a real lawyer, to the professorial rhetoric of Augustine, just because it is more genuine — at least according to our modern ideas.)

Thus, in the firm establishment of the Old Testament in the Canon, and in the building of the Church on this double scripture (Old Testament and New Testament) the stubbornness of the Jews is in fact brought out as the other half of the Christian dogma (its formal consciousness of itself — the dogma of the Church — if we may point to the creed as the dogma of Christianity).

But could this same idea (that of the stubbornness of the Jews) also be a Jewish dogma? Yes, it could be, and in fact it is. But this Jewish consciousness of being rejected has quite a different place in our dogmatic system, and would correspond to a Christian consciousness of being chosen to rule, a consciousness that is in fact present beyond any doubt. The whole religious interpretation of the significance of the year 70[1] is tuned to this note. But the parallel that you are looking for is something entirely different. A dogma of Judaism about its relation to the Church must correspond to the dogma of the Church about its relation to Judaism. And this you know only in the form of the modern liberal-Jewish theory of the "daughter religion" that gradually educates the world for Judaism. But this theory actually springs from the classical period in the formation of Jewish dogma — from the Jewish high scholasticism which, in point of time and in content, forms a mean between Arab and Christian scholasticism (al-Ghazali — Maimonides — Thomas Aquinas). For it was only then that we had a fixing of dogma, and that corresponds with the different position that intellectual conceptions of faith hold with us and with you. In the period when you were developing dogma, we were creating our canon law, and vice versa. There is a subtle connection running all through. For instance, when you were systematizing dogma, we were systematizing law; with you the mystical view of dogma followed its definition, while with us the mystical view preceded definition, etc.,

---

[1] That is, the date of the destruction of the Temple.

etc. This relation is rooted throughout in the final distinction between the two faiths. Indeed with us, too, this theory is not part of the substance of our dogma; with us, too, it was not formed from the content of the religious consciousness but belongs only to a second stratum, a stratum of learning concerning dogma. The theory of the daughter religion is found in the clearest form in both of the great scholastics. Beyond this, it is found, not as dogma but as a mystical idea (see above), in the literature of the old Synagogue, and likewise in the Talmudic period. To find it is no easy task, however. For whereas the substantial dogma in our scholasticism was based on trials, the connection between the old mysticism and medieval philosophy is brought about by the free religious spirit of the people, not by a fettered relationship to the past. But I should like to quote you one such legend. The Messiah was born exactly at the moment when the Temple was destroyed, but when he was born, the winds blew him forth from the bosom of his mother. And now he wanders unknown among the peoples, and when he has wandered through them all, then the time of our redemption will have come.

So that Christianity is like a power that fills the world (according to the saying of one of the two scholastics, Yehudah ha-Levi: it is the tree that grows from the seed of Judaism and casts its shadows over the earth; but its fruit must contain the seed again, the seed that nobody who saw the tree noticed). This is a Jewish dogma, just as Judaism as both the stubborn origin and last convert is a Christian dogma.

But what does all that mean for me, apart from the fact that I know it? What does this Jewish dogma mean for the Jew? Granted that it may not belong to the dogmas of the substantial group, which like the corresponding Christian dogmas can be won from an analysis of the religious consciousness. It is rather like the corresponding Christian one, a theological idea. But theological ideas must also mean something for religion. What, then, does it mean?

What does the Christian theological idea of Judaism mean for the Christian? If I am to believe E. R.'s letter before last (or before the one before the last?): Nothing! For there he wrote that nowadays König and he are the only people who still take Judaism seriously. The answer is already on the point of my pen — that it was not here a question of theoretical awareness, but whether there was a continual realization of this theological idea by its being taken seriously in actual practice. This practical way, in which the theological idea of the stubbornness of the Jews works itself out, is *hatred of the Jews*. You know as well as I do that all its realistic arguments are only fashionable cloaks to hide the single true metaphysical ground: that we will not make common cause with the world-conquering fiction of Christian dogma, because (however much a fact) it *is* a fiction (and *"fiat veritas, pereat realitas,*[2] since "Thou God art truth"[3]) and, putting it in a learned way (from Goethe in *Wilhelm Meister*[4]): that we deny the foundation of contemporary culture (and *"fiat regnum Dei, pereat mundus,"*[5] for "ye shall be to me a kingdom of priests and a holy people" [Lev. 19:6]); and putting it in a popular way: that we have crucified Christ and, believe me, would do it again every time, we alone in the whole world (and *"fiat nomen Dei Unius, pereat homo,"*[6] for "to whom will you liken me, that I am like?" [Isa. 40:25]).

And so the corresponding Jewish outcome of the theological idea of Christianity as a preparer-of-the-way is the *pride of the Jews*. This is hard to describe to a stranger. What you see of it appears to you silly and petty, just as it is almost impossible for the Jew to see and judge anti-Semitism by anything but its vulgar and stupid expressions. But (I must say again, *believe me*) its metaphysical basis is, as I have said, the three articles: (1) that we have the truth, (2) that we are at the goal, and (3) that any and every Jew feels in the depths of his soul that the Christian relation to God, and so in a sense their religion, is particularly and extremely pitiful, poverty-stricken, and ceremonious; namely, that as a Christian one has to learn from someone else, whoever he may be, to call God "our Father." To the Jew, that God is our Father is the first and most self-evident fact — and what need is there for a third person between me and my father in Heaven? That is no discovery of modern apologetics but the simplest Jewish instinct, a mixture of failure to understand and pitying contempt.

These are the two points of view, both narrow and limited just as points of view, and so in theory both can be surpassed; one can understand why the Jew can afford his unmediated closeness to God and why the Christian may not; and one can also understand how the Jew must pay for this blessing. I can elaborate this argument in extreme detail. It can be intellectualized through and through, for it springs in the last resort from that great victorious breaking in of the spirit into what is not spirit that one calls "Revelation."

---

[2]Let there be truth, and let reality perish.

[3]From the High Holiday prayers; cf. Jeremiah 10:10.

[4]In *Wilhelm Meisters Wanderjahre* a scheme of education is proposed for a group of emigrants who want to realize their ideal society in America. The teaching of the Christian religion is to be made mandatory in order to hold together society and to solve the problem of accommodating oneself to the inevitable through faith, hope, and love. "To this religion we firmly hold. . . . In this sense . . . we tolerate no Jew among us; for how should we grant him participation in the highest culture, the source and tradition of which he denies" (book 3, chap. 11). —F. A. R.

[5]Let there be the kingdom of God, and let the world pass away.

[6]Let the name of one God exist, and let man pass away.

But now I want to formulate your question in a way that seems profitable to me — but is not such intellectualizing, as an activity of knowing, preparing, acting on the future, like every cultural activity, a Christian affair, not a Jewish affair? Are you still a Jew in that you do it? Is not part of the price that the Synagogue must pay for the blessing in the enjoyment of which she anticipates the whole world, namely, of being already in the Father's presence, that she must wear the bandages of unconsciousness over her eyes? Is it sufficient if you carry the broken staff in your hand, as you do — I am willing to believe it — and yet take the bandages away from your eyes?

Here the polished clarity of antitheses ends; here begins the world of more and less, of compromise, of reality, or, as the Jewish mysticism of the late Middle Ages very finely said for "World of Reality, of Thinghood," "World of Activity, of Matter of Fact" [*'olam ha-'asiyah*] ; and as I should prefer to say, the "World of Action." Action alone can here decide for me, but even if it has decided for me, I still need — indulgence! Not as if thought is here entirely left behind; but it no longer goes as before along a proud, sure king's highway, with vanguard, flanks and countless trains of attendants; it goes lonely along the footpath in pilgrim dress. Something like this:

You recollect the passage in the Gospel of John where Christ explains to his disciples that they should not leave the world, but should remain within it. Even so, the people of Israel — who indeed could use all the sayings of the Gospel — could speak to its members in such a way, and as a matter of fact it does so: "to hallow the name of God in the world," is a phrase that is often used. From this follows all the ambiguity of Jewish life (just as all the dynamic character of the Christian life follows from it). The Jew, insofar as he is "in the world," stands under these laws and no one can tell him that he is permitted to go just so far and no farther, or that there is a line that he may not cross. Such a simple "as little as possible" would be a bad standard, because if I wished to govern all of my actions by the standard "as little as possible from outside Judaism" it would mean, in the circumstances, a diminution of my inner Jewish achievement. So I say to myself as a rule: "as much as possible of the inner Jewish life" — though I well know that in the particular case I cannot anxiously avoid a degree of life outside Judaism. I also know that thereby, in your eyes, I open the way to a charge of soullessness. I can only answer fully at the center and source of my activity; at the periphery it escapes me. But should I then let the citadel fall in order to strengthen these precarious outworks? Should I "be converted," when I have been "chosen" from birth? Is that a real alternative for me? Have

I only been thrown into the galley?[7] Is it not *my* ship? You became acquainted with me on land, but you have scarcely noticed that my ship lies in harbor and that I spend more time than is necessary in sailors' taverns, and therefore you could well ask what business I have on the ship. And for you really to believe that it is my ship, and that I therefore belong to it (*pour faire quoi? y vivre et y mourir*) — for you really to believe me will only be possible if the voyage is once more free and I launch out.

Or only when we meet out on the open sea? You might! . . .

To Eugen Rosenstock

Tuesday–Thursday, November 7–9, 1916

. . . [T]he nineteenth century formed an -ism for *ethnos* for the first time, namely, *nationalism*. But that no longer means what *ethnismos* would have meant in the year 0, namely, the creation of the idea of Paganism, but the complete Christianizing of the conception of a "people." For nationalism expresses not merely the peoples' belief that they come *from* God (that, as you rightly say, the pagans also believe), but that they go *to* God. But now peoples do have this belief, and hence 1789 is followed by 1914–1917, and yet more "from . . . to's"; and the Christianizing of the concept of a "people" is not yet the Christianizing of the people themselves.[1] . . .

That is why even today, when the idea of being elected has become a coloring reagent in every nation, the election of the Jews is something unique, because it is the election of the "one people," and even today our peculiar pride or peculiar modesty, the world's hatred or the world's contempt, rejects an actual comparison with other peoples. Though its content has not become something universal, it has lost nothing of its metaphysical weight. (Its atavism was only a symbol, and only Messianism had real meaning for it.) For it still remains, and will always remain, the only visible actual embodiment of the attained goal of unity (the

---

[7] A reference to the *Pédant joué* of Cyrano de Bergerac, imitated by Molière in *Les fourberies de Scapin* (act II, scene ii). The father, when told that his son has been kidnapped by the Turks on a galley, keeps repeating: "Que diable allait-il faire dans cette galère?" This motif of the galley (in the case standing for Judaism) recurs in other passages of the correspondence.

[1] That is, modern nationalism has provided a secular substitute for the conceptions of Messianism and Election.

one people on earth, as it calls itself in the Sabbath prayer), whereas the peoples are only on the way to this desired goal, and must be so, if it is indeed ever really to be attained.

For the Jewish idea of election is from the outset anything but naïve. If it had been, you would have been right in comparing it with the race born from Zeus and nurtured by Zeus. But it is not in the least naïve. It discovers its "origin" only when it has learnt about its "destiny." If it were naïve, i.e., atavistic, in its meaning, then hatred of the Jews would be inexplicable, since one crow does not peck out another's eyes. But on *Sinai* (not, say, by the terebinths of Mamre), so says an old punning legend, Israel has inherited the " *sinna*," the hatred of the peoples. The Jews are the only *un*-naïve people in antiquity, and so of course Christianity, which takes away from antiquity the ingenuous confidence of its *pou stō*,[2] is to that extent a "Judaizing of the pagans."

Your description of paganism corresponds, then, notwithstanding the different ways we put it, very much to what I take my own point of view to be. That I was not sure of it may be attributable to the fact that I could not follow what you made of the philosophical background of "language." This has changed in the meantime; now my mind also plays on language in a lively way. But now I should like to explain the idea of the pagans once more, with reference to the idea of the peoples, as you do too, because by always harking back to Israel's being a people, you inadvertently reduce it to the idea of paganism.

Augustine in one passage contrasts his own political philosophy with that of Cicero. I think it is in the book before the last in the City of God (this is a passage, moreover, that, apart from the transformation of chiliastic ideas in the same context, I consider to be the key passage of the whole thing — I take the older interpretation, as against Troeltsch). In one section, now lost, of the *De Republica*, Cicero allotted to the State the two absolute ends of self-preservation (*salus*) and fidelity to contracts (*fides*), which ends can obviously come into conflict with one another (e.g., Saguntum), and then fidelity must be preferred before safety. Thus in the *civitas terrena*; but in the *civitas Dei*[3] a conflict between faith and salvation is not possible. Here Augustine could have quoted Isaiah 7:9, if the Latin translator had not offered another text (from which the *credo ut intelligam*"[4] is usually obtained). Luther translates it very finely: "If you do not believe, you do not abide." "To believe" and "to abide" are one and the same. The secularizing of this idea is modern nationalism,

---

[2]The Archimedean point: "where I stand."
[3]City on earth . . . city of God.
[4]I believe, that I may understand.

which becomes imperialism in order to have a good conscience. The defenders of the citadel of Jerusalem hoped up to the last moment for a miracle; not for them was the great, awe-inspiring naïveté of pagan faith, which lives to the end and dies, and asks no more, hopes no more — the impulse that inspired Thermopylae, Carthage, Saguntum. In the world of revelation there is no "abiding" without "believing," because all belief is anchored in an abiding reality; the anchor could hardly have been an ancient symbol of hope, since hope, when present, is autonomous and not anchored.

Now what I want to continue, I find that everything that I want to write is something I can't express to you. For now I would have to show you Judaism from within, that is, to be able to show it to you in a hymn, just as you are able to show me, the outsider, Christianity. And for the very reason that you can do it, I cannot. Christianity has its soul in its externals; Judaism, on the outside, has only its hard protecting shell, and one can speak of its soul only from within. So it can't be done — and you must take my word for it that the, as it were, abstract character of the religious life is the same with us and with you. Beginning and end, if I may so express it, are the same with us and with you; to use Newton as affording a parable, the continually approaching and the continually vanishing curves have the same formula with both of us, and you know that one can define the whole curve from an equation of this kind, but you and we choose different points on the path of the curve in order to describe it, and therein lies our difference. You rightly put your finger on this difference in speaking of Moriah and Golgatha. But you have read your Genesis 22 badly. You have confused Abraham and Agamemnon. The latter indeed sacrificed what he had for the sake of something else that he wanted, or, if you like, that he considered it his duty to want. Indeed, he did not perform the sacrifice himself; he only gave it up, and stood with veiled head close by. But Abraham did not offer something, not "a" child, but his only son, and what is more, the son of the promise, and sacrificed him to the God of this promise (the traditional Jewish commentary reads this paradox into the text); the meaning of the promise according to human understanding becomes impossible through this sacrifice. Not for nothing is this story associated with our highest festivals; it is the prototype of the sacrifice not of one's own person (Golgatha), but of one's existence in one's people, of the "son" and of all future sons (for we base our claims before God on this sacrifice, or rather on this readiness to sacrifice, and it is the sacrifice of the father [not of the son], as is emphasized in the story). The son is given back; he is now only the son of the promise. Nothing else happens, no Ilium falls, only the promise remains firm; the father was ready to sacrifice not for the sake of some

181

Ilium, but for the sake of nothing. Agamemnon sacrifices something "that he had"; Abraham, all that he could be; Christ, all that he is.[5] Yes, that is really, as you say, "the whole difference." To the "naïve" laying claim to an inalienable right before God corresponds, you forget, just as naïve a taking up of a yoke of inalienable sufferings, which we — "naïvely"? — know is laid upon us (cf. the traditional commentary on Isaiah 53) "for the redemption of the world." (Lucifer? Please don't mix up those symbols!) And yet we do not work at this redemption, though it will also mean our redemption from suffering. On the contrary: to the holy restlessness of your work corresponds in us a holy dread that the redemption might not come "before the time" (in which connection there are the most peculiar and even grotesque legends, both old and new) — a dread that forms the metaphysical ground of our relation to Christianity, just as your restlessness forms the ground of your relation to Judaism.

Now to return to the subject: the two sacrifices, that on Moriah and that on Golgatha have this in common, then, as against all pagan sacrifices: that nothing was got out of them (since what was sacrificed is identical with what was given back), but the sacrifice itself becomes in effect the abiding object of faith, and thereby that which abides. That which abides is different; on the one hand, an external community, and on the other an external man — and the consequences of this make mutual understanding so difficult that the one side is always being seduced into classifying the other with those that know of nothing abiding. Perhaps the readiest, if not also the most correct, antidote against this error of either side regarding the other as pagans is simply to reflect on our mutual possession of the Book.

Your whole description of the Synagogue since A.D. 70 forgets, or refuses to recognize, that we consciously take upon ourselves "the yoke of the kingdom of heaven," that we pay the price for the sin of pride of non-cooperation, of walking without mediator in the light of God's countenance. We pay subjectively through suffering the consciousness of being shut out, of being alienated, and objectively, in that we are to you the ever-mindful memorial of your incompleteness (for you who live in a church triumphant need a mute servant who cries out every time you believe that you have partaken of God in bread and wine, "*despota, memnēso tōn eschatōn*").[6]

---

[5]Cf. Eugene Rosenstock-Huessy, *The Christian Future* (Harper Torchbook edition, 1966), 182ff.

[6]"Master, remember the last things," a play on Herodotus' story of how Xerxes had a servant who stood behind him at table and said, "Master, remember the Athenians." [The translation of this sentence has been corrected by me. —F. A. R.].

I myself have written fully already of how our whole part in the life of the peoples can only be *clam, vi, precario*.[7] No doubt all we can do is hack's work; we must accept the verdict of what people think of us, and we cannot be our own judges (because it is not our own history at which we are working). All very true, and the world draws the consequences, even when some of us (not I) refuse to accept them so far as they are concerned. But that, generally speaking, we should take some sort of passive part in the life of the peoples (and, as time goes on, particularly their Christian life), is inevitable if we are to live at all (and, of course, we always hang on to life "in an unbounded way," but — your legend of the eternal Jew, if you don't falsify it, tells you this — you don't do it from hunger to live, but from duty to live a metaphysical duty: according to your opinion, damnation, according to ours, election. Life has not been given us because we are hungry for life, but hunger for life has been given to us because we must live.) Such participation cannot be avoided even by your ideal Polish Jew, with his marriage at eighteen (or, better, fourteen and, in earlier time, freedom from military service).

But along with this external life, which is in the deepest sense unethical, goes a pure inner Jewish life in all that serves the maintenance of the people, of its "life" insofar as it is not purchased from without, but must be worked out from within. Here belongs the inner Jewish task of ordering communal life, here Jewish theology, here the art of the Synagogue (yes, its "beauty"!). These phenomena may comprise much that is strange — yet Judaism cannot but assimilate this strange element to itself; it acts like this of its own accord, even when it doesn't in the least want to do so. The prodigious strength of the tradition has this effect on us even when we are in fact unaware of it. The forms of the inner Jewish life are, however, quite distinct from all apparent parallels in civilization. The art of the Synagogue does not enter into living relation with other art, nor Jewish theology with Christian theology, and so on; but Jewish art and theology, taken together, build up the Jews into a united whole and maintain them in their form of life (which isn't any living movement but just life, plain and simple), and only then do they work as a ferment on Christianity and through it on the world.

How far the Jew takes part in the life of the peoples is something he does not prescribe for himself; they prescribe it for him. For individuals it is very much a question of tact, and even sometimes of conscience (since it is partly a matter of the imponderable relationships of fellowship, and not of duties laid down in black and white by the law). I myself, since

---

[7]Secret, perforce, precarious (a formula from Roman law for the invalid and unprotected ways of acquiring possession).

you mention it, conduct myself merely dutifully towards the State; I do not take a post in one of its universities, and do not offer myself as a volunteer in the army, but go to the International Red Cross, and leave it when I have the chance of doing so when the State calls up my age group, and I have to say to myself that but for my voluntary service with the Red Cross, I should now be being legally called up by the State....

...It lies within my power to determine whether I as an individual take upon myself the metaphysical destiny, "the yoke of the Kingdom of Heaven" to which I have been called from my birth; whether I want to live *principaliter* and *essentialiter* as a Jew, even if it isn't possible *consequentialiter* and *accidentialiter*; whether I want to take the natural call up into the sphere of metaphysical choice. The cycle of institutional practices makes it easier to carry out such a resolve. I would not have the courage to take the step for myself, a step that . . . has taken with his larger possession of inherited tradition and (as a Zionist) field of Jewish activity. But "where is there the metaphysics of the seed of Abraham?" I had to smile; if you had to experience this at close quarters as I did, you would have experienced an outbreak of this metaphysics which you would not have anticipated in these particular people. The naïve feeling of the quite "modern Jews" here out-Talmuds the Talmud, and the traditional religious law seems to me (with regard to this border problem) quite consistent in that it must keep open the possibility of proselytism, because of the messianic character of Judaism. According to this the blood relationship is maintained only on account of its symbolic meaning; but the law must rigidly insist that the proselyte only "comes of his own accord," he is not fetched, not "converted," for he is indeed a parable of the proselytized humanity at the "End of the Days" (with regard to this, incidentally, the living religious sense of our common prayers knows almost nothing about "praying in Jerusalem" but only about "prays to Thee alone," and about "entering together into one fellowship").

So much for "Franz R." I told you last time that it is premature and therefore pointless to speak about him. No doubt you will not believe this F. R., and will treat my letters more and more as descriptions of how I think I ought to live rather than how I actually do. That can scarcely be helped. That was the point of my seafaring similes; if I had meant them in a general sense (as you understood them) I would have been able to describe to you more closely a ship that cannot go astray and whose crew cannot suffer shipwreck; there is only one ship of its kind, it travels on all seas, and its crew only comes on deck at night — you said is quite correctly, it is the Ghost Ship, and up to date — 1914, '15, '16 — it has not yet found Senta. But the Flying Dutchman will always return to land again, and one day we will find her (Habakkuk 2:4 — for he is both "stiff-necked" and "upright" in one person). *Lasciava ogni cosa* — except for — *speranza*.[8] Before the Throne of God the Jew will only be asked one question: Hast thou hoped for the salvation? All further questions — the tradition doesn't say so, but I do — are addressed to you. . . .

To Gertrud Oppenheim

May 1, 1917

For all those for whom the choice was not already made for them in their blood, Christianity has erected the image of the first Man, that is, of the first Man of Decision. All those for whom the choice was not already made in the blood — that means all human beings with the exception of the chosen people (for us, personal choice, as Meyrink[1] describes it, is only an anamnesis, a recognition of the choice in our blood. This is the only way in which we experience it). Christianity then clothed this first Man in the royal mantle of the last Man, of the Finisher — in order that everyone know what is happening to them when it does happen that the choice falls on them. For, if the choice had fallen upon a heathen, he would not have been able to make sense out of it; he would have believed that he had become a god (examples unnecessary), whereas, in reality, he would only have become a *man*, a member of the never-ending community of humanity. Christians, however, know that it is only in the act of being chosen that they become men. Yet they do not know the difference between the first and the last Man. They believe that in the choice it is finished, that in faith redemption takes place, and their thinkers teach that choice, the "good will" is "worthy of admiration and respect."[2] Then the Jew comes along, that eternal *enfant terrible* of church history (eternal *enfant* — he was there when it all started) and shouts: the mantle was stolen! it belongs to the *last* man, the world has *not* yet been redeemed, men are still enroute, faith makes them men, but not "more" than men, the "good will" is *not* "worthy of admiration," a good *being* would be. The Jew's forefathers were chosen and chose themselves, and thus, by virtue of the "merits of the fathers," or better, the "worthiness of

---

[8]He gave up everything except hope.

[1]Gustav Meyrink (originally Meyer) 1868–1932, authored novels on Jewish motifs, e.g., *Das grüne Gesicht* (1916); *Der Golem* (1915); English translation: *The Golem* (London: Victor Gollancz, 1928).

[2]Rosenzweig refers to the moral philosophy of Immanuel Kant (1724–1804). See the beginning of his *Foundations of the Metaphysics of Morals* (1785). —*Tr.*

the fathers," he is, as a son of Israel, also a man. But he knows something which he has to tell humanity again and again (if humanity knew this itself, then it would lose the *image*, under which and in which alone it remains on the path of choice) and that is: that to be human does not necessarily mean to be redeemed, and that humanity is yet *waiting* for its redemption. *He* is able to *know* that, because his humanity is *not* based on a visible image, clothed in the usurped royal mantle of fulfillment. And this special status of his obligates him to function as an eternal exposé of this the most pious of all deceptions, and thereby to salvage the truth until such time as the pious deception renders itself superfluous. That will occur when the deception changes from a lie into truth; that will be precisely the moment when the place of the first man, who holds sway over the will, will be taken by the last man, who holds sway over being. Without the impact of the first man, that would never happen; for it is only when all will has become choice that Being forfeits its power (coincidence). Yet without the eternal monitor, the eternal *enfant terrible*, the impact of the first man would have been drowned in his pretension of fulfillment, and the world would never be finished.

2

The Star of Redemption

1921

THE RAYS OR THE ETERNAL WAY

The Eternity of Realization

No man has the power to grasp the thought of the Creator for "his ways are not our ways and his thoughts are not our thoughts." This description of God's ways concludes the great survey of the entire contents of oral and written law which Maimonides has presented to us as the "Repetition of the Law." It introduces the subsequent sentences about the way of the true Messiah and about the great error of worshiping another besides God into which the world was led, according to the prophecy of the Book of Daniel, "by apostate sons of your people, who presume to fulfill the vision — and shall stumble." And our great teacher continues thus:[1] All these matters only served to clear the way for King Messiah, to prepare the whole world to worship God with one accord, as it is written, "Yea, at that time I will change the speech of the peoples to a pure speech, that all of them may call on the name of the Lord and serve him with one accord" [Zeph. 3:9]. Thus the Messianic hope, the Torah and the commandments have become familiar topics, topics of conversation among the inhabitants of the far isles and many peoples, uncircumcised

---

[1]After A. M. Herschman, *The Code of Maimonides Book Fourteen* (Yale Judaica Series III), xxiiif. The passage is usually expunged from the censored editions. [See above, p. 4.] —*Tr.*

187

of heart and flesh. They are discussing these matters and the command-ments of the Torah. Some say, "Those commandments were true, but have lost their validity and are no longer binding"; others declare that they had an esoteric meaning and were not intended to be taken literally, that the Messiah has already come and revealed their occult significance. But when the true King Messiah will appear and succeed, be exalted and lifted up, they will forthwith recant and realize that they have inherited naught but lies from their fathers.

The Way Through Time: Christian History

The rays shoot forth from the fiery nucleus of the Star. They seek out a way through the long night of the times. It must be an eternal way, not a temporary one, even though it leads through time. Not that it may deny time — after all, it is meant to conduct through time — but time must not gain power over it. On the other hand, it must not create its own time, and thus liberate itself from time, after the fashion of the eternal people, continually reproducing itself in itself. Thus there remains for it only one thing: it must master time. But how could that happen? How could a way which traverses time partition time instead of being itself partitioned by time?

Epoch

The question already embraces the answer. The tempo of time deter-mines everything occurring in it only, after all, because time is older and younger than everything that occurs. Were an occurrence with a begin-ning and an end outside it to confront it, then the pulse of this occurrence could regulate the hours of the world clock. Such an occurrence would have to originate beyond time and run its course into a temporal beyond. True it would be within time in any present, but knowing itself indepen-dent of time in its past and in its future, it feels itself strong against time. Its present stands between past and future. The moment, however, does not stand. Rather it vanishes with the speed of an arrow. As a result it is never "between" its past and its future: it has vanished before it could be between anything. The course of the world knows a between only in the past. Only the point in past time is a point-in-time, an epoch, a stop. Living time knows of no points: as fast as it begins to be traversed with the speed of a flying arrow by the moment, every point is already traversed. But in the past the hours stand in that motionless juxtaposi-tion. Here there are epochs, stations in time. They may be recognized by the fact that time precedes them and time follows them. They are between time and time.

Time, however, attains gravity only as such a between. Now it can no longer vanish like an arrow. The epoch no longer passes before I become aware of it, nor transforms itself before I notice it. Rather it signifies something. Something: in other words it has substantiality, is like a substance. In the past the course of the world assumes the form of immovable "substances," of eras, epochs, great moments. And this it can do only because in the past the vanishing moments are captured as stops, held between a before and an after. As a between they can no longer escape, as a between they have stability, they stand still like hours. Time has lost its power over the past, which consists entirely of betweens. It can still add to the past, but it can no longer change the past except, at the most, through what it adds. It can no longer take a hand in the inner structure of the past, for that is fixed, point by integrated point. The synchronized cadence of the years may appear to dominate the present so thoroughly that the impatience of a world reformer, the plaint of one haplessly aware of his change of fortune, bridle against it in vain. In the past, however, this cadence loses its power. In the past, events dominate time, and not vice versa. An epoch is that which stands — stands still — between its before and after. It little cares how many years it is assigned by the chronicle; every epoch weighs the same whether it lasts centuries or decades or only years. Here events rule time by marking it with their notches. Yet the event exists only within the epoch; the event stands between before and after. And a stationary between exists only in the past. If then the present too were to be elevated to the mastery of time, it too would have to be a between. The present — every present — would have to become "epoch-making." And time as a whole would have to become the hour, this temporality. As such it would have to be yoked into eternity, with eternity its beginning, eternity its end, and all of time but the between between that beginning and that end.

Christian Chronology

Thus it is Christianity that has made an epoch out of the present. Only the time before Christ's birth is now still past. All the time that succeeds, from Christ's earthly sojourn to his second coming, is now that sole great present, that epoch, that standstill, that suspension of the times, that interim over which time has lost its power. Time is now mere temporality. As such it can be surveyed in its entirety from any one of its points, for beginning and end are equidistant from each of its points. Time has become a single way, but a way whose beginning and end lie beyond time, and thus an eternal way. On ways which lead from within time to within time, by contrast, only the next segment can ever be surveyed. Every point on the eternal way is, moreover, a midpoint, since beginning and end are, after all, equidistant, no matter how time advances. It is a midpoint not because it is at the precise moment, the present point — not at all, for then it would be midpoint for one moment and already in the next instant no longer midpoint. That would amount to the kind of vitality with which time rewards a life that submits to it: a purely temporal vitality. It is the vitality of a life in the moment to be life in time, to let itself be carried off by the past, to summon up the future. Men and nations live thus. God withdrew the Jew from this life by arching the bridge of his law high above the current of time which henceforth and to all eternity rushes powerlessly along under its arches.

The Christian, however, takes up the contest with the current. He lays the track of his eternal way alongside of it. He who travels this road gauges the spot of the river which he is just looking at only by its distance from the points of departure and destination. He himself is ever and only en route. His real concern is only that he is still and yet on the way, still and yet between departure and goal. As often as he glances out the window, the current of time, ever yet passing by outside, tells him this, and nothing more. He who travels the current itself can only see from one bend to the next. For him who travels the iron tracks, the current as a whole is but a sign he is still en route, only a sign of the between. Beholding the current, he can never forget that the place whence he comes as well as the place whither he travels lie beyond the current's territory. If he asks himself where he may be now, at this moment, the current gives him no answer, while the answer which he gives himself is never anything but: en route. As long as the current of this temporality still runs at all, just so long he is himself with every moment midway between beginning and end of his course. Beginning and end are both equally near to him at every moment, for both are in the eternal, and it is only thereby that he knows himself as midpoint at every moment — as midpoint, not of a horizon which he surveys, but of a stretch which consists entirely of midpoint, which is, indeed, all middle, all Between, all path. He can and must sense every point along this path as a midpoint only *because* his path is all middle and because he knows this. The entire stretch, by consisting entirely of midpoints, is in short but a single midpoint. "Were Christ born a thousand times in Bethlehem and is not also born within you — you would still be lost" — this dictum of *The Cherubinic Wanderer*[2] is for the Christian a paradox only in the bold pithiness of its expression, not in its spirit. For the Christian the moment becomes the representative of eternity not

---

[2] A popular collection of religious poems by Angelus Silesius (Johannes Scheffler) published in 1657 and 1675, which Rosenzweig quotes from memory. The correct text is "Wird Christus tausendmal zu Bethlehem geboren / Und nicht in dir, du bleibst noch ewiglich verloren" (Book I, no. 61). —F. A. R..

as moment but as midpoint of the Christian world-time. And since it stays and does not perish, this world-time consists of such "midpoints." Every event stands midway between beginning and end of the eternal path and, by virtue of this central position in the temporal middle realm of eternity, every event is itself eternal.

Thus Christianity gains mastery over time by making of the moment an epoch-making epoch. From Christ's birth on, there is henceforth only present. Time does not bounce off Christianity as it does off the Jewish people, but fugitive time has been arrested and must henceforth serve as a captive servant. Past, present, and future — once perpetually interpenetrating each other, perpetually transforming themselves — are now become figures at rest, paintings on the walls and vaults of the chapel.[3] Henceforth all that preceded the birth of Christ, prophets and Sibylline oracles included, is past history, arrested once and for all. And the future, impending hesitantly yet inescapably attracted, is the Last Judgment. The Christian world-time stands in between this past and this future as a single hour, a single day; in it all is middle, all equally bright as day. Thus the three periods of time have separated into eternal beginning, eternal middle, and eternal end of the eternal path through this temporality. Temporality itself is disabused of its self-confidence and allows this form to be forced on it in the Christian chronology. It ceases to believe that it is older than Christianity and counts its years from the birthday of Christianity. It suffers all that preceded this to appear as negated time, as unreal time so to speak. Hitherto it had re-counted the past by counting the years; now this counting becomes the prerogative of the present, of the ever present path. And Christianity treads this path, treads it deliberately, certain of its own eternal presence, ever in the middle of occurring world, ever in the event, ever *au courant*, ever with the imperious glance of the consciousness that it is the eternal way which it treads, and on which time now follows it as its obedient pedometer.

Christendom

But what is Christendom if not people, successive generations, nations, states, persons differing in age, condition, sex, in color, education, breadth of vision, in endowments and capacities? And are these nevertheless to be henceforth at every moment one, gathered into a single midpoint and this midpoint in its turn the midpoint of all other midpoints of this one great middle? This question touches on the formative element in this community of Christianity. In the preceding book we raise the question of the formative element in the communion of Ju-

---

[3]Refers to Michelangelo's frescoes in the Sistine chapel. —F. A. R.

daism, which Jewish dogma might have answered with "the Torah." But we were not entitled to be satisfied with that answer, and the dogmatic answer "Christ" would avail us no more here. Rather, it is precisely the manner in which a communion founded on dogma gives itself reality which we wish to fathom. More exactly still — for we know it has to be an eternal communion — we asked again, as in the preceding book, how a communion can found itself for eternity. We fathomed this for the communion of the eternal life; now we ask it concerning the communion of the eternal way.

The difference cannot simply be found in the fact that at every point of the way there is a midpoint. After all, at every moment in the life of the [Jewish] people there was the whole life. God led every individual out of Egypt [m.Pes. 10:5]: "I make this covenant . . . not with you alone but both with those who are not standing here with us this day . . . and with those who are with us here this day" [Deut. 29:13f.]. Both the eternal life and the eternal way have this in common: they are eternal. Eternity is after all just this: that everything is at every point and at every moment. Thus the difference does not lie here. In the final analysis it must lie in that which is eternal, not in its eternal character. And so it is. Eternal life and eternal way are as different as the infinity of a point and the infinity of a line. The infinity of a point can only consist of the fact that it is never erased; thus it preserves itself in the eternal self-preservation of procreative blood. The infinity of a line, however, ceases where it would be impossible to extend it, it consists of the very possibility of unrestricted extension. Christianity, as the eternal way, has to spread ever further. Merely to preserve its status would mean for it renouncing its eternity and therewith death. Christianity must proselytize. This is just as essential to it as self-preservation through shutting the pure spring of blood off from foreign admixture is to the eternal people. Indeed proselytizing is the veritable form of its self-preservation for Christianity. It propagates by spreading. Eternity becomes eternity of the way by making all the points of the way, one by one, into midpoints. In the eternal people, procreation bears witness to eternity; on the eternal way this witness must really be attested to as witness. Every point of the way must once bear witness that it knows itself as midpoint of the eternal way. There the physical onward flow of the one blood bears witness to the ancestor in the engendered grandson. Here the outpouring of the spirit must establish the communion of testimony in the uninterrupted stream of baptismal water coursing on from each to another. Every point which this outpouring of the spirit reaches must be able to survey the whole path as an eternal communion of testimony. But the way can be surveyed only if it is itself the content of the testimony. In the witness of the communion the way must be attested at the same time. That communion becomes a single one through the attested belief. The belief is a belief in the path. Everyone in the communion knows that there is no eternal way other than the way which he is going. Only he belongs to Christianity who knows his own life to be on the way which leads from Christ come to Christ coming.

Belief

This knowledge is belief. It is belief as the content of a testimony. It is belief in something. That is exactly the opposite of the belief of the Jew. His belief is not the content of a testimony, but rather the produce of a reproduction.[4] The Jew, engendered a Jew, attests his belief by continuing to procreate the Jewish people. His belief is not in something: he is himself the belief. He is believing with an immediacy which no Christian dogmatist can ever attain for himself. This belief cares little for its dogmatic fixation: it has existence and that is worth more than words. But the world is entitled to words. A belief which seeks to win the world must be belief in something. Even the tiniest union of units united to win a piece of the world requires a common faith, a watchword by which those united can recognize themselves. Anyone who wants to create a piece of way of his own in the world must believe in something. Merely to believe would never allow him to attain to something in the world. Only he who believes in something can conquer something — namely, what he believes in. And it is exactly so with Christian belief. It is dogmatic in the highest sense, and must be so. It may not dispense with words. On the contrary: it simply cannot have enough of words, it cannot make enough words. It really ought to have a thousand tongues. It ought to speak all languages. For it has to wish that everything would become its own. And so the something in which it believes must be — not a something but everything. For this very reason it is the belief in the way. By believing in the way, Christian belief paves the way for the way into the world. Bearing witness, it first generates the eternal way in the world. Jewish belief, on the other hand, follows after the eternal life of the people as a product.

The Church

Thus Christian belief, the witness to the eternal way, is creative in the world. It unites those who bear witness into a union in the world. It unites them as individuals, for bearing witness is always an individual matter.

---

[4] The original play on words involves the homophonous roots *zeugen* = testify and *zeugen* = (re)produce, and cannot be translated in its entirety. —Tr.

Moreover the individual is here supposed to bear witness concerning his attitude to an individual, for the testimony, after all, concerns Christ. Christ is the common content of all the testimonies of belief. But though they were united as individuals, belief now directs them toward common action in the world. For the paving of the way is the common labor of all the individuals. Each individual can, after all, set foot on only one point of the eternal way — his point — and make of it what the whole way must become in order to be the eternal way: middle. And thus belief established that union of individuals, *as* individuals, for common labor which rightfully bears the name of *ecclesia*. For this original name of the church is taken from the life of the ancient city-states, and designates the citizens assembled for common deliberation. God's People designated its festivals as "sacred convocation" [Exod. 12:16 et al.] with what was essentially a similar term. But for itself it used words, like people or congregation [Deut. 5:19 et al.], which once designated the people-in-arms, that entity, in other words, in which the people appears as the self-contained whole into which the individuals have dissolved. In the *ecclesia*, however, the individual is and remains an individual, and only its resolve is common and becomes — *res publica*.

Christ

Now Christianity gives itself precisely this name of *ecclesia*, the name of an assembly of individuals for common labor. Still, this labor only comes to pass by virtue of each one acting in his place as individual. In the assembly, similarly, the common resolve emerges only by virtue of the fact that each expressed his opinion and votes entirely as an individual. Thus, too, the community of the church presupposes the personality and integrity — we may safely say: the soul — of its members. Paul's analogy of the congregation as the body of Christ [Eph. 1:22f., Rom. 12:5, 1 Cor. 12:27, 29 et al.] does not imply some kind of division of labor like, say, the famous parable of stomach and limbs by Menenius Agrippa. Rather it alludes precisely to this perfect freedom of each individual in the Church. It is illuminated by the great "For though everything belongs to you . . . yet you belong to Christ" [1 Cor. 3:21–23]. Everything is subservient to Christianity because Christianity, and every individual Christian within it, proceeds from the crucified one. Every Christian is privileged to know himself on the way, not merely at any arbitrary point, but rather at the absolute middle of the way which, after all, is itself wholly middle, wholly between. But inasmuch as Christianity and the individual [Christian] still await the second coming, those who have just been manumitted as lords of all things at once know themselves again as everyone's slave. For what they do to the least of His brothers, that they do to him who will return to judge the world.[5]

How then will the *ecclesia* constitute itself on the basis of that freedom and integrity of the individuals which must be preserved? How is the bond which connects each to each within it to look? It must, after all, leave the individuals free while it binds them; indeed, in truth, it must first make them free. It must leave everyone as it finds him, man as man, woman as woman, the aged old, the youths young, the master as master, the slave as slave, the wealthy rich, the paupers poor, the sage wise and the fool foolish, the Roman a Roman and the barbarian a barbarian. The bond must not place anyone in the status of another, and yet it must bridge the chasm between man and wife, between parents and child, between master and slave, between rich and poor, sage and fool, Roman and barbarian. It must free each one as he is, in all his natural and God-given dependencies with which he stands in the world of creation. It must set him in the middle of that way which leads from eternity to eternity.

It is the bond of brotherliness which thus takes men as it finds them and yet binds them together across differences of sex, age, class, and race. Brotherliness connects people in all given circumstances — independently of these circumstances, which simply continue to exist — as equals, as brothers "in the Lord." From being men they become brothers, and the common belief in the common way is the content for this. In this Christian covenant of brotherhood, Christ is both beginning and end of the way, and thereby content and goal, founder and master of the covenant, as well as the middle of the way, and therefore present wherever two have met together in his name.[6] Wherever two have met together in his name, there is the middle of the way. There the whole way may be surveyed. The beginning and end are equidistant because he who is beginning and end abides in midst of those assembled here. Thus in the middle of the way Christ is neither founder nor master of his Church, but rather a member of it, himself a brother of his covenant. As such he can also be with the individual in brotherliness: even the individual — and not only two who have met together — already knows himself as Christian. Though seemingly alone with himself, he yet knows himself as member of the church because this solitude is togetherness with Christ.

Christ is near to this individual in that form to which his brotherly feelings can most readily direct themselves. The individual is, after all, to remain what he is: the man a man, the woman a woman, the child

---

[5]Cf. Matthew 25:40.
[6]Cf. Matthew 18:20.

a child.[7] Thus Christ is a friend to the man, a spiritual bridegroom to the woman, a holy infant to the child. Tied to the historical Jesus, Christ may forego this identification with the familiar figure of the neighbor, the object of brotherly love; but there the saints substitute for Christ himself. At least they do so in the Petrine Church of love, the Church which holds its believers most ardently to the way and allows them to remember less of its beginning and end. There man is privileged to love Mary as the pure virgin, and woman to love her as the divine sister, and each to love the saint of his class and nation from within his class and nation. Indeed, everyone is there privileged to love his saintly namesake as a brother from within the narrowest confines of the Self as it is contained within his Christian name. This Church of love is even more intrinsically a Church of the way than the others. And in it the figure of the living world-wanderer pushes itself ahead even of the deceased God on the cross; in it — more than in the sister churches — this wanderer becomes an example to be followed like an exemplary human brother; in it, at the same time, the whole crowd of saints interceding for their frail brothers and sisters, surges before the judge of the last judgment, where the way reaches the goal.

The Christian Act

Thus brotherliness weaves its bond among men of whom none equal each other. Nor is this brotherliness by any means identity of everything with human countenance, but rather the harmony precisely of men of the most diverse countenances. One thing is necessary, of course, but only one: that men have a countenance at all, that they see each other. The church is the communion of all those who see each other. It joins men as coevals, as contemporaries at disparate loci of the ample space. Contemporaneity is something which in temporality does not even exist. In temporality there is only before and after. The moment in which one catches sight of oneself can only precede or follow the moment where one catches sight of another. Simultaneously to catch sight of oneself and of another at the same moment is impossible. That is the profoundest reason for the impossibility of loving one's neighbor as oneself in the heathen world which is, after all, precisely temporality. In eternity, however, there is also contemporaneity. It goes without saying that, seen from its shore, all time is simultaneous. But that time too which, as eternal way, leads from eternity to eternity admits of simultaneity. For only insofar as it is middle between eternity and eternity is it possible for people to meet in it. Thus he who catches sight of himself on the way is on

---

[7]Cf. 1 Corinthians 7:18–24.

the same point —- that is, on the exact midpoint — of time. It is brotherliness which transports men into this midpoint. Time, already overcome, is placed at its feet; it is left for love only to traverse the separating space. And thus it traverses in its flight the hostility of nations as well as the cruelty of gender, the jealousy of class as well as the barrier of age. Thus it permits all the hostile, cruel, jealous, limited ones to catch sight of each other as brothers in one and the same central moment of time.

The Jewish Act

The contemporaries catch sight of one another in the middle of time.[8] At the boundaries of time, similarly, those had encountered each other for whom the differences of space did not mean a separation that first had to be overcome. For there these differences had already been overcome, from the start, in the innate communion of the people. There the labor of love — both of divine love for men and of human love for each other — had to be directed solely toward the preservation of this communion through time, toward the creation of contemporaneity of the sequences of generations separated in temporality. That is the covenant between scion and ancestor. By virtue of this covenant the people becomes an eternal people. For in catching sight of each other, scion and ancestor catch sight in each other at the same moment of the last descendant and the first ancestor. Descendant and ancestor are thus the true incarnation of the eternal people, both of them for each other, and both together for him who stands between them, just as the fellow-man become brother is the Church incarnate for the Christian. We experience our Judaism with immediacy in elders and children. The Christian experiences his Christianity in the sensation of that moment which leads the brother to him at the height of the eternal way. For him, all of Christianity seems to crowd together there. It stands where he stands, he stands where it stands: at the middle of time between eternity and eternity. We too are shown eternity by the moment, but differently: not in the brother who stands closest to us, but rather in those who stand furthest from us in time,[9] in the oldest and the youngest, in the elder who admonishes, in the lad who asks, in the ancestor who blesses and in the grandson who receives the blessing. It is thus that the bridge of eternity does its spanning for us: from the starry heaven of the promise[10] which arches over

---

[8]Cf. Hölderlin's poem *Patmos* (1802): Since the peaks of time cluster / High all around / And loved ones dwell / Near, languishing / On mountains farthest apart . . . (translated by Christopher Middleton [University of Chicago Press, 1972], 75). —F. A. R.

[9]M. Pes. 10:4: "Here the son asks. . . . " The traditional four questions of the Passover Seder by the youngest child.

[10]Cf. Genesis 15:5.

that moment of revelation whence sprang the river of our eternal life, unto the limitless sands of the promise[11] washed by the sea into which that river empties, the sea out of which will rise the Star of Redemption when once the earth froths over, like its flood rides, with the knowledge of the Lord [Isa. 11:9].

Cross and Star

In the final analysis, then, that tension of beginning and end withal strives mightily toward the end. Though as tension it originates only in both, it finally gathers nevertheless at one point, namely, at the end. The child with its questions is in the final analysis still and all a more powerful admonisher than the elder. No matter how we may perpetually draw nourishment from the inexhaustible treasure of the elder's inspired life, no matter how we may maintain and fortify ourselves on the merit of the fathers: the elder turns into a memory, the child alone compels. God establishes his kingdom only "out of the mouths of babes and sucklings" [Ps. 8:3].[12] In the final analysis the tension after all concentrates itself entirely at the end, on the latest sprout at last, on the Messiah whom we await. So too the Christian agglomeration at the midpoint at long last does not remain glued to that spot after all. Let the Christian discern Christ in his brother[13]: in the final analysis he is after all driven beyond the brother to Christ himself, without mediation. Let the middle be but middle between beginning and end: it gravitates, for all that, toward the beginning. Let man discern cross and last judgment alike from the middle of the way in eternal proximity: he cannot let that satisfy him. He steps directly under the cross, and will not rest till the image of the crucified one cover all the world for him. In this turning to the cross alone, he may forget the judgment: he remains on the way for all that. For though it still belongs to the eternal beginning of the way, the cross is after all no longer the first beginning; it is itself already on the way and whoever steps under it thus stands at its middle and beginning at the same time. Thus Christian consciousness, all steeped in belief, presses toward the beginning of the way, to the first Christian, the crucified one, just as Jewish consciousness, all gathered up in hope, presses toward the man of the end of time, to David's royal sprout. Belief can renew itself eternally at its beginning, just as the arms of the cross can be extended to infinity. Hope, however, eternally unites itself out of all the multiplicity of time in the one near and far moment-in-space (*Augenpunkt*) of the

---

[11]Cf. Genesis 22:17.
[12]Cf. Resh Laqish's statement in the name of R. Judah the Prince (b. Shab. 119b).
[13]Cf. Matthew 10:40, Mark 9:37, Luke 9:48.

end, just as the Star on the shield of David gathers all into the fiery nucleus. Rootedness in the profoundest self — that had been the secret of the eternity of the [eternal] people. Diffusion throughout all that is outside — this is the secret of the eternity of the [eternal] way.

The Two Roads: The Essence of Christianity

Expansion to the exterior, and not: as far as possible but rather — whether possible or not — expansion into each and everything that is outside, and that, in each respective present, can only at most be a still-outside — if this expansion is all that unconditional, all that limitless, then what was true of the Jewish rootedness in its own interior is manifestly valid also for it, namely, that nothing may remain outside as something contradictory. Here too all contradictions must somehow be drawn into its own boundaries. But such boundaries as may have been possessed by the personal self, rooting itself in itself, are alien, nay they are unthinkable for this expansion into the exterior. Where is the boundless to have boundaries? It bursts all bounds every time! Admittedly, the expansion itself cannot have boundaries, but that exterior into which the expansion takes place, can have them: the boundaries of the All. But these boundaries are not reached in the present nor in any future present, for eternity can erupt today or tomorrow but not the day after tomorrow. And the future is always mere day after tomorrow.

Thus the manner in which the contradictions are alive must also be different here from what it was in the absorption in the self. There the contradictions were at once harnessed into the internal structures of God, world, man; the three contradictions were alive as if in constantly alternating currents between those three poles. Here, on the other hand, the contradictions must already inhere in the nature of the expansion if they are to be effective wholly and at every moment. The expansion must take place along each of two discrete and even opposite ways. Beneath Christianity's footsteps into each of the countries God, man, and world there must bloom respectively two different sorts of flowers. Indeed, these steps themselves must diverge in time, and two forms of Christianity must traverse those three countries, each along its own path, hopeful of reuniting again one day, but not within time. Within time they march their separate ways and only by marching separately are they certain of traversing the entire All without losing themselves in it. Judaism was able to be the one people,[14] the eternal people [Isa. 44:7], only because it already bore all the great contradictions within itself; for the peoples of the world, on the other hand, these contradic-

---

[14] 2 Samuel 7:23, and the Sabbath afternoon Standing Prayer.

tions emerge only where they part company one from another. Just so Christianity too, to be really all-embracing, must harbor within itself the contradictions with which other associations each delimit themselves against all others already in name and purpose. Only thus can Christianity distinguish itself as the all-embracing association and withal the only one of its kind. God, world, and man can become Christian God, Christian world, Christian man only if they disgorge the contradictions in which life moves out of themselves and work each one out individually. Otherwise Christendom would be no more than a club, entitled perhaps to its particular purpose and its special area, but without a claim to expansion to the ends of the world. And again, if Christianity were to try to expand beyond these contradictions, then its way, though it would not need to bifurcate, would not be the way through the world, the way along the current of time; it would rather be a way leading to the trackless ocean of the winds where the All is without content even if it be also without limits or contradictions. And the way of Christianity must lead elsewhere, into the living All that surrounds us, the All of life, the All composed of God, man, and world.

Son and Father

The way of Christianity into the country labelled God thus divides into two ways. It is a duality which is simply incomprehensible to the Jew, albeit Christian life rests precisely on it. It is incomprehensible to us for though we too know a contradiction in God, a juxtaposition of justice and mercy,[15] of creation and revelation, this contradiction is within him, it is in ceaseless connection precisely with itself. There is an alternating current oscillating between God's attributes; one cannot equate him with the one or the other; he is, rather, One precisely in the constant equalization of apparently opposite "attributes." For the Christian, however, the division into "Father" and "Son" signifies much more than merely a separation into divine sternness and divine love. The Son is, after all, also the judge of the world, the Father "so loved" the world that he gave his own son [John 3:16]. Thus sternness and love are not really divided between the two persons of the deity at all. And no more can they be divided according to creation and revelation. For the Son is not without participation in creation, nor the Father in revelation. Rather it is Christian piety which follows different paths according as it is with the Father or with the Son. The Christian approaches only the Son with

---

[15] The rabbinic concepts of *middat ha-din* (the attribute of strict justice) and *middat ha-raḥamim* (the attribute of mercy), e.g., Gen. R. 12:15 (Theodor ed., 1:112f.), 21:8 (1:202), and 33:3 (1:308). —F. A. R.

that familiarity which seems so natural to us in our relationship to God that we for our part can barely conceive of the existence of persons who mistrust this trust. The Christian dares to enter the presence of the Father only by means of the Son; he believes he can reach the Father only through the Son. If the Son were not a man he would avail nothing to the Christian.[16] He cannot imagine that God himself, the holy God, could so condescend to him as he demands, except by becoming human himself. The inextinguishable segment of paganism which is innermost in every Christian bursts forth here. The pagan wants to be surrounded by human deities; he is not satisfied with being human himself: God too must be human. The vitality which the true God too shares with the gods of the heathen becomes credible to the Christian only if it becomes flesh [John 1:14] in a human-divine person of its own. Once this God has become man, the Christian proceeds through life as confidently as we and — unlike us — full of conquering power. For flesh and blood will only be subdued by flesh and blood, and precisely the indicated "paganism" of the Christian qualifies him to convert the pagans.

But at the same time he is also proceeding along another path, the one which is immediate to the Father. In the Son, the Christian drew God immediately into the brotherly nighness of his own I: before the Father he may once more divest himself of everything personal. In his nighness he ceases to be I. Here he knows himself in the orbit of a truth which makes a mockery of everything that is I. He satisfies his need for the nighness of God by means of the Son, but the Father provides him with divine truth. Here he attains that pure remoteness and objectivity of cognition and action which, in apparent contradiction to the heartfelt-ness of love, designates Christianity's other way through the world. For knowledge as for action life is systematized into fixed orders under the sign of God the Father. On this path too, the Christian feels the glance of God directed toward him, of God the Father, that is, not the Son. It is un-Christian to confuse these two ways to God. It is a matter of "tact" to distinguish them and to know when it is proper to walk the one and when the other. The Christian does not know those unexpected reversals out of the consciousness of divine love into that of divine righteousness and vice versa which, quick as lightning, are of the essence of Jewish life. His approach to God remains twofold and, if the compulsion of this twofold path should tear him apart, he is permitted to decide clearly for one of them and to devote himself entirely to it rather than to waver back and forth in the twilight between the two. The world, his fellow-Christians,

---

[16]John 14:6: Jesus said to him, "I am the way, and the truth, and the life; no one comes to the Father, but by me." Cf. the letter to E. Rosenstock, above p. 177.

will no doubt see to it that the balance is restored. For that which, in God, is here revealed as a separation of the divine persons corresponds, in the Christian world, to a twofold order, and in the Christian man to a dual form of life.

Priest and Saint

In Jewish man, man was one, and a living one at that, for all his contradictions, for all the ineradicable conflicts between his love by God and his love for God, between his Judaism and his humanism, between patriarch and messiah. But in Christianity, this man separates into two figures, not necessarily two mutually exclusive and antagonistic figures, but two figures going their separate ways, separate even when they meet in a single person as is always possible. And these separate ways again lead through all that broad country of humanity in whose districts form and freedom appear to be in perpetual conflict. Precisely this contradiction is given free reign in Christianity in the two figures of the priest and the saint. And again it is not simply a case of the priest being merely the human vessel of revelation, or of the saint's love merely supplying the warmth to ripen the fruit of redemption. For the priest is not simply the man in whom the word of the divine mouth awakens the slumbering soul with a kiss. Rather he is the man redeemed to his destiny as image of God, prepared to become the vessel of revelation. And the saint can redeem the world in love only on the basis of a revelation which has just, and always just, come to him, only in the nearness of his Lord which always anew becomes something he can taste and see. He cannot just act as though there were no God to put into his heart what to do, anymore than the priest could wear his priestly garment if he were not able to acquire redemption in the visible forms of the Church, and with that the feeling that he discharges his office in the image of God. A bit of heretical caprice is concealed in that consciousness of divine inspiration which is borne by the saint; a bit of the self-apotheosis of the Grand Inquisitor is donned with the priestly garb as this implies the claim to be in the image of God. The outer limits of form and freedom are ceremonial and super-personal self-apotheosis on the one hand and momentary, personal caprice on the other — on the one hand the emperor of Byzantium, exalted above everything mundane and incidental by the greatest pomp and strictest etiquette, and on the other the revolutionary, hurling the torch of his momentary demand into millennial buildings. The broad realm of the soul stretches between these outer limits, and the bifurcated path of Christianity traverses it all.

State and Church

For the Jew, the world is full of smooth transitions from "this world" to the "world to come" and back; for the Christian, it is organized into the great dualism of state and Church. Not without justification it has been said of the pagan world that it knew neither the one nor the other. The *polis* was both state and Church for its citizens, as yet without any contradiction. But in the Christian world, these two separated from the beginning. The history of the Christian world thereafter consists of the attempt to maintain this separation. It is not as if only the Church were Christian and not the state. "Render unto Caesar that which is Caesar's" [Matt. 22:1 et al.] weighed no less heavily in the course of the centuries than the second half of this dictum. For the law to which the peoples submit proceeds from Caesar. And creation, the work of divine omnipotence, is consummated in the universal rule of law on earth. The very Caesar to whom one was to render what was his had already commanded a world which was a single constituency. The Church itself transmitted to a later age the memory of this state of affairs together with the longing for its restoration. It was the Pope who placed the diadem of the Caesars on the brows of the Frankish Charlemagne. It rested on the heads of his successors for a millennium, bitterly disputed by the Church itself, which postulated its own preeminent domain and title and defended it against the very claim to universal imperial jurisdiction which she herself had nurtured. While these two equally universal jurisdictions battled for the world there grew up new structures, "states" which presumed to fight for jurisdiction not, like the empire, over the world, but only over themselves. These states thus emerged as rebels against a world created by a single creative power and whose jurisdictional unity had been turned over to the emperor for safekeeping. And when these states were free to believe that they had found a firm foundation in creation, when they had found their niche in the natural nation, at that very moment the crown was removed from the head of the Roman emperor once and for all, and the neo-Frankish national emperor crowned himself with it.[17] Others imitated him as representatives of their nations, but the imperial drive seemed now to have transferred to the peoples together with the title of emperor: now the peoples themselves became bearers of supra-national, world-oriented volition. And by the time this imperial drive has been eroded in the mutual friction of the peoples, it will assume a new form. For it is doubly anchored, once in the divine Creator of the world whose power it reflects, and again in the world's longing for redemption, which

---

[17] Alludes to the fact that the Pope put the crown on the head of Charlemagne; Napoleon at his coronation placed it on his head himself. —F. A. R.

it serves. Thus it opens up one of the two essential paths of Christianity, leading into that part of the All which is the World.

The other path leads through the Church. The Church too is in the world. It must therefore come into conflict with the state. It cannot dispense with a legal constitution of its own. On the contrary, it is a visible system and of a sort which the state cannot tolerate — say because it were to limit itself to a particular sphere — but rather a system which claims to be not a whit less universal than the state. Church law, no less than Caesar's, sooner or later applies to everyone. The Church drafts man for the labor of redemption and assigns to this labor a place in the created world. Stones must be brought from the mountains and trees felled in the forest if there is to be a house in which man will serve God. The Church is in the world, visible and with a universal law of its own, and thus not a whit more than Caesar's empire itself the kingdom of God. It grows toward the latter in its history which is secular both in the sense of worldly and of centuries-long; it remains a segment of the world and of life, and it becomes eternal only through its animation by the human act of love. Ecclesiastical history is no more the history of the kingdom of God than is imperial history. In the strict sense there is in fact no history of the kingdom of God. The eternal can have no history, at most a prehistory. The centuries and millennia of ecclesiastical history are no more than the earthly form, changing with time, around which the ecclesiastical year spins the halo of eternity. . . .

THE STAR OR THE ETERNAL TRUTH

Spirit (Psychology)

Limits of Humanity

. . . To the truth which is God's seal[18] there corresponds the Truly as man's seal. He may and must say his Truly, his Yes and Amen. He is not permitted any if's and but's. In his mouth, "if" is a vile word, and he is entitled to decline to answer to a moralistic cross-examination confronting him with "what would you do if." It is enough for him to know what he must do when any of these if's has become a "thus" for him. . . .

Configuration of Humanity: The Jew

In revelation, truth coursed into the Here and Now, and there was a dual possibility for it to unite with the Truly of Man. The locus where man was located, the station where he stood, could be found in himself; his nature could be such as was created for and in him at birth, something

---

[18]B. Shab. 55a: Truth is a the seal of the Holy One, blessed be He.

he could carry around with him, an inner home which he could no more cast aside than the snail its house or, to use a better analogy, a magic circle which he could no more escape than the circuit of his blood, precisely because, like the latter and with the latter, he carries this with him wherever he may go or stand. If then man carries his inner home, his inner station, with him, then the decisive moment, the moment of his second birth, of his rebirth, must lie for him beyond the confines of his personality, before his own life. The rebirth of the Jew — and it is of him that we are here speaking — is not his personal one, but the transformation of his people for freedom in the divine covenant of revelation. On that occasion the people experienced a second birth, and he in it, not he personally as an individual. The patriarch Abraham heard the call of God and answered it with his "Here I am" [Gen. 22:1], and the individual only in Abraham's loins. Henceforth the individual is born a Jew. He no longer needs to become one in some decisive moment of his individual life. The decisive moment, the great Now, the miracle of rebirth, lies before the individual life. In the individual life there is found only the great Here, the viewpoint, the station, the house and the circuit, in short all that is granted to man in the mystery of his first birth.

Configuration of Humanity: The Christian
It is just the contrary with the Christian. In his personal life there occurs to him at a given point the miracle of rebirth, and it occurs to him as an individual. Direction is thereby injected into the life of one born heathen by nature. "A Christian is made, not born." This beginning of his having become a Christian, whence originate ever new beginnings, a whole chain of beginnings, this he carries with him, but otherwise nothing. He never "is" a Christian, although there is a Christianity. Christianity exists without him. The individual Jew generally lacks that personal vitality which only comes to a man in the second birth, with the "intrusion of the self." For although the [Jewish] people has the defiantly demonic self in full measure, the individual [Jew] has it not at all. Rather he is from his first birth on whatever he is as Jew, in a sense, then by virtue of his personality, not of his character. Correspondingly, the Christian loses everything "natural," everything innate, in his Christianity. There are Christian characters, men, that is, in whose features one can read the struggles in which the Christian in them was born. But in general there are no Christian personalities; an artificial expression like "Johannine nature" is the exception that proves this rule. What is Christian by nature has its being outside him, in secular and ecclesiastical institutions; he does not carry it around with him on the outside. The mystery of birth, which occurs in the Jew precisely to the individual, here precedes every

individual in the miracle of Bethlehem. There, in the origin of revelation which is common to all, the first birth common to all occurred. The undeniable, the given, the original and enduring being of their Christianity they find, not in themselves, but in Christ. They themselves had, each of them, to become Christian. They are relieved of being-Christian before birth by the birth of Christ, just as, contrariwise, the Jew is relieved of becoming-Jew in the protohistory of his people's revelation, while he possesses his being Jew in himself from birth on and carries it with him.

Law of Humanity: Birth and Rebirth

This contradictory relationship of Here and Now, of birth and rebirth, also determines each and every further contrast in effect between Jewish and Christian life. Christian life begins with rebirth. Birth lies outside it in the first instance. Thus it must seek to lay a foundation for its birth and its rebirth. It must remove the birth from the manger in Bethlehem into its own heart. "Were Christ born a thousand times in Bethlehem, but not also in you, you would still be lost."[19] This whole Here that is still without, this whole world of naturalness must be drawn into the series of becoming-Christian's which begins with the great Now of the rebirth. Christian life leads the Christian into the outside. The rays radiate evermore, till all the outside shall be irradiated. Jewish life is just the opposite. Birth, the whole natural Here, the natural individuality, the impartible participation in the world — already exists here, and this broad and full existence must be conducted into the narrow instant of the rebirth. This conducting becomes a re-duction, for rebirth precedes the personal and individual birth by time out of mind. The reliving of the quondam common rebirth here takes the place of the transfer of the quondam common birth into the personal reborn heart. Thus instead of the past being made present, the present is conducted back into the past. Everyone is to know that the Eternal brought him personally out of Egypt [m. Pes. 10:5]. The present Here dissolves in the great Now of the remembered experience. The Christian way becomes expression and expropriation and irradiation of the outermost, while Jewish life becomes memory and internalization and inspiration of the innermost.

The Shape of Verification: Eschatology

The rays of the Star thus break forth to the exterior, the fire glows toward the interior, and neither rests till it has arrived at the end, the outermost or the innermost. Both draw everything into the circle filled with their effect. But the rays do so by dividing on the outside, scattering, and going

---

[19]Cf. above, p. 190.

their separate ways, ways which only reunite beyond the outer space of the protocosmos when that has been traversed in its entirety. The fire, on the other hand, does so by gathering and in-gathering within itself the rich multiplicity of existence, in the flickering play of its flame, as contradictions of the inner life, contradictions which likewise find their resolution only there where the flame may be quenched because the world has ceased to glow and no longer provides it with fuel, and the hissing life of the flame dies out in what is more than human-worldly life: in the divine life of truth. For with this we are concerned here, with the truth, and no longer with the bifurcation of the way in the visible world, or with the inner contradictoriness of life. But truth never appears before the end. The end is its locus. For us it is not the given but the result. For to us it is a Whole; only to God it is im-parted. For him it is not the result, but the given, given, that is, by him, gift. But we never see the truth until the end. Thus we must now accompany both the bifurcation and the contradictoriness to the end; we may no longer be content with what we encountered hitherto on our journey of discovery, with life and the way.

The Christian Way

The forks in the road were threefold, according to the three forms that the All assumed after it had burst into pieces for us. The centrifugal way of Christianity embraced God, world, and man, all three incommensurable as far as intellect was concerned. And wherever the apostles of Christendom drew a portion of the All into Christianity, the old gods, the old world, the old Adam were nailed to the cross, and those born in paganism were reborn in Christianity for the new God, the new world, the new man. The obscure designations which only remained as tablets inscribed by pagan hands at the tops of the three crosses were read by Christianity in their own manifest sense as the concealed God, the secluded man, the enchanted world.

Spiritualized God

The ways of the Father and the Son unveiled the All of the Concealed God. They radiated outward from the Star of Redemption, but they radiated apart, and appeared intent on constituting themselves the contrast between two persons. In its face, admittedly, paganism collapsed because of its fundamental indefiniteness, and collapsed each time anew, as each new indefiniteness was caught in this ever-open Either-Or. The worldly materialistic bases for the creation of new gods were caught up in the belief in the Father, the human-personal ones in the belief in the Son. Thus paganism was really at the end of its wisdom, but Christianity appeared to triumph over it only by adapting its concept of God to it;

207

it purchased the end of pagan wisdom only at the cost of the curse of ever having to remain at the beginning of the way. In the concept of the Spirit, which emanates from both Father and Son, Christianity itself thus designates the point where both, Father and Son, will meet again when once the world has gathered under this cross, beyond the way. The Christian credo had to accommodate itself to a pagan impulse in order to win over the pagans, and this impulse is quenched by the worship of God in the Spirit and the truth, by the promise that the Spirit would lead Christendom. It is quenched, however, only to make room for a new danger: a deification of the Spirit or rather a spiritualization of God. This would forget God himself in favor of the Spirit; it would lose the living power of God, incalculably creating and quickening life, in the hope of a glimpse; intoxicated with the hope of seeing him and with the fullness of the Spirit it would lose touch with the constantly growing world and with the soul renewing itself in belief. The Eastern Church, true to its origin in the Apostle John and the Greek Church Fathers, assumed the function of the conversion of wisdom; henceforth it displays the great illustration of this danger of spiritualizing God, seeking refuge in hope and a glimpse from an anarchic world, a chaotic soul.

Deified Man

The ways of priest and saint disclosed the All of the secluded man. Though they likewise emanated from the same ray of the Star of Redemption, they too radiated apart, and appeared to constitute themselves into the contradiction which, among men, divides man from man. And here too paganism, which divided men among themselves in a hundred different ways, collapsed again and again in the face of this [single] contrast. For paganism made all its divisions according to the permanent criterion of shape and color, class and language, or according to the fleeting emotions of the moment, in hate and love. But all these permanent criteria came to nought before the one indestructible character of the priest, a character setting him apart from the laity; all the tempestuous emotions of the moment shattered on the saint's one great passion, his ever-new passion of love. The wealth of pagan forms paled into insignificance before the weight of that [one] form; every caprice of pagan passions disappeared before this [one] passion and came to nought. But the contrast still remained. Though it caught and appeased the pagan frenzy of humanity, the struggle continued between those who now lay there in stillness. Between form and freedom, between priest and saint, peace remained just as unaccomplished in the All of humanity as it did between the single form and the wealth of figures, between the one freedom and the passions. Here again, unity beckoned only there where the two ways met again beyond every way in order to gather mankind under this cross. Thence beckoned the image of him who had said to Christendom: "I am the truth" [John 14:6]. The Son of man was the only one whose high priesthood did not suffer from the servant-form, and whose humanity, on the other hand, was not reduced by his divinity. The figures of priest and saint, always separated in their campaigns of conquest through the country of the soul, were thus united in view of this image of one who would be true man and true God, and in imitation of him. In the duality of these figures, and in all the divisions which this duality in turn posited within the soul, man, who was still and yet as divided within himself as in paganism, could thus shape himself in an image approaching the longed-for image of a unity of the heart, at least in imitation and hope. At least in the longing and hope for a unity of the heart, the last conflict of the pagan soul thus appears to be resolved before the image of the Son of Man. But here too a new danger again threatens; a deification of man and a humanization of God which would forget God himself in favor of man, which threatened to lose the straightforward belief in the superhuman God and the activity-minded love for a figure-poor world in favor of a credulous longing to descend into the still chamber whence spring the manifold rivulets of the soul. The Northern [i.e., Protestant] Church, true to its origin in Paul and the German Fathers, had assumed the function of converting the Spiritual, of the poet in man; henceforth it displays the great illustration of that danger of a humanization of God which deifies man, seeking refuge in the still corner of longing and in one's own heart from a world bereft of soul and from the Lord of the spirits of all flesh.

Idolized World

The ways of state and Church freed the enchanted world from enchantment. These too, though emanating from the one ray of the Star, radiated apart, and appeared to constitute themselves the contrast which, in the world, divided order from order, world from world. And once more paganism which, in the world, divides all from all, state from state, people from people, class from class, each from each, collapsed again and again before this uniform contradiction. Before the one essential division between natural and supernatural order, all the divisions of paganism became inessential. If henceforth they wished to embellish their zeal against one another with so much as the appearance of justification, they had to borrow the reflected glory of a higher justice from that contradiction; they had to attempt to provide power with spiritual content. Thus the pagan "struggle of all against all" was sublimated into a higher struggle for higher stakes, but it remained a struggle. Only at the end of

209

all history there looms the prospect of a kingdom free of struggle and contradiction in which God will be all-in-all.[20] The fullness of the pagan world would have simply refused to dissolve in a "kingdom of priests and a holy nation" [Exod. 19:6]. To comprehend this wealth fully within itself, Christianity had to walk the two separate but parallel ways, the way of the state and the way of the Church, and these meet there at the end of all history. Thus the two ways cannot unite until the fullness of the pagans has dissolved. But in this prospect of a future one-and-universal world freed from contradictions, of a day when God will be all-in-all, there once more lies a danger for Christianity. It is the last of the three great dangers which are unavoidable because inseparable from its greatness and strength: making the world divine or God worldly. It would forget the One above all[21] in favor of the All-in-All; it would forfeit the pious confidence in the free inner strength of the soul which renews itself, and in the providence of God which goes its own way above all human insight, in favor of the lovingly active unification of what the world has separated into the one-and-universal building of the kingdom. The Southern [i.e., Roman Catholic] Church, true to its origin in Peter and the Latin Church Fathers, had assumed the function of converting the visible legal system of the world; henceforth it illustrates that danger of making God worldly by making the world divine, seeking refuge in the act of love which sustains the world and in the joy of the effectively effected [good] work from a freedom of the soul which it mistrusts and from a God whose sway is beyond finding out.

The Christian Dangers

Threefold was the division of the way, threefold the reunification which is always in the Beyond, threefold the danger. That the Spirit leads onto all ways, and not God; that the Son of man be the truth, and not God; that God would become All-in-All [1 Cor. 15:28] and not One above all — these are the dangers. They originate at the end points of the way, in the Beyond where the rays at last unite which never meet in the Here of God as of the soul and of the world. Thus they are dangers which Christianity never overcomes — spiritualization of God, apotheosis of man, pantheification of the world — just as it never overcomes the division of the churches into the Church of the spiritual truth, that of the Son of Man, and that of the kingdom of God. Each of these, immersed respectively in hope, faith, and love, must neglect the other two

---

[20] 1 Corinthians 15:28: When all things are subjected to Him, then the Son himself will also be subjected to Him, that God may be all in all.

[21] Cf. Zechariah 14:9: And the Lord shall be King *over* (Heb. *ʿal*) all the earth. . . .

forces in order to live all the more strongly in the one, and in order to administer its portion in the work of bringing about the rebirth of the protocosmos which was born in paganism. Christianity radiates in three divided directions. It presses toward an Outermost in pursuing its self-expropriating course to the outside, but this Outermost is not something simple. Like the protocosmos in which the pagan finds himself, it is something threefold. Revelation bridged the gap between those three Alls of the protocosmos, connecting the three points in the one immovable order of the Day of the Lord. But Christianity completes its expropriation into the All, and the rays which were scattered on their way through time gather together again by making God spiritual, human, worldly, and these three points can no longer be connected, as we shall see. Though they are in a fixed order with respect to each other, unlike the three points of paganism, and the Perhaps has long ago fallen silent forever, yet Christianity no longer offers them a fluent interconnection which would again lift these three separated ones too into a unity, at least not completely. Before we turn to this ultimate understanding of the rays which are radiated into the outside, let us now return to contemplate the glow with which the flame of the fire glows in itself.

Jewish Life

The flame too flashed in threefold blaze. In three contradictions of its own burning life, it internalized the tripartite life of the outer All. The might and humility of the Jewish God, the election and the redemptive vocation of Jewish man, the this-worldly and eschatological character of the Jewish world — in these three flashes, the flame gathered, mirror-like, all possible contradictions into its interior as simple contradictions. For in contrast to all earthly flames, it does not simply burn out its warmth by radiating outward. Rather, because eternally feeding on itself, it simultaneously gathers the blaze into its innermost interior as supreme perfervid fire. And by thus gathering its blaze inwardly, it in turn smelts the blazing, flashing contradictions more and more into a unitary, still glow.

The God of the [Jewish] People

The contradiction between creative power and revealing love is itself still inherent in the original transformation from the concealed God of paganism to the manifest God of revelation. It is Jewish in the narrower sense only in the fitful and unpredictable transitions between his two aspects. In the inner warmth of the Jewish heart, this contradiction is melted down in the invocation of God as "our God

211

and God of our fathers."[22] This God is indistinguishably the God of creation and of revelation. He is not invoked here by his revealed name, but as God in general. Yet as God in general he nonetheless becomes "our" God. And this his quality of being ours is in turn made to root in his very beginning so that the revelation whereby he is our God is based in its own creative origin in the revelation to the Patriarchs. Precisely this whole intricate structure of belief is a perfectly simple emotion in the Jewish heart. It is no ultimate unity; it is not an Outermost which emotion can just barely attain. It is something inner, a simple, inner unity. It is not something supreme; it is the Jew's everyday consciousness of God. So far from being something supreme and ultimate, it is on the contrary something extremely "constricted." The whole constriction of direct, naïve Jewish consciousness consists in this ability to forget that there is anything else in this world, indeed that there is any world outside of the Jewish world and the Jews. Our God and God of our fathers — of what concern is it to the Jew at the moment when he thus invokes God that this God is the "king of the universe,"[23] the One God of the future, as he otherwise again and again says and knows. In this invocation he feels himself entirely alone with him in the most constricted circle, and has lost consciousness of all wiser circles, not perchance because he only has him in the way in which God revealed himself to him and God's creativity thus remains outside for him; no, for the creative power is quite there with him. But the Creator has constructed himself into Creator of the Jewish world, and revelation only occurred to the Jewish heart. The paganism which had been embraced by the ways of Christianity, radiating outward and then radiating back together again, is here left entirely behind, entirely outside. The glow which glows inward knows nothing of the darkness that surrounds the Star on the outside. Jewish feeling has here poured creation and revelation entirely into the most intimate space between God and his people.

The Man of Election

Like God, man too constricts himself for Jewish feeling when this seeks to unite him into a unitary glow out of the dual consciousness, still flaming into one another, of Israel and the Messiah, of the gracious gift of revelation and the redemption of the world. One concept leads from

---

[22] A formula with which a number of Jewish prayers, especially the Standing Prayer (ᶜamidah) begin. —F. A. R.

[23] A standard expression in many benedictions recited on various occasions.

Israel to the Messiah, from the people that stood below Mount Sinai[24] to that day when the house of Jerusalem "shall be called a house of prayer for all peoples."[25] This concept emerged under the prophets and has governed our inner history since then: the remnant. The remnant of Israel, the faithful remnant, the true Israel within the people, this is at every moment the assurance that a bridge connects the two poles. For the rest, Jewish consciousness may well flicker back and forth in hot-blooded transitions between those two poles of life which were determined in the original inner conversion of the secluded man of paganism into the determined and disclosed man of revelation, the poles respectively of the personal discovery of divine love and of the dedicated effectuation of love in the sanctity of conduct. But the remnant represents both at the same time: the assumption of the yoke of the commandment and that of the yoke of the kingdom of heaven.[26] If the Messiah should come "today,"[27] the remnant will be ready to receive him. In defiance of all secular history, Jewish history is the history of this remnant; the word of the prophet, that it "will remain," ever applies to it. All secular history deals with expansion. Power is the basic concept of history because in Christianity revelation began to spread over the world, and thus every expansionist urge, even that which consciously was purely secular, became the unconscious servant of this expansionist movement. But Judaism, and it alone in all the world, maintains itself by subtraction, by contraction, by the formation of ever new remnants. This happens quite extensively in the face of the constant external secession. But it is equally true also within Judaism itself. It constantly divests itself of un-Jewish elements in order to produce out of itself ever new remnants of archetypal Jewish elements. Outwardly it constantly assimilates only to be able again and again to set itself apart on the inside. In Judaism there is no group, no tendency, nay barely an individual who does not regard his manner of sacrificing incidentals in order to hold on to the remnant as the only true way, and himself therefore as the true "remnant of Israel."[28] And so he is. In Judaism, man is always somehow a remnant. He is always somehow a survivor, an inner something, whose exterior was seized by the current

---

[24] Exodus 19:17, understood as meaning literally "standing *underneath* the mountain" in b. Shab. 88a and Av. Zarah 2b: God lifted up Mount Sinai and held it over the assembled people, threatening them with destruction if they should refuse to accept the Torah. —F. A. R.

[25] Isaiah 56:7: for my house shall be called a house of prayer for all peoples.

[26] Cf. m. Ber. 2:2.

[27] Cf. b. Sanh. 98a.

[28] Cf. Isaiah 11:11.

of the world and carried off while he himself, what is left of him, remains standing on the shore. Something within him is waiting. And he has something within himself. What he is waiting for and what he has he may call by different names; often enough he may barely be able to name it. But he has a feeling that both the waiting and the having are most intimately connected with each other. And this is just that feeling of the "remnant" which has the revelation and awaits the salvation. The strange questions which, according to tradition, will one day be presented to the Jew by the divine judge, indicate these two aspects of the feeling. The first, "Have you derived sentence from sentence?" means: was the consciousness alive in you that whatever may happen to you was somehow already given to you before birth in the gift of revelation? And the other, "Have you awaited salvation?"[29] means that pointing toward the future advent of the kingdom which is placed in our blood at birth. In this duo-unity of feeling, man has thus wholly constricted himself into Jewish man. Once more the paganism which was embraced by the divergent and finally reconverging ways of Christianity lies outside in the darkness. Jewish man is wholly by himself. The future which otherwise weighs so heavily on his soul has here fallen silent. In the feeling of being the remnant, his heart is wholly at one in itself. There the Jew is Jew alone. The revelation which was his, the redemption for which he has been summoned, both have completely merged in the constricted space between him and his people.

The World of Law

And like God and man, so the world too becomes quite intimately constricted for Jewish feeling so soon as it seeks to escape into the unity of a worldly existence from the flame flickering restlessly back and forth between this world and the world to come. That the world, this world, is created and withal in need of the future redemption is a dual idea whose disquieting character is quieted in the unity of the law. Though as content of revelation and claim on the individual it is commandment, seen as world it is law. The law, then, in its multiplicity and strength ordering everything, comprising everything "external," that is all the life of this world, everything that any worldly jurisdiction may conceivably comprise, this law makes this world and the world to come indistinguishable. God himself, according to Rabbinic legend, "studies" in the

---

[29] B. Shab. 31a: Rava said: When a man is led in for judgment [in the world to come] he will be asked: "...have you hoped for salvation? ...have you deduced one thing from another [in study]?"

law.[30] For in the law everything of this world that is comprised in it, all created existence, is already given life and soul directly as content of the world to come. Jewish feeling is oblivious to the fact that the law is only Jewish law, that this finished and redeemed world is only a Jewish world, and that the God who rules the world has more to do than merely to study in the law, and this quite apart from whether the law is meant in its traditional sense or whether the old concept has been filled with new life. For even in the latter case, Jewish feeling takes only this world for unfinished, while it takes for finished and unalterable the law that it presumes to impose on this world so that it might be transformed into the world to come. Even if the law appears in the highly modern garb of some contemporary Utopianism, the law then stands in sharp contrast to that Christian lack of law which can and wants to be taken by surprise, which still distinguished the Christian-turned-politician from the Jew-turned-Utopian, and which endows the latter with the greater power to shake up, the former with the greater readiness to attain. The Jew always thinks that what counts is only to turn his legal doctrines this way and that; sooner or later it would turn out to have "everything in it" [m. Avot 5:22]. The law turns its back on the paganism which Christianity embraces, it knows nothing of it and does not wish to know anything of it. The idea of the transition from this world into the world to come, the idea of the messianic age which is suspended over life as a Today[31] that is ever to be awaited, this idea coalesces here and becomes an everyday object as the Law in the obedience to which the seriousness of that transition recedes, the more complete the obedience. For precisely the How of the transition is already determined. The life of the pious man, like that of God in the legend, may now also be exhausted in the ever more complete "study" of the law. The whole world, that which is created for existence as well as that which is still to be endowed with soul, and which grows toward redemption, is combined into one by his feeling, and poured into the intimately familiar space between the law and his people, the people of the law.

The Jewish Dangers
Everything twofold, everything internally all-comprehending within Jewish life has thus become very constricted and simple for this innermost of Jewish feelings. One would have to say too simple and too constricted, and one would need to detect dangers in this constriction as

---

[30]Cf. b. Av. Zarah 3b: Rabbi Judah said in the name of Rav: The Day has twelve hours; for the first three hours the Holy One, blessed be He, sits and busies himself with [the study of] the Torah.
[31]Cf. b. Sanh. 98a.

much as in the Christian latitude. If the concept of God was threatened there, his world and his man appear to be in danger here. By radiating apart to the outside, Christianity threatens to lose itself in individual rays far from the divine nucleus of truth. By glowing toward the inside, Judaism threatened to gather its warmth to its own bosom, far away from the pagan reality of the world. If there the dangers were spiritualization of God, humanization of God, secularization of God — here they are denial of the world, disdain of the world, mortification of the world. It was denial of the world if the Jew, in the proximity of his God, felt himself anticipating redemption, and forgot that God is Creator and Revealer, that as Creator he supports the entire world, and that as Revealer he ultimately does turn his countenance to man as such. It was disdain of the world for the Jew to regard himself as the remnant, and thus as the true man, originally created in the image of man and awaiting the end in this original purity, thereby withdrawing from the very man to whom befell, in his God-forsaken obduracy, the revelation of divine love, and who now had to act out this love in the limitless work of redemption. Finally it was mortification of the world if the Jew, possessed of the law which had been revealed to him and had become flesh and blood in his spirit, now dared venture to regulate the existence of things, renewed at every moment, and their silent growth, or even but to judge them. All three of these dangers are the necessary consequences of an inwardness turned away from the world, as those of Christianity are the consequence of an externalization of the self turned toward the world. For the Jew it is essential to encase himself thus. It is the last step in that internalization,[32] that rooting in his own self, whence he draws the strength of eternal life, just as that evanescence is, for the Christian, the necessary consequence of his unimpeded egress and progress on the eternal way.

Harmlessness of the Dangers

But this rootedness in one's own self is nevertheless something entirely different from the Christian externalization of the self. Granted, for the individual personality our self-encasement may represent a grave danger while the Christian personality need hardly suffer from those dangers of Christianity. But in truth our dangers represent no danger at all for us in the final analysis. For here it turns out that the Jew simply cannot descend into his own interior without at the same time ascending to the Highest. This is, in fact, the profoundest difference between Jewish and Christian man: the Christian is by nature or at least by birth —

---

[32] A pun on the German word *Erinnerung* used by Hegel to signify "internalization" in addition to its usual meaning, "remembrance." —*F. A. R.*

a pagan; the Jew, however, is a Jew. Thus the way of the Christian must be a way of self-externalization, of self-renunciation;[33] he must always take leave of himself, must forfeit himself in order to become a Christian. The life of the Jew, on the other hand, must precisely not lead him out of himself; he must rather live his way ever deeper into himself. The more he finds himself the more he turns his back on paganism, which for him is on the outside not, as with the Christian, on the inside; the more, that is, he becomes Jewish. For though he is born a Jew, his "Jewishness" is something which he too must first live and experience for himself, something which becomes wholly visible in looks and traits only in the aged Jew. The type of the aged Jew is as characteristic for us as the youthful type is for the Christian nations. For Christian life de-nationalizes the Christian, but Jewish life leads the Jew deeper into his Jewish character.

Jewish Life in the Mystery of the Highest

Thus the Jew internalizes himself into his interior only for the sake of his Most High, for God's sake. And therewith those dangers now prove to be dangerous at most to him as individual. He can, that is, become hard, say, or proud or rigid. But they are no dangers to Judaism. To set up his God, his man, his world as God, man, world in general are three ways of turning his back on the exterior, of turning inward to the interior, practiced respectively on God, man, and the world. But this triple fanning of the flames of his Jewish sentiment is not itself an Ultimate; it does not end there. These are not, like God, world, and man in paganism, three points devoid of relation and order. Between these last three elements, rather, there courses a connecting current, an orbit, that is, comparable to that on which the elements of paganism entered into the relationship which led from creation via revelation to redemption. And in this interconnection, the apparently exclusively-Jewish aspect of this three-fold sentiment, apparently constricted and exclusive and isolated, now closes ranks again into the one all-illuminating stellar image of truth.

The Tale of the Chariot

Jewish mysticism bridges the gap between the "God of our Fathers" and the "Law" in a manner all its own. It replaces the general concept of creation with that of the mysterious creation, the "tale of the chariot"[34] as it is called in an allusion to the vision of Ezekiel. There the created

---

[33] Both meanings are inherent in the original's *Selbstentäusserung.* —Tr.

[34] *Ma^{c}aseh merkavah* and *ma^{c}aseh bereshit* are the terms for the esoteric topics based on the description of the divine Throne-Chariot described in Ezekiel 1, and the story of Creation in Genesis 1:1–2:3, first used in m. Ḥagigah 2:1 and passages of the Tosefta, Babylonian, and Palestinian Talmud dealing with this Mishnah. Jewish mysticism both in antiquity,

world itself is full of mysterious relations to the law, and the law is not alienated from this world but the key to this enigma of the world. The plain wording of the law conceals a hidden meaning which expressed nothing so much as the essence of the world. For the Jew, the book of the law can thus, as it were, replace the book of nature or even the starry heavens from which the men of yore once thought they could interpret terrestrial matters by intelligible omens. That is the basic idea of countless legends with which Judaism expands the apparently constricted world of its law into the whole world, and on the other hand, precisely because it finds this world presaged in its law, already sees the world-to-come in it. All modes of exegesis are pressed into service, especially of course that infinitely applicable one of numerology and reading the letters in accordance with their numerical values. One hardly knows where to begin to give examples. The seventy offerings of Tabernacles [Num. 19:12–38] are offered for the seventy "nations of the world" — as counted by legend[35] on the basis of the Tabula Gentium in Genesis [chap. 10]. The number of the bones of the human body are juxtaposed to the numerical value of a passage in the prayer book so that the words of the psalmist be fulfilled and all bones praise the Eternal.[36] The revealed name of God is concealed in the words which recount the completion of creation. One could continue endlessly. In itself, this biblical exegesis appears peculiar and even ridiculous to the observer unaccustomed to it. But its sense is none other than that the entire creation is interpolated between the Jewish God and the Jewish law, and that God and his law thereby both prove to be equally all-embracing as — creation.

The Wanderings of the Shekhina

Mysticism bridges the gap between the "God of our Fathers" and the "Remnant of Israel" with the doctrine of the Shekhina. The Shekhina, God's descent upon man and his sojourn among men, is pictured as a dichotomy taking place in God himself. God himself separates himself from himself, he gives himself away to his people, he shares in their sufferings,[37] set forth with them into the agony of exile, joins their wanderings.[38] The Torah was thought to have been created prior to the

---

the Middle Ages, and thereafter, has developed its views on theosophy, ecstasy, theurgy, and cosmogony as explications of these two *topoi.* —F. A. R.

[35]Cf. b. Sukkah 55b.

[36]Cf. Midr. Tanhuma to Leviticus 19:2 and Psalm 35:10.

[37]Cf. Psalm 91:15 and Ex. R. 115 ad loc.

[38]Cf. b. Meg. 29a: R. Simeon ben Yoḥai said: Come and see how precious Israel is to the Holy One, blessed be He; every place to which they were exiled the Shekhinah was with them. Cf. Moshe Idel's interpretation of this passage in his essay "Franz Rosenzweig and

world,[39] and the world for its part on behalf of the Torah;[40] in this conception, the law had become, for Jewish feelings, more than just the Jewish law; it was really sensed as a fundamental pillar of the world, and even the notion that God himself studies his law thus now gained a general, supra-Jewish sense. Just so the pride of the "remnant of Israel" now arrives, in the concept of the Shekhina, at a more general implication. For the sufferings of this remnant, the constant requirement to separate and exclude oneself, all this now becomes a suffering for God's sake, and the remnant is the bearer of this suffering. The idea of the wanderings of the Shekhina, of the sparks of the original divine light being scattered about the world, this casts all of revelation between the Jewish God and Jewish man, and thereby anchors both, God as well as the remnant, in all the depth of — revelation. In mysticism, the expansion of the Jewish to the universal occurred to creation by means of that multiplicity of meanings and interpretations of the Law. In the same mysticism it occurs to revelation by means of the profound insight which detects in God's self-dedication to Israel a divine suffering which really should not be permitted, and in Israel's separating itself into a remnant the establishment of a dwelling-place for the exiled God. Precisely this divine suffering marks the relationship between God and Israel as constricted, as too slight. Nothing would be more natural for the "God of our Fathers" than that he should "sell" himself for Israel and share its suffering fate. But by doing so, God himself puts himself in need of redemption. In this suffering, therefore, the relationship between God and the remnant points beyond itself.

The Uniting of God

But the redemption would then have to occur in the relationship of the "remnant" to the "law." How is this relationship conceived? What does fulfilling the law mean to the Jew? How does he conceive it? Why does he fulfill it? For the sake of heavenly reward? "Be not as the servants who serve their masters for the sake of the reward" [m. Avot 1:3]. For the sake of earthly satisfaction? "Say not: I do not like pork; say rather: I like it well enough, but my Father in heaven has forbidden it" [Sifra to Lev. 20:26, Weiss ed., 93d]. The Jew, however, fulfills the endless customs

---

the Kabbalah" in *The Philosophy of Franz Rosenzweig*, Paul Mendes-Flohr, ed. (Hanover and London: University Press of New England, 1988), esp. 165–167. —F. A. R.

[39]B. Pes. 54a where the Torah is numbered among the seven things created before even the world was created. Cf. G. Scholem, "The Meaning of the Torah in Jewish Mysticism," in *On the Kabbalah and Its Symbolism*, chap. 2 (London, 1965). —F. A. R.

[40]Cf. Gen. R. 1:1 (Theodor ed., 1:2.).

and precepts "for the sake of uniting the holy God and his Shekhina."[41] With this formula, the individual, the remnant, prepares his heart, "in awe and love," to fulfill, "in the name of all Israel" whatever command- ment is at the moment incumbent on him. He will gather the glory of God, dispersed all over the world in countless sparks, out of the disper- sion and one day bring it back home to Him who has been stripped of his glory. Every one of his deeds, every fulfilling of a commandment, achieves a portion of this reunion. To confess God's unity — the Jew calls it: to unify God. For this unity is as it becomes, it is Becoming Unity. And this Becoming is enjoined on the soul and hands of man. Jewish man and Jewish law — nothing less than the process of redemption, embracing God, world, and man, transpires between the two. The ful- filling of the commandment is inaugurated and stamped as an act which brings redemption nearer, with a formula in which the individual ele- ments, such as they are absorbed into this last One, once more resound individually: the "holy God" who has given the law, the "Shekhina" which he expropriated from himself to the remnant of Israel, the "awe" with which this remnant turned itself into the dwelling-place of God, the "love" with which he thereupon proceeded to fulfill the law, he the individual, the "I" which fulfills the law, yet he "in the name of all Israel" to which the law was given and which was created through the law. The most constricted has all expanded into the whole, the All, nay better: has redeemed itself for the unification of the One. The descent into the Innermost has disclosed itself as an ascent to the Highest. The merely Jewish feeling has been transfigured into world-redemptive truth. In the innermost constriction of the Jewish heart there shines the Star of Redemption.

Christian Eschatology

Here the Star blazes. The Ultimate, the Innermost, the apparently con- stricted and rigid nature of emotion is set in motion. It coalesces into a structure illuminating the world. By comprehending God, world, and man via creation and revelation through to redemption, it expressed the content of Judaism; now it likewise also illuminates the Innermost of the Jewish soul. Thus the Star of Redemption is the image of being, but it continues to glow also in the inner sanctum of emotion. That is here very different than in Christianity. There too the Star of Redemption

---

[41]Cf. Gershom G. Scholem, *On the Kabbalah and its Symbolism* (London, 1963), 108f. for an exposition on the doctrine of redemption as the reunion of God and his *Shekhinah*. The formula expressing the intention to bring this about became a standard pronouncement accompanying the fulfillment of nearly every religious act. Cf. also Louis Jacobs, *Hasidic Prayer* (London and New York, 1973), chap. 12. —F. A. R.

designates the content, the inner being, whence it radiates outward into the world of reality as something real. But these rays reunite at three disparate points, at true end points, points which are also goals for emotion. And these points can no longer be interconnected. Mysticism can no longer bridge the gap between these outermost prospects of emotion. That God is spirit stands isolated from the notion that he is all-in-all, and also from the notion that the Son who is the way is also the truth. The idea of creation does not mediate between the former disjointedness, nor that of revelation between the latter. At the most a certain connection is established in mythological images such as that of the "spirit hovering over the waters" [Gen. 1:2] or the pouring out of the spirit in the Johannine baptism [Matt. 3:16]. But this remains image; it does not merge into an emotional unity. Only between the two last ideas, the divinity of the Son and the promise that God will be All-in-All, does a bridge arch. The first theologian of the new religion[42] teaches that the Son, when once all will have submitted to him, will turn over his dominion to the Father, and then God will be All-in-All. But one can see at once that this is a theologism. For Christian piety it is meaningless. It depicts a distant, far distant future. It deals with the last things by explicitly depriving them of all influence on time. For the dominion belongs to the Son, as yet and for all time, and God is not All-in-All. It depicts an eternity wholly beyond time. And thus this sentence has never meant more in the history of Christianity than precisely — a theologism, an idea. It was not and could not be a bridge on which emotion might move to and fro between one shore and the other. The two shores were structurally too diverse for this, the one too exclusively temporal, the other too exclusively eternal. True, it was an idea that the Son of Man would one day turn over his dominion, but this does not alter the fact that, within time, he was deified. True, it was an idea that God would one day be All-in-All, but this does not alter the fact that he was granted precious little influence on the Aught-in-Aught of this temporality where his *locum tenens* was lord. Emotion did not step on the bridge. Here as everywhere it confined itself to the individual points in which it gathered its last rapture. The rapture did not carry further than these end and gathering points. Christianity has produced spiritualistic, individualistic, and pantheistic mysticism, but these three did not enter into a mutual relationship. Emotion can find satisfaction in any one of the three, just as a discrete form of the Church corresponds to each of them, and none is made superfluous by the other two. Emotion everywhere attains its goal. And well it may. For where it attains its goal, there a piece of the protocosmos is renewed in

---

[42]Paul (cf. note 20).

death and resurrection: dead is the myth and resurrected in the venera-
tion of the Spirit, dead is the hero and resurrected in the word from the
cross, dead is the cosmos and resurrected in the one-and-universal All
of the kingdom. That these three, each in itself, imply an attenuation of
the truth or, more precisely, that God is Lord of the Spirits [Num. 16:22],
not Spirit, giver of sufferings [b. Qid. 40b] and not the crucified one, one
and not All-in-All — who would want to raise such objections to a faith
which marches triumphantly through the world and for which the gods
of the nations — national myth, national hero, national cosmos — are
no match? Who would indeed!

The Law of Verification: Theology

The Meaning of Bifurcation

And withal: the Jew does it. Not with words, for what would words
still avail in this realm of vision! But with his existence, his silent existence. This existence of the Jew constantly subjects Christianity to the
idea that it is not attaining the goal, the truth, that it ever remains —
on the way.[43] That is the profoundest reason for the Christian hatred of the Jew, which is heir to the pagan hatred of the Jew. In the
final analysis it is only self-hate, directed to the objectionable mute
admonisher, for all that he but admonishes by his existence; it is hatred of one's own imperfection, one's own not-yet. By his inner unity,
by the fact that in the narrowest confines of his Jewishness the Star
of Redemption nonetheless still burns, the Jew involuntarily shames
the Christian, who is driven outwards and onwards, to the utter dis-
sipation of the original fire, into the outermost reaches of emotion, an
emotion which no longer knows of a whole in which it might find itself at one with every other emotion to a truth beyond all feeling, but
rather an emotion which itself was already blissful. The uttermost in
Christianity is this complete losing oneself in the individual emotion,
this immersion, be it in the divine spirit, the divine man, the divine
world. No current of action any longer runs between these emotions;
they themselves already stand beyond all action. True, that attenuation of emotion is essential, just as its constriction is in Judaism. But
whereas the latter finds its resolution in Jewish life itself, in the world-
redemptive meaning of a life-in-the-law, the former, the attenuation, no
longer finds its resolution in any life, since it itself is already an uttermost
experience.

---

[43]Cf. Rosenzweig's letter to Eugen Rosenstock of November 7–9, 1916, above, p. 179f.
—F. A. R.

The Eternal Protest of the Jew

If, therefore, the Christian did not have the Jew at his back he would lose his way wherever he was, just as the three Churches which, after all, are none other than the earthly domiciles of those ultimate three emotions, experience their affinity through the Jew; without him they might at most know it but not feel it. The Jew forces on Christianity the knowledge that that emotional satisfaction remains denied to it. The Jew sanctified his flesh and blood under the yoke of the law,[44] and thereby lives constantly in the reality of the heavenly kingdom; the Christian's constantly pro-fane flesh and blood sets itself in opposition to redemption, and he learns that he himself is not permitted to anticipate redemption emotionally. By anticipating redemption, the Jew purchases the possession of truth with the loss of the unredeemed world; he gives the lie to the Christian who, on his march of conquest into the unredeemed world, has to purchase his every forward step with illusion.

The Two Testaments

Christianity is well aware of this relationship, of the dependence of its own development on the existence — and no more than the existence — of Judaism. It was always the hidden enemies of Christianity, from the Gnostics to the present day, who wanted to deprive it of its "Old Testament." A God who was only spirit, and no longer the Creator who gave his law to the Jews, a Christ who was only Christ and no longer Jesus, a world which was only All and its center no longer the Holy Land — though it would no longer offer the slightest resistance to deification and divinization, there would be nothing left in them to recall the soul from the dream of this deification into unredeemed life; the soul would not just get lost, it would remain lost. And the mere Book would not render this service to Christianity, or rather: it renders this service only because it is not mere book, because our life is living testimony that it is more than a mere book. The historical Jesus must always pull out from under the feet of the ideal Christ the pedestal on which his philosophic or na-tionalistic worshipers would like to set him. For an "idea" can after all be united with any theory or self-conceit to lend it its own halo. But the historical Jesus, that is precisely Jesus Christ in the dogmatic sense, does not stand on a pedestal; he really walks the streets of life and forces life to submit at his glance. It is exactly the same with the "spiritual" God in whom all those believe gladly and easily who hesitate to believe in Him "who created the world that he might reign over it." In his spirituality, that spiritual God is a very agreeable partner who leaves us entirely free

---

[44]Cf. m. Avot 3:5.

to dispose of a world which is not "purely spiritual" and thus not his but consequently presumably the devil's. And this world itself — how gladly one would like to regard it as All, and oneself as the gloriously irresponsible "speck of dust in the All," rather than as its responsible center about which everything rotates or as the pillar on whose stability the world rests.

The Eternal Hatred for the Jew

It is always the same. And as that ever-present struggle of the Gnostics shows, it is the Old Testament which enables Christianity to withstand this its own danger, and the Old Testament only because it is more than mere book. A mere book would easily fall victim to the arts of allegorical exegesis. Had the Jews of the Old Testament disappeared from the earth like Christ, they would [now] denote the idea of the People, and Zion the idea of the Center of the World, just as Christ denotes the idea of Man. But the stalwart, undeniable vitality of the Jewish people, attested in the very hatred of the Jews, resists such "idealizing." Whether Christ is more than an idea — no Christian can know it. But that Israel is more than an idea, that he knows, that he sees. For we live. We are eternal,[45] not as an idea may be eternal: if we are eternal, it is in full reality. For the Christian we are thus the really indubitable. The pastor [Christian Fürchtegott Gellert] who was asked for the proof of Christianity by Frederick the Great argued conclusively when he answered: "Your majesty, the Jews!" The Christians can have no doubts about us. Our existence stands surety for their truth. That is why, from the Christian point of view, it follows logically that Paul should let the Jews remain to the end — till "the fullness of the peoples shall have come in" [Rom. 11:25], that is, to that moment when the Son shall return the dominion to the Father. The theologism from the beginnings of Christian theology enunciates what we have here explained: that Judaism, by its eternal endurance through all time, the Judaism attested in the "Old" Testament and itself attesting livingly to it, that this is the One Nucleus whose glow provides invisible nourishment to the rays which, in Christianity, burst visibly and divisibly into the night of the pagan proto- and hypocosmos.

The Meaning of Verification

Before God, then, Jew and Christian both labor at the same task. He cannot dispense with either. He has set enmity between the two for all

---

[45] A statement inspired by the words that Rosenzweig's teacher, the philosopher Hermann Cohen, exclaimed when he concluded his last lecture on "Plato and the Prophets" in Berlin on January 7, 1918: "But we [the Jews] are eternal!" (cf. Rosenzweig's Introduction to Cohen's *Jüdische Schriften*, vol. 1 [Berlin, 1924], lxii). —F. A. R.

time, and withal has most intimately bound each to each. To us [Jews] he gave eternal life[46] by kindling the fire of the Star of his truth in our hearts. Them [the Christians] he set on the eternal way by causing them to pursue the rays of that Star of his truth for all time unto the eternal end. We [Jews] thus espy in our hearts the true image of the truth, yet on the other hand we turn our backs on temporal life, and the life of the times turns away from us. They [the Christians], for their part, run after the current of time, but the truth remains at their back; though led by it, since they follow its rays, they do not see it with their eyes. The truth, the whole truth, thus belongs neither to them nor to us. For we too, though we bear it within us, must for that very reason first immerse our glance into our own interior if we would see it, and there, while we see the Star, we do not see — the rays. And the whole truth would demand not only seeing its light but also what was illuminated by it. They [the Christians], however, are in any event already destined for all time to see what is illuminated, and not the light.

And thus we both have but a part of the whole truth. But we know that it is in the nature of truth to be im-parted, and that a truth in which no one had a part would be no truth. The "whole" truth, too, is truth only because it is God's part. Thus it does not detract from the truth, nor from us, that it is only partially ours. A direct view of the whole truth is granted only to him who sees it in God. That, however, is a view beyond life. A living view of the truth, a view that is at the same time life, can become ours too only from out the immersion into our own Jewish heart and even there only in image and likeness. As for the Christians, they are denied a living view altogether for the sake of a living effectiveness of the truth. Thus both of us, they as much as we, we as much as they, are creatures precisely for the reason that we do not see the whole truth. Just for this we remain within the boundaries of mortality. Just for this we — remain. And remain we would. We want to live. God does for us what we want for so long as we want it. As long as we cling to life, he gives us life. Of the truth he gives us only what we, as living creatures, can bear, that is our portion.[47] Were he to give us more, to give us his portion, the whole truth, he would be hoisting us beyond the boundaries of humanity.[48] But precisely as long as he does not do this, just so long

---

[46]Cf. the benediction after reading from the Torah: "Eternal life He has planted in our midst" (m. Soferim 13:8).

[47]Cf. Ex. R. 29: 1 on Ps. 29:4 and Pesiqta derav Kahana, ed. Mandelbaum I, 224; English translation by W. G. Braude and I. J. Kapstein (Philadelphia, 1975), 249f.

[48]An allusion to Goethe's poem "Grenzen der Menschheit" (Limits of humanity, 1781). Our first selection from Book 3 of *The Star of Redemption* bears the title. Now near the end, words and motifs from this poem are again employed, though with meanings that differ

we too harbor no desire for it. We cling to our creatureliness. We do not gladly relinquish it. And our creatureliness is determined by the fact that we only take part, only are part. Life had celebrated the ultimate triumph over death in the Truly with which it verifies the personally vouchsafed truth imparted to it as its portion in eternal truth. With this Truly, the creature fastens itself to its portion which was imparted to it. In this Truly, it is creature. This Truly passes as a mute mystery through the whole chain of beings; it acquires speech in man. And in the Star it flares up into the visible, self-illuminating existence. But it remains ever within the boundaries of creatureliness. Truth itself still says Truly when it steps before God. But God himself no longer says Truly. He is beyond all that can be imparted, he is above even the whole, for this too is but a part with him; even above the Whole, he is the One.

---

from Goethe's more "pagan" intentions. They are used to point out the tension between the Biblical and Rabbinic expressions of God as the "alpha and omega" whose seal is Truth as the whole (*'mt*) (Isa. 44:6; b. Shab. 55a) and the fact that human beings participate in the truth existentially as it is imparted to them as Jews or Christians. The following quotations from the Goethe poem will show that Rosenzweig had them clearly in mind, though giving them a changed meaning:

> For with gods
> No man should ever
> Dare to measure himself . . .
> What then distinguishes Gods from men?
> That many waves
> Before them move,
> An eternal stream:
> Us the wave gathers,
> Us the wave swallows,
> And we sink.
>
> A little ring
> Confines our life
> And many generations
> Link up, enduring
> On their existence's
> Endless chain.

(Adapted from Vernon Watkins's translation in J. W. von Goethe, *Selected Poems*, ed. Christopher Middleton, vol. 1 [Boston: Suhrkamp/Insel, 1987], 83–85). —F.A.R.

3

A Note on
Anthropomorphism

1928

...History has shown that "anthropomorphism" is the protective wall for safeguarding "monotheism."[1] Or rather, to use more explicit language, it has shown that, failing the courage to attribute one's genuinely perceived experiences of God to their genuine and immediate source in God, these experiences assume an independent existence and seek for themselves their own supporting entity or entities alongside God Himself whom they had assumed incapable of sustaining them. The farther into the distance God is banished, the more permissible it seems for man to populate with demi-gods and godlings that space between himself and God which is so full of the currents of divine energy.

The ancient translations, from the Septuagint to the Targums, document the first period of an internal Jewish struggle with Biblical "anthropomorphism." It is of course no coincidence, in light of what has been said, that this is the period which gave birth to Christianity. Philo's Logos was the necessary corollary to his spiritualized God. The gospel of the Logos enunciated the statement "God is Spirit" [John 4:24], a proposition that was fateful to Christianity because of the temptation to turn it

---

[1]The best commentary on this "Note" is found in Professor Moshe Idel's article "Franz Rosenzweig and the Kabbalah" in *The Philosophy of Franz Rosenzweig*, ed. Paul Mendes-Flohr (Hanover, N.H. and London, 1988), esp. 169–171. —F. A. R.

on its head. And inasmuch as Paul was the first Jew to have viewed the God of the Bible as the God of harsh and merciless justice — incomprehensible to us even now! — it was inevitable that he would associate the Mediator with that divine love which, based on his own experience, he could hardly have denied. Judaism saved itself from the two extremes of the Hellenistic-Jewish spirit-god and the Judaeo-Christian god-man by taking refuge in the daring "anthropomorphisms" of the Talmudic aggadah, i.e., in the unshakable certitude that everything we experience of God comes indeed from Him. It is to this certainty, along with the Law and study, that we owe our continued existence as Jews.

Both the Hellenistic spiritualization of God, as well as the Christian humanization of God which responded to it, occurred on the border between Israel and the nations; in the second period of struggle with "anthropomorphism" both word and response took place within Israel itself. Medieval Jewish religious philosophy was called into action as a response to the grotesque aberration of early Kabbalah — a classical, purely Jewish case of a genuine, i.e., representational, anthropomorphism (without quotation marks) — which attempted to quantify and measure the "shape" of God. The philosophical reaction culminated in Maimonides' effort — successful as far as possible within Judaism — to codify dogmatically the "incorporeality" of God. Then came the rejoinder from the classical and late Kabbalah. Having acquired from religious philosophy the concept of the Godhead as totally without qualities and defined only negatively — in the language of Kabbalah, "*En Sof*," the Absolute — it discovered below this highest degree an increasingly colorful heavenly throng of lower and intermediate degrees.

Since the beginning of the Emancipation, Judaism finds itself in the third period of its struggle with "anthropomorphism." This time the struggle is linked to precisely those latest excesses of Kabbalah. Living in the midst of this period, we cannot yet give a definite historical answer. But from personal experience I would suggest that it is given through the outstanding Jews who converted to Christianity in the nineteenth, and alas the twentieth century as well.[2] . . .

---

[2]Since the Emancipation Jewish theology, reacting to the excesses of Kabbalah, denied those elements of the tradition which had given Judaism vitality and "religious availability," to use Whitehead's term. Against this background of a watered-down and abstract version of the ancestral faith he explains the phenomenon of some outstanding Jewish personalities adopting the Christian religion to satisfy their quest for a living faith. —F. A. R.

4

The Significance of the Bible
in World History

1929

It will always be futile to attempt to explain the unique position claimed
for the Bible in its very name of Bible, the Book, on the grounds of the
quality of its content. For to apply a superlative to a book because of content presupposes dogmatic prejudice. Mohammedanism, for instance,
dogmatically states that the Koran is the most beautiful of all books. The
only way in which the scholar can grasp and prove the significance of
the Bible is by its effect and its destiny: namely, by its effect on, and its
destiny in, the course of world history.

Their very first encounters, springing from war or from trade relations,
establish certain spiritual contacts among peoples, without however
creating between them a world historical bond. For this, more than a
haphazard flow of influences is required; the creation of such a bond demands the conscious transfer into one's sphere of something recognized
as alien; in other words, it requires *translation*. The historical moment of
the birth of world literature, and hence of supernational consciousness,
occurred, in the full light of history, with two events, one of which was
only symptomatic while the other had constitutive significance as well. It
came when two books, each the very foundation of its national literature,
were first translated into another language. At just about the same time,
a prisoner of war in Rome translated the Odyssey from Greek into Latin,

and Jewish settlers in Alexandria translated the Book of their people into Greek. Whatever unity of spirit and purpose exists on the five continents of this earth today derives from the fusion of these two events, and the consequences thereof, events originally related only because in them the Greeks played the double role of giving and taking.

The origin of the Greek Bible falls between the beginning of the movement that tried to bring Judaism to other peoples and the ebb of that movement before one that was stronger, one that, while accepting the Jewish Bible as its ever present foundation, regarded it merely as the "old" Testament. And from this time on we must distinguish between the direct effects of the Jewish Bible, and the indirect effects springing from its fusion — technical as well as chemical — with the New Testament. Viewed from the standpoint of world history, the former effects are sporadic, no matter how strong they may be at certain junctures, while the latter constitute the indispensable mortar that cements world history into a whole.

Let us first discuss the direct effect. Even that is not direct in the true meaning of the word, for every return to the Jewish Bible occurs with reference to the New Testament, though often in a spirit of opposition. Here we have a more or less deliberate, though rarely fundamental, return to the "Law." Wherever the demands of Christian communal life were not satisfied by the all too primitive model community described in the Acts of the Apostles and in the Epistles, or by the critical attitude toward the world pronounced in the Gospels (critical in both the social and moral aspects), it was — and still is — natural to revert to the Old Testament, to law born of prophecy. The Christian church, the Christian state, Christian economics, and Christian society could not and cannot be established upon the New Testament, which sees the world only in crisis, only face to face with Judgment. In contrast to the pointed paradoxes of the New Testament, the Jewish Bible, sprung from the richness of the life of a whole people, of a whole national literature, offered a solid ground for building the world, and for building in the world, in that its faith in creation was both living and profound — even within the sphere of prophetic criticism and polemics. And so, just because of the manifold origins of the Book, the various edifices could be as different, even opposed to one another, as the various sides and aspects of national life; monarchists and monarchomachists, churches and sects, popes and heretics, reactionaries and revolutionists, protectors of property rights and social reformers, war-enthusiasts and pacifists could and can, did and do, cite the Book as their authority.

But its indirect effect by way of the New Testament is far more important than all these influences and references. The New Testament writings originated in protest against the Jewish Bible, in the belief that salvation had come, that "the time was full," a belief whose burning fervor condensed the long-breathed hope for redemption to a brief span. That Christianity could persist after "this generation" has passed away, while "this world" did not come to an end; or, to express it in terms of Bible history, that the New Testament writings became the canonical New Testament — this Christianity and the New Testament owe to their bond with Judaism. For the way back to the still persisting Creation could be found only if the God of Genesis and he "who has spoken through the prophets" was the same as the one invoked in the Lord's Prayer and not, as the Gnostics claimed, an old God dethroned by the God of a new era. Connection with the created world — this and nothing less is at stake for Christianity both in the theological identification expressed in the dogma of the Trinity and in the identifying of the "word" that "was God" with the Messiah from David's stem. It is no mere chance that in the struggle for these identifications, in this struggle against Marcion's "alien God" — and this "alien" means alien to the Old Covenant — the church created her canon of the New Testament as a counterpart to the Old Testament. This counterpart was not, however, intended to supersede the Old Testament, but only to supplement and outrange it. Whatever cultural strength Christianity has displayed in the two millennia since then, and cultural strength here implies strength to become integrated in the world and to integrate the world into itself, is due to the effort to retain *its* Old Testament.

And so it is no longer a problem of conscious references to the Jewish Bible, or of relationships that could be traced or proved in detail, but of the entire sphere of whatever — in any degree — might be called a cultural effect of Christianity. What matters here is that Christianity has been able to synthesize with the world. What matters is the fruitful tension of such syntheses, which has given Christian Europe her spiritual dominance in the world. Nothing is altered by the fact that Christianity itself has always regarded this tension as a torment it wished to evade. If Christianity ever succeeded in its perpetual attempt to escape from the limitations and strangeness of the Old Testament into the wide region of philosophy or the circumscribed pale of nationalism [*völkische Nähe*], then Christendom would come to an end, and with it the Bible's including the Jewish Bible's participation in world history. For while the course of the one world history that began with this Book may change its protagonists, it cannot lose connection with its origin and each successive step of its development. This connection is precisely what we call world history. No future can undo the past, just as no past can prevent the coming of that which is to come.

231

It is quite possible that the secularization of religious communities, which began a hundred and fifty years ago, will march on, and that church and synagogue in the old traditional sense will persist only for a small nucleus, while a worldly agent, the "church people," or, in our case, the "Jewish people," will become the general community. If this should take place, the significance of the Holy Scriptures would not lessen but would even grow — as has already been shown both by church and synagogue in the last century and a half. When dogma and Law cease to be the all-embracing frame of the community and serve only as props from within, the Scriptures must not merely fulfil the task of all Scriptures: to establish a connection between generations; they must also assume another which is likewise incumbent on all Scriptures: they must guarantee the connection between the center and the periphery of the community. Thus, even if church and synagogue no longer flanked the portal on the road of humanity,[1] the Bible would still continue to stand ready, so that humanity could consult it about this very road, "turn its pages again and again," and find "everything in it."[2]

---

[1]See the illustration on p. 168.
[2]Quoted from the Sayings of the Fathers (Avot 5:22).

Will Herberg (1901–1977)

Courtesy of Drew University

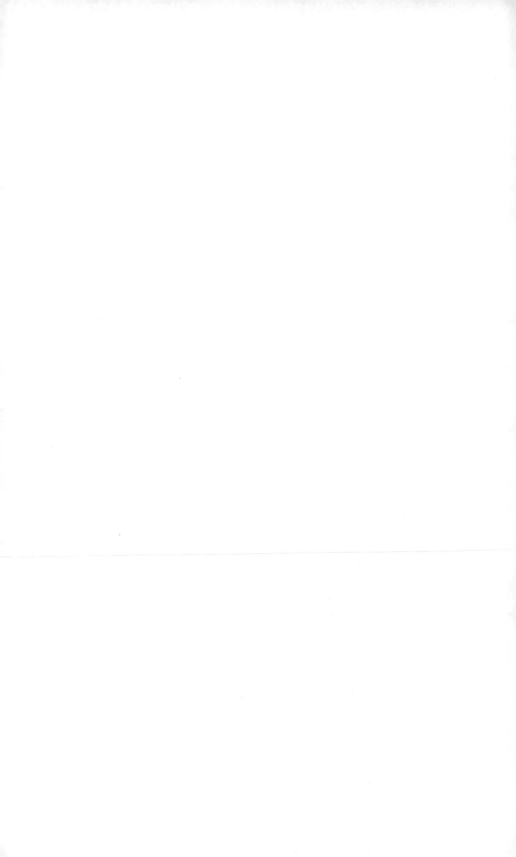

Introduction

by Bernhard W. Anderson

Will Herberg, in a sense, was one who could become "all things to all men," to quote an expression of the Apostle Paul. To the secular humanist, he was a critic who himself had roots in the liberal tradition. To the Marxist, he was a critic of ideology who himself stood in the prophetic perspective out of which Marxism arose. To the Jew he was a critic of Jewish isolationism who himself stood conservatively in the Jewish tradition. And to the Christian he was a critic of Christian triumphalism who himself stood close to the Christian faith, so close that he could have said, as King Agrippa hinted to Paul, that it would not take much to win him over to Christianity (Acts 26:28).

I

The proper place to begin to understand Herberg's view of Christianity is with his own life-story. Once he was a convinced Marxist, indeed a card-carrying Communist, but during his days as research analyst and educational director of the International Ladies' Garment Workers' Union he became critical of the Communist party's misuse of power for the sake of the collective whole (totalitarianism). Rejecting "the god that failed," he responded — as did many intellectuals of the time — to the thought of Reinhold Niebuhr of Union Theological Seminary in New York. This Christian theologian spoke to his condition because he advocated, with a passion and incisiveness comparable to Israel's ancient prophets, the transcendent judgment of all human powers by the Holy God, worshipped alike by Jews and Christians.

This Niebuhrian interpretation of the biblical-Christian faith sorely tempted Herberg to become a Christian. Indeed, he might have taken the step, had it not been for the belief, enforced by Niebuhr himself, that he should first be a Jew in a full theological sense. This led to a wrestling with the great modern philosopher of Judaism, Franz Rosenzweig, who — after a similar crisis of faith — had come to the realization that Judaism and Christianity have a complementary relationship in the divine economy. While Rosenzweig understood the relationship ontologically — Jewish existence is a being in eternity and Christian existence is a being in history — Herberg shifted to the biblical mode of covenant: the Jewish people are called to be a community that is faithful to God's Torah, while the vocation of the Christian community is to go out into the world for the purpose of inviting others into the fold of the covenant. He described this as a "double covenant": the covenant of faithfulness (Judaism) and the covenant of mission (Christianity), both callings being essentially related to, and supportive of, each other.

II

With this double allegiance, Herberg was, when speaking to Christians, a staunch defender of orthodox Christianity, as illustrated in his famous sermon on "The Incarnate Word," given to the 1961 graduating class of Drew Theological Seminary (reproduced in *Faith Enacted as History*, 95–98). He insisted that Christians take their own faith with radical seriousness, without yielding to the liberal influences that, he maintained, had eroded Christianity, both Catholic and Protestant, in the modern period. He was equally critical of those who attempted to convert the Christian faith into a "social gospel" (actualizing the Kingdom of God on earth) and those who, under the influence of Rudolf Bultmann, sought to reduce divine revelation to existentialist categories. His witness made a beneficial contribution to the Christian community, although his forceful and even uncompromising stand on "liberal" issues may have had the effect at times of alienating some who wanted to be on "the creative edge" during the ferment of the sixties.

This was especially true in the field of social action. His reaction to the idolatrous claims of Marxism sent him to the opposite extreme of social conservatism. His "reactionary" stand on political, social, and economic issues was based on a profound understanding of traditional Christianity: the view that original sin corrupts the finest human achievements and brings all thought and action under the judgment of God. This prophetic "orthodoxy" he shared with Niebuhr, who however was more open to liberalizing developments in the political and economic sphere. Doubtless many Christian theologians, standing on the same platform of conviction, would be critical of Herberg's tendency to condemn those liberal forces, whether in the church or in society, that seek to bring about change. With his double-covenant view, however, Herberg was keenly aware of the dangers to which the Christian faith is exposed when it goes out into the world and seeks to win people by accommodating to prevailing fashions of thought and behavior.

Herberg's view of the "double covenant" holds tremendous possibilities for Jewish-Christian dialogue. To be sure, one may question whether on New Testament grounds his view stands "on all fours" exegetically and whether, in the last analysis, it provides a sufficient theological basis for understanding the relationship between the Jewish and Christian communities. It should be noted that the Apostle Paul, in his agonized wrestling with the Jewish/Christian question in Romans 9–11, does not use this language but speaks, rather, of the mystery of divine election in which the two communities are embraced (11:25). The double covenant appears to be a rationalizing of this mystery of God's freedom which, for Paul, includes Israel's priority in the history of salvation (11:15–16, 28–29), God's freedom to "harden the heart" of at least a part of Israel (9:18, 22), and Israel's final redemption in the mystery of divine freedom (11:25–26). For my part, I believe that this theme of the mystery of the divine purpose, in which both communities participate, deserves to be carried further — even beyond the confines of Paul's exposition. If both communities are co-related in the mystery of divine election (calling), this precludes premature, rational explanations, just as it rules out enthusiastic efforts at conversion, at one extreme, or of defensive encampment in confessional positions, at the other.

Be that as it may, Herberg has attempted in his own way and in his own time to provide a theological basis for the co-existence of the Christian and Jewish communities. It must be added, however, that he was dubious about whether it is possible now for creative and frank dialogue to take place. This matter came up during our luncheon conversations (*Tischreden*), which began immediately after my departure from Drew University (beginning in the Fall of 1968), where we were colleagues. In one conversation I was telling about my experience in a dialogue involving about twenty Jews, Protestants, and Catholics at Princeton Theological Seminary. He responded that he was not particularly optimistic about such conversations, for the "time" had not yet come, owing to the sad history behind us and the need for all three conversants — Protestants, Catholics, and Jews — to do more work in biblical theology. In addition, he felt that "the rabbinical mind," with its interest in the ongoing tradition, could not easily be reconciled with "the biblical theological mind," which insists on the primacy of Scripture.

III

Any evaluation of Herberg's contributions to Christianity and the Jewish-Christian dialogue would have to include a consideration of the post-war "neo-orthodox" movement, of which he was a part. Indeed, he was sometimes known as "the Reinhold Niebuhr of Judaism." This movement, and the related "biblical theology movement," have been eclipsed, so it seems, by trends of the seventies and eighties in which no clear theological direction is apparent. Herberg was not unaware of these new developments but viewed them with the equanimity of a sage. "What is called biblical theology," he wrote to me (June 18, 1970), "is not just an intellectual fashion, although it has been that in theological circles for the past three decades. It is a faithful attempt to see the Christian faith in terms of its authentic tradition, which takes its rise from, and must remain true to, the Holy Scriptures." "The impression of biblical theology," he ventured, "cannot be effaced, but it remains, and will remain, the foundation of a valid understanding of Christian faith (and of the Jewish faith as well). Nothing can change that."

Some of Herberg's insights provide a lasting basis for conversation. One of these is his awareness of the abuses and limitations of the exercise of power in any arena. Judaism and Christianity, which share the witness of Israel's prophets, stand together in opposition to any power which denies human beings their inalienable freedom to be and to become and, more than that, any power that claims totalitarian sovereignty over the world or, in the language of a prophetic poem, attempts to usurp the throne of God (Isa. 14:12–20).

Furthermore, Herberg profoundly understood the relative standpoints of every position of faith, including the Jewish and the Christian. His Rosenzweig-like insight that "truth is one for God only" made him a defender of a theocentric Christianity over against the "Christomonism" which, down through history, has often led to Christian triumphalism. My good friend Will has helped me to see that a firm commitment to Jesus Christ as "the way, the truth, and the life" (John 14:6) does not need to find expression in an exclusive christology. After all, the earliest Christian creed, the Apostles', begins theocentrically with the Creator, not christocentrically with the "Son."

Above all, Herberg has helped Jews and Christians alike to realize that faith is not assent to abstract truths or dogmatic formulations but is personal and existential. Furthermore, he always inveighed against "mysticism" — if this means a retreat from the world into some sort of divine-human relationship that lifts one beyond history. Biblical faith is — to use one of his favorite expressions — "faith enacted as history" — a response to God's call to be co-workers in the divine purpose whose goal is the redemption of humanity and a "new creation."

1

Judaism and Christianity: Their Unity and Difference

1952

The Double Covenant in the Divine Economy of Salvation

I

No one who examines Judaism and Christianity in a broad religio-historical perspective can fail to be impressed by the profound likeness of the two religions. However significant the differences between them may be when seen at close range, the essential similarity they exhibit becomes very striking when the two, taken together, are contrasted with the nonbiblical "religions of the world." In such a perspective, they strike one as being virtually identical in their structure of faith. Let me briefly formulate this common structure as it is exhibited in both Judaism and Christianity in their authentic forms:

1. They both affirm the living God, the God of Abraham, Isaac, and Jacob, the God of Israel, as Creator, King, Judge, and Redeemer.

2. They both see in Abraham's coming out of the pagan world in response to the divine call the crucial break with the religions and philosophies of the world and the establishment of the covenant that defines man's authentic relation to God.

3. They both assert that true knowledge of God is accessible only through his self-revelation in encounter with man and that scripture is in some sense both vehicle and record of such revelation.

4. They both see man as a unitary, self-transcending, dynamic, responsive, and responsible creature, in contrast to both the mystical-idealist and the naturalist views of man.

5. They both see man as originally (in the order of creation) ordained to God and therefore at one with the world and himself. They both see this primal harmony upset and all creation "spoiled" by man's sin, which is essentially self-will in rebellion against God, the idolatrous diversion of ultimate allegiance from God to something that is not God. They therefore see no way out for man from the misery of sinful existence except through repentance and a restoration of the proper relation to God in total love and obedience. And, for both, such restoration is possible only through the grace of a loving and merciful God.

6. They both share a realistic and actualistic emphasis: they both see the world, and human action within it, as real and important, though of course they hold the world to be the creation of God and therefore without any claims to ultimacy or self-subsistence in its own right.

7. For both, an ethic of obedience is central in the requirement of faith, and the demand of God is a moral demand for righteousness and love in action. In this they differ from the nature religions, which do not rise to ethics but seek a unity with the divine through harmony with the rhythms of nature, as well as from the mystical religions, which pretend to transcend ethics in a self-dissolving union with the divine.

8. Both are eschatological: they look forward to a transhistorical "end" of history, which is both judgment and fulfillment, and in which the full meaning of life and history is revealed.

9. In both, faith is defined by and expressed through a saved and saving community, which is understood as an instrument of God with a divine vocation in history. And both see Israel as such an elect community of God.

10. Both are historical religions in the profound sense that for both religion is *faith enacted as history*, incapable of being expressed, understood, or communicated apart from the history in and through which it is enacted. For both, the context of sacred history is basically the same, the history of the People Israel. And both see the entire human enterprise as part of a great three-phase process of *Heilsgeschichte* [salvation history] — of creation, fall, and redemption. Both look back to a crucial redemptive and revelatory act in the past, which was also the community-creating event, an event that came as prefigurement and instrument of the fulfillment of God's purpose. In both, therefore, the very quintessence of faith is (to use Buber's phrase) the attitude of remembrance and expectation — remembrance of God's gracious act of

redemption in the past and expectation of the full and final redemption to come.

In all of these respects, and they are surely basic, Judaism and Christianity are at one with each other and poles apart from the nonbiblical "religions of the world." Is it any wonder that Christian theologians speak of Judaism and Christianity as "not, fundamentally, two different religions but one" (Frederick C. Grant)[1] and note with emphasis "the identity of structure at all points and the identity of content in most" of the two faiths (Tillich),[2] or that a Jewish theologian (Finkelstein) refers to Judaism and Christianity as "twin religions" and indeed speaks of them as constituting "one system"?[3] There can be little doubt that the two religions belong together in a most intimate way. Yet in their very likeness they are different, and to define this difference within the framework of their unity now becomes our task.

II

It is necessary, in the first place, to note and to evaluate some of the attempts that have been made to establish criteria by which Judaism and Christianity may be validly distinguished. Martin Buber's recent and Hermann Cohen's earlier attempts[4] to make this distinction in terms of a basic difference between Jewish 'emunah and Christian pistis seem to me to fail because of the discrepancy in terms of comparison; they take 'emunah in its authentic Hebraic meaning of utter trust and self-commitment, but pistis they take not in its true biblical sense but as overlaid with Greek intellectualism. Nor is the distinction, made by Parkes and others,[5] that Judaism is corporate while Christianity is individual valid in any but a very relative sense; in both, the tension between the corporate and the personal is to be found, though naturally expressed in somewhat different ways. Most fallacious, it seems to me, is the attempt, familiar through the centuries, to distinguish the two religions by making Judaism, especially the Judaism of New Testament times, into a religion of dead legalism and justification through works, in contrast to Christianity as a religion of grace and faith. "It was quite

---

[1]Frederick C. Grant, "The Teaching of Jesus and First-Century Jewish Ethics," in *The Study of the Bible Today and Tomorrow*, H. R. Willoughby, ed. (University of Chicago Press, 1947), 312.

[2]Paul Tillich, "Is There a Judaeo-Christian Tradition?" *Judaism* 1, no. 2 (1952): 109.

[3]Louis Finkelstein, *Akiba: Scholar, Saint, and Martyr* (Covici & Friede, 1936), 6; *Tradition in the Making* (Jewish Theological Seminary of America, 1937), 12.

[4]Martin Buber, *Two Types of Faith* (London: Routledge & Kegan Paul, Ltd., 1951); Simon Kaplan, "Hermann Cohen's Philosophy of Judaism," *Judaism* 1, no. 2 (1952), esp. 145–146.

[5]James Parkes, *Judaism and Christianity* (University of Chicago Press, 1948).

generally held," Hans-Werner Bartsch comments in his summary of recent Protestant theological thinking, "that the religion of later Judaism [he means the Judaism of New Testament times] was dominated entirely by thoughts of righteousness for reward, and so provided the dark background for Jesus' proclamation of forgiveness. But now Erik Sjöberg has shown (*Gott und Sünder im palästinischen Judentum nach dem Zeugnis der Tannaiten*) that the idea of repentance and forgiveness was present in late Judaism as well. This confronts New Testament scholarship with the task of presenting the significance of the proclamation of Jesus Christ."[6] It was hardly necessary to wait for Sjöberg's researches, valuable as they are, to reach this conclusion; the same lesson might have been learned from the writings of such well-known scholars as George Foot Moore, Claude Montefiore, and Travers Herford.[7] The fact of the matter is that the demand of the law and the gospel of grace are to be found in both religions; indeed, as Luther once exclaimed, where is the man who can properly distinguish between law and gospel?

The real distinction between Judaism and Christianity seems to me to lie elsewhere. To see the two in their proper relation, it is necessary to relate each and both to the divine economy of salvation as that is biblically understood.

The central category of biblical thinking is covenant. "Never imagine that you have rightly grasped a biblical idea," Paul Ramsey has said, "until you have reduced it to a corollary of the idea of 'covenant.' "[8] And this is supremely true of biblical thinking about salvation. In the biblical view, man has, so to speak, standing with God, and a direct personal relation to him, only by virtue of his membership in the people of God, the redeemed and redeeming community. "The individual Israelite," Alan Richardson points out quite emphatically, "approached God in virtue of his membership in the holy people. . . . In the whole of the Bible, in the Old Testament as well as the New, there is no such thing as a private personal relation between an individual and God apart from his membership in the covenant-folk."[9] Man's relation to God is essentially responsive; it is God's call expressed in the grace of election that gives

---

[6]Hans-Werner Bartsch, *Handbuch der evangelisch-theologischen Arbeit, 1938 bis 1948* (Stuttgart: Evangelisches Verlagswerk, 1949).

[7]See, e.g., George Foot Moore, *Judaism in the First Centuries of the Christian Era*, 3 vols. (Harvard University Press, 1927–1930); and R. Travers Herford, *Pharisaism: Its Aim and Its Method* (G. P. Putnam's, 1912), *Talmud and Apocrypha* (London: Soncino Press, Ltd., 1933), *The Pharisees* (Macmillan Company, 1924), *Judaism in the New Testament Period* (London: Lindsey Press, 1928).

[8]Paul Ramsey, "Elements of a Biblical Political Theory," *Journal of Religion* 29, no. 4 (1949): 258.

[9]Alan Richardson, "Instrument of God," *Interpretation* 3, no. 3 (1949): 278.

man the possibility of, from his side, entering into personal relationship with God. Modern religious existentialism, in its very welcome emphasis on personal confrontations, tends to forget that such confrontation is, humanly speaking — there can be no question of limiting God's grace — possible only within, and on the basis of, the covenant. In the biblical view, people outside the covenant, properly called gentiles, cannot — apart from the uncovenanted grace of God, which is virtually covenant-creating — of themselves find their way to God or meet him in personal confrontation. In our modern intellectualistic and therefore inadequate terminology, this is equivalent to saying that only the religion of Israel brings men to God; other, pagan, religions, the "religions of the world," lead them away from God.

The covenant of Israel is understood by the prophets, and perhaps much earlier, as the covenant of a redeemed and redeeming community; the purpose it defines is a universal purpose and the people it brings into being is an instrument of God for the redemption of mankind. All of mankind is to be brought into the covenant and, within the covenant, restored to a right relation to God.

The paradox of Israelite religion was that a covenant of such universal scope and purpose was actualized in a particular folk or ethnic community. To affirm the God of Israel involved coming under the covenant and that meant becoming part of the Israelitish, or Jewish, people in the folk sense of the term. Despite all rabbinic efforts to establish half-way covenants and categories in order to facilitate proselytizing and thus help realize the universal vocation of Israel, this fact remained a fact and could not basically be altered. In this situation, Christianity emerged to break through the paradox and bring the "nations of the world" to the God of Israel by bringing them under the covenant of Israel in a new form. Through Christianity, God's covenant with Israel was opened to all mankind — without requiring a change of ethnic or "national" status. This is simply a historical fact, and has been noted as such by quite unbelieving historians; but it is also the conclusion of Paul, who in true Hebraic spirit attempts to discern the purposes of God in the course of historic events.

God's covenant with Israel is opened to all mankind through Christ. I hesitate to touch upon this tremendous question; I will say in advance that my comments relate to only one aspect of Christ's vocation, but that aspect is, I think, very relevant to the purposes of the present discussion.

As the one by whom and through whom the covenant of Israel is opened to mankind, Christ appears in early Christian thinking as, quite literally, an incarnate or one-man Israel, the Remnant-Man. Through union in faith with him, the gentile believer becomes part of Israel; he therefore comes under the covenant and thereby becomes heir to the promises of God to Israel. "So remember," Paul tells recent gentile converts, "that at that time when you were without Christ, you were aliens to the commonwealth of Israel and strangers to the covenants of promise.... But now through your union with Christ Jesus, you, who were once far away, have ... been brought near ... so that you are no longer strangers and foreigners but fellow citizens of God's people and of the family of God" (Eph. 2:12–19). "And if you are Christ's," he says elsewhere, "then you are Abraham's seed, heirs according to the promise" (Gal. 3:29). A modern Jewish scholar has put what he takes to be Paul's meaning in these words: "He so broadened the term 'Jew' as to include in it, as an honorable fellowship, all those who transformed their lives by being faithful Christians."[10]

Through Christ, a new covenant-community is created — the Church, the "Body of Christ." Through Christ, Israel's *Heilsgeschichte* becomes the redemptive history of the pagan-turned-Christian, who thus becomes in effect an Israelite. "Through Jesus Christ," writes H. Richard Niebuhr, "Christians of all races recognize the Hebrews as their fathers; they build into their lives as Englishmen or as Americans, as Italians or Germans, the memories of Abraham's loyalty, of Moses' heroic leadership, of prophetic denunciations and comfortings. All that has happened to the strange and wandering people of God becomes a part of their own past."[11]

Christian faith thus brings into being and defines a new covenant, which is new not in the sense of supplanting the old but in the sense of extending and enlarging it, very much as we speak of the New World side by side with the Old World. For with the emergence of Christianity, the election and vocation of Israel are not annulled. On this, Jews of course insist, and on this Christian theologians as far apart as H. Wheeler Robinson and Karl Barth agree. "Israel," says the former, remains an elect nation by virtue of the divine choice and that choice is sufficiently vindicated by that which Israel's history has produced."[12] "Is Israel's mission thereby suspended?" asks the latter. "No, on the contrary, through everything ... God's election holds and will hold to all eternity.... God keeps faith [with Israel] right through all stages of its wanderings.... [So] God's faithfulness in the reality of Israel is in

---

[10]Solomon Grayzel, "Christian-Jewish Relations in the First Millennium," in *Essays on Antisemitism*, K. S. Pinson, ed. (Conference on Jewish Relations, 1942), 27.

[11]H. Richard Niebuhr, *The Meaning of Revelation* (Macmillan Company, 1946), 115–116.

[12]H. Wheeler Robinson, *Inspiration and Revelation in the Old Testament* (Oxford: Clarendon Press, 1946), 159.

fact the guarantee of his faithfulness to us and to all men."[13] The election of Israel remains, and its vocation remains, though it assumes a form in the Christian world different from that which it possessed in the pre-Christian world.

It is not without significance that the bringing of the gospel to the world and the opening of the covenant of Israel to all mankind came only after a vigorous conflict within the early Christian community; the restrictive conceptions which dominated this community were such that, had they triumphed, Christianity would have been doomed to remain just another Jewish sect. It was Paul preeminently who saw the purpose of God and strove to bring Christ, and therefore the covenant and the God of Israel, to the non-Jewish world. Yet it was not until the fall of Jerusalem, and the virtual elimination of the earlier Jewish-Christian "Mother-Church of that city, that Paul's victory was assured. With the church of Jerusalem, though at the other pole, were eliminated also the Sadducees, whose existence was tied to the Temple. We may pause a moment to marvel how the very same catastrophic event — the fall of Jerusalem and the destruction of the Temple — served as the historical instrument for assuring the victory, each in its own community, of the "twin religions," rabbinic Judaism and Pauline Christianity. How unsearchable indeed are God's judgments and his ways past finding out! [See Rom. 11:33].

III

We may now resume the original line of argument. What I have been trying to say can be summarized as follows: Judaism and Christianity represent one religious reality, Judaism facing inward to the Jews and Christianity facing outward to the gentiles, who, through it, are brought to the God and under the covenant of Israel, and therefore cease to be gentiles. This is the unity of Judaism and Christianity.

What, then, are the differences? They are differences of mediation, of vocation, and of orientation. And these differences, though they emerge within the framework of the unity of the two faiths, are of crucial importance.

In both Judaism and Christianity, as I have pointed out, there is no such thing as a direct and unmediated relation to God; this relation must in some way be mediated through one's covenant status. In Judaism,

---

[13] Karl Barth, *Dogmatics in Outline*, translated by G. T. Thomson (Philosophical Library, 1949), 79; see also Maria F. Sulzbach, "Karl Barth and the Jews," *Religion in Life* 21, no. 4 (1952): 585–593.

however, it is by virtue of his being a member of the People Israel that the believer approaches God and has standing before him; in Christianity, it is by virtue of his being a member of Christ. This is clearly brought out in the structure of prayer of the two faiths. Both Christian and Jew open their prayers with an invocation to God, go on to their petitions, and conclude with a kind of commendatory plea. But the Christian says "through" or "for the sake of Christ our Lord," whereas the Jew concludes with "for the sake of Israel thy people"; the one recalls the "merits of Christ," the other the "merits of the fathers" (Abraham, Isaac, and Jacob; i.e., Israel). To be a Jew means to meet God and receive his grace in and through Israel; to be a Christian means to meet God and receive his grace in and through Christ.

In the matter of orientation, authentic Judaism is therefore Israel-centered (I mean, of course, the covenant-people Israel, not the State of Israel), while authentic Christianity is Christ-centered. In neither need this centrality lead to a diversion from God, because in both it is through mediation that God is approached.

There is also a corresponding difference in their *Heilsgeschichten*, which structurally are so alike. Both Judaism and Christianity anchor their faith in a redemptive, revelatory, and community-creating event, which becomes the center of history: in Judaism, it is the Sinai-event; in Christianity, the Christ-event.[14] Both have an eschatology that is "realized" and futuristic at the same time, though the "realized" aspect is obviously stronger in Christianity and the futuristic in Judaism.

Everything converges on the problem of vocation. The vocation of both Judaism and Christianity can be defined in common terms: to stand witness to God amidst the idolatries of the world, or in the familiar rabbinic formula, *kiddush ha-Shem* — the sanctification of the Name. But the Jew fulfills his vocation by "staying with God," while the Christian can fulfill his only by "going out" to conquer the world for God. (I use the concepts and terminology of Franz Rosenzweig, the great German-Jewish philosopher and theologian whose profound insights in the relationship of Judaism and Christianity I am trying to present.) What does this distinction basically mean? I think I can best indicate my meaning by quoting from a recent essay by Roger Shinn: "Inevitably [says Roger Shinn] Hitler found in the Jews (*by their very existence*) and

---

[14]Both Martin Buber, *Israel and the World* (Schocken Books, 1948), 94, and Oscar Cullmann, *Christ and Time*, rev. ed. (Westminster Press, 1964), *passim*, deny that there is any real "midpoint" or "center" in Israel's *Heilsgeschichte*, and indeed make this absence a point of difference between Judaism and Christianity. I do not see how the structure of Jewish faith permits any such interpretation.

in *faithful* Christians (*by their religious protests*) a reminder of the universalism . . . he could not tolerate" (emphasis added).[15]

I call your attention to the words I have emphasized. What do they imply? They imply that whereas to fulfill his witness the Christian must be "faithful" and must make a "religious protest," the Jew stands witness by his very being, simply by being. Because of his anomalous status in the non-Jewish world — and this, too, cannot be understood as historical accident, but must be seen, through the eyes of faith, as reflecting the purposes of God — the Jew is forced to live the "semi-detached" existence — in the world, but never quite of it — to which the Christian aspires. Recall the picture of Christian life given in the Epistle to Diognetus: "The Christians dwell in all countries, but only as sojourners. As citizens, they share in all things with others and yet endure all things as if they are strangers. Every foreign land is to them as a native country, and every land of their birth is as a land of strangers." This is the Christian life as it should be, but it is the Jewish actuality. The Christian may very easily make his peace with the world at the expense of his faith; he then lapses into idolatry and worships the "gods of space," as Tillich puts it. The Jew, so long as he remains and is known as a Jew, cannot do that, however much he may desire to. The Jew is, whether he will or not, a standing reproach to the pagan in man and society, an unassimilable element in any culture engaged in deifying itself — and he is that simply by being a Jew and quite apart from his personal faith or desire, "by [his] very existence," as Roger Shinn puts it. The choice for him is authentic or unauthentic Jewish existence, God's witness in self-affirmation or in self-repudiation — but God's witness he remains nevertheless. Such is the "mystery of Israel."

The Jew's vocation is to "stand," the Christian's to "go out" — both in the same cause, the cause of the Kingdom. This difference of vocation, combined with the parallel differences in mediation and orientation, make for a series of other differences which are also equivalences. The liturgical pattern reflects in a particularly faithful manner the identity of structure yet difference of content to which Tillich refers. In both Judaism and Christianity, the central liturgical pattern is the reenactment of the crucial revelatory redemptive, and community-creating event — the Exodus-Sinai-event in Judaism, the Christ-event in Christianity. Pesaḥ, Sukkot, and Shavuot [Passover, Tabernacles, Weeks], the three great pilgrim festivals, reenact phases of the Sinai-event that brought Israel into being; Good Friday, Easter, and Pentecost, with perhaps Christmas pre-

---

[15]Roger Shinn, "Religious Faith and the Task of the Historian," in *Liberal Learning and Religion*, Amos N. Wilder, ed. (Harper & Brothers, 1951), 70.

fixed, reenact phases of the Christ-event that brought the Church into being. In both cases, the believer reenacts these events liturgically in order to appropriate them existentially as part of his own being and history. "All this I do," says the Jew reciting the Passover Haggadah, "because of what God did for *me* in bringing me out of Egypt." And the Mishnah comments: "In every generation, a man must so regard himself as if he himself came forth from Egypt."[16] This is, of course, equivalent to the familiar Christian concept which Pascal formulates in these words: "Everything that happened to Jesus Christ must take place in the soul and in the body of every Christian.... Everything that happens to the Church happens also to every Christian as an individual."[17] Existential appropriation of *Heilsgeschichte* in contemporaneity is the basic principle of Jewish and Christian liturgy alike, the difference arising from the difference in the *heilsgeschichtliche* event that forms the core of each faith.

The alleged distinction between Judaism as corporate and Christianity as individual finds its relative validation but also its limitation in this context. In both Judaism and Christianity, normative religious existence is corporate; no one — not even the hermit in the desert — can be a Christian all by himself apart from the Church, any more than the Jew can be a Jew all by himself apart from Israel. In both, the personal confrontation with God, which is at the heart of faith, occurs normatively only within the context of the corporate covenant group. Yet there is the difference: the Jew is born a Jew, the Christian is born a pagan and becomes a Christian through accepting Christ. The Christian's religious experience, therefore, normatively begins with a personal confrontation and a personal act of faith, even if (as in infant baptism) that act is vicariously performed by a sponsor. For the Jew, however, religious existence is normatively corporate from the beginning, since the Jew is born into the covenant. (The pagan convert to Judaism constitutes the exception that, so to speak, proves the rule, since the pagan who becomes a Jew, like the pagan who becomes a Christian, but in contrast to the Jew born a Jew, begins with a personal act of faith and its appropriate ritual expression.) This difference is not without its effect on the *ethos* of the two faiths.

But, of course, the most familiar difference between Judaism and Christianity is a difference that is felt to be somehow related to the difference between law and grace, between *halakhah* and *agapē*. It is easy to misunderstand and misrepresent this difference. It is not as if law

---

[16]M. Pesaḥim 10.5.
[17]Blaise Pascal, "Letter to M. and Mme. Perier" (October 17, 1651), in *The Great Shorter Works of Pascal*, translated by Emile Cailliet and John C. Blankenagel (Westminster Press, 1948), 89, "Letter to M. and Mme. de Rouannez" (September 1656), ibid., 143.

can be assigned to Judaism and grace to Christianity: both affirm law in some sense and both see law transcended and fulfilled in grace and love. Judaism is not salvation by works — the rabbis tell us that "our father Abraham inherited this world and the world-to-come solely by virtue of his faith";[18] and the observant Jew prays every morning, "Our Father, our King, be gracious unto us, for we have no works. Save us according to thy grace." On the other hand, Christianity does not disregard works — does not Paul himself tell us that everyone will be judged according to "the things done in his body, according to what he has done, whether it be good or bad" (2 Cor. 5:10)? The difference goes much deeper than such superficial distinctions: it is a difference directly related to the basic difference in covenant character and vocation.

The Jew's relatively "static" vocation — he "stays with" God — is reflected in the regulative principle of *halakhah*, which is central to normative Jewish faith. It is *halakhah* as a holy discipline of life that maintains Israel's existence as covenant-people and therefore enables it to fulfill its vocation. But the Church's vocation is essentially to "go out"; its function is to shatter the pagan patterns of life and re-create everything in and under Christ; for that it needs the unbound weapon of the free *charisma* of grace. Yet there remains in both an inescapable polarity: Judaism has its *charisma* of grace, which was particularly evident in its periods of proselytizing activity; and Christianity has its *halakhah* and law, which come to the fore when the Christian community, as in Calvinist Geneva, settles down to a relatively static existence. But the weights assigned to the two poles are very different, and that is everything.[19]

It is in terms of this difference that the ritual acting out of personal incorporation into the covenant community is defined. The Jew born a Jew is circumcised as a mark of the covenant; he, so to speak, appropriates his covenant existence through the ongoing pattern of halakhic observance — that is how he affirms, maintains, and ever renews his belonging to Israel, the People of God. The Christian, on his part, becomes a Christian through baptism (or its equivalent), he appropriates his covenant existence through the one observance that, in Christian faith, replaces the entire *halakhah* — the Lord's Supper. Precisely because, in Christian faith, Christ "fulfills the law," *all* ritual observances, for the Christian, are performed in the one sacrament of Christ, by which the believer renews his union with Christ and his belonging to the

---

[18]Mekilta to Ex. 14:31, Jacob Z. Lauterbach, *Mekilta de Rabbi Ishmael* (Philadelphia: Jewish Publication Society, 1933), 1:253.

[19]See the very significant article by Monford Harris, "Two Ways: *Halakhah* and *Charisma*," *Judaism* 1, no. 1 (1952): 80–84.

Church, the new people of God. Halakhic observance and the Lord's Supper are thus essentially equivalents.

Within the same framework, we may understand something of the characteristic perils and corruptions of the two covenant communities. In respect to the covenant, the Jew's characteristic peril is the pride of exclusive possession — God's election was his from the beginning and his to keep for himself; the Christian's is the pride of supersession — the election is now his alone, the Jew having been disinherited. Again in respect to the covenant, but now negatively: the Jew who revolts against the "yoke of the Kingdom" expressed it in the so-called self-hatred that reflects both rejection of his vocation and bitter resentment at having been "separated" by God and forced to be "different"; the Christian, on the other hand, expresses his resentment against the claim of God through anti-Semitism. "Whenever the pagan within the Christian soul rises in revolt against the yoke of the Cross," Rosenzweig points out, "he vents his fury on the Jew"[20] as Christ-bringer. This is virtually identical with the view expounded by a number of recent Christian theologians, particularly A. Roy Eckardt, in his important work *Christianity and the Children of Israel* [1948], to which I am so much indebted.

In respect to the distinction between law and grace, the characteristic peril of the Jew is legalism, the notion that one can rely upon the meticulous performance of his obligations under the law to put him in a right relation with God; for the Christian, the analogous peril is antinomianism, the belief that grace absolves the believer from all obligations under the law.

I will not attempt to continue the list of similarities, differences, and equivalences. My purpose is not to present an exhaustive account, but simply to stress that these similarities, differences, and equivalences are not really intelligible except in terms of the fundamental unity of Judaism and Christianity, which yet involves an essential distinction in vocation, mediation, and orientation.

IV

Let me now try to bring all the threads together by reformulating the relationship of Judaism and Christianity in their unity and difference, in their interdependence of function and witness.

"Israel," says Franz Rosenzweig, "can bring the world to God only

---

[20]Jacob B. Agus, "Franz Rosenzweig," in *Modern Philosophies of Judaism* (New York: Behrman's Jewish Book House, 1941), 194.

through Christianity."[21] Despite all hostility through the ages, Jewish tradition has always "freely acknowledged the divine mission of Christianity" as "Israel's apostle" to the nations.[22] This, if one may venture to put it that way, is Christianity's service for Judaism.

But there is also Judaism's service for Christianity. "Christianity," Franz Rosenzweig continues, "could not long remain a force for redemption without Israel in its midst."[23]

It is important [Paul Tillich asserts] that there always be Judaism. It is the corrective against the paganism that goes along with Christianity. . . . The Church is always in danger of adoring the gods of space in which she is ruling. . . . The Church is always in danger of losing her prophetic spirit. . . . Therefore, the prophetic spirit included in the tradition of the Synagogue is needed so long as the gods of space are in power, and that means to the end of history. . . . Synagogue and Church should be united in our period in the struggle for the Lord of time.[24]

That the witness of the Jew through his very being a Jew is also a witness, and a very necessary witness, against the ever-present temptation of the Church to make its peace with the "gods of space," all recent history goes to show; and one must be grateful for the insight and integrity that have led so many Christian writers — Barth, Berdyaev, Tillich, Maritain, Eckardt — to draw this lesson of history and proclaim it to the Church and the world. "If, as Christians, we thought that Church and Synagogue no longer affect one another," says Barth, "everything would be lost. And where the separation . . . has been made complete, it is the Christian community which has suffered. The whole reality of the revelation of God is then secretly denied and as a result philosophy and ideology take the upper hand and Christianity of the Greek or German or some other kind is invented."[25] "Whenever the Church is in danger of drawing away from its source and forgetting its origins," the French Jesuit L. Richard asserts, "Israel is there to recall it thereto."[26] This is Judaism's service for Christianity.

Yet this interdependence is, after all, secondary. Primarily, each faith is the authentic form of religious existence for those who belong to the

[21] Ibid., 193, Nahum N. Glatzer, *Franz Rosenzweig: His Life and Thought* (Schocken Books, 1953), 341. [This formulation is Agus's, not Rosenzweig's! —F. A. R.]

[22] A. A. Neuman, "Judaism," in *The Great Religions of the Modern World*, Edward J. Jurji, ed. (Princeton University Press, 1946), 228–229.

[23] Agus, "Franz Rosenzweig," 193; Glatzer, *Franz Rosenzweig: His Life and Thought*, 343–344.

[24] Quoted in A. Roy Eckardt, *Christianity and the Children of Israel* (King's Crown Press, 1948), 146–147.

[25] Barth, *Dogmatics in Outline*, 75.

[26] L. Richard, "Israël et le Christ," in H. de Lubac et al., *Israël et la foi chrétienne* (Fribourg: Librairie de l'Université, 1942), 118.

covenant community which it defines. "Granted that Judaism and Christianity are dialectically related, and hence that it is wrong to say that Christianity has taken the place of Judaism, a particular individual will nevertheless affirm confessionally why he must subscribe to Christianity rather than to Judaism or to Judaism rather than to Christianity. Were this not the case, the tension between the two faiths would not be real or meaningful."[27] These words of A. Roy Eckardt seem to me thoroughly valid and never to be forgotten as we stress the inescapable interdependence of the two faiths.

The last word, therefore, is difference in unity and unity in difference. "The two religions," says Franz Rosenzweig, "are equal representations of the truth — equal before God."[28] With God, truth is one, but for men it is irreducibly split (*entzweit*), since the truth as men see it is confessional and conditioned by one's covenantal position. This is not a vicious relativism, nor does it assert for one moment that all religions are equally true or equally valid. On the contrary, as Rosenzweig puts it, man is either a pagan or a Jew or Christian. (Islam presents a problem; Rosenzweig does not regard it as a distinct way, nor do I; I think rather it is a kind of Jewish-Christian heresy.) The pagan, as pagan, does not rise to the level of the *Überwelt* [transcendent] (Franz Rosenzweig's term), where the Jew and Christian find themselves — although, of course, God in his grace may reach out to him. On this level of the *Überwelt*, Jew and Christian has each his assigned position, defined in the covenant that relates him to God. Their positions, their "standpoints," being different, their views of the one truth will be different — although they will be views of the same truth, just as two people standing in the same room but in different corners will see the room in different perspectives and therefore somewhat differently. Each will be loyal to the truth if he speaks out about the truth as he sees it, though recognizing that his truth is never quite identical with the full truth of God. "Truth is a noun only to God," says Franz Rosenzweig; "to men it is really best known as an adverb, 'truly' (*wahrlich*), as the measure of inner faithfulness."[29] "Granted that Judaism and Christianity are dialectically related," I repeat the words of A. Roy Eckardt quoted above, "a particular individual will nevertheless affirm confessionally why he must subscribe to Christianity rather than to Judaism or to Judaism rather than to Christianity." This does not derogate from the "finality" of either Judaism or Christianity, if

---

[27] A. Roy Eckardt, "Christian Faith and the Jews," *The Journal of Religion* 30, no. 4 (1950): 245.
[28] Glatzer, *Franz Rosenzweig: His Life and Thought*, xxv–xxvi.
[29] Agus, "Franz Rosenzweig," 191.

that is properly understood; it merely prevents the idolization of either. For, strictly speaking, God alone is absolute, and our knowledge of the Absolute need not itself be absolute knowledge.

In short, each of us — the Jew on his part and the Christian on his — sees that aspect of the truth which is to be apprehended from his perspective, as that is defined by his covenantal position and vocation. Each of us must stand by his truth and confess it, recognizing that insofar as we do so in integrity and wholeness of heart, we remain faithful to the God whose truth it is. Naturally, we will see the same reality in somewhat different ways; naturally, too, each may see an aspect of reality hidden to the other, and even interpret the same things differently. But perhaps this is part of the purpose of God in placing Jew and Christian on different sectors of the fighting front of the Kingdom.

If what I have said makes any sense at all, it must follow that the authentic differences between Judaism and Christianity are not the result of ignorance or blindness, but are irreducible differences which must persist until the final clarification. Judaism and Christianity, as a young Jewish theologian has put it, are parallel lines meeting only at infinity. In the final clarification, we both believe, the two will be one — and then perhaps (let us be humble enough to admit it) neither "our" truth nor "their" error will prove to be quite as we see it today.

Again, if all this is at all valid, there can be no proselytizing between the Jewish and Christian communities. Finkelstein has connected the cessation of Jewish proselytism with the emergence of the "monotheistic faiths" of Christianity and Islam.[30] Eckardt has presented the Christian argument against the "mission to the Jews" in the book I have mentioned and in other writings. "The missionary view," he says, "is . . . challenged [not alone by "liberalism," but also] by some who accept Christian faith as in a certain sense final. . . . What is usually involved here is the contention that the Jews have a unique function in the divine economy. . . . The claim [that if the "mission to the Jews" is abandoned] it logically follows that missionary endeavor has to cease for all people, is seen as failing to realize that Judaism and other religions are not on the same plane. Christianity and Judaism have a relationship lacking between Christianity and other religions."[31] Not "mission to the Jews" or "mission to the Christians," but "Jewish-Christian conversation."[32] Each — the Jew on his part and the Christian on his — is obliged to

---

[30]Louis Finkelstein, "The Beliefs and Practices of Judaism," in Louis Finkelstein et al., *The Religions of Democracy* (Devin-Adair Company, 1941), 6.

[31]Eckardt, "Christian Faith and the Jews," 236, and *Christianity and the Children of Israel*, 158.

[32]It is gratifying to note that this conception is beginning to make itself felt among

make a confessional statement of his faith and to make it in "conversation," so to speak, with the other. Neither Judaism nor Christianity is "higher" or "more perfect" than the other — such criteria make no sense in biblical thinking; but from the standpoint of each, it is always possible to see the specific shortcomings and perils of the other, and, in all charity, to bear witness against them. "From a human point of view" — I quote Eckardt again — "certain shortcomings will be discerned in the alternate view. . . . I have no interest in trying to convert the Jews to Christianity. The intention here is to show why some of us must be Christians rather than Jews. Frank confession may help to further understanding."[33] The heart of each may ache, perhaps, that the other is not in his camp, fighting side by side with him on his sector of the front, but he must also recognize that though the other fights on another sector, he is also fighting for the living God and that it is perhaps by the providence of God that they are thus separated.

And so Jew and Christian stand separated yet united. The unity far transcends the separation, for we are united in our common allegiance to the living God and in our common expectation of, and longing for, the One who is to come. Jew and Christian — to recall Tillich's words — stand united until the end of history in the struggle for the Lord of time against the "gods of space."

---

continental Protestants; see J. H. Grolle, *Het Gesprek met Israël* (The Hague: 's-Gravenhage, Boekencentrum, 1949).

[33] Eckardt, "Christian Faith and the Jews," 245.

2

A Jew Looks at Jesus

1966

"Who do you say that I am?" Jesus asked his disciples (Matt. 16:15), and this question, which led to Peter's confession of faith, still remains a crucial question, for the Jew no less than for the gentile, today no less than nineteen hundred years ago. It is this question I should like to discuss here. Speaking as a Jew, from out of what I take to be the authentic tradition of Jewish faith, what can I say about Jesus, the man of Nazareth whom Peter hailed as the Christ?

I

Jesus was, first of all, a great and incomparable moral teacher. Of that there cannot be, and indeed never has been, any doubt. His exhortations and discourses stand unrivaled in the ethical literature of mankind. Men of all cultures and religions have paid tribute to the inexhaustible truth and power of his moral teaching. The Sermon on the Mount is known wherever men anywhere have concerned themselves with the moral life, and nowhere has it failed to stir the imagination and raise the heart to the self-giving love which Jesus preached. By the common testimony of mankind, this Jewish rabbi from Nazareth nineteen hundred years ago reached the high-water mark of moral vision and ethical teaching.

But if that were all there was to it, there would be no question to ask and no problem to discuss. For, as a moral teacher, Jesus stands merely as one among many, one of the rabbis of Judaism, entirely in the line of rabbinical tradition. Scholars, both Jewish and non-Jewish, have shown beyond the shadow of a doubt that all his moral teachings, even the most exalted, have their sources and parallels in the contemporary religious literature of the Jews, from whom he sprang and among whom he taught. It is not enough to point to the consummate synthesis that this teacher of genius achieved in his teaching. This may be granted, but it is not simply, or even primarily, as a moral teacher that Jesus confronts us as a problem and a challenge. As a moral teacher, he is a Jewish rabbi of great power and insight, drawing upon the traditional wisdom of his people. That is a great deal, but it is not enough to answer the question we are asking. We must look further.

Jesus was, on the next level, in the line of the prophets of Israel. If the prophet is the God-possessed man standing over against the community to which he belongs, bringing to bear upon it the word of the Lord in judgment and promise, then Jesus of Nazareth was a prophet in Israel, in the succession of Amos, Hosea, Isaiah, and Jeremiah. His denunciations of the corruptions and idolatries of the age, his call to repentance, his promise of divine grace for those of a broken heart and a contrite spirit, his proclamation of the new age to come as judgment and fulfillment, follows, as it was meant to follow, the pattern of the great prophets. There is, indeed, something new because of the new situation; but this newness, this speaking out of and to the condition of the time, is precisely what characterizes the living word of prophecy. Jesus, the rabbinic teacher, is also among the prophets of Israel, with clear affinities to the great prophets of the past.

But again, if that were all there was to it, there would be no question to ask and no problem to discuss, for again, neither as prophet nor as moral teacher is Jesus anything more than one among many. It is not here that his uniqueness, if uniqueness there be, is to be discovered. Jesus' prophetic proclamations follow the prophetic word of his predecessor; his denunciations of the self-righteous "scribes and Pharisees" can be abundantly paralleled in the literature of rabbinic self-criticism; the promise he held out of divine mercy for the repentant sinner was a promise which every contemporary Jew could understand even if he could not prevail upon himself to take hold of it. No, not here can we find the answer to our question — we must look still further.

II

The Jesus that confronts us as a problem is the Jesus whom Peter confessed as the Christ and whom the Fourth Gospel represents as declaring: "I am the way . . . ; no one comes to the Father, but by me" (John 14:6). What can a Jew make of this confession and this claim?

257

It seems to me obvious that this claim and this confession have no meaning outside the context of the faith of Israel, as defined in the Hebrew Bible, in which Judaism and Christianity alike are grounded. The persistent attempt through the centuries to throw out the Old Testament and replace it with some other so-called "preparation for the gospel," such as Greek philosophy, Hindu mysticism, or modern science, is inevitably and inescapably, however unwittingly, an attempt to destroy the biblical substance of the Christian faith, and to convert Christianity into a pagan salvation cult. Christian faith is biblical and Hebraic, or it is nothing at all.

Viewing it from the biblical-Hebraic standpoint, and in the light of a biblically defined understanding of God's redemptive purpose, what can a Jew say of the Christian church and the Christ it proclaims? It is hard to avoid the conviction that Christianity emerges, in God's plan of redemption, to open the covenant of Israel to the "nations of the world." *In biblical faith it is in and through membership in the covenanted people of God that — humanly speaking — man has his standing with God and can avail himself of God's grace for redemption. "The individual Israelite," Alan Richardson has pointed out, "approaches God in virtue of his membership in the holy people.... In the whole of the Bible, in the Old Testament as well as the New, there is no such thing as a private personal relation between an individual and God apart from this membership in the covenant folk."[1] Man's relation to God is essentially responsive; it is God's call, expressed in the grace of election, that gives man the possibility — *from his side* — of entering into personal relations with God. (Modern existentialism, in its very welcome emphasis on personal confrontation, has tended to forget that such confrontation is, humanly speaking, possible only *within*, and on the basis of, the covenant.) In the biblical view people outside the covenant, properly called gentiles, cannot — apart from the uncovenanted grace of God — of themselves find their way to God or meet him in personal encounter. In our modern intellectualistic, and therefore inadequate, terminology this is equivalent to saying that only the religion of Israel brings men to God; other, pagan religions, the "religions of the world," lead men away from him.

The covenant of Israel is understood by the prophets, and perhaps much earlier, as the covenant of a redeemed and redeeming community; the purpose it defines is a universal purpose, and the people it brings into

---

*The following section repeats passages found in the essay "Judaism and Christianity," above, sect. II, pp. 243ff. F. A. R
[1] Alan Richardson, "Instrument of God," *Interpretation* 3 (1949): 278.

being are an instrument of God for the redemption of mankind. All are to be gathered into the covenant and, within the covenant, restored to a right relation to God. It is in this context that the Jew finds it possible to understand the providential role of the Christian church, and the church to understand the never-failing providential function of Jewry. Through Christ God's covenant with Israel is — in the fullness to time — opened to all mankind. As the one by whom and through whom the covenant of Israel is opened to mankind, Christ appears in early Christian thinking as, quite literally, an incarnate or one-man Israel. Through union in faith with him the gentile believer, the pagan of yesterday, becomes part of Israel; he therefore comes under the covenant, and thereby becomes heir to the promise of God to Israel. "If you are Christ's," Paul says, "then you are Abraham's offspring, heirs according to the promise" (Gal. 3:29). "That the blessing of Abraham might come on the gentiles through Jesus Christ"; that is how the apostle describes this aspect of Christ's redemptive work (Gal. 3:14, KJV). He admonishes recent gentile converts:

Remember that you were at that time separated from Christ, alienated from the commonwealth of Israel, and strangers to the covenants of promise. . . . But now in Christ Jesus you who once were far off have been brought near . . . so [that] you are no longer strangers and sojourners, but you are fellow citizens with the saints and members of the household of God. (Eph. 2:12–19)

Solomon Grayzel, a modern Jewish writer, has — I think quite correctly — put what he takes to be Paul's meaning in these words: "He so broadened the term 'Jew' as to include in it . . . all those who transformed their lives by being faithful Christians."

Attempting to understand what has happened in terms of the divine purpose, the Jew can see Christ as the one in whom God was, and is, acting for the redemption of the peoples. Through Christ a new covenant community is created — the church, the "Body of Christ." Through Christ, Israel's redemptive history becomes the redemptive history of the pagan-turned-Christian, who becomes in effect an Israelite. "Through Jesus Christ," H. Richard Niebuhr points out, "Christians of all races recognize the Hebrews as their fathers. . . . All that has happened to that strange and wandering people of God becomes part of their own past."[2]

Christian faith thus brings into being and defines a new covenant; but it is new not in the sense of supplanting the old, but in the sense of extending and enlarging it, very much as we speak of the new world side by side with the old. For with the emergence of Christianity the election and vocation of Israel are not annulled, nor does the church supersede

---

[2]H. Richard Niebuhr, *The Meaning of Revelation* (Macmillan Company, 1946), 115–116.

the people of the "old covenant." The notion that it does, not only renders unintelligible the survival of Jewry these nineteen hundred years; it is itself a manifestation of that spiritual pride, the pride of supersession, that goes a long way toward corrupting the meaning and power of the gospel that is proclaimed. The election of Israel remains, and its vocation remains, though it assumes a very different form in the Christian world from that which it possessed in the pre-Christian.

It is in terms of this conception of the double covenant that the Jew can see Jesus on the level of his uniqueness. He is indeed the way — the way by and through which the people of the world may enter the covenant of Israel and come to serve the God of Israel, who is the Creator of the universe and the Lord of all being. "Israel," Franz Rosenzweig, the great Jewish religious philosopher, has said, "can bring the world to God only through Christianity."[3] And this "Christianity" is, of course, the extension into history of the Jesus whom Peter hailed as the Christ.

But there is also the other side of the medal. "Christianity," Rosenzweig continues, "could not long remain a force for redemption without Israel in its midst,"[4] and what that means can best be seen in the words of Paul Tillich, who speaks from the Christian commitment:

It is important that there always be Judaism. It is the corrective against the paganism that goes along with Christianity. . . . The Church is always in danger of adoring the gods of space in which she is ruling. . . . The Church is always in danger of losing her prophetic spirit. . . . Therefore, the prophetic spirit included in the tradition of the Synagogue is needed so long as the gods of space are in power, and that means to the end of history.[5]

Against all idolatries, Judaism proclaims: "Hear, O Israel, the Lord is our God, the Lord alone"; and this is a word which the church as well as the world — and the church because it is so immersed in the world — never ceases to need Judaism's witness to the living God, which it is compelled to bear by its divine calling as that is expressed in history, is a witness that cannot end until all things are brought to the end of judgment and fulfillment.

Yes, each needs the other: Judaism needs Christianity, and Christianity needs Judaism. The vocation of both can be defined in common terms: to bear witness to the living God amidst the idolatries of the world. But, since the emergence of the church, and through the emergence of the

---

[3] Nahum N. Glatzer, ed., *Franz Rosenzweig: His Life and Thought* (Schocken Books, 1953), 341.

[4] Ibid.

[5] Quoted in A. Roy Eckardt, *Christianity and the Children of Israel* (King's Crown Press, 1948), 146–147.

church, this vocation has, as it were, been split into two parts. The Jew fulfills his vocation by "staying with God," "giving the world no rest so long as the world has not God" — to recall Jacques Maritain's unforgettable phrase.[6] The Christian can fulfill his vocation only by "going out" to conquer the world for God. The Jew's vocation is to "stand," the Christian's to "go out" — both in the same cause of the kingdom of God. Judaism and Christianity thus represent one faith expressed in two religions — Judaism facing inward to the Jews, and Christianity facing outward to the gentiles, who, through it, are brought to the God, and under the covenant, of Israel, and therefore cease to be gentiles in the proper sense of the term. This is the unity of Judaism and Christianity, and this is why a Jew is able to see and acknowledge Jesus in his uniqueness as the way to the Father.

I know that what I say here will not satisfy those who are Christians, although they will, I hope, recognize its truth so far as it goes. And, indeed, it should not satisfy the Christian, since to the Christian, Jesus as the Christ must necessarily mean much more than he can possibly mean to the Jew. For the Jew sees Jesus as emerging from Israel and going forth; he sees him from the rear, as it were. The Christian, on the other hand, precisely because he is a Christian, will see Christ as coming toward him, in the fullness of divine grace, to claim, to judge, and to save; he meets him as Paul met him on the road to Damascus or as Peter outside Rome, face to face in confrontation. Yet this difference of perspective should not blind us to the fact that it is the same reality we see. And indeed — here again I refer to Franz Rosenzweig — the two religions relate to the same truth, being equal representations of it — equal before God.[7] With God, truth is one; but for men it is irreducibly split, since the truth as men see it is confessional and conditioned by one's community of faith. This is not a vicious relativism, nor does it assert for one moment that all religions are equally valid or equally true. On the contrary, as Rosenzweig puts it, man is either a pagan or a Jew or Christian.[8] The pagan, as pagan, is outside the scope of the covenant — that is what being a pagan means — though God, in his mercy, may, of course, reach out to him. Jew and Christian, on the other hand, has each his assigned position, defined in the covenant that relates him to God. Their positions, their "standpoints," being different, their views of the one truth and the one reality will be different — although both will be

---

[6]Jacques Maritain, *A Christian Looks at the Jewish Question* (Longmans, Green & Company, 1939), 29.
[7]Glatzer, *Franz Rosenzweig: His Life and Thought*, 341.
[8]Ibid.

views of the same truth and the same reality, just as two people standing in the same room but in different corners will see the room in different perspectives and therefore somewhat differently. Each will be loyal to the truth if he speaks out the truth as he sees it, though recognizing that his truth is never quite identical with the full truth of God. This approach does not derogate from the "finality" of either Judaism or Christianity, if that is properly understood; it merely prevents our making an idol of either; both are seen as instruments in the redemptive purpose of God, though each in a different way.

In short, each — the Jew on his part and the Christian on his — sees the truth as it is to be apprehended from his perspective, defined by his covenant and his vocation. Each must stand by his truth and confess it, recognizing that insofar as he does so in integrity and wholeness of heart, he remains faithful to the God whose truth it is. Naturally, since the two see the same reality in somewhat different ways, each may see an aspect of the truth hidden to the other, and even interpret the same truth differently. But perhaps that is part of God's purpose in placing the Jew and Christian on different sectors of the fighting front of the Kingdom, so that each may bear not only the common witness to God, but also a witness against the perils, inadequacies, and temptations of the other. The witness of Christianity against the legalistic, moralistic tendencies in Judaism is a witness for which the Jew must always be grateful. And the Christian, too, it seems to me, ought to see the value of the Jewish word in this dialogue. The Christian who tends to be impatient with the Jew for refusing to see in Jesus the fulfillment and completion of God's redemptive work might pause a moment to consider whether this Jewish "obstinacy" was not itself important as an indispensable reminder of the very incompleteness of this completion, of a redemption which may indeed have come but is nevertheless yet to come. The heart of each, Jew and Christian alike, may ache, perhaps, that the other is not in his camp, seeing things his way and fighting side by side with him on his sector of the front; but he ought also to recognize that though the other fights on a different sector, he is also fighting the same battle for the same God, and that it is perhaps by the providence of God that they are thus separated.

III

This, then, is how a Jew may see Jesus and the faith and church built upon the confession of him as the Christ. I realize how difficult it is for one to communicate what he has to say on this matter. "Christ," Franz Kafka, the Jew, once exclaimed, "is an abyss filled with light; one must close one's eyes if one is not to fall into it."[9] And yet speak one must. In Jesus — not merely Jesus the moral teacher, or Jesus the prophetic voice, but also the Jesus whom Christians confess the Christ — Jew and Christian find their unity . . . and their difference. In answering the question "Who do you say that I am?" Jew and Christian stand separated, yet united. The unity far transcends the separation, however real that may be, for the two are united in their common allegiance to the living God and in their common expectation of, and longing for, the One who is to come: for the Christian, the One who came and is to come again, for the Jew the One who is promised to Israel; but for both the same Promised One. In this one faith and hope, Jew and Christian — to recall Paul Tillich's words — stand united until the end of time in the struggle for the Lord of history against the pagan and idolatrous powers that threaten to overwhelm us on every side.

---

[9]Gustav Janouch, *Conversations with Kafka* (Frederick A. Praeger, 1953), 93.

Abraham J. Heschel (1907–1972)

Courtesy of Sylvia (Mrs. Abraham J.) Heschel

Introduction

by John C. Merkle

Christianity can be properly understood only in relation to Judaism; the true meaning of the church can be known only in connection with the Jewish people and its divinely appointed role in history. This is because the movement that emerged in response to Jesus of Nazareth was a Jewish sectarian movement; it was one of a variety of ways of expressing Jewish faith and hope in the first century of the common era. Before long, this movement, at first comprised solely of Jews, began to attract Gentile converts. Eventually, it became a predominantly Gentile church separated from the Jewish fold. As it consolidated its own identity independent of Judaism, the church underwent a process of "dejudaization" whereby many of its authentic Jewish components were eclipsed by elements of the Hellenistic and Roman world views it assimilated. Furthermore, the church attempted to legitimize its independent status by presenting itself as the "new Israel" that had displaced the Jews as the "old Israel." In point of fact, the church always has defined its identity in relation to Judaism and the Jewish people. Unfortunately, the church has usually misunderstood and misrepresented Judaism and has failed to appreciate the ongoing dynamism and validity of Jewish religious life.

But we are now living at a pivotal moment in the history of Jewish-Christian relations. For a little more than two decades, ever since the Second Vatican Council, the church has been in a process of reversing its perspective on Judaism and its nearly two millennia long relationship with the Jewish people. To be sure, this is a painful process, for it cuts to the core of Christian self-understanding, which was built in large part upon the notion of Christianity having superseded Judaism. Now that the church acknowledges the abiding validity of Judaism, it is imperative that we reevaluate the meaning of Christianity in relation to Judaism. However painful this reevaluation might be, it is necessary, for in it lies

267

the key to authentic Christian renewal. By contact with Judaism, the faith of Jesus, we Christians can water the roots of our own spiritual lives.

I

There have been many Jews whose influence on the church has contributed to this great reversal of the church's perspective on Jews and Judaism, but perhaps none more than Abraham Joshua Heschel (1907–1972). Indeed, it may be that Heschel did more to inspire an enhanced appreciation of Judaism among Christians than any other Jew in post-biblical history. Although other Jews have represented the grandeur of Judaism perhaps as much as Heschel did, it seems that he succeeded in communicating it to Christians more than anyone else. Living as he did in the midst of an ecumenical revolution, wherein Christians more than ever before began to reevaluate their perspectives on Judaism, Heschel had the opportunity to reach the Christian world in ways unknown to Jews in previous generations. And while he is only one of many Jewish religious thinkers of this century to influence Christians, he more than the others has been regarded by Christians as a spokesman for his tradition. This is indeed fitting, at least for those of us who agree with prominent Jewish scholar Jacob Neusner that Heschel is "the greatest Judaic theologian of this century."[1]

Prior to the publication of *Man Is Not Alone* (1951), Abraham Heschel was hardly known outside the world of Jewish scholarship. Yet in a review of that book, which Reinhold Niebuhr described as a "masterly analysis of faith," Niebuhr predicted that Heschel would become "a commanding and authoritative voice not only in the Jewish community but in the religious life of America."[2] During the next two decades Heschel fulfilled that expectation, emerging, in the words of this book's editor, as "the outstanding Jewish thinker of his generation" and "a major spiritual force in contemporary America."[3]

---

[1] Jacob Neusner, *Stranger at Home: "The Holocaust," Zionism, and American Judaism* (Chicago: University of Chicago Press, 1981), 82.

[2] Reinhold Niebuhr, "Masterly Analysis of Faith," *New York Herald Tribune Book Review*, April 1, 1951, 12.

[3] Fritz A. Rothschild, "Abraham Joshua Heschel (1907–1972): Theologian and Scholar," in *American Jewish Yearbook*, 74, Morris Fine and Milton Himmelfarb, eds. (Philadelphia: Jewish Publication Society of America, 1973), 533. This necrology by Rothschild and his introduction to *Between God and Man: An Interpretation of Judaism from the Writings of Abraham J. Heschel*, Fritz A. Rothschild, ed., rev. ed. (New York: The Free Press, 1976) are principal sources of the biographical information included here. For a longer introduction to Heschel's life and works (based on Rothschild and other sources) see chap. 1 of John C. Merkle, *The Genesis of Faith: The Depth Theology of Abraham Joshua Heschel* (New York: Macmillan Publishing Co., 1985).

Born in Warsaw in 1907, Heschel was the descendent of a long line of scholars and religious leaders. He grew up in an atmosphere of genuine ḥasidic piety and learning. By the age of ten he not only was at home in the world of the Bible and the Talmud but also had become acquainted with the world of Jewish mysticism, the Kabbalah. At the age of twenty, he moved to Berlin and enrolled at both the Hochschule für die Wissenschaft des Judentums and the University of Berlin. His dual enrollment signified what was to become a lifelong task: to combine the fruits of modern Western scholarship with a faithful and profound understanding of his Jewish heritage. He earned his doctorate in philosophy from the University in 1933. His dissertation, *Die Prophetie* (published in 1936), is a brilliant analysis of prophetic consciousness and forms the basis of the latter half of his monumental book, *The Prophets* (1962), hailed by Bernhard Anderson as "the most penetrating study of the subject that has appeared."[4]

In 1934 Heschel was ordained a rabbi and became an instructor in Talmud at the Hochschule where he had studied. In 1937 he succeeded Martin Buber at the Jüdische Lehrhaus (founded by Franz Rosenzweig) in Frankfurt am Main, where he taught until deported by the Nazis in October 1938 and returned to Poland. In April 1939 he was invited to join the faculty at the Hebrew Union College in Cincinnati. That summer, just six weeks before the Nazi invasion of Poland, Heschel left for England en route to his new post in the United States, which he assumed in the spring in 1940.

For five years Heschel served as Associate Professor of Philosophy and Rabbinics at the Hebrew Union College. In 1945, the year be became a citizen of the United States, Heschel joined the faculty of the Jewish Theological Seminary of America in New York, where he subsequently became Professor of Jewish Ethics and Mysticism and where he taught until his death in 1972.

Heschel was a prolific writer who made scholarly contributions to the study of the Bible, rabbinic literature, medieval philosophy, Jewish mysticism, and Ḥasidism. He also advanced a creative religious philosophy for our time. Along with the works already cited, some of Heschel's most important books are *The Sabbath* (1951), a profound study of the "architecture of time"; *Man's Quest for God* (1954), a penetrating analysis of prayer and symbolism; *Man Is Not Alone* (1951) and *God in Search of Man* (1955), his magnum opus as a creative religious philosopher, described by Neusner as "the single best introduction to the intellectual heritage

---

[4]Bernhard W. Anderson, "Confrontation with the Bible," *Theology Today* 30 (October 1973): 270.

of Judaism";[5] *Torah min ha-shamayim be-ispaklaryah shel ha-dorot* (vol. 1, 1962; vol. 2, 1965; in Hebrew), his magnum opus as a historical theologian; and *A Passion for Truth* (1973), a remarkable comparative study of the Baal Shem Tov (the founder of Ḥasidism), Reb Mendl of Kotzk (a ḥasidic master) and Søren Kierkegaard.

Heschel's writings are genuinely religious because his was an authentic religious life: a harmony of study, prayer, and action. His action consisted primarily in the unsung *mitzvot* of a pious Jew. But he also took a public and courageous stand on a number of social issues. This began early in his life and was particularly evident in an anti-Nazi lecture that he delivered in Frankfurt am Main in March 1938. Yet it was only in the last decade of his life that Heschel emerged as a recognized ethical leader of national and international prominence. This began in 1963 when he delivered the keynote address at the National Conference on Religion and Race, which led to widespread clergy participation in the great "march on Washington." He was passionate and persistent in his support of civil rights and in his condemnation of racism. He appeared with Martin Luther King, Jr., and he marched by his side from Selma to Montgomery. Heschel also protested the American involvement in the Vietnam war. He co-authored *Vietnam: Crisis of Conscience* (1967) and he was a national co-chairman of Clergy and Laity Concerned about Vietnam, an organization that helped to bring the moral and religious implications of this war to the attention of the American people.

Heschel was also the first major Jewish figure to urge world Jewry to come to the aid of the Jews in the Soviet Union. At a 1963 convocation of the Rabbinical Assembly he sounded the battle cry against the "spiritual genocide" being inflicted on Jews in the Soviet Union. Recalling Heschel's address to the Assembly, Fritz Rothschild writes: "His passionate plea for massive public action received wide publicity in the press and led to the subsequent formation of the American Conference on Soviet Jewry."[6]

Zionism was another cause to which Heschel was deeply committed. His book *Israel: An Echo of Eternity* (1968) is but one eloquent expression of that commitment. But Heschel not only challenged non-Jews to support Israel's right to exist; he also called upon both Jews and Arabs to acknowledge each other's basic human rights and to work together for peace.

Heschel was also active ecumenically. Most noteworthy is the promi-

---

[5] Jacob Neusner, *The Way of Torah: An Introduction to Judaism* (Belmont, Calif.: Dickenson Publishing Co., 1979), 104.
[6] Fritz A. Rothschild, "Abraham Joshua Heschel (1907–1972): Theologian and Scholar," 535

nent role he assumed in the negotiations between Jewish organizations and the hierarchy of the Catholic church before and during the Second Vatican Council. In Rome during the Council, Heschel represented the American Jewish Committee in its effort to improve Jewish-Christian relations and to eliminate anti-Judaism from church teachings. The American Jewish Committee realized that the church's attitude toward Jews was related to basic questions of theology and therefore chose Heschel, on account of his theological acumen, to represent the Committee at the Council. Late in November 1961 Heschel met with Augustin Cardinal Bea, the head of the Secretariat for Christian Unity, who invited Heschel to submit suggestions to the Council to improve Catholic-Jewish relations. Concerning Heschel's response to Bea, Fritz Rothschild writes:

Heschel's memorandum, prepared in cooperation with the American Jewish Committee, made three important recommendations. It urged the Council "to reject and condemn those who assert that the Jews as a people are responsible for the crucifixion. . . ." It suggested that the Council "acknowledge the integrity and permanent preciousness of the Jews and Judaism" so that the Jews be accepted *as Jews*. This meant that the Church would reconsider its missionary attitude and refrain from regarding Jews primarily as potential converts. And finally, it called for programs "to eliminate abuses and derogatory stereotypes" by promoting scholarly cooperation and the creation of church agencies to combat religious prejudice.[7]

Throughout the Council Heschel remained the most influential American Jewish delegate. Although the final conciliar decree on the Jews did not fulfill Heschel's expectations, "he nevertheless felt that it was a landmark in Jewish-Catholic relations and opened the path for a new era of better understanding and mutual respect."[8] This landmark was due largely to Heschel's presence and effort at the Council.

II

Convincing Christians to change their traditional perspective on Judaism was largely a by-product of Heschel's primary task of bearing witness to God. Nevertheless, it was an important item on his theological agenda. He was committed to fostering what he called "the new Christian understanding of Judaism."[9] In 1966 Heschel spoke to a Jewish audience of an

---

[7] Ibid., 535–536.

[8] Ibid., 536. Concerning Heschel's influence at Vatican II and the broader effect of his work on Jewish-Christian relations, see also Eva Fleischner, "Heschel's Significance for Jewish-Christian Relations," in *Abraham Joshua Heschel: Exploring His Life and Thought*, John C. Merkle, ed. (New York: Macmillan Publishing Co., 1985), 142–164.

[9] Abraham J. Heschel, "From Mission to Dialogue," *Conservative Judaism* 21 (Spring 1967): 9; hereafter cited as "Dialogue."

ecumenical revolution that was occurring wherein Jews had a unique opportunity, "unprecedented in almost two thousand years," to enter into
dialogue with Christians who are "eager to hear the message of Jewish
thought."[10] Heschel's desire to share Jewish insights with Christians was
not aimed at converting them to Judaism. "We abstain from conversion
and regard any attempt at depriving a person of a noble faith, of his heritage, as an act of arrogance," said Heschel.[11] But he knew that Judaism,
which had already given the world so many spiritual treasures, still had
unique contributions to offer not only Jews but all people. For these
contributions to be received by Christians, Heschel knew that they had
to develop a new and more accurate understanding of Judaism. There
are many ways in which he himself contributed to this development,
most importantly by what he conveyed about the three central realities
around which Judaism revolves: God, the Torah, and the people Israel.

Concerning Heschel's understanding of God, the well-known philosopher Charles Hartshorne expressed the view of many Christians when
he said: "If there has been a theology whose supreme principle is divine love, that it is."[12] So much for the age-old Christian polemic that
Christianity has a view of God superior to that found in Judaism! What
Reinhold Niebuhr called Heschel's "masterly analysis of faith" is essentially an analysis of the way of Torah. So much for the contrast between
Judaism as a religion of law and Christianity as a religion of faith! To encounter Heschel, said the Protestant biblical scholar W. D. Davies, was to
experience "the mysterious greatness of the Jewish tradition."[13] So much
for the Christian myth that the church is "the new house of God" that
has displaced Israel as "the previous people of God"![14] When Christians
discover that the Jewish understanding of God is infinitely richer than
has been depicted in Christian polemics; that the way of Torah, which in
traditional Christian literature has been declared abrogated, continues to
bear the fruit of holiness; and that the Jewish people, whose divinely appointed mission has supposedly been superseded by the church, have
endured through untold persecutions precisely because of their spiritual and moral vitality; when Christians discover these facts they must
develop a new theology of Judaism and the Jewish people.

To read Heschel is to feel the spiritual vitality and grandeur of Judaism; it is to be persuaded that the Jewish people are still covenanted

---

[10]"Dialogue," 11.

[11]"Dialogue," 1.

[12]Charles Hartshorne, in a letter to John C. Merkle (June 18, 1965).

[13]W. D. Davies, "Conscience, Scholar, Witness," *America* (March 10, 1973), 214.

[14]Karl Rahner, *Foundations of Christian Faith: An Introduction to the Idea of Christianity* (New York: Seabury Press, 1978), 157.

to God and have an indispensable part to play in the divinely inspired drama of redemption. In light of this, Christians must ask themselves how they are to interpret the role of Christianity in that drama. The time-worn idea that Christianity has superseded Judaism and that Christians have displaced Jews as God's elect cannot survive an honest reading of Heschel. Indeed, it cannot survive any genuine encounter with Judaism. But, again, perhaps more than anyone else, Heschel has communicated the splendor of his tradition to Christians. Only in recent decades have Christians finally begun turning to Jews for their understanding of Jewish faith rather than to Christian critics of Judaism. In doing so, many have found Heschel to be a preeminent guide. Moreover, apart from the desire to understand Judaism, countless Christians have turned to Heschel for guidance in their own life of faith. As a side-effect of being spiritually enriched by a Jew devoted to his tradition, Christians must reject the Christian myth that Judaism is an obsolete religion and that those who adhere to it in spite of the Christian alternative are spiritually blind or stubborn. On the contrary, they must acknowledge the spiritual depth and theological veracity of the Judaism that nurtured Heschel's religious life and understanding.

III

Here is where Heschel has made his greatest contribution to the Christian world: he has inspired deep appreciation for Judaism among count-less Christians. And since the church's identity has been built in large part upon misinformation about Judaism, this new Christian appreci-ation of Judaism must inevitably cause a revolution in Christian self-understanding. How is the church to legitimize its identity and mission if not by portraying itself as the "new Israel" that has displaced the "old Israel" as God's chosen people?

Heschel himself has proposed an answer for Christians to consider. And what he has written about Christianity presents a challenge to Christian self-understanding. "The vital challenge for the Church," said Heschel, "is to decide whether Christianity came to overcome, to abol-ish, or to continue the Jewish way by bringing the God of Abraham and His will to the Gentiles."[15] In order to appreciate Heschel's view of Christianity and its purpose in history, it is necessary to consider it in relation to his view of the role of the Jewish people and their covenant.

---

[15] Abraham J. Heschel, "The Jewish Notion of God and Christian Renewal," in *Renewal of Religious Thought*, vol. 1 of *Theology of Renewal*, L. K. Shook, ed. (New York: Herder and Herder, 1968), 111; hereafter cited as "Renewal"; see also below, p. 328.

According to Heschel, God's "revelation to Israel continues as revelation through Israel."[16] The Jewish people have been charged with the task of giving witness to God by way of Torah. But just as biblical and rabbinic authors reminded the people that their special election did not imply either Israel's superiority in relation to other peoples or an exclusive relationship with God, Heschel pointed out that it did not imply that Israel was the only vehicle of God's revelation.[17] Heschel believed we should be open to the revelation of the divine wherever it may be discerned, and that such openness is an expression of trust in the God of our biblical heritage who transcends all traditions. God's revelation is to be found in many unexpected places, particularly, according to Heschel, wherever justice and love are promoted and enhanced.

It is clear, then, that for Heschel the purpose or end of divine revelation is human redemption. He claimed that "diversity of religions is the will of God" because "the task of preparing the kingdom of God" requires such diversity.[18] If this is so, does it not follow that peoples of various faiths have been chosen by God for various tasks? Speaking specifically about Christianity, Heschel said: "The Jewish attitude enables us to acknowledge the presence of a divine plan in the role of Christianity within the history of redemption."[19]

Notice that Heschel spoke of the *history* of redemption. From his Jewish perspective, redemption is not only an event that will occur at the end of history, but a process that may go on all the time — enhanced or spoiled by human deeds. It is a process in which both Judaism and Christianity have eminent roles to the extent that they bear witness to the God of Israel and foster human living in accord with divine concern. But while Christianity focuses on one event within the process as the prolepsis of "the end of days," Judaism stresses the fact that no matter how many redemptive events have occurred (Exodus, Sinai, etc.) the process is still terribly incomplete.

In early Christianity, when the church was predominantly Jewish, there was great longing for the fulfillment of this world's redemption. The resurrected Jesus, who was acclaimed the Messiah because his followers sensed in him the coming of God's kingdom, was expected to return and inaugurate the messianic age. Before long, as the church became Hellenized, this emphasis on his "second coming" gave way to a stress on the personal salvation that had been won for believers

---

[16] Abraham J. Heschel, "No Religion Is an Island,'" *Union Seminary Quarterly Review* 21 (January 1966): 129; hereafter cited as "Religion"; see below, p. 320.

[17] Cf. "Religion," 126–127; see below, p. 321.

[18] "Religion," 126; see below, p. 318.

[19] "Religion," 131; see below, p. 322.

through the death and resurrection of Christ. Heschel, noting this transition, lamented the fact that "Christians have become less and less messianic."[20] He often reminded us that "the ultimate concern of the Jew is not personal salvation but universal redemption."[21] He thereby challenged the church to recapture the original hope of Jesus and his disciples for the coming of God's reign in this world. Such a church would feel a closer kinship with the Jewish people who are keenly aware of the world's lack of redemption and yet keep alive the hope for the messianic age.

Since the church has its roots in the Jewish covenant, Heschel suggested that the church might "consider itself an extension of Judaism."[22] Still, he was emphatic about this: Christianity is no substitute for Judaism. Even in a world where the church continues the Jewish way, Israel retains her own unique vocation: to bear witness to God by way of Torah.

But this implies that Christianity, which Heschel acknowledges "as part of God's design,"[23] has its own unique role in the history of redemption. The church has a vocation that is compatible with but distinct from the vocation of Israel. This means that while it is meant "to continue the Jewish way," it may — indeed, it must — do this according to its own distinctive form of covenantal life. For most of its history the church has stressed the discontinuity between Israel and itself, even to the point of claiming to represent a new covenant that has replaced the Jewish covenant. But if we are inspired by Heschel's view and think of the church as "an extension of Judaism," we will reject the idea that a new covenant has replaced the Jewish one. Rather, we will think of Christianity as a new way, coexisting with the Jewish way, of living in covenant with the God of Israel. If such a view were to be adopted by the church it would constitute a radical transformation in self-understanding, but it would be closer to the vision of the earliest Christians who, like Jesus, continued to live within the Jewish covenant.

When, at the Second Vatican Council, for the first time in its history, the Catholic church recognized the validity of Judaism, it did by implication affirm the abiding significance of the Jewish covenant; and since then this has been explicitly affirmed in Vatican statements. Nevertheless, there still exists within the churches, including the Catholic church,

---

[20]"Renewal," 120; see below, p. 336.
[21]Abraham J. Heschel, *The Insecurity of Freedom: Essays on Human Existence* (New York: Schocken Books, 1966) 146; hereafter cited as *Freedom*. The theme is reiterated often throughout Heschel's works.
[22]*Freedom*, 169.
[23]"Religion," 132; see below, p. 323.

the widespread conviction — expressed in both official and unofficial theological writings — that the Jewish covenant has been fulfilled by a new Christian covenant. Judaism remains a valid way to God, but is considered to be inferior to Christianity. The Jewish covenant is not superseded but surpassed. This theory is rooted in the belief that Jesus is the Messiah of Jewish expectations through whom a new covenant has been established. So, although Judaism is a valid religion, Jews would do well to accept Jesus as the Christ and thereby embrace Christianity as the fulfillment of Judaism. But have the messianic expectations of Israel been fulfilled? And did Jesus really establish a new covenant apart from the Jewish covenant?

The "new covenant" of which Jesus spoke (Luke 22:20) should be understood as covenantal renewal and as anticipation — not fulfillment — of the messianic realization of the covenant envisioned by the prophets Jeremiah and Ezekiel (Jer. 31:31–34; Ezek. 16:59–63). Commenting on the new covenant prophesied by Jeremiah, Heschel said: "what the prophet seems to predict is not abolition of the Torah but inner identification with it. . . . Days are coming . . . when man will become torah."[24] These will be messianic days. Jesus was caught up in the Jewish messianic expectations of his day. The new covenant for which he longed was not another covenant that would replace or be an alternative to the Jewish covenant.[25] Rather, it was the new messianic form of that covenant. Obviously, this has not come to pass. The messianic expectations of Judaism which inspired Jesus' hopes — the end of all idolatry, war, suffering, etc. — have not been fulfilled. Jesus probably lived with a lively expectation of messianic fulfillment, and indeed we Christians believe that he had — and continues to have — a central role to play in the messianic drama. But we must admit that the messianic realization of the covenant — anticipated by Jeremiah, Ezekiel, and Jesus — is still but a hope, and not a reality, for Christians as well as Jews. Moreover, according to Heschel, it is imperative that we translate our messianic hope into a program of action since God, having endowed us with freedom, needs our help in redeeming the world.[26]

The time has come for Christians to acknowledge the fact that Christianity is valid not because it supersedes or even surpasses Judaism but, on the contrary, to the extent that it extends covenantal life with Israel's God to the Gentile world. This is not to say that Judaism is closed

---

[24] *Freedom*, 174.
[25] Cf. Rosemary Ruether, *Faith and Fratricide: The Theological Roots of Anti-Semitism* (New York: Seabury Press, 1974), 253.
[26] This is a recurrent theme in Heschel's writings; cf., e.g., "Renewal," 119; see below, p. 335.

to Gentiles. Anyone who desires to respond to God by way of Torah may convert to Judaism. The fact remains, however, that Christianity has made covenantal life accessible to more Gentiles than has Judaism. Moreover, it is our conviction as Christians that God wills a way of covenantal life for Gentiles that is distinct from Israel's way of living in covenant.

Jews keep their covenant with God alive by way of Torah. We Christians have come to know God through the Gospel of and about Jesus, so we will do our part to keep the covenant alive by recalling the crucified and resurrected messianic herald, and by embracing the covenantal faith and hope for which he lived and died. Thus we will keep alive the Christian tradition that keeps alive his memory and celebrates his resurrected presence. But we must also transform the church, purging it of its chronic anti-Judaism, and making it a more identifiable offspring of Jewish faith and a true ally of the Jewish people. In order to do this we must understand the Jewish way. For this, the writings of Abraham Joshua Heschel are an invaluable legacy.

1

More Than Inwardness

1955

By Faith Alone?

The claim of Judaism that religion and law are inseparable is difficult for many of us to comprehend. The difficulty may be explained by modern man's conception of the essence of religion. To the modern mind, religion is a state of the soul, inwardness; feeling rather than obedience, faith rather than action, spiritual rather than concrete. To Judaism, religion is not a feeling for something that is, but *an answer* to Him who is asking us to live in a certain way. It is in its very origin a consciousness of total commitment; a realization that all of life is not only man's but also God's sphere of interest.

"God asks for the heart."[1] Yet does he ask for the heart only? Is the right intention enough? Some doctrines insist that love is the sole condition for salvation (Sufi,[2] Bhakti-marga), stressing the im-

---

[1] *Sanhedrin* 106b.
[2] Ignaz Goldziher, *Vorlesungen über den Islam* (Heidelberg, 1910), 167ff.; D. S. Margoliouth, "The Devil's Delusion of Ibn Al-Jauzi," *Islamic Culture* 10 (1936): 348. "The Brethren of the Free Spirit," who emerged in the thirteenth century taught that God could best be served in freedom of spirit, and that the sacraments and ordinances of the Church were not needed. "As man is essentially divine and is able through contemplation and withdrawal from things of sense to know himself united with God, he can in his freedom do what God does, and must act as God works in him. There is, therefore, for the free man neither virtue not vice. God is all, and all is God, and all is His." "Such is the virtue of love and charity that whatever was done in their behalf could be no sin. . . . Have charity and do what thou pleasest" (J. Herkless, *Encyclopedia of Religion and Ethics* 2:842f.; H. Ch. Lea, *A History of the Inquisition* (New York, 1909), 2:321.

portance of inwardness, of love or faith, to the exclusion of good works.

Paul waged a passionate battle against the power of law and proclaimed instead the religion of grace. Law, he claimed, cannot conquer sin, nor can righteousness be attained through works of law. A man is justified "by faith without the deeds of the law."[3]

That salvation is attained by faith alone was Luther's central thesis. The antinomian tendency resulted in the overemphasis of love and faith to the exclusion of good works.

The Formula of Concord of 1580, still valid in Protestantism, condemns the statement that good works are necessary to salvation and rejects the doctrine that they are harmful to salvation. According to Ritschl, the doctrine of the merit of good deeds is an intruder in the domain of Christian theology; the only way of salvation is justification by faith. Barth, following Kierkegaard, voices Lutheran thoughts, when he claims that man's deeds are too sinful to be good. There are fundamentally no human deeds, which, because of their significance in this world, find favor in God's eyes. God can be approached through God alone.

The Error of Formalism

In trying to show that justice is not identical with our predilection or disposition, that it is independent of our interest and consent, we should not commit the common error of confounding the relation of man to justice with the relation of justice to man. For although it is true that we ought to do justice for its own sake, justice itself is for the sake of man. To define justice as that which is worth doing for its own sake is to define the motive, not the purpose. It is just the opposite: the good, unlike play, is never done for its own sake, but for a purpose. To think otherwise is to make an idol of an ideal; it is the beginning of fanaticism. Defining the good by the motive alone, equalizing the good with the good intention and ignoring the purpose and substance of the good action, is a half-truth.

Those who have only paid attention to the relation of man to the ideals, disregarding the relation of the ideals to man, have in their theories seen only the motive but not the purpose of either religion or morality. Echoing the Paulinian doctrine that man is saved by faith alone, Kant and his disciples taught that the essence of religion or morality would consist in an absolute quality of the soul or the will, regardless of the actions

---

[3]Romans 3:20: "By the deeds of the law there shall no flesh be justified in his sight; for by the law is knowledge of sin." On the theological implications of the whole problem, see E. LaB. Cherbonnier, *Hardness of Heart* (New York, 1955), chap. 11.

that may come out of it or the ends that may be attained. Accordingly, the value of a religious act would be determined wholly by the intensity of one's faith or by the rectitude of one's inner disposition. The intention, not the deed, the *how*, not the *what* of one's conduct, would be essential, and no motive other than the sense of duty would be of any moral value. Thus acts of kindness, when not dictated by the sense of duty, are no better than cruelty, and compassion or regard for human happiness as such is looked upon as an ulterior motive. "I would not break my word even to save mankind!" exclaimed Fichte. His salvation and righteousness were apparently so much more important to him than the fate of all men that he would have destroyed mankind to save himself. Does not such an attitude illustrate the truth of the proverb, "The road to hell is paved with good intentions?" Should we not say that a concern with one's own salvation and righteousness that outweighs the regard for the welfare of one human being cannot be qualified as a good intention?

Judaism stresses the relevance of human deeds. It refuses to accept the principle that under all circumstances the intention determines the deed. However, the absence of the right intention does not necessarily vilify the goodness of a deed of charity.[4] The good deeds of any man, to whatever nation or religion he may belong,[5] even when done by a person who has never been reached by a prophet and who therefore acts on the basis of his own insight,[6] will be rewarded by God.

No Dichotomy

The cause of nearly all failures in human relations is this — that while we admire and extol the tasks, we fail to acquire the tools. Neither the naked hand nor the soul left to itself can effect much. It is by instruments that work is done. The soul needs them as much as the hand. And as the instruments of the hand either give motion or guide it, so the instruments

---

[4]Said Rabbi Eleazar ben Azariah: "Scripture says (Deut. 24:19), 'When you reap your harvest in your field, and have forgotten a sheaf in the field, you shall not go back to get it; it shall be for the stranger, for the fatherless and the widow.' You see, it states immediately afterwards, 'that the Lord your God may bless you.' Scripture thus gives the assurance of a blessing to one through whom a meritorious deed came about (the feeding of the stranger), though he had no knowledge of what he was doing (since he forgot to remove the sheaf from the field). You must now admit that if a *Sela*[c] (a coin) was tied up in the skirt of one's garment and it fell from it and a poor man finds it and supports himself by it, the Holy One, blessed be He, gives the assurance of blessing to the man who has lost the *Sela*[c]" (*Sifra* to 5:17, ed. Weiss, 27a; cf. *Sifre* on Deut., ed. Finkelstein, 300).

[5]Halevi, *Kuzari*, 1, III.

[6]Maimonides, *The Guide of the Perplexed*, part III, chap. 17; see, however, *Mishneh Torah*, Melakim 8, 11.

of the soul supply either suggestions or cautions. The meaningfulness of the mitsvot consists of their being vehicles by which we advance on the road to spiritual ends.

Faith is not a silent treasure to be kept in the seclusion of the soul, but a mint in which to strike the coin of common deeds. It is not enough to be dedicated in the soul, to consecrate moments in the stillness of contemplation.

The dichotomy of faith and works which presented such an important problem in Christian theology was never a problem in Judaism. To us, the basic problem is neither what is the right action nor what is the right intention. The basic problem is: what is right living? And life is indivisible. The inner sphere is never isolated from outward activities. Deed and thought are bound into one. All a person thinks and feels enters everything he does, and all he does is involved in everything he thinks and feels.

Spiritual aspirations are doomed to failure when we try to cultivate deeds at the expense of thoughts or thoughts at the expense of deeds. Is it the artist's inner vision or his wrestling with the stone that brings about a work of sculpture? Right living is like a work of art, the product of a vision and of a wrestling with concrete situations.

Judaism is averse to generalities, averse to looking for meaning in life detached from doing, as if the meaning were a separate entity. Its tendency is to make ideas convertible into deeds, to interpret metaphysical insights as patterns for action, to endow the most sublime principles with bearing upon everyday conduct. In its tradition, the abstract became concrete, the absolute historic. By enacting the holy on the stage of concrete living, we perceive our kinship with the divine, the presence of the divine. What cannot be grasped in reflection, we comprehend in deeds. . . .

The Law

In Judaism allegiance to God involves a commitment to Jewish law, to a discipline, to specific obligations. These terms, against which modern man seems to feel an aversion, are in fact a part of civilized living. Every one of us who acknowledges allegiance to the state of which he is a citizen is committed to its law, and accepts the obligations it imposes upon him. His loyalty will on occasion prompt him to do even more than mere allegiance would demand. Indeed, the word loyalty is derived from the same root as "legal," *ligo*, which means "to be bound." Similarly, the word "obligation" comes from the Latin *obligo*, to bind, and denotes the state of being bound by a legal or moral tie.

The object of the prophets was to guide and to demand, not only to

1

console and to reassure. Judaism is meaningless as an optional attitude to be assumed at our convenience. To the Jewish mind life is a complex of obligations, and the fundamental category of Judaism is *a demand* rather than *a dogma, a commitment* rather than a feeling. *God's will* stands higher than *man's creed.* Reverence for the authority of the law is an expression of our love for God.

However, beyond His will is His love. The Torah was given to Israel as a sign of His love. To reciprocate that love we strive to attain *ahavat Torah.* . . .

2

A Hebrew Evaluation of Reinhold Niebuhr

1956

Once upon a time a king received a shocking report about the new harvest: Whoever eats of the crop becomes mad. So he called together his counselors. Since no other food was available, the alternative was clear. Not to eat of the new harvest would be to die of starvation, to eat would be to become mad. The decision reached by the king was: We will all have to eat, but let at least a few of us continue to keep in mind that we are mad. This parable by Rabbi Nahman of Bratslav (1772–1811) comes to my mind in opening an essay on the meaning of Reinhold Niebuhr to our generation. He reminds us what we are.

In boldness of penetration, depth of insight, fullness of vision and comprehensiveness, Reinhold Niebuhr's system excels everything which the whole of American theology has hitherto produced. A pioneer for his generation, he speaks of the eternal in a world of spiritual absenteeism, compelling it to listen to him. It is not easy to listen to him because he not only plants new truths but also roots out old errors, even the most comfortable and satisfying ones. Yet the degree to which Niebuhr does influence American thinking is one of the most significant facts of contemporary American history.

In an age that "has no vantage point from which to understand the

283

predicament of modern man,"[1] Niebuhr not only helps many of his contemporaries to see through their delusions, deceptions, and pretensions;
he also succeeds in recovering some of the insights of prophetic thinking that are of tremendous aid in understanding the central issues of
existence from a religious perspective.[2]

In the following pages an attempt is made to examine some of
Niebuhr's views in the light of Jewish thinking. We shall confine ourselves to a few aspects of his doctrine of evil, particularly those of
common conviction and concern.

I

Niebuhr reminds us that "there is a mystery of evil in human life to
which modern culture has been completely oblivious."[3]

It may have been possible prior to 1914 to believe with Herbert
Spencer, who in his *Evanescence of Evil* asserted that "evil perpetually
tends to disappear."[4] The certainty of evil's gradual extinction through
the growth of culture and education was a part of the belief in the steady
progress of mankind, of the belief in "redemption through progress." But
the horrors through which we have lived in the past forty years have
totally discredited such simple, easy-going optimism.

"Therefore he who is prudent will keep silent in such a time; for it
is an evil time" (Amos 5:13). But Niebuhr is not prudent. The road to
disaster is paved with pleasant illusions, and the way to deal with evil
is not to ignore it. Indeed, the effort to minimize the power of evil has
had fateful results in the past. It has not only weakened our alertness to
the dangers of existence but also impaired our sense of guilt, our ability
to repent, and our power to pray, "Forgive us for we have sinned."

Niebuhr's distinctive contribution to contemporary thinking lies in
his comprehension of "the dimension of depth in life," in his tracing every problem with which he deals "to some ultimate origin." He

---

[1] *Faith and History* (New York, 1949), 9.

[2] "I have as a Christian theologian sought to strengthen the Hebraic-prophetic content
of the Christian tradition" (Reinhold Niebuhr, introduction to Waldo Frank's *The Jew in
Our Time* [New York, 1944]).

[3] *An Interpretation of Christian Ethics*, 119.

[4] "All evil results from the non-adaptation of constitution to conditions. . . . Eventually
true is it that evil perpetually tends to disappear. In virtue of an essential principle of life,
this non-adaptation of an organism to its conditions is ever being rectified; and modification
of one or both continues until the adaptation is complete. Whatever possesses vitality, from
the elementary cell up to man himself, inclusive, obeys this law. . . . This universal law of
physical modification is the law of mental modification also. . . . Progress, therefore, is not
an accident but a necessity. Evil and immorality must surely disappear; man must surely
become perfect" (Herbert Spencer, *Social Statics* [New York, 1897], 28–32).

stresses the antinomies and ambiguities of man's historic existence and denies that they can be overcome in history itself. He has shown that the tragic aspect of man cannot be reduced either to a psychological or to a biological quality; that it is rather an aspect of history, of the structure of existence. The question that is going to occupy us is to what degree Niebuhr's thought is within the biblical and prophetic tradition.

Many modern theologians have consistently maintained that the Bible stands for optimism, that pessimism is alien to its spirit.[5] There is, however, very little evidence to support such a view. With the exception of the first chapter of the Book of Genesis, the rest of the Bible does not cease to refer to the sorrow, sins, and evils of this world. As Maimonides pointed out (in a different context and order), the ideas that apply to the world in the state of its coming into being do not apply to the world that is in being. The design of the Creator was for a world that was to be good, very good; but then something mysterious happened, to which Jewish tradition alludes in many ways, and the picture of the world profoundly changed. When the prophets look at the world, they behold "distress and darkness, the gloom of anguish" (Isa. 8:22). When they look at the land, they find it "full of guilt against the Holy One of Israel" (Jer. 51:5). "O Lord, how long shall I cry for help, and Thou wilt not hear? Or cry to Thee 'violence!' and Thou wilt not save? Why dost Thou make me see wrongs and look upon trouble? Destruction and violence are before me; strife and contention arise. So the law is slacked and justice never goes forth. For the wicked surround the righteous, so justice goes forth perverted" (Hab. 1:2–4). This is a world in which the way of the wicked prosper and "all who are treacherous thrive" (Jer. 12:1); a world which made it possible for some people to maintain that "Everyone who does evil is good in the sight of the Lord, and He delights in them," and for others to ask, "Where is the God of justice?" (Mal. 2:17).

The psalmist did not feel that this was a happy world when he prayed: "O God, do not keep silence; do not hold peace or be still, O God. For, lo, Thy enemies are in uproar; those who hate thee have raised their heads" (Ps. 83:2–3).

The terror and anguish that came upon the psalmist were not caused by calamities in nature but by the wickedness of man, by the evils in history:

---

[5]To my knowledge Schopenhauer was one of the first to claim that the Hebrew spirit was characteristically optimistic, whereas Christianity was pessimistic. *Die Welt als Wille und Vorstellung*, II, chap. 48; *Parerga and Paralipomena*, Gusbach ed., II, 397. *Sämtliche Werke*, Frauenstädt ed., III, 712f.

Fearfulness and trembling come upon me,
Horror has overwhelmed me.
And I said, Oh that I had wings like a dove!
Then would I fly away, and be at rest.
Psalm 55:6–7

These are the words of Moses in his last days: "I know how defiant and stiffnecked you are.... I know that, when I am dead, you will act wickedly, and turn aside from the path which I enjoined upon you; and in time to come misfortune will befall you, for having done evil in the sight of the Lord" (Deut. 31:27–29). It is not a sweet picture of man that Isaiah paints, saying: "You have never heard, you have never known, for of old your ear has not been opened. For I knew that you would deal very treacherously, and that from birth you were called a rebel" (Isa. 48:8).

There is one line that expresses the mood of the Jewish man throughout the ages: *"The earth is given into the hand of the wicked"* (Job 9:24).[6]

How does the world look in the eyes of God? Are we ever told that the Lord saw that the righteousness of man was great in the earth, and that He was glad to have made man on the earth? The general tone of the biblical view of history is set after the first ten generations: "The Lord saw how great was man's wickedness on earth, and how every plan devised by his mind was nothing but evil all the time. And the Lord regretted that He had made man on earth, and His heart was saddened" (Gen. 6:5–6; cf. 8:21). One great cry resounds throughout the Bible: The wickedness of man is great on the earth. It is voiced by the prophets; it is echoed by the psalmist.

The two dominant attitudes of prophetic faith are gratitude and contrition; gratitude for creation and contrition before judgment; or, in other words, confidence that life is good in spite of its evil and that it is evil in spite of good. In such faith both sentimentality and despair are avoided.[7]

The absence of the awareness of the mystery of evil is a tragic blindness of modern man. In his vocabulary the word is missing. But without an awareness of sin, without the fear of evil, there can be no repentance.

II

A major concern of Niebuhr's thinking is the problem of realism and the lack of realism in our contemporary "nominalistic" culture. An example of the sentimentality and unreality that dominate the political opinions

---

[6]Raba, in *Baba Bathra*, 9a, referred to the end of the verse as denying divine Providence.
[7]*An Interpretation of Christian Ethics*, 106.

of the liberal world is the belief that the power of man's lust and ambitions is no more than some subrational impulse, which can be managed with more astute social engineering or more psychiatric help. In contrast, Niebuhr insists that the freedom of the self is a radical one and is not easily brought under the control of reason, just as it is not easily kept within the confines of nature's harmonies.

The utopianism and deductive thinking of the modern mentality are best illustrated in its relation to the problem of egocentricity, the universality of which is "empirically respected by all men of affairs who are charged with any responsibility in business or government."[8] Yet academic empiricism continues to insist that the universal tendency to egocentricity is due to faulty education and that it could be overcome either by adequate psychiatric technique or social reforms.

The fact that the phenomenon of self-seeking may be related, not to specific forms of insecurity, but to the insecurity of life itself, seems to be obscured in even the most sophisticated psychological theory, which is why psychological theories are so irrelevant to political theory.

Such sentimentality and unreality have often been considered a distinctly biblical attitude, while in truth the Bible constantly reminds us of man's frailty and unreliability. "All flesh is grass, and all the strength thereof is as the flower of the field. The grass withers, the flower fades . . . surely the people is grass" (Isa. 40:6–7). "Put not your trust in princes, nor in the son of man, in whom there is no help" (Ps. 146:3). Isaiah calls upon us not to trust the world; the psalmist tells us not to rely on man.

What the rabbis thought about the nature of man may be shown in the following comment. We read in Habakkuk 1:14, *And Thou makest man as the fishes of the sea, and as the creeping things, that have no ruler over them?* "Why is man here compared to the fishes of the sea? . . . Just as among fishes of the sea, the greater swallow up the smaller ones, so with men, were it not for fear of government, men would swallow each other alive. This is just what we have learned: Rabbi Hanina, the Deputy High Priest, said, 'Pray for the welfare of the government, for were it not for fear thereof, men would swallow each other alive.'"[9]

According to Rabbi Jacob, "This world is like a vestibule before the world to come; prepare yourself in the vestibule, so that you may enter the banquet hall."[10] There is no reward for good deeds in this world.[11]

---

[8] *Christian Realism and Political Problems*, 7–8.
[9] *Abodah Zarah*, 3b–4a; see also *Aboth*, 3:2.
[10] *Aboth*, 4:21.
[11] *Erubin*, 22a.

The time for reward promised in the Bible is the life to come.[12] According to Rav, "The world was created for the extremely pious or the extremely wicked, for men like Rabbi Hanina ben Dosa [a saint who lived in the first century of the common era] or for men like King Ahab; this world was created for the extremely wicked, the world to come was created for the extremely pious."[13] "In this world war and suffering, evil inclination, Satan, and the angel of death hold sway."[14]

In the Jewish mystical literature of the thirteenth century the doctrine is advanced that world history consists of seven periods (*shemitah*), each lasting seven thousand years, which in the Jubilee, the fifty thousandth year, will reach its culmination. The current period is one which is dominated by the divine quality of "stern judgment." In it the evil urge, licentiousness, arrogance, forgetfulness, and unholiness prevail.[15]

According to Rabbi Shneur Zalman of Ladi: "Anything that refuses to regard itself as nothing beside God but, on the contrary, asserts itself as an entity separate from God does not receive the light of its vitality from the inner holiness and essence of God." It receives the light of its vitality, so to speak, from the "hind-part" of his holiness, and only after it has gone through myriad channels of emanation and has been so obscured and contracted that it is capable of living "in exile," apart from God. And that is why this material world is called a "world of shells" (*kelipoth*), "the other side" (*sitra aḥra*). And this is why all the things that happen in this world are harsh and evil, and this is why the wicked prevail.[16]

The pious Jews put no trust in the secular world. "They realized quite well that the world was full of ordeals and dangers, that it contained Cain's jealousy of Abel, the cold malevolence of Sodom, and the hatred of Esau, but they also knew that there was in it the charity of Abraham and the tenderness of Rachel. Harassed and oppressed, they carried deep within their hearts a contempt for the world, with its power and pomp, with its bustling and boasting. . . . They knew that the Jews were in exile, that the world was unredeemed."[17] Dazzled by the splendor of Western civilization, the modern Jew has been prone to forget that the world is unredeemed, and that God is in exile. The present generation which has witnessed the most unspeakable horrors committed by man and sponsored by an extremely civilized nation is beginning to realize

---

[12]*Kiddushin*, 39b.

[13]*Berakhot*, 61b. This world is often compared to "night"; it is even called "the world of falsehood."

[14]*Midrash Vayosha, Beth Hamidrash*, Jellinek, ed., 2d ed. (Jerusalem, 1938), I, 55.

[15]*Temunah* (Koretz, 1784), 39b.

[16]Rabbi Shneur Zalman of Ladi, *Tanya*, 10b.

[17]Heschel, *The Earth Is the Lord's* (New York, 1950), 96.

how monstrous an illusion it was to substitute faith in man for faith in God.

We do not feel "at home" in the world. With the psalmist we pray, "I am a stranger on earth, hide not Thy commandments from me" (119:19). Indeed, if not for our endless power to forget and our great ability to disregard, who could be at ease even for one moment in a lifetime? In the face of so much evil and suffering, of countless examples of failure to live up to the will of God, in a world where His will is defied, where His kingship is denied, who can fail to see the discrepancy between the world and the will of God?

And yet, just because of the realization of the power of evil, life in this world assumed unique significance and worth. Evil is not only a threat; it is also a challenge. It is precisely because of the task of fighting evil that life in this world is so preciously significant. True, there is no reward for good deeds in this world; yet this does not mean that the world is a prison. It is rather a prelude, a vestibule, a place of preparation, of initiation, of apprenticeship to a future life, where the guests prepare to enter *tricilinium*, or the banquet hall.[18] Life in this world is a time for action, for good works, for worship and sanctification, as eternity is a time for retribution. It is eve of the Sabbath, on which the repast is prepared for the Lord's day; it is the season of duty and submission, as the morrow shall be that of freedom from every yoke. More precious, therefore, than all of life to come is a single hour of life on earth — an hour of repentance and good deeds. Eternity gives only in the degree that it receives. This is why the Book of Ecclesiastes pronounced the dead lion less happy than the living dog.[19]

III

Niebuhr's central problem is not the problem of sin or the problem of evil. His problem is not good *and* evil, but the evil within the good, or more accurately the *confusion* of good and evil.

More frustrating than the fact that evil is real, mighty, and tempting is the fact that it thrives so well in the disguise of the good, and that it can draw its nutriment from the life of the holy. In this world, it seems, the holy and the unholy do not exist apart but are mixed, interrelated, and confounded; it is a world where idols are at home, and where even the worship of God may be alloyed with the worship of idols.

In Jewish mysticism we often come upon the view that in this world

---

[18]*Aboth*, 4:22.
[19]*Shabbat*, 30a.

neither good nor evil exists in purity, and that there is no good without the admixture of evil nor evil without the admixture of good. The confusion of good and evil is the central problem of history and the ultimate issue of redemption. The confusion goes back to the very process of creation. "When God came to create the world and reveal what was hidden in the depths and disclose light out of darkness, they were all wrapped in one another, and therefore light emerged from darkness and from the impenetrable came forth the profound. So, too, from good issues evil and from mercy issues judgment, and all are intertwined, the good impulse and the evil impulse."[20]

Ezekiel saw in his great vision that "a stormy wind came out of the north, and a great cloud, with brightness [*nogah*] round about it, and fire flashing forth continually" (1:4). He first beheld the powers of unholiness. A *great cloud* represents "the power of destruction"; "it is called *great*, on account of its darkness, which is so intense that it hides and makes invisible all the sources of light, thus overshadowing the whole world. The *fire flashing forth* indicates the fire of rigorous judgment that never departs from it. *With brightness round about it* . . . that is, although it is the very region of defilement, yet it is surrounded by a certain brightness . . . it possesses an aspect of holiness, and hence should not be treated with contempt, but should be allowed a part in the side of holiness."[21] Even Satan contains a particle of sanctity. In doing his ugly work as the seducer of man, his intention is "for the sake of heaven," for it is for a purpose such as this that he was created.[22]

The great saint Rabbi Hrish of Zydatschov once remarked to his disciple and nephew: "Even after I had reached the age of forty — the age of understanding — I was not sure whether my life was not immersed in that mire and confusion of good and evil [*nogah*]. . . . My son, every moment of my life I fear lest I am caught in that confusion."[23]

All of history is a sphere where good is mixed with evil. The supreme task of man, his share in redeeming the work of creation, consists in an effort to separate good from evil and evil from good. Since evil can only exist parasitically on good, it will cease to be when that separation will be accomplished. Redemption, therefore, is contingent upon the *separation* of good and evil.

---

[20]*Zohar*, III, 80b; see also I, 156a.
[21]Ibid., II, 203a–203b; see 69a–69b. The *kelipoth*, or the forces of the unholy, are unclean and harmful from the aspect of man. However, from the aspect of the holy, they exist because of the will of the Creator and for His sake. A spark of holiness abides in them and maintains them. Rabbi Abraham Azulai, *Haḥamah* (Przemysl, 1897), II, 218a.
[22]*Baba Bathra*, 16a.
[23]Rabbi Eisik Safran, *Zohar Ḥai*, I.

IV

Most high religions make an effort to present the world and life as a unified whole and to regard all discord and incongruities as provisional or illusory. They seek a universal principle of meaning and are pantheistic either in the cosmic or in the acosmic sense. In contrast, the emphasis in Jewish mysticism is upon the contradictory, the paradoxical, and the unresolved mystery. The temporal world comes into existence through God's creation. "Thereby a realm of freedom and mystery is indicated beyond the capacity of reason to comprehend."[24] The final irrationality of the givenness of things is frankly accepted.

The pinnacles of faith embodying paradox and contradiction, and straining at the limits of rationality, are made plausible when understood as the keys which make the drama of human life comprehensible and without which it either is given too simple a meaning or falls into meaninglessness.

To Jewish tradition, too, paradox is an essential way of understanding the world, history, and nature. Tension, contrast, contradiction characterize all of reality. This is why, in the language of the *Zohar*, our universe is called *ᶜalma de-peruda*, "the world of separation." Strife, tension, and contradiction afflict all of life, including the study of the Torah; even the sages of the Talmud disagree on many details of the law. "God has also set one thing against the other; the good against the evil, and the evil against the good; good from good and evil from evil; the good marks out the evil and the evil marks out the good; good is reserved for the good ones and evil is reserved for the evil ones."[25] The passage in Ecclesiastes 7:14, "God has made the one as well as the other," inspired a medieval Jewish author to compose a treatise (*Temurah*) for the purpose of proving that contrast and contradiction are necessary to existence. "All things cleave to one another, the pure and the impure. There is no pure except through impurity; a mystery which is expressed in the words: *a clean thing out of an unclean* (Job 14:4). The brain is contained in a shell, a shell which will not be broken until that time when the dead shall rise again. Then will the shell be broken and the light shine out into the world from the brain, without any covering on it."[26] However, there is a polarity in everything except God. For all tension ends in God. He is beyond all dichotomies.

But it is true that not only the world He created but even His relation to the world is characterized by the polarity of justice and mercy, of law

---

[24]*Christian Realism and Political Problems*, 181.
[25]*Yetsirah*, vi, 6.
[26]*Zohar*, II, 69b.

and love. When His justice is imposed, His mercy is afflicted.[27] Yet in His own being He is One. Thus the pinnacle of Jewish truth is a mystery of divine unity. "Thou art One and none can penetrate . . . the mystery of Thy unfathomable unity" (Ibn Gabirol).

Evil, Niebuhr claims, is much more inextricably bound up with good than most psychological systems realize. There is an element of perversity in all human action; there is "the inevitability of sin in all human striving." "The corruption of evil is at the heart of human personality."[28] Thus "the supposedly objective and dispassionate ideas of the world of culture . . . are always subject to the corruption of man's spiritual pretension, to human sin."[29] This becomes manifest in the fact that "the tragedies in human history, the cruelties and fanaticisms, have not been caused by the criminals . . . but by the good people . . . by the idealists who did not understand the strange mixture of self-interest and ideals which is compounded in all human motives." Niebuhr warns, therefore, against making the cause of religion appear to be "a contest between God-fearing believers and unrighteous unbelievers." He points to the fact that biblical religion has emphasized "the *inequality of guilt* just as much as the equality of sin." "Especially severe judgments fall upon the rich and the powerful, the mighty and the noble, the wise and the righteous."[30] Indeed, the most horrible manifestation of evil occurs when it acts in the guise of good. In dealing with the problem of evil religious living must include an effort in two directions: separation and purification. By separation is meant the detachment of good from evil; by purification is meant the elimination of evil from good.

Judaism is also aware of the danger of evil's intrusion into the instrument of good. Therefore at the great ritual on the Day of Atonement the high priest would cast lots upon the two goats: one lot for the Lord and the other lot for Azazel. The purpose of the ritual of the goat on which the lot fell for Azazel was *to atone for the evil*. The High Priest would lay both his hands upon the head of the goat, on which the lot fell for Azazel, "and confess over him all the iniquities of the children of Israel, all their transgressions, all their sins." While the purpose of the goat upon which the lot fell for the Lord was "to make atonement *for the holy place*, because of the uncleannesses of the children of Israel, and because of their transgressions, even all their sins; and so shall he do for the tent of meeting, that dwells with them in the midst of their uncleannesses"

---

[27] See *Sanhedrin*, 4:5.
[28] *Faith and History*, 205, 122.
[29] *An Interpretation of Christian Ethics*, 123; see also 76.
[30] *The Nature and Destiny of Man*, 1:222ff.

(Lev. 16:16). At the most sacred day of the year the supreme task was *to atone for the holy*. It preceded the sacrifice, the purpose of which was to atone for the sins.

The ambiguity of human virtue has been a central issue in the lives of many Jewish thinkers, particularly in the history of Hasidism. "God asks for the heart."[31] Yet our greatest failure is in the heart. "The heart is deceitful above all things, it is exceedingly weak — who can know it?" (Jer. 17:9). The regard for the ego permeates all our thinking. Is it ever possible to disentangle oneself from the intricate plexus of self-interests? Indeed, the demand to serve God in purity, selflessly, "for His sake," on the one hand, and the realization of our inability to detach ourselves from vested interests, represent the tragic tension in the life of piety.[32] In this sense, not only our evil deeds, but even our good deeds precipitate a problem.

What is our situation in trying to carry out the will of God? In addition to our being uncertain of whether our motivation — *prior to the act* — is pure, we are continually embarrassed *during the act* with "alien thoughts" which taint our consciousness with selfish intentions. And even following the act there is the danger of self-righteousness, vanity, and the sense of superiority, derived from what are supposed to be acts of dedication to God.

It is easier to discipline the body than to control the soul. The pious man knows that his inner life is full of pitfalls. The ego, the evil inclination, is constantly trying to enchant him. The temptations are fierce, yet his resistance is unyielding. And so he proves his spiritual strength and stands victorious, unconquerable. Does not his situation look glorious? But then the evil inclination employs a more subtle device, approaching him with congratulations: What a pious man you are! He begins to feel proud of himself. And there he is caught in the trap (Rabbi Raphael of Bersht).

"For there is not a righteous man upon this earth, that does good and sins not" (Eccles. 7:20). The commentators take this verse to mean that even a righteous man sins on occasion, suggesting that his life is a mosaic of perfect deeds with a few sins strewn about. The Baʿal Shem, however, reads the verse: *For there is not a righteous man upon earth that does good and there is no sin in the good*. "It is impossible that the good should be free of self-interest."[33] Empirically, our spiritual situation looks hopeless:

---

[31] *Sanhedrin*, 106b.

[32] The essence of idolatry is to regard something as a thing in itself, separated from the holiness of God. In other words, to worship an idol does not mean to deny God; it means not to deny the self. This is why pride is idolatry (*Tanya*, 28b).

[33] Rabbi Yaakov Yosef of Polnoye, *Toldoth Yaakov Yosef* (Lemberg, 1863), 150d.

"We are all as an unclean thing, and all our deeds of righteousness are as filthy rags" (Isa. 64:5).

"Even the good deeds we do are not pleasing but instead revolting. For we perform them out of the desire for self-aggrandizement and for pride, and in order to impress our neighbors."[34]

Who can be trustful of his good intention, knowing that under the cloak of *kavanah* there may hide a streak of vanity? Who can claim to have fulfilled even one *mitzvah* with perfect devotion? Said Rabbi Elimelech of Lizhensk to one of his disciples, "I am sixty years old and I have not fulfilled one *mitzvah*."[35] *There is not a single mitzvah which we fulfill perfectly* ... except circumcision and the Torah that we study in our childhood,[36] for these two acts are not infringed upon by "alien thoughts" or impure motivations.

The mind is never immune to alien intentions, and there seems to be no way of ever weeding them out completely. A Hasidic Rabbi was asked by his disciples, in the last hours of his life, whom they should choose as their master after his passing away. He said, "If someone should give you the way to eradicate 'alien thoughts,' know he is not your master."

We shall not know with what we are to worship the Lord until we arrive there (Exod. 10:26). "All our service, all the good deeds we are doing in this world, we do not know whether they are of any value, whether they are really pure, honest or done for the sake of heaven — until we arrive there — in the world to come; only there shall we learn what our service was here."[37]

The human will cannot circumvent the snare of the ego nor can the mind disentangle itself from the confusion of bias in which it is trapped. It often looks as if God's search for the righteous man will end in a cul-de-sac.[38]

Should we, then, despair because of our being unable to attain perfect purity? We should if perfection were our goal. Yet we are not obliged to be perfect once for all, but only to rise again and again. Perfection is

---

[34]Rabbi David Kimḥi, *Commentary on Isaiah, ad locum.* Similarly S. D. Luzzatto in his commentary. Cf. N. J. Berlin, *Commentary on Sheeltoth,* sec. 64, 420. According to *Sheeltoth* the meaning of the verse is that our deeds of righteousness are as a cloth put together in patches, not woven together properly.

[35]Rabbi Yaakov Aaron of Zalshin, *Beth Yaakov* (Pietrkov, 1899), 144; *Aboth*, 2:20.

[36]*Midrash Tehillim*, 6, 1.

[37]Rabbi Isaac Meir of Ger.

[38]Moments of despair were known to the prophets. Elijah, fleeing from Jezebel, fled to the wilderness and there he sat down under a broom-tree and said, "It is enough; now, O Lord, take away my life, for I am not better than my fathers" (1 Kings 19:4). Jeremiah exclaims, "Cursed be the day wherein I was born" (20:14). Cf. also Psalms 22; 39; 88; Job 9:21, 10:20f.; 14:6f.; Ecclesiastes 4:2.

divine, and to make it a goal of man is to call on man to be divine. All we can do is to try to wring our hearts clean in contrition. Contrition begins with a feeling of shame at our being incapable of disentanglement from the self. To be contrite at our failures is holier than to be complacent in perfection.

It is a problem of supreme gravity. If an act to be good must be done exclusively for the sake of God, are we ever able to do the good? Rabbi Nahman of Kossov gave an answer in the form of a parable. A stork fell into the mud and was unable to pull out his legs until an idea occurred to him. Does he not have a long beak? So he stuck his beak into the mud, leaned upon it, and pulled out his legs. But what was the use? His legs were out, but his beak was stuck. So another idea occurred to him. He stuck his legs in to the mud and pulled out his beak. But what was the use? The legs were stuck in the mud. . . .

Such is exactly the condition of man. Succeeding in one way, he fails in another. We must constantly remember: We spoil, and God restores. How ugly is the way in which we despoil, and how good and how beautiful is the way in which He restores!

And yet, Judaism insists upon the deed and hopes for the intention. Every morning a Jew prays, "Lord our God, make the words of Thy Torah pleasant in our mouth . . . so that we study Thy Torah for its own sake."

While constantly keeping the goal in mind, we are taught that for pedagogic reasons one must continue to observe the law even when one is not ready to fulfill it "for the sake of God." For the good, even though it is not done for its own sake, will teach us at the end how to act for the sake of God. We must continue to perform the sacred deeds even though we may be compelled to bribe the self with human incentives. Purity of motivation is the goal; constancy of action is the way.

The ego is redeemed by the absorbing power and the inexorable provocativeness of a just task which we face. It is the deed that carries us away, that transports the soul, proving to us that the greatest beauty grows at the greatest distance from the center of the ego.

Deeds that are set upon ideal goals, that are not performed with careless ease and routine but in exertion and submission to their ends, are stronger than the surprise and attack of caprice. Serving sacred goals may eventually change mean motives. For such deeds are exacting. Whatever our motive may be in beginning such an act, the act itself demands an undivided attention. Thus the desire for reward is not the driving force of the poet in his creative moments, and the pursuit of pleasure or profit is not the essence of a religious or moral act.

At the moment in which an artist is absorbed in playing a concerto, the thought of applause, fame, or remuneration is far from his mind.

The complete attention of the artist, his whole being, is involved in the music. Should any extraneous thought enter his mind, it would arrest his concentration and mar the purity of his playing. The reward may have been on his mind when he negotiated with his agent, but during the performance it is only the music that claims his complete concentration.

Similar may be man's situation in carrying out a religious or moral act. Left alone the soul is subject to caprice. Yet there is a power in the deed that purifies desires. It is the act, life itself, that educates the will. The good motive comes into being while doing the good.

If the antecedent motive is sure of itself, the act will continue to unfold, and obtrusive intentions could even serve to invigorate the initial motive which may absorb the vigor of the intruder into its own strength. Man may be replete with ugly motives, but a deed and God are stronger than ugly motives. The redemptive power discharged in carrying out the good purifies the mind. The deed is wiser than the heart.

This, then, seems to be the attitude of Judaism. Though deeply aware of how impure and imperfect all our deeds are, the fact of our doing is cherished as the highest privilege, as a source of joy, as that which endows life with ultimate preciousness. We believe that moments lived in fellowship with God, acts fulfilled in imitation of God's will, never perish; the validity of the good remains regardless of all impurity.

V

Central to Niebuhr's thinking is the insight that "the possibilities of evil grow with the possibilities of good,"[39] and that *"every higher principle of order* to which the soul might attach itself, in the effort to rescue meaning from chaos, *is discovered,* upon analysis, *to have new possibilities of evil in it."*[40]

That "the possibilities of evil grow with the possibilities of good" is an insight of which Jewish tradition was aware. The good is presumably used both in the worldly and in the spiritual sense. In the first sense, the idea is expressed by Hillel who used to say, "The more flesh, the more worms [in the grave]; the more property, the more anxiety."[41] According to rabbinic legends, the wantonness of the antediluvian generations was due "to the ideal conditions under which mankind lived before the Flood. They knew neither toil nor care, and as a consequence of their extraordinary prosperity they grew insolent. In their insolence they rose

---

[39] *An Interpretation of Christian Ethics,* 97.
[40] Ibid., 68.
[41] *Aboth,* 2:7.

up against God."[42] In the scriptural sense, the Talmud teaches that *the greater the man, the greater his evil inclination*,[43] for the evil inclination is more eager to attack "the great," "the scholars," than to attack the simple people.

However, Niebuhr speaks not only of "the possibilities of evil" in the good; he characterizes evil as an inevitable fact of human existence. Now, if every good action is liable to corruption, what would be the worth and relevance of the worship and service of God? Does not the grace of God consist precisely in its guarding the sacred acts from being vitiated by evil? It is profoundly true that goodness may turn to cruelty, piety to fanaticism, faith to arrogance. Yet this, we believe, is a perpetual possibility rather than a necessity, a threat rather than an inevitable result.

Biblical history bears witness to the constant corruption of man; *it does not, however, teach the inevitable corruptibility of the ultimate in the temporal process.* The holiness of Abraham, Isaac, and Jacob, and the humility of Moses are the rock on which they rely. *There are good moments in history that no subsequent evil may obliterate.* The Lord himself testified to it. The integrity of Job proved it. Abraham could not find ten righteous men in Sodom by whose merit the city would have been saved. Yet there is not a moment in history without thirty-six righteous men, unknown and hidden, by whose merit the world survives. We believe that there are corners full of light in a vastness that is dark, that unalloyed good moments are possible. It is, therefore, difficult from the point of view of biblical theology to sustain Niebuhr's view, *plausible and profound as it is.*

If the nature of man were all we had, then surely there would be no hope for us left. But we also have the word of God, the commandment, the *mitzvah.* The central biblical fact is *Sinai*, the covenant, the word of God. Sinai was superimposed on the failure of Adam. Is not the fact that we were given the knowledge of His will a sign of some ability to carry out His will? Does the word of God always remain a challenge, a gadfly? Is not the voice of God powerful enough to shake the wilderness of the soul, to strip the ego bare, to flash forth His will like fire, so that we all cry, "Glory"?

To the Jew, Sinai is at stake in every act of man, and the supreme problem is not good and evil but God, and His commandment to love good and to hate evil. The central issue is not the sinfulness but the obligations of man.

---

[42]Louis Ginzberg, *The Legends of the Jews* (Jewish Publication Society edition), 1:152f.; 5:173.

[43]*Sukkah* 52a; see also *Ecclesiastes Rabba* I, 16, and *Genesis Rabba* 19, 3.

While insisting upon the contrast between God's power and man's power, God's grace and human failure, Judaism stresses a third aspect, the *mitzvah*. It is a *mitzvah* that gives meaning to our existence. The *mitzvah*, the carrying out of a sacred deed, is given to us as a constant opportunity. Thus there are two poles of piety: the right and the wrong deed; *mitzvah* and sin. The overemphasis upon sin may lead to a deprecation of "works"; the overemphasis upon *mitzvah* may lead to self-righteousness. The first may result in a denial of the relevance of history and in an overly eschatological view; the second in a denial of messianism and a secular optimism. Against both dangers Judaism warns repeatedly.

We must never forget that we are always exposed to sin. "Be not sure of yourself till the day of your death," said Hillel.[44] We have been taught that one may be impregnated with the spirit of the holy all the days of his life, yet one moment of carelessness is sufficient to plunge into the abyss. *There is but one step between me and death* (1 Sam. 20:3). On the other hand, we are taught to remember that we are always given the opportunity to serve Him. Significantly, Jewish tradition, while conscious of the possibilities of evil in the good, stresses the *possibilities of further good in the good*. Ben Azzai said, "Be eager to do a minor *mitzvah* and flee from transgression; for one *mitzvah* leads to [brings on] another *mitzvah*, and one transgression leads to another transgression; for the reward of a *mitzvah* is a *mitzvah*, and the reward of a transgression is a transgression."[45]

Judaism, in stressing the fundamental importance of the *mitzvah*, assumes that man is endowed with the ability to fulfill what God demands, at least to some degree. This may, indeed, be an article of prophetic faith: the belief in our ability to do His will. "Surely this Commandment [*mitzvah*] which I enjoin upon you this day is not too baffling for you, nor is it beyond reach. It is not in the heavens, that you should say, 'Who among us can go up to the heavens and get it for us and impart it to us, that we may observe it?' Neither is it beyond the sea that you should say, 'Who among us can cross to the other side of the sea and get it for us and impart it to us, that we may observe it?' No, the thing is very close to, in your mouth and in your heart, to observe it" (Deut. 30:11–14). Man's actual failures rather than his essential inability to do the good are constantly stressed by Jewish tradition, which claims that man is able to acquire "merit" before God. The doctrine of merits implies the certainty that for all imperfection the worth of good deeds remains in all eternity.

---

[44] *Aboth*, 2:5.
[45] Ibid., 4:2.

It is true that the law of love, the demand for the impossible, and our constant failures and transgression create in us grief and a tension that may drive us to despair. Yet, is not the reality of God's love greater than the law of love? Will He not accept us in all our frailty and weakness? "For He knows our nature [*Yetzer*]; He remembers that we are dust" (Ps. 103:14).

"In liberal Christianity there is an implicit assumption that human nature has the resources to fulfill what the Gospel demands. The Kantian axiom, 'I ought, therefore I can,' is accepted as basic to all analyses of the moral situation. In classical Christianity the perfectionism of the Gospel stands in a much more difficult relation to the estimate of human resources. The love commandment stands in juxtaposition to the fact of sin. It helps, in fact, to create the consciousness of sin."[46]

Judaism, too would reject the axiom, "I ought, therefore I can"; it would claim, instead, "Thou art commanded, therefore thou canst." It claims, as I have said, that man has the resources to fulfill what God commands, at least to some degree. On the other hand, we are continually warned lest we rely on man's own power and believe that the "indeterminate extension of human capacities would eventually alter the human situation." Our tradition does not believe that the good deeds alone will redeem history; it is the obedience to God that will make us worthy of being redeemed by God.

If Judaism had relied on the human resources for the good, on man's ability to fulfill what God demands, on man's power to achieve redemption, why did it insist upon the promise of messianic redemption? Indeed, messianism implies that any course of living, even the supreme human efforts, must fail in redeeming the world. In other words, history is not sufficient to itself.

Yet the Hebraic tradition insists upon the *mitzvah* as the instrument in dealing with evil. At the end of days, evil will be conquered by the One; in historic times evils must be conquered one by one.

This is what the prophets discovered: History is a nightmare. There are more scandals, more acts of corruption, than are dreamed of in philosophy. It would be blasphemous to believe that what we witness is the end of God's creation. It is an act of evil to accept the state of evil as either inevitable or final. Others may be satisfied with improvement; the prophets insist upon redemption. The way man acts is a disgrace, and it must not go on forever. Together with condemnation, the prophets offer a promise. The heart of stone will be taken away, a heart of flesh will be given instead (Ezek. 11:19). Even the nature of the beasts will change to

---

[46] *An Interpretation of Christian Ethics*, 65.

match the glory of the age. The end of days will be the end of fear, the end of war; idolatry will disappear, knowledge of God will prevail.

The inner history of Israel is a history of waiting for God, of waiting for His arrival. Just as Israel is certain of the reality of the Promised Land, so is she certain of the coming of "the promised day." She lives by a promise of "the day of the Lord," a day of judgment followed by redemption, when evil will be consumed and an age of glory will ensue.

The climax of our hopes is the establishment of the kingship of God, and a passion for its realization must permeate all our thoughts. For the ultimate concern of the Jew is not personal salvation but universal redemption. Redemption is not an event that will take place all at once at "the end of days" but a process that goes on all the time. Man's good deeds are single acts in the long drama of redemption, and every deed counts. One must live as if the redemption of all men depended upon the devotion of one's own life. Thus life, every life, we regard as an immense opportunity to enhance the good that God has placed in His creation. And the vision of a world free of hatred and war, of a world filled with understanding for God as the ocean is filled with water, the certainty of ultimate redemption must continue to inspire our thought and action.

A full appreciation of the significance of Reinhold Niebuhr will have to take into account not only his teachings but also his *religious epistemology*. It will, furthermore, turn not only to his books but also to his deeds. For all his profundity, his prophetic radicalism, his insights into the ultimate aspect of human destiny, his sense for the dimension of eternity, Niebuhr has maintained a concern for the immediate problems of justice and equity in human relations. His spirituality combines heaven and earth, as it were. It does not separate soul from body, or mind from unity of man's physical and spiritual life. His way is an example of one who does justly, loves mercy, and walks humbly with his God, an example of the unity of worship and living.

3

Protestant Renewal: A Jewish View

1963

The world has never yet seen a religious structure which has not at some critical moment revealed the need for repair; we see that realization radiating from the words of the prophets of Israel. It is in the spirit of reverence for what I consider to be at stake in the religious life of the Protestant community that I offer the suggestions that follow. It is an encouraging sign for renewal of the concern of Protestantism for its origins in Judaism that a Jewish scholar should be invited to write on this issue. Indeed, some of the problems I shall touch upon afflict Jews as well as Christians.

I shall write of the situation resulting from the convergence of two trends: the age-old process of dejudaization of Christianity, and the modern process of desanctification of the Hebrew Bible. Then I shall touch upon the polarity of mystery and history, and upon the issue of dedogmatization.

Dejudaization

There was early in the history of the Christian church a deliberate cultivation of differences from Judaism, a tendency to understand itself in the light not of its vast indebtedness to but rather of its divergences from Judaism. With the emergence and expansion of Christianity in the Greco-Roman world, gentile Christians overwhelmed the movement, and a continuous process of accommodation to the spirit of that world was set in motion. The result was a conscious or unconscious dejudaization of Christianity, affecting the church's way of thinking and its inner life as well as its relationship to the past and present reality of Israel — the father and mother of the very being of Christianity. The children did not arise and call the mother blessed; instead, they called the mother blind. Some theologians continue to act as if they did not know the meaning of "honor your father and your mother"; others, anxious to prove the superiority of the church, speak as if they suffer from a spiritual Oedipus complex.

The Christian message, which in its origins intended to be an affirmation and culmination of Judaism, became very early diverted into a repudiation and negation of Judaism; obsolescence and abrogation of Jewish faith became conviction and doctrine; the new covenant was conceived not as a new phase or disclosure but as abolition and replacement of the ancient one; theological thinking fashioned its terms in a spirit of antithesis of Judaism. Contrast and contradiction rather than acknowledgment of roots, relatedness and indebtedness, became the perspective. Judaism a religion of law, Christianity a religion of grace; Judaism teaches a God of wrath, Christianity a God of love; Judaism a religion of slavish obedience, Christianity is universalism; Judaism seeks work-righteousness, Christianity preaches faith-righteousness. The teaching of the old covenant a religion of fear, the gospel of the new covenant a religion of love; a *Lohnordnung* over against a *Gnadenordnung*.

The Hebrew Bible is preparation; the gospel fulfillment. In the first is immaturity, in the second perfection; in the one you find narrow tribalism, in the other all-embracing charity.

The process of dejudaization within the church paved the way for abandonment of origins and alienation from the core of its message.

The vital issue for the church is to decide whether to look for roots in Judaism and consider itself an extension of Judaism or to look for roots in pagan Hellenism and consider itself as an antithesis to Judaism.

The spiritual alienation from Israel is most forcefully expressed in the teaching of Marcion, who affirmed the contrariety and abrupt discontinuity between the God of the Hebrew Bible and the God whom Jesus had come to reveal. Marcion wanted a Christianity free from any vestige of Judaism. He saw his task as that of showing the complete opposition between the Hebrew Bible and the Gospels. Although in the year 144 of the Christian era the church expelled the apostle of discontinuity and anathematized his doctrines, Marcion remains a formidable menace, a satanic challenge. In the modern Christian community the power of Marcionism is much more alive and widespread than is generally realized.

Notwithstanding the work of generations of dedicated scholars who have opened up new vistas in the understanding of the history and literature of ancient Israel and their relation to Christianity, there is an abiding tendency to stress the *discontinuity* between the Hebrew Bible and the New Testament. According to Rudolf Bultmann (as summarized by Bernhard W. Anderson), "for the Christian the Old Testament is not revelation, but is essentially related to God's revelation in Christ as hunger is to food and despair is to hope.... The God who spoke to Israel no longer speaks to us in the time of the new Covenant."[1] Here is the spiritual resurrection of Marcion. Was not the God of Israel the God of Jesus? How dare a Christian substitute his own conception of God for Jesus' understanding of God and still call himself a Christian?

What is the pedigree of the Christian gospel? These are the words with which the New Testament begins: "The book of the genealogy of Jesus Christ, the son of David, the son of Abraham" (Matt. 1:1; see also 1 Cor. 10:1–3; 1 Pet. 1:10ff.). Yet the powerful fascination with the world of Hellenism has led many minds to look for origins of the Christian message in the world derived from Hellas. How odd of God not to have placed the cradle of Jesus in Delphi, or at least in Athens!

Despite its acceptance of *sola scriptura* which ought to have protected it from dejudaization, Protestantism has often succumbed to an individualistic hellenized conception of the Christian tradition, to a romantic oversimplification of the problem of faith and inwardness, to pantheism and sentimentality. Only a conscious commitment to the roots of Christianity in Judaism could have saved it from such distortions. To the early Christians the premise of their belief that the word became flesh was in the certainty that the spirit had become the word. They were alive and open to the law and the prophets.

In modern times there is a tendency to look for the spirit everywhere except in the words of the Hebrew Bible. There is no *religio ex nihilo*, no ultimate beginning. There is no science without presupposition and no religion without ultimate decisions. An ultimate decision for Jew or Christian is whether to be involved in the Hebrew Bible or to live away from it. The future of the Western world will depend on the way in which we relate ourselves to the Hebrew Bible.

The extent of Christianity's identification with the Hebrew Bible is a

---

[1] B. W. Anderson, "The New Covenant and the Old," in *The Old Testament and Christian Faith* (New York: Harper & Row, 1963), 227.

test of its authenticity — as well as of Jewish authenticity. Lack of such identification lies at the heart of the malaise of Protestantism today.

The Desanctification of the Bible

Into his studies of the Bible the modern scholar brings his total personality, his increased knowledge of the ancient Near East, his power of analysis, his historic sense, his honest commitment to truth — as well as inherent skepticism of biblical claims and tradition. In consequence, we have so much to say *about the Bible* that we are not prepared to hear what the Bible has to say about us. We are not in love with the Bible; we are in love with our own power of critical acumen, with our theories about the Bible. Intellectual narcissism is a disease to which some of us are not always immune. The sense of the mystery and *transcendence* of what is at stake in the Bible is lost in the process of analysis. As a result, we have brought about the desanctification of the Bible.

The basic presupposition of much modern Protestant study of Scripture, which has contributed enormously to our historical and theological discernment, is that one should treat the Bible like any other book — with objectivity and detachment. Yet objectivity is not devoid of ambiguities; it claims to be value-free, though the attitude of being value-free is itself a valuational attitude.

My mother is and is *not* like any other mother to me, and the Bible is and is *not* like any other book to me. A pianist should study musicology but remain an artist. The words of the Bible are not made of paper. In order to know them I must submit them to my judgment; in order to understand them I must stand under their judgment.

The Hebrew Bible is quoted in sermons but is absent from minds. Its intellectual relevance is ignored. Its way of thinking has not affected modern man and has remained, it seems, outside the intellectual concern of many present-day theologians. What we face is a profound alienation from the Bible. The prophets' categories have become unknown and strange. To believe, we need God, a soul and the Word. Having rejected the notion of the Bible as a paper pope, many are left with the Bible as a collection of ill-composed records on a mass of paper.

The Bible is holiness in words. How are we to preserve within our involvement in critical studies the awareness of the holy; how are we to cultivate the understanding that the authority of the Bible is not merely an issue of either philology or chronology? More decisive than the dogmatic attempt to define the date and authorship of the biblical document is the openness to the *presence of God* in the Bible. Such openness is not acquired offhand. It is the fruit of hard, constant care, of involvement; it is the result of praying, seeking, craving. Where and how is modern man guided to search for it today?

The words are still with us. Scripture may have vanished from our hearts. Yet the miracle of re-engagement is possible.

The Polarity of Mystery and History

The substance of the Christian gospel contains both proclamation and instruction: it proclaims *events* — the life, death and resurrection of Jesus — and it offers instruction — guidance, teaching full of demands. The events represent the *mystery* with which Christian existence is involved, while the teaching is concerned with this world, with the sphere of *history*, within which the commandment of love is to be fulfilled. Christianity is bound to this polarity of mystery and history. Without the mystery it would be moral teaching; without the history it would be an otherworldly movement of the spirit. Is it easy to maintain the right balance between two heterogeneous poles? It seems to me that in the history of the Christian church preoccupation with the mystery has often led to withdrawal from history and to attenuation of the demands posed by the teaching.[2]

Disregard for the supremacy of the demand has often led theologians to read an attitude of disregard for Torah in the words of the prophets. I cite a classical example:

Behold, the days are coming, says the Lord, when I will make a new covenant with the house of Israel and the house of Judah, not like the covenant which I made with their fathers when I took them by the hand to bring them out of the land of Egypt, my covenant which they broke, though I was their husband, says the Lord. But this is the covenant which I will make with the house of Israel after those days, says the Lord: I will put my law within them, and I will write it upon their hearts; and I will be their God, and they shall be my people. (Jer. 31:31–33)

Is this really what the prophet meant: "the end of the previous covenant of God with his people"? Is this really what Jeremiah envisaged: "inwardness of faith," "a change in the human heart," "a personal relationship between God and people?" Let us beware of interpreting the prophets in the images of the twentieth century.

"I will write it upon their hearts." Moses wrote the words of the covenant upon "tables of stone" (Exod. 34:1); now God will write the covenant upon the hearts. The heart is the person. What the prophet seems to predict is not abolition of the Torah but inner identification

---

[2]See Leo Baeck, *Judaism and Christianity* (1958), 171ff.; W. D. Davies, "The Gospel Tradition," in *Neotestamentica et Patristica* (1962), 33.

with it. To the biblical mind nothing in the world was as holy as the Tablets; they were placed in the Ark. Days are coming when man will become the Tables, when man will become Torah.

The sharp contrast drawn between the Torah (teaching, law) and grace, between works and faith, represents a major divergence from the Hebrew way of thinking. The preoccupation with personal salvation has, it seems, a tendency to weaken one's openness to history as it unfolds in its secular and social aspects. Social ills produced in the wake of major economic, political and social revolutions seem to stir and to arouse the sensitivity of the so-called secularists sooner than they do the conscience of the pious — a situation parallel to that in Judaism when preoccupation with ritual may weaken sensitivity to social issues. In biblical days prophets were astir while the world was asleep; today the world is astir while church and synagogue are busy with trivialities.

Perhaps the demand for the "priesthood of all believers" should be supplemented by a demand for the *prophethood of all believers*.[3] Prophets make up the vanguard, standing in the first line of the battle to achieve the fulfillment of the will of God here and now. The true sanctuary has no walls; spirit and commitment must be alive in homes as well as in churches; man's total existence is the challenge.

There must be an end to the scandal of the presence of sentimentality in the face of divine grandeur, an end to the encouragement of easy assurance of salvation. God is either of extreme importance or of no importance.

The first word in God's approach to man is: "The Lord God commanded the man ... " (Gen. 2:16). It is the commandment we must first listen to.

Do not sell salvation too cheaply. Let us disavow easy decisions and come to realize that religious existence is arduous and full of demands, that existence as such is at the brink of the abyss. Luther had to fight against the traffic in indulgences; today he would have to fight the epidemic of self-indulgence.

The great principle of the Reformation was that knowledge of God is direct and personal. Yet ours is a civilization of indirect knowledge and of depersonalization. There is no stillness, no privacy, no cultivation of concentration or receptivity. Moreover, no person is a *tabula rasa*. The substance and the mode of religious experience are colored by and contingent upon the total direction and content of one's existence. The

---

[3]See Moses' exclamation: "Would that all the Lord's people were prophets, that the Lord would put His spirit upon them" (Num. 11:29).

individual encounter may be false and idolatrous. There is the danger of false religiosity; it is not personal faith or "religious experience" alone on which we can rely. Indeed, the individual "encounter" may be an encounter with idolatry. The source of identification is the intimate union of the Word and the conscience.

Dedogmatization

The need within Protestantism for re-examination, revision and renewal is of extreme urgency. Yet renewal must not be permitted to degenerate into a trend to religion à la mode, and it must not be guided exclusively by concern for preservation of the church. The greater problem today is not how to preserve the church but how to preserve humanity, threatened not only by the possibility of nuclear explosion but also by liquidation of the inner man.

The problems we all face are both new and radical; they are religious as well as total. We have passed through the stage of social conformity and are entering that of political and intellectual automation, trapped as we are already in glittering clichés. The issue is not the incarnation; it is the elimination of God. For many people God is a forgotten myth; for many the terms in which the creed speaks seem to lie beyond the frame of modern discourse. Society and religion seem to be as remote from each other as is Cape Kennedy from the moon. On the other hand, this is a great moment for outburst and return. The absurdity of human arrogance, the deep sense of insecurity and shame, lie like dormant revelations in many souls. We have satellites in the air and a weird dread of man in our hearts.

Religion is neither a self-subsisting entity nor an end in itself. Its institutions, rituals, symbols, creeds, derive their vitality from the deep roots of human existence. Detached from its roots, religion becomes irrelevant. Our predicament is due to our having forfeited the antecedents of religious faith, the prerequisites of insight and commitment. We live a life which tends to suppress rather than to cultivate the moments that precede reflection and responsiveness to ultimate demands.

The primary issue of theology is pretheological; it is the total situation of man and his attitudes toward life and the world.[4] The power to praise precedes the power of faith. Without a continuous cultivation of a sense of the ineffable, it is hard to remain open to the meaning of the holy. Each time before uttering the word "God" we must first take the mind out of the prison of platitudes and labels, must honestly sense the sheer

---

[4]See my book *Man Is Not Alone* (New York: Farrar, Straus, 1951), 168ff.; see also, "Depth Theology," in *The Insecurity of Freedom* (New York: Farrar, Straus & Giroux, 1966), 116.

mystery of being alive, of facing the world. The antecedents of faith include a perspective upon the world, certain ultimate questions, spiritual traditions — as well as hard-won personal insights and moments of participation in the religious life of the community. In the Western world most of these prerequisites go back to a book, the Bible.

Are dogmas unnecessary? We cannot be in rapport with the reality of the divine except for rare, fugitive moments. How can those moments be saved for the long hours of functional living, when the thoughts that feed like bees on the inscrutable desert us and we lose both the sight and the drive? Dogmas are like amber in which bees, once alive, are embalmed, and they are capable of being electrified when our minds become exposed to the power of the ineffable. For problems remain with which we must always grapple: How are we to communicate those rare moments of insight to all hours of our life? How are we to commit intuition to concepts, the ineffable to words, communion to rational understanding? How are we to convey our insights to others and unite with them in a fellowship of faith: It is the creed that attempts to answer these questions.

The adequacy of dogmas depends on whether they claim to formulate or to allude; in the first case they flaunt and fail, in the second they indicate and illumine. To be adequate they must retain a telescopic relation to the theme to which they refer, must point to the mysteries of God rather than picture them. All they can do is indicate a way, not mark an end, of thinking. Unless they serve as humble signposts on the way dogmas are obstacles. They must be allusive rather than informative or descriptive. Taken literally, they either turn flat, narrow and shallow, or become ventriloquistic myths. For example, the dogma of creation has often been reduced to a tale and robbed of its authentic meaning; but as an allusion to ultimate mystery it is of inexhaustible relevance.

There must be honest admission that the truth, the meaning, and the joy are to be found in what can be neither conceived nor achieved. The righteous lives by his faith, not by his creed. And faith is not an allegiance to a verbal formulation; on the contrary, it involves profound awareness of the inadequacy of words, concepts, deeds. Unless we realize that dogmas are tentative rather than final, that they are accommodations rather than definitions, intimations rather than descriptions; unless we learn how to share the moment and the insight to which they are trying to testify, we stand guilty of literalmindedness, of pretending to know what cannot be put into words; we are guilty of intellectual idolatry. The indispensable function of the dogmas is to make it possible for us to rise above them. The time has come to break through the bottom of theology into depth theology.

4

No Religion Is an Island

1965

I speak as a member of a congregation whose founder was Abraham, and the name of my rabbi is Moses.

I speak as a person who was able to leave Warsaw, the city in which I was born, just six weeks before the disaster began. My destination was New York, it would have been Auschwitz or Treblinka. I am a brand plucked from the fire, in which my people was burned to death. I am a brand plucked from the fire of an altar of Satan on which millions of human lives were exterminated to evil's greater glory, and on which so much else was consumed: the divine image of so many human beings, many people's faith in the God of justice and compassion, and much of the secret and power of attachment to the Bible bred and cherished in the hearts of men for nearly two thousand years.

I speak as a person who is often afraid and terribly alarmed lest God has turned away from us in disgust and even deprived us of the power to understand His word. In the words Isaiah perceived in his vision (6:9–10):

Then I said, "Here I am! Send me." And he said, "Go, and say to this people: Hear and hear, but do not understand; see and see, but do not perceive. Make the heart of this people fat, and their ears heavy, and shut their eyes; lest they see with their eyes, and hear with their ears, and understand with their hearts, and turn and be healed."

Some of us are like patients in the state of final agony — who scream in delirium: the doctor is dead, the doctor is dead.

309

I speak as a person who is convinced that the fate of the Jewish people and the fate of the Hebrew Bible are intertwined. The recognition of our status as Jews, the legitimacy of our survival, is only possible in a world in which the God of Abraham is revered.

Nazism in its very roots was a rebellion against the Bible, against the God of Abraham. Realizing that it was Christianity that implanted attachment to the God of Abraham and involvement with the Hebrew Bible in the hearts of Western man, Nazism resolved that it must both exterminate the Jews and eliminate Christianity, and bring about instead a revival of Teutonic paganism.

Nazism has suffered a defeat, but the process of eliminating the Bible from the consciousness of the western world goes on. It is on the issue of saving the radiance of the Hebrew Bible in the minds of man that Jews and Christians are called upon to work together. *None of us can do it alone.* Both of us must realize that in our age anti-Semitism is anti-Christianity and that anti-Christianity is anti-Semitism.

Man is never as open to fellowship as he is in moments of misery and distress. The people of New York City have never experienced such fellowship, such awareness of being one, as they did last night in the midst of darkness.[1]

Indeed, there is a light in the midst of the darkness of this hour. But, alas, most of us have no eyes.

Is Judaism, is Christianity, ready to face the challenge? When I speak about the radiance of the Bible in the minds of man, I do not mean its being a theme for "Information, please" but rather an openness to *God's presence in the Bible*. The continuous ongoing effort for a breakthrough in the soul of man, the guarding of the precarious position of being human, even a little higher than human, despite defiance and in face of despair.

The supreme issue is today not the *halakhah* for the Jew or the Church for the Christian — but the premise underlying both religions, namely, whether there is a *pathos*, a divine reality concerned with the destiny of man which mysteriously impinges upon history; the supreme issue is whether we are alive or dead to the challenge and the expectation of the living God. The crisis engulfs all of us. The misery and fear of alienation from God make Jew and Christian cry together.

Jew must realize that the spokesmen of the Enlightenment who attacked Christianity were no less negative in their attitude toward Judaism. They often blamed Judaism for the misdeeds of the daughter religion. The casualties of the devastation caused by the continuous on-

---

[1]A reference to a city-wide power failure. —*F. A. R.*

slaughts on biblical religion in modern times are to be found among Jews as well as among Christians.

On the other hand, the Community of Israel must always be mindful of the mystery of aloneness and uniqueness of its own being. "There is a people that dwells apart, not reckoned among the nations" (Num. 23:19), says the Gentile prophet Balaam. Is it not safer for us to remain in isolation and to refrain from sharing perplexities and certainties with Christians?

Our era marks the end of complacency, the end of evasion, the end of self-reliance. Jews and Christians share the perils and the fears; we stand on the brink of the abyss together. Interdependence of political and economic conditions all over the world is a basic fact of our situation. Disorder in a small obscure country in any part of the world evokes anxiety in people all over the world.

Parochialism has become untenable. There was a time when you could not pry out of a Boston man that the Boston state-house is not the hub of the solar system or that one's own denomination has not the monopoly of the holy spirit. Today we know that even the solar system is not the hub of the universe.

The religions of the world are no more self-sufficient, no more independent, no more isolated than individuals or nations. Energies, experiences and ideas that come to life outside the boundaries of a particular religion or all religions continue to challenge and to affect every religion.

Horizons are wider, dangers are greater. . . . *No religion is an island.* We are all involved with one another. Spiritual betrayal on the part of one of us affects the faith of all of us. Views adopted in one community have an impact on other communities. Today religious isolationism is a myth. For all the profound differences in perspective and substance, Judaism is sooner or later affected by the intellectual, moral and spiritual events within the Christian society, and vice versa.

We fail to realize that while different exponents of faith in the world of religion continue to be wary of the ecumenical movement, there is another ecumenical movement, world-wide in extent and influence: nihilism. We must choose between interfaith and inter-nihilism. Cynicism is not parochial. Should religions insist upon the illusion of complete isolation? Should we refuse to be on speaking terms with one another and hope for each other's failure? Or should we pray for each other's health, and help one another in preserving one's respective legacy, in preserving a common legacy?

The Jewish diaspora today, almost completely to be found in the Western world, is certainly not immune to the spiritual climate and the state of religious faith in the general society. We do not live in isolation, and the way in which non-Jews either relate or bid defiance to God has a profound impact on the minds and souls of the Jews. Even in the Middle Ages, when most Jews lived in relative isolation, such impact was acknowledged. To quote, "The usage of the Jews is in accordance with that of the non-Jews. If the non-Jews of a certain town are moral, the Jews born there will be so as well." Rabbi Joseph Yaabez, a victim of the Spanish Inquisition, in the midst of the Inquisition was able to say that "the Christians believe in Creation, the excellence of the Patriarchs, revelation, retribution and resurrection. Blessed is the Lord, God of Israel, who left this remnant after the destruction of the second Temple. But for these Christian nations we might ourselves become infirm in our faith."

We are heirs to a long history of mutual contempt among religions and religious denominations, of religious coercion, strife and persecutions. Even in periods of peace, the relationship that obtains between representatives of different religions is not just reciprocity of ignorance; it is an abyss, a source of detraction and distrust, casting suspicion and undoing efforts of many an honest and noble expression of good will.

The Psalmist's great joy is in proclaiming: "Truth and mercy have met together" (Ps. 85:11). Yet so frequently faith and the lack of mercy enter a union, out of which bigotry is born, the presumption that my faith, my motivation, is pure and holy, while the faith of those who differ in creed — even those in my own community — is impure and unholy. How can we be cured of bigotry, presumption, and the foolishness of believing that we have been triumphant while we have all been defeated?

Is it not clear that in spite of fundamental disagreements there is a convergence of some of our commitments, of some of our views, tasks we have in common, evils we must fight together, goals we share, a predicament afflicting us all?

On what basis do we people of different religious commitments meet one another?

First and foremost we meet as human beings who have so much in common: a heart, a face, a voice, the presence of a soul, fears, hope, the ability to trust, a capacity for compassion and understanding, the kinship of being human. My first task in every encounter is to comprehend the personhood of the human being I face, to sense the kinship of being human, solidarity of being.

To meet a human being is a major challenge to mind and heart, I must recall what I normally forget. A person is not just a specimen of the species called *homo sapiens*. He is all of humanity in one, and whenever one man is hurt we are all injured. The human is a disclosure of the divine, and all men are one in God's care for man. Many things on earth are precious, some are holy, humanity is holy of holies.

To meet a human being is an opportunity to sense the image of God, *the presence* of God. According to a rabbinical interpretation, the Lord said to Moses: "Wherever you see the trace of man there I stand before you...."

When engaged in a conversation with a person of different religious commitment I discover that we disagree in matters sacred to us, does the image of God I face disappear? Does God cease to stand before me? Does the difference in commitment destroy the kinship of being human? Does the fact that we differ in our conceptions of God cancel what we have in common: the image of God?

For this reason was man created single (whereas of every other species many were created)...that there should be peace among human beings: one cannot say to his neighbor, my ancestor was nobler than thine (Sanhedrin 37a).

The primary aim of these reflections is to inquire how a Jew out of his commitment and a Christian out of his commitment can find a religious basis for communication and cooperation on matters relevant to their moral and spiritual concern in spite of disagreement.

There are four dimensions of religious existence, four necessary components of man's relationships to God: (a) the teaching, the essentials of which are summarized in the form of a creed, which serve as guiding principles in our thinking about matters temporal or eternal, the dimension of the doctrine; (b) faith, inwardness, the direction of one's heart, the intimacy of religion, the dimension of privacy; (c) the law, or the sacred act to be carried out in the sanctuary in society or at home, the dimension of the deed; (d) the context in which creed, faith and ritual come to pass, such as the community or the covenant, history, tradition, the dimensions of transcendence.

In the dimension of the deed there are obviously vast areas for cooperation among men of different commitments in terms of intellectual communication, of sharing concern and knowledge in applied religion, particularly as they relate to social action.

In the dimension of faith, the encounter proceeds in terms of personal witness and example, sharing insights, confessing inadequacy. On the level of doctrine we seek to convey the content of what we believe in; on the level of faith we experience in one another the presence of a person radiant with reflections of a greater presence.

I suggest that the most significant basis for meeting of men of different religious traditions is the level of fear and trembling, of humility and contrition, where our individual moments of faith are mere waves in the endless ocean of mankind's reaching out for God, where all for-mulations and articulations appear as understatement, where our souls are swept away by the awareness of the urgency of answering God's commandment, while stripped of pretension and conceit we sense the tragic insufficiency of human faith.

What divides us? What unites us? We disagree in law and creed, in commitments which lie at the very heart of our religious existence. We say "No" to one another in some doctrines essential and sacred to us. What unites us? Our being accountable to God, our being objects of God's concern, precious in His eyes. Our conceptions of what ails us may be different; but the anxiety is the same. The language, the imagination, the concretization of our hopes are different, but the embarrassment is the same, and so is the sigh, the sorrow, and the necessity to obey.

We may disagree about the ways of achieving fear and trembling, but the fear and trembling are the same. The demands are different, but the conscience is the same, and so is arrogance, iniquity. The proclamations are different, the callousness is the same, and so is the challenge we face in many moments of spiritual agony.

Above all, while dogmas and forms of worship are divergent, God is the same. What unites us? A commitment to the Hebrew Bible as Holy Scripture. Faith in the Creator, the God of Abraham, commitment to many of His commandments, to justice and mercy, a sense of contrition, sensitivity to the sanctity of life and to the involvement of God in history, the conviction that without the holy the good will be defeated, prayer that history may not end before the end of days, and so much more.

There are moments when we all stand together and see our faces in the mirror: the anguish of humanity and its helplessness; the perplexity of the individual and the need of divine guidance; being called to praise and to do what is required.

In conversations with Protestant and Catholic theologians I have more than once come upon an attitude of condescension to Judaism, a sort of pity for those who have not yet seen the light; tolerance instead of reverence. On the other hand, I cannot forget that when Paul Tillich, Gustave Weigel, and myself were invited by the Ford Foundation to speak from the same platform on the religious situation in America, we not only found ourselves in deep accord in disclosing what ails us, but above all without prior consultation, the three of us confessed that our guides in this critical age are the prophets of Israel, not Aristotle, not Karl Marx, but Amos and Isaiah.

The theme of these reflections is not a doctrine or an institution called Christianity, but human beings all over the world, both present and past, who worship God as followers of Jesus, and my problem is how

I should relate myself to them spiritually. The issue I am called upon to respond to is not the truth of dogma but the faith and the spiritual power of the commitment of Christians. In facing the claim and the dogma of the Church, Jews and Christians are strangers and stand in disagreement with one another. Yet there are levels of existence where Jews and Christians meet as sons and brothers. "Alas, in heaven's name, are we not your brothers, are we not the sons of one father and are we not the sons of one mother? . . . "

To be sure all men are sons of one father, but they have also the power to forfeit their birthright, to turn rebels, voluntary bastards, "children with no faithfulness in them" (Deut. 32:20). Is it not flesh and blood but honor and obedience that save the right of sonship. We claim brotherhood by being subject to His commandments. We are sons when we hearken to the Father, when we praise and honor Him.

The recognition that we are sons in obeying God and praising Him is the starting-point of my reflection. "I am a companion of all who fear Thee, of those who keep Thy precepts" (Ps. 119:63). I rejoice wherever His name is praised, His presence sensed, His commandment done.

The first and most important *prerequisite of interfaith is faith*. It is only out of the depth of involvement in the unending drama that began with Abraham that we can help one another toward an understanding of our situation. Interfaith must come out of depth, not out of a void absence of faith. It is not an enterprise for those who are half learned or spiritually immature. If it is not to lead to the confusion of the many, it must remain a prerogative of the few.

Faith and the power of insight and devotion can only grow in privacy. Exposing one's inner life may engender the danger of desecration, distortion and confusion. Syncretism is a perpetual possibility. Moreover, at a time of paucity of faith, interfaith may become a substitute for faith, suppressing authenticity for the sake of compromise. In a world of conformity, religions can easily be levelled down to the lowest common denominator.

Both communication and separation are necessary. We must preserve our individuality as well as foster care for one another, reverence, understanding, cooperation. In the world of economics, science and technology, cooperation exists and continues to grow. Even political states, though different in culture and competing with one another, maintain diplomatic relations and strive for coexistence. Only religions are not on speaking terms. Over a hundred countries are willing to be part of the United Nations; yet no religion is ready to be part of a movement for United Religions. Or should I say, not yet ready? Ignorance, distrust, and disdain often characterize their relations to one another. Is disdain for the opposition indigenous to the religious position? Granted that Judaism and Christianity are committed to contradictory claims is it impossible to carry on a controversy without acrimony, criticism without loss of respect, disagreement without disrespect? The problem to be faced is: how to combine loyalty to one's own tradition with reverence for different traditions? How is mutual esteem between Christian and Jew possible?

A Christian ought to ponder seriously the tremendous implications of a process begun in early Christian history. I mean the conscious or unconscious dejudaization of Christianity, affecting the Church's way of thinking, its inner life as well as its relationship to the past and present reality of Israel — the father and mother of the very being of Christianity. The children did not arise to call the mother blessed; instead, they called the mother blind. Some theologians continue to act as if they did not know the meaning of "honor your father and mother"; others, anxious to prove the superiority of the church, speak as if they suffered from a spiritual Oedipus complex.

A Christian ought to realize that a world without Israel will be a world without the God of Israel. A Jew, on the other hand, ought to acknowledge the eminent role and part of Christianity in God's design for the redemption of all men.

Modern Jews who have come out of the state of political seclusion and are involved in the historic process of Western mankind cannot afford to be indifferent to the religious situation of our fellow-men. Opposition to Christianity must be challenged by the question: What religious alternative do we envisage for the Christian world? Did we not refrain for almost two thousand years from preaching Judaism to the Nations?

A Jew ought to ponder seriously the responsibility involved in Jewish history for having been the mother of two world religions. Does not the failure of children reflect upon their mother? Do not the sharp deviations from Jewish tradition on the part of the early Christians who were Jews indicate some failure of communication within the spiritual climate of first century Palestine?

Judaism is the mother of the Christian faith. It has a stake in the destiny of Christianity. Should a mother ignore her child, even a wayward, rebellious one? On the other hand, the Church should acknowledge that we Jews in loyalty to our tradition have a stake in its faith, recognize our vocation to preserve and to teach the legacy of the Hebrew Scripture, accept our aid in fighting Marcionite trends as an act of love.

Is it not our duty to help one another in trying to overcome hardness of heart, in cultivating a sense of wonder and mystery, in unlocking doors to holiness in time, in opening minds to the challenge of the Hebrew Bible, in seeking to respond to the voice of the prophets?

No honest religious person can fail to admire the outpouring of the love of man and the love of God, the marvels of worship, the magnificence of spiritual insight, the piety, charity and sanctity in the lives of countless men and women, manifested in the history of Christianity. Have not Pascal, Kierkegaard, Immanuel Kant or Reinhold Niebuhr been a source of inspiration to many Jews?

Over and above mutual respect we must acknowledge indebtedness to one another. It is our duty to remember that it was the Church that brought the knowledge of the God of Abraham to the Gentiles. It was the Church that made Hebrew Scripture available to mankind. This we Jews must acknowledge with a grateful heart.

The Septuagint, the works of Philo, Josephus, as well as the Apocrypha and Pseudepigrapha, and the *Fons vitae* by Ibn Gabirol would have been lost had they not been preserved in monasteries. Credit for major achievements in modern scholarship in the field of Bible, in biblical as well as hellenistic Jewish history, goes primarily to Protestant scholars.

The purpose of religious communication among human beings of different commitments is mutual enrichment and enhancement of respect and appreciation rather than the hope that the person spoken to will prove to be wrong in what he regards as sacred.

Dialogue must not degenerate into a dispute, into an effort on the part of each to get the upper hand. There is an unfortunate history of Christian-Jewish disputations, motivated by the desire to prove how blind the Jews are and carried on in a spirit of opposition, which eventually degenerated into enmity. Thus any conversation between Christian and Jew in which abandonment of the other partner's faith is a silent hope must be regarded as offensive to one's religious and human dignity.

Let there be an end to disputation and polemic, an end to disparagement. We honestly and profoundly disagree in matters of creed and dogma. Indeed, there is a deep chasm between Christians and Jews concerning, e.g., the divinity and Messiahship of Jesus. But across the chasm we can extend our hands to one another.

Religion is a means, not the end. It becomes idolatrous when regarded as an end in itself. Over and above all being stands the Creator and Lord of history, He who transcends all. To equate religion and God is idolatry.

Does not the all-inclusiveness of God contradict the exclusiveness of any particular religion? The prospect of all men embracing one form of religion remains an eschatological hope. What about here and now? Is it not blasphemous to say: I alone have all the truth and the grace, and all those who differ live in darkness, and are abandoned by the grace of God?

Is it really our desire to build a monolithic society: one party, one view, one leader, and no opposition? Is religious uniformity desirable or even possible? Has it really proved to be a blessing for a country when all its citizens belonged to one denomination? Or has any denomination attained a spiritual climax when it had the adherence of the entire population? Does not the task of preparing the kingdom of God require a diversity of talents, a variety of rituals, soul-searching as well as opposition?

Perhaps it is the will of God that in this aeon there should be diversity in our forms of devotion and commitment to Him. In this aeon diversity of religions is the will of God.

In the story of the building of the Tower of Babel we read: "The Lord said: They are one people, and they have all one language, and this is what they begin to do" (Gen. 11:6). These words are interpreted by an ancient rabbi to mean: What has caused them to rebel against me? The fact that they are one people and they have all one language. . . .

For from the rising of the sun to its setting My name is great among the nations, and in every place incense is offered to My name, and a pure offering; for My name is great among the nations, says the Lord of hosts (Mal. 1:11).

This statement refers undoubtedly to the contemporaries of the prophet. But who were these worshippers of One God? At the time of Malachi there was hardly a large number of proselytes. Yet the statement declares: All those who worship their gods to not know it, but they are really worshipping Me.

It seems that the prophet proclaims that men all over the world, though they confess different conceptions of God, are really worshipping One God, the Father of all men, though they may not be aware of it.

Religions, I repeat, true to their own convictions, disagree profoundly and are in opposition to one another on matters of doctrine. However, if we accept the prophet's thesis that they all worship one God, even without knowing it, if we accept the principle that the majesty of God transcends the dignity of religion, should we not regard a divergent religion as His Majesty's loyal opposition? However, does not every religion maintain the claim to be true, and is not truth exclusive?

The ultimate truth is not capable of being fully and adequately expressed in concepts and words. The ultimate truth is about the situation that pertains between God and man. "The Torah speaks in the language of man." Revelation is always an accommodation to the capacity of man. No two minds are alike, just as no two faces are alike. The voice of God reaches the spirit of man in a variety of ways, in a multiplicity of languages. One truth comes to expression in many ways of understanding.

A major factor in our religious predicament is due to self-righteousness and to the assumption that faith is found only in him who has arrived, while absent in him who is on the way. Religion is often inherently guilty of the sin of pride and presumption. To paraphrase the prophet's words, the exultant religion dwelt secure and said in her heart: "I am, and there is no one besides me."

Humility and contrition seem to be absent where most required — in theology. But humility is the beginning and end of religious thinking, the secret test of faith. There is no truth without humility, no certainty without contrition.

Ezra the Scribe, the great renovator of Judaism, of whom the rabbis said that he was worthy of receiving the Torah had it not been already given through Moses, confessed his lack of perfect faith. He tells us that after he had received a royal *firman* from King Artaxerxes granting him permission to lead a group of exiles from Babylonia: "I proclaimed a fast there at the river Ahava, that we might afflict ourselves before our God, to seek of Him a right way for us, and for our little ones, and for all substance. For I was ashamed to require of the King a band of soldiers and horsemen to help us against the enemy in the way: because we had spoken unto the king, saying, the hand of God is upon all them for good that seek Him" (Ezra 8:21–22).

Human faith is never final, never an arrival, but rather an endless pilgrimage, a being on the way. We have no answers to all problems. Even some of our sacred answers are both emphatic and qualified, final and tentative; final within our own position in history, tentative — because we can only speak in the tentative language of man.

Heresy is often a roundabout expression of faith, and sojourning in the wilderness is a preparation for entering the promised land.

Is the failure, the impotence of all religions, due exclusively to human transgression? Or perhaps to the mystery of God's withholding His grace, of His concealing even while revealing? Disclosing the fullness of His glory would be an impact that would surpass the power of human endurance.

His thoughts are not our thoughts. Whatever is revealed is abundance compared with our soul and a pittance compared with His treasures. No word is God's last word, no word is God's ultimate word.

Following the revelation at Sinai, the people said to Moses: "You speak to us, and we will hear; let not God speak to us, lest we die" (Exod. 20:19).

The Torah as given to Moses, an ancient rabbi maintains, is but an unripened fruit of the heavenly tree of wisdom. At the end of days, much that is concealed will be revealed.

The mission to the Jews is a call to the individual Jews to betray the fellowship, the dignity, the sacred history of their people. Very few Christians seem to comprehend what is morally and spiritually involved in supporting such activities. We are Jews as we are men. The alternative to our existence as Jews is spiritual suicide, extinction. It is not a change into something else. Judaism has allies but no substitutes.

The wonder of Israel, the marvel of Jewish existence, the survival of holiness in the history of the Jews, is a continuous verification of the marvel of the Bible. Revelation to Israel continues as a revelation through Israel.

The Protestant pastor, Christian Fürchtegott Gellert, was asked by Frederick the Great, "Prove to me the truth of the Bible, but briefly, for I have little time." Gellert answered. "Your Majesty, the Jews."

Indeed, is not the existence of the Jews a witness to the God of Abraham? Is not our loyalty to the law of Moses a light that continues to illumine the lives of those who observe it as well as the lives of those who are aware of it?

Gustave Weigel spent the last evening of his life in my study at the Jewish Theological Seminary. We opened our hearts to one another in prayer and contrition and spoke of our own deficiencies, failures, hopes. At one moment I posed the question: Is it really the will of God that there be no more Judaism in the world? Would it really be the triumph of God if the scrolls of the Torah would no more be taken out of the Ark and the Torah no more read in the Synagogue, our ancient Hebrew prayers in which Jesus himself worshipped no more recited, the Passover Seder no more celebrated in our lives, the law of Moses no more observed in our homes? Would it really be *ad majorem Dei gloriam* to have a world without Jews?

My life is shaped by many loyalties — to my family, to my friends, to my people, to the U.S. constitution, etc. Each of my loyalties has its ultimate root in one ultimate relationship: loyalty to God, the loyalty of all my loyalties. That relationship is the covenant of Sinai. All we are we owe to Him. He has enriched us with gifts of insight, with the joy of moments full of blessing. He has also suffered with us in years of agony and distress.

None of us pretends to be God's accountant, and His design for history and redemption remains a mystery before which we must stand in awe. It is arrogant to maintain that the Jews' refusal to accept Jesus as the Messiah is due to their stubbornness or blindness as it would be presumptuous for the Jews not to acknowledge the glory and holiness in the lives of countless Christians. "The Lord is near to all who call upon Him, to all who call upon Him in truth" (Ps. 145:18).

Fortunately there are some important Christian voices who expressed themselves to the effect that the missionary activities to the Jews be given up. Reinhold Niebuhr may have been the first Christian theologian who at a joint meeting of the faculties of the Union Theological Seminary and the Jewish Theological Seminary declared that the missionary "activities are wrong not only because they are futile and have little fruit to boast for their exertions. They are wrong because the two faiths despite differences are sufficiently alike for the Jew to find God more easily in terms of his own religious heritage than by subjecting himself to the hazards of guilt feelings involved in conversion to a faith which, whatever its excellencies, must appear to him as a symbol of an oppressive majority culture. . . . Practically nothing can purify the symbol of Christ as the image of God in the imagination of the Jew from the taint with which ages of Christian oppression in the name of Christ have tainted it."[2] Tillich has said,

Many Christians feel that it is a questionable thing, for instance, to try to convert Jews. They have lived and spoken with their Jewish friends for decades. They have not converted them, but they have created a community of conversation which has changed both sides of the dialogue.[3]

And a statement on "relations with the Roman Catholic Church" adopted by the Central Committee of the World Council of Churches in its meeting in Rochester, New York in August, 1963, mentions proselytism as a "cause of offence," an issue "which must be frankly faced if true dialogue is to be possible."[4]

The ancient rabbis proclaim: "Pious men of all nations have a share in the life to come."

"I call heaven and earth to witness that the Holy Spirit rests upon each person, Jew or Gentile, man or woman, master or slave, in consonance with his deeds."

Holiness is not the monopoly of any particular religion or tradition. Wherever a deed is done in accord with the will of God, wherever a thought of man is directed toward Him, there is the holy.

The Jews do not maintain that the way of the Torah is the only way of serving God. "Let all the peoples walk each one in the name of its god, but we will walk in the name of the Lord our God for ever and ever" (Mic. 4:5).

"God loves the Saint" (Ps. 146:8) — "They love Me, and I love them. . . . If a person wishes to be a Levite or a priest, he cannot become one; a saint, even if he is a gentile, he may become. For saints do not

---

[2]Reinhold Niebuhr, *Pious and Secular America* (New York: Scribner's, 1958), 108.

[3]Paul Tillich, *Christianity and the Encounter of the World Religions* (New York: Columbia University Press, 1963), 95.

[4]*Ecumenical Review* 16, no. 1 (October 1963): 108.

derive their saintliness from their ancestry; they become saints because they dedicate themselves to God and love Him." Conversion to Judaism is no prerequisite for sanctity. In his Code Maimonides asserts: "Not only is the tribe of Levi (God's portion) sanctified in the highest degree, but any man among all the dwellers on earth whose heart prompts him and whose mind instructs him to dedicate himself to the services of God and to walk uprightly as God intended him to, and who disencumbers himself of the load of the many pursuits which men invent for themselves." "God asks for the heart, everything depends upon the intention of the heart... all men have a share in eternal life if they attain according to their ability knowledge of the Creator and have ennobled themselves by noble qualities. There is no doubt that he who has thus trained himself morally and intellectually to acquire faith in the Creator will certainly have a share in the life to come. This is why our rabbis taught: a gentile who studies the Torah of Moses is (spiritually) equal to the High Priest at the Temple in Jerusalem."

Leading Jewish authorities, such as Jehuda Halevi and Maimonides, acknowledge Christianity to be a *praeparatio messianica*, while the Church regarded ancient Judaism to have been a *praeparatio evangelica*. Thus whereas the Christian doctrine has often regarded Judaism as having outlived its usefulness and the Jews as candidates for conversion, the Jewish attitude enables us to acknowledge the presence of a divine plan in the role of Christianity within the history of redemption. Jehuda Halevi, though criticizing Christianity and Islam for retaining relics of ancient idolatry and feast days, "they also revere places sacred to idols," compares Christians and Mohammedans to proselytes who adopted the roots, but not all the branches (or the logical conclusions of the divine commandments). "The wise providence of God towards Israel may be compared to the planting of a seed of corn. It is placed in the earth, where it seems to be changed into soil, and water, and rottenness, and the seed can no longer be recognized. But in very truth it is the seed that has changed the earth and water into its own nature, and then the seed raises itself from one stage to another, transforms the elements, and throws out shoots and leaves.... Thus it is with Christians and Moslems. The Law of Moses has changed them that come into contact with it, even though they seem to have cast the Law aside. These religions are the preparation and the preface to the Messiah we expect, who is the fruit himself of the seed originally sown, and all men, too, will be fruit of God's seed when they acknowledge Him, and all become one mighty tree."

A similar view is set forth by Maimonides in his authoritative Code: "It is beyond the human mind to fathom the designs of the Creator; for our ways are not His ways, neither are our thoughts His thoughts. All these matters relating to Jesus of Nazareth and the Ishmaelite (Mohammed) who came after him, served to clear the way for King Messiah, to prepare the whole world to worship God with one accord, as it is written, *For then will I turn to the peoples a pure language, that they may all call upon the name of the Lord to serve Him with one consent* (Zeph. 3:9). Thus the messianic hope, the Torah, and the commandments have become familiar topics — topics of conversation (among the inhabitants) of the far isles and many people...."

Christianity and Islam, far from being accidents of history or purely human phenomena, are regarded as part of God's design for the redemption of all men. Christianity is accorded ultimate significance by acknowledging that "all these matters relative to Jesus of Nazareth and Mohammed... served to clear the way for King Messiah." In addition to the role of these religions in the plan of redemption, their achievements within history are explicitly affirmed: Through them: "the messianic hope, the Torah, and the commandments have become familiar topics — [among the inhabitants] of the far isles and many peoples." Elsewhere Maimonides acknowledges that "the Christians believe and profess that the Torah is God's revelation (*torah min hashamayim*) and given to Moses in the form in which it has been preserved; they have it completely written down, though they frequently interpret it differently."

Rabbi Johanan Ha-Sandelar, a disciple of Rabbi Akiba, says: "Every community which is established for the sake of heaven will in the end endure; but one which is not for the sake of heaven will not endure in the end."

Rabbi Jacob Emden [1697–1776] maintains that heretical Jewish sects such as the Karaites and the Sabbatians belong to the second category whereas Christianity and Islam are in the category of "a community which is for the sake of heaven" and which will "in the end endure." They have emerged out of Judaism and accepted "the fundamentals of our divine religion... to make known God among the nations..., to proclaim that there is a Master in heaven and earth, divine providence, reward and punishment..., Who bestows the gift of prophecy... and communicates through the prophets laws and statutes to live by.... This is why their community endures.... Since their intention is for the sake of heaven, reward will not be withheld from them." He also praises many Christian scholars who have come to the rescue of Jews and their literature.

Rabbi Israel Lipschütz of Danzig (1782–1860) speaks of the Christians, "our brethren, the gentiles, who acknowledge the one God and revere

323

His Torah which they deem divine and observe, as is required of them, the seven commandments of Noah...."

What, then, is the purpose of interreligious cooperation?

It is neither to flatter nor to refute one another, but to help one another; to share insight and learning, to cooperate in academic ventures on the highest scholarly level, and what is even more important to search in the wilderness for well-springs of devotion, for treasures of stillness, for the power of love and care for man. What is urgently needed are ways of helping one another in the terrible predicament of here and now by the courage to believe that the word of the Lord endures for ever as well as here and now; to cooperate in trying to bring about a resurrection of sensitivity, a revival of conscience; to keep alive the divine sparks in our souls, to nurture openness to the spirit of the Psalms, reverence for the words of the prophets, and faithfulness to the Living God.

5

The Jewish Notion of God
and Christian Renewal

1967

. . . The prophets of Israel had no theory or "notion" of God. What they
had was an *understanding*. Their God-understanding was not the result
of a theoretical inquiry, of a groping in the midst of alternatives. To the
prophets, God was overwhelmingly real and shatteringly present. They
never spoke of Him from a distance. They lived as witnesses, struck
by the words of God, rather than as explorers engaged in an effort to
ascertain the nature of God; their utterances were the unloading of a
burden rather than glimpses obtained in the fog of groping. To them,
the attributes of God were drives, challenges, commandments, rather
than timeless notions detached from His Being. They did not offer an
exposition of the nature of God, but rather an exposition of God's insight
into man and His concern for man. They disclosed attitudes *of* God rather
than notions *about* God.

I am not going to speak about notions. To quote from Isaiah. "You are
My witnesses, says the Lord, I am the Lord" (Isa. 43:10–11).

There are no proofs for the existence of the God of Israel. There are
only witnesses. You can only think of Him by seeking to be present to
Him. You cannot define Him, you can only invoke Him. He is not a
notion but a name.

Now there are voices in our own days, all over the country, suggesting
that we eliminate and get rid of the traditional name, "God," to refer to

the ultimate Presence. After all, who needs that word, that name? This is being done for the telephone exchanges in the United States: to get rid of names! So let us abolish names altogether. Let us call every human being by a number, and worship zero.

You know what goes on in our days about words. Certain chapters from certain books are considered obsolete because the words are not understandable anymore. For example, "The Lord is my shepherd; I shall not want." An impossible verse; who has seen a shepherd? Children grow up without ever having heard of a shepherd. I therefore offer an emendation and suggest that we read: "The Lord is my plumber, I shall not want." In the same spirit, artificial fertilization may substitute the test tube for the mother. There will be no mothers. All men will be organization members.

The supreme issue is not the question whether in the infinite darkness there is a ground of being which is an object of man's ultimate concern, but whether the reality of God confronts us with a pathos — God's ultimate concern with good and evil; whether God is mysteriously present in the events of history; whether being is transcended by creation; whether creation is transcended by care; whether my life is dependent on God's care; whether in the course of my life I come upon a trace of His guidance.

God is either of no importance or of supreme importance. God is He whose regard for me is more precious than life. Otherwise, He is not God. God is the meaning beyond the mystery.

How can I speak of a notion? To speak adequately about God one would have to sense all the horrors and all the joys of all creatures since the beginning of time, and to intuit how God is relevant to all this.

The ambiguities are numerous and drive us to despair — almost. Yet the God of Israel does not leave us to ourselves. Even when He throws us into darkness, we know that it is *His* darkness, that we have been cast into it by *Him*. Thus we do not pretend to know His secrets or to understand His ways. Yet we are certain of knowing His Name, of living by His love and receiving His grace, as we are certain of receiving His blows and dying according to His will. Such is our loyalty, a loyalty that lives as a surprise in a world of staggering vapidity, in an hour of triumphant disloyalty.

The Covenant is a holy dimension of existence. Faith is the consciousness of living in that dimension, rather than an assent to propositions. Important as is the intellectual crystallization of faith in terms of creed, what characterizes Judaism, I believe, is the primacy of faith over creed.

Faith is both certainty and trial: certainty in spite of perplexities, a trial demanding sacrifice, strain, wrestling. For certainty without trial becomes complacency, lethargy, while trial without certainty is chaos, presumption, as if God had never reached us, as if history were always a monologue. Faith is a mode of being alive to the meaning beyond the mystery, commitment to total existence, and the dynamics of faith is the ongoing shaping and modification of one's existence. Faith also involves fear: fear lest He discard us, lest He forsake us. Then we must learn how to despise the convenience of belief. We have again and again experienced His wrath. "Thou hast made us like sheep for slaughter . . . " (Ps. 44:12–13).

We remain faithful in spite of the demonic darkness that often engulfs us, in spite of the vapidity of the holy that often affects us. God is one, but man is torn to pieces by temptation and ambiguity. We are both haunted and exalted by the words of Job: "Though He slay me yet will I trust in Him" (Job 13:15).

Faith is a high ladder and at times all the rungs seem to have been taken away. Can we replace the rungs? Can we recover the will to rise? And if the rungs cannot be replaced, shall we learn how to reach the truth at the top of the ladder?

Let me illustrate. In 1492, the Jews of Spain were placed before the choice: to be converted or to be expelled. The overwhelming majority left their homeland. Ships overcrowded with fugitives found difficulty landing, because disease had broken out among them on board ship. One of the boats was infested with the plague, and the captain of the boat put the passengers ashore at some uninhabited place. There most of them died of starvation, while some of them gathered up all their strength and set out on foot in search of some settlement. There was one Jew among them who struggled on foot together with his wife and two sons. The wife grew faint and died, not being accustomed to so much difficult walking. The husband picked up his children and carried them in his arms until he and they fainted from hunger. When he regained consciousness, he found that his sons had died also. In great grief he rose to his feet, raised his eyes to the heavens, and cried out: "Lord of the universe, much have you done to make me desert my faith. But know this of a certainty, that a Jew I am and a Jew I shall remain! And nothing which you have brought upon me, or are likely to bring upon me, will be of any avail!"

The meaning of the saying "the God of Israel" differs essentially from a phrase such as "the God of Aristotle" or "the God of Kant." It does not mean a doctrine of God conceived of or taught by Israel. It means God with whom Israel is vitally, intimately involved, an involvement transcending the realm of thinking, not reducible to human consistency,

327

and one which does not simplify itself in order to accommodate common sense.

Furthermore, the saying "God of Israel" has no possessive or exclusive connotation: God belonging to Israel alone. Its true meaning is that the God of all men has entered a Covenant with one people for the sake of all people. It is furthermore clear that "Israel" in this saying does not mean Israel of the past, a people living in ancient Palestine which has long ceased to exist. Israel is a people in whom the past endures in the present tense. The exodus occurs now. We are still on the way, and cannot accept any event as a final event. We are God's stake in human history, regardless of merit and often against our will.

Israel is a people that shares the Name of God. Of the two words in Hebrew for the Jews, "Israel" and "Yehudi," the "*el*" in Israel means "God," whereas the Hebrew word for "Jew," "*Yehud*," has the three letters that combine to make up the four in the ineffable name. It is a people that can only endure in a world in which the name of God is revered. The disappearance of God would mean the disappearance of the Jew. But we know of God's commitment and of His faithfulness.

Christian Renewal

The term "renewal" has many meanings, but I shall suggest only briefly that what is taking place in the movement of Christian renewal is certainly a shift from evasion to confrontation, a willingness to recognize the validity of principles long disparaged or disregarded, which it is unnecessary to enumerate here.

It is clear, however, that renewal is not an act carried out once and for all, but rather a constant happening, *semper a novo incipere*. It is furthermore a process, not only in relation to others, but above all one that affects the inner life and substance of the Christian.

I believe that one of the achievements of this age will be the realization that in our age religious pluralism is the will of God, that the relationship between Judaism and Christianity will be one of mutual reverence, that without denying profound divergences, Jew and Christian will seek to help each other in understanding each one's respective commitment and in deepening appreciation of what God means. And I should like to make some suggestions in the hope they will be taken in the right spirit. Although I may be critical, I shall be offering the critique of a friend.

My own suggestion, first, is that Christian renewal should imply confrontation with Judaism out of which it emerged. Separated from its source, Christianity is easily exposed to principles alien to its spirit. The vital challenge for the Church is to decide whether Christianity came to overcome, to abolish, or to continue the Jewish way by bringing the God of Abraham and His will to the Gentiles.

Now, in a real sense, I believe there is a battle going on in this twentieth century which centers around the Hebrew Bible. The prohibition and suppression of the Hebrew Bible in Soviet Russia is symbolic of that battle.

There is an old challenge to the Christian church going back to Marcion, a challenge that has never died out. The recurrent tendency to bring about a disengagement of the New Testament from the context of Judaism in which it came into being is evidence of what may be an unresolved tension. Marcion's spirit resounds in words recently uttered by a distinguished Catholic writer, that "it would be inexact . . . to suppose that the Christian *Theos* is the same" as the God of the Old Testament.[1] Marcion's criticism of the Old Testament or the Hebrew Bible proceeded from his conviction that the Gospel was something absolutely and utterly new. However, the Catholic Church of the second century appreciated the heritage, and rejected the one-sidedness of Marcion's doctrines.

Although I do not presume to judge matters of Christian doctrine, it seems utterly strange to assert that the community of Israel, "the Synagogue," did not have the capacity to determine the canonicity of holy Scripture. If this were the case, there could not have been any legitimacy in the scriptural text which the New Testament, and Jesus as depicted in it, quoted to authenticate their claims. Without the existence of a scriptural canon which is presupposed by the New Testament, the arguments of Jesus would be bereft of their foundation. And to turn a disagreement about the identity of this "Anointed" to an act of apostasy from God Himself seems to me neither logical nor charitable.

I would go beyond that and make a suggestion that what I believe the hour calls for is a renewal of understanding, renewed acknowledgement of the primacy of the Hebrew Bible. It was the Torah and the prophets that Jesus himself expounded, preached about. It was the Torah and the prophets that he revered as sacred Scripture, and it is in the words of the psalmist that Christians pray. To be sure, according to conciliar doctrine, equal reverence is required for all books, both of the Hebrew Bible and of the New Testament. And still, what lingers on in the theology is the assumption that the worth of the Hebrew Bible is in its being a preparation, a prehistory, not in its own grandeur.

Let me mention an example. At Vatican Council II each morning after Mass, an ancient copy of the Gospel was carried down the nave of

---

[1] Leslie Dewart, *The Future of Belief: Theism in a World Come of Age* (New York, 1966), 138.

329

St. Peter's Church and deposited on a golden throne on the altar. It was the Gospel only and no other book.[2]

According to Karl Rahner, "ultimately God effected the production of the Old Testament books to the extent that they were to have a certain function and authority in regard to the New Testament,"[3] not in their own majesty and preciousness, but only to the degree to which they play a role in the New Testament. Now this statement reminds me of the proof of divine providence that was offered in the seventeenth century by an Anglican bishop. He said, "You see, you can see Divine Providence in the fact that wherever there is a city, Providence supplied a river. . . . " I think this is a perspective that makes the infinite power of the Hebrew Bible conform to a rather narrow ecclesiastic principle.

Why is the Hebrew Bible indispensable to our existence? It is because the Bible urges us to ask and to listen: What does God require of me? And if there is any validity to my claim to be human it is the fact that I am aware of this problem: What does God require of me? It is through the Bible that I learn how to say "Here I am!"

The place and power of the Hebrew Bible is so important, because all subsequent manifestations and doctrines, whether in Judaism or Christianity, derive their truth from it, and unless they are continually judged and purified by it, tend to obscure and distort the living relationship of God to the world.

Now, the Bible is absent from contemporary thinking. It is quoted for edification, as a pretext for a sermon. It does not live as a power judging our lives. The Bible is respected as a source of dogma, not as living history. The Psalms are read, but the prophets are not. They are revered as forerunners, not as guides and teachers.

The Bible is on-going disclosure. Yet the word will not speak in a vacuum. It is a sledgehammer to the prophet, when he knows how to be an anvil. The words speak. The words are not signs, but outcries. The words stand for Him, they extend from Him, pleading unceasingly. The words are gates disclosing possibilities, possibilities of engagement to Him and the staccato of His presence and His concealments.

---

[2]See *Dialogue on the Way*, George A. Lindbeck, ed. (Minneapolis, 1965), 137 and 222.

[3]Karl Rahner, *Inquiries* (New York, 1964), 56. Equally astonishing is Rahner's statement: "Now the Synagogue, unlike the Church, does not have the authority to testify infallibly to the inspiration of the Scriptures. Even prior to the death of Christ, there existed no authoritative teaching *office* in the Old Testament, in the sense of a permanent institution formally endowed with inerrancy. There were individual prophets, but no infallible Church, for the eschatological event, the final and irreversible salvation act of God, had not yet occurred. It was possible for the Synagogue to apostatize from God, to turn a "No" to him and to his "Anointed" into its own official "truth," thus bringing about its own end as a divine institution" (ibid., 54).

An important root of contemporary nihilism is the age-old resistance to the Hebrew view of the world and of man. The Hebrew Bible has destroyed an illusion, the illusion that one can be an innocent bystander or spectator in this world. It is not enough to be a consumer in order to be a believer. The Bible has destroyed the ancient tradition in which the relation to the gods came with ease, in which gods accommodated themselves to our notions and standards, in which religion was above all a *guarantee*.

God is Judge and Creator, and not only Revealer and Redeemer. Detached from the Hebrew Bible, people began to cherish one perspective of the meaning of God, preferably His promise as Redeemer, and became oblivious to His demanding presence as Judge, to His sublime transcendence as Creator. The insistence upon His love without realizing His wrath, the teaching of His immanence without stressing His transcendence, the certainty of His miracles without an awareness of the infinite darkness of His absence — these are dangerous distortions. To believe too much is more perilous than to believe too little.

With your permission, I should like to say that it is difficult for a Jew to understand when Christians worship Jesus as the Lord, and this Lordship takes the place of the Lordship of God the Creator. It is difficult for a Jew to understand when theology becomes reduced to Christology. It is significant that quite a number of theologians today consider it possible to say, "we can do without God and hold on to Jesus of Nazareth."[4]

The overriding issue of this hour in the world and western civilization is the *humanity of man*. Man is losing his true image and shaping his life in the image of anti-man. Is there anything in the human situation today that makes reverence and responsibility a vital necessity? Is being human a supreme purpose? Does not man cease to be human if reverence and responsibility are gone?

The task of Christian renewal, I should like to hope, is above all the renewal of man, and the renewal of man is the *renewal of reverence*. How shall we prevent and heal man's discarding the power of freedom, his massive disposal of his power to decide? How shall we teach him to be involved in living engagement with the challenge and mystery of what being alive demands of him? The task is to deliver the mind from the illusion that availability and transparency are the exclusive attributes of being. False lucidity misguides us more than plain obscurity.

---

[4] "We do without God and hold to Jesus Christ" (Thomas Altizer and William Hamilton, *Radical Theology and the Death of God* [New York, 1966], 33).

The Renewal of Man

The renewal of man involves a renewal of language. To the man of our age, nothing is as familiar and trite as words. Of all things they are the cheapest, most abused, and least esteemed. They are the objects of perpetual defilement. We all live in them, feel in them, think in them, but since we fail to uphold their independent dignity, they turn waif, elusive — a mouthful of dust. When placed before the Bible, the words of which are like dwellings made of rock, we do not know how to find the door. There is no understanding the God of Israel without deep sensitivity to the holiness in words. For what is the Bible? Holiness in words. And we destroy all the gates of the Bible by the on-going desecration of the power of the word. The effect, I believe, is that we are all engaged, all involved, in the process of liquidating the English language. Promiscuity of expression, loss of sensitivity to words, has nearly destroyed the fortress of the spirit. And the fortress of the spirit is the *dabar*, the word. Words have become slums. What we need is a renewal of words.

The hour calls for *the renewal of the antecedents of faith*. The task is pre-theological. Revival and cultivation of basic antecedents of faith will help us to rediscover the image of man.

The renewal of man involves renewal of the sense of wonder and mystery of being alive, taking notice of the moment as a surprise. The renewal of man must begin with rebellion against reducing existence to mere fact or function. Why do I speak about the renewal of man? Because the Hebrew Bible is not a book about God. It is a book about man. Paradoxical as the Bible is, we must accept its essential premise: that God is concerned about man. If God had asked me for advice, I would have told him right after the first experience with Adam and Eve, "Don't bother with that species." But He goes on patiently, waiting for man. I say we need a revival of the premises and antecedents of faith because it is useless to offer conclusions of faith to those who do not possess the prerequisites of faith. It is useless to speak of the holy to those who have failed to cultivate the ingredients of being human.

Prior to theology is depth theology; prior to faith are premises or prerequisites of faith, such as a sense of wonder, radical amazement, reverence, a sense of mystery of all being. Man must learn, for example, to question his false sense of sovereignty.

The biblical message remains unacceptable unless seen in the context of essential attitudes and sensibilities. The tendency to rely completely, in our religious thinking, upon the so-called "contemporary experience" must be questioned. Contemporary experience is stunted experience, it is largely devoid of the higher qualities of experience.

Human beings have never been so bewildered about issues that challenge them most deeply. The famous dictum of Dietrich Bonhoeffer "that a world that has come of age...could live without the tutelage" of God presupposes a view of our world which is, I believe, naïve. Can you regard a world of Auschwitz and Hiroshima, of Vietnam and intercontinental ballistic missiles as a world that has come of age?

The most radical question we face does not really concern God but man — has not man proved to be incompatible or incongruous with the civilization that has emerged? Contemporary consciousness has not come to terms with its own experience. Overwhelmed by the rapid advancement in technology, it has failed to develop an adequate anthropology, a way of insuring the independence of the human being in the face of forces hostile to it.

The level of experience is wide but shallow. Man is gradually losing his ability to be in charge of his own life. He is beginning to regard himself not only as a self-contradiction but as an impossibility. To what degree is the predicament of man of this civilization, which is shaped by Judaism and Christianity, due to the failure of the Jewish and the Christian faith? Too many events happening too rapidly bombarded our consciousness too frequently for us to be able to ponder their significance. Contemporary experience is lacking in adequate corresponding reflection. In facing the tension between faith and the everyday world, we must not forget that our everyday experience is a problem rather than a norm. It is not assumed that we must renounce technology, but rather that we must ask whether man's image can be derived from technology.

I mention all this because, where ancient religions were concerned with a single aspect or some aspects of the human, the Hebrew Bible is concerned with all of human existence. In a sense, there is no preoccupation with the "religious" in the Bible; in the Bible what counts is the secular.

Sacramental — Prophetic

I should like here to touch briefly on a few other subjects I believe of concern to us here. Men of faith frequently succumb to a spectacular temptation: to personalize faith, to localize the holy, to isolate commitment. Detached from and irrelevant to all emergencies of being, the holy may segregate the divine.

Is the world of faith a realm of its own, an oasis of peace in the wilderness of the world? Is its task accomplished in being concerned for the holy, in offering spiritual comfort, while remaining aloof from the material and secular issues of this world?

In Israel there are two orientations, I believe, two directions of living for the sake of God, exemplified by the prophet and by the psalmist. I would suggest, therefore that the right goal would be to bring about some kind of balance or polarity — the proper polarity of the sacramental and the prophetic.

The psalmist is mostly guided by personal impulse. His own life, his concern for his spiritual situation, forms the background of his experiences. His attainments, his insights, and his purification constitute self-enhancement of significance to his existence as an individual. He exemplifies the individual's secret love affair with God.

The prophet's existence, by contrast, involves public affairs. Its content, aim, and events have an eminently super-personal character. Prophecy is not a private affair of the experience. The prophet is not concerned with his own salvation. His aim is not personal illumination, but the illumination of the people; not spiritual self-enhancement, but leading the people to the service of God. The prophet is nothing without his people. The prophet is a person who holds God and man in one thought at one time — and at all times.

When the people Israel arrived at the wilderness of Sinai, the Lord called to them out of the mountain, saying: "You shall be to me a kingdom of priests and a holy nation" (Exod. 19:6). A whole nation of priests? A people who so recently were slaves are told to be priests! And yet to Moses, our teacher, the charge was not radical enough. His vision of what the people ought to be was of a grandeur unsurpassed in the history of self-reflection. When Joshua the son of Nun, the minister of Moses, appealed to him to curb the prophetic outpourings of Eldad and Medad, Moses said to him: "Would that all the Lord's people were prophets, that the Lord would put His spirit upon them!" (Num. 11:29).

The two central ideas proclaimed in the Bible are *demand* and *promise*. Theologically, the demand precedes the promise. God first said to Abraham: "Go from your country . . . to the land that I will show you," and then " . . . and I will make of you a great nation . . . " (Gen. 12:1–2).

Existentially, the commandment is the link of man to God. Man's existence has a touch of eternity if God is waiting for his deeds. God's expectation, God's waiting for man, comes to expression in His commandments. Indeed, the transcendence alluded to in man's existence is that mysterious waiting, that divine expectation.

The Hebrew Bible records God's "mighty acts" in history. What is overlooked is that on every page of the Bible we come upon God's hoping and waiting for *man's* mighty acts.

This is the meaning of human existence. The world is unredeemed and deficient, and God is in need of man to be a partner in completing, in aiding, in redeeming. Of all the forms of living, doing is the most patent way of aiding. Action is truth. The deed is elucidation of existence, expressing thirst for God with body and soul. The Jewish *mitzvah* is a prayer in the form of a deed. The *mitzvot* are the Jewish sacraments, sacraments that may be performed in common deeds of kindness. Their nature is intelligible if seen in the light of God's care for man. The good act, ritual as well as moral, is a *mitzvah*, a divine offer, a divine representative.

Ultimate issues confront us in immediate situations. What is urgent for the Jew is not the acceptance of salvation but the preparing of redemption, the preparing *for* redemption.

The prophet Samuel would not abide in the security of his own home, of his piety. He moved from place to place, mixing with those who were not pious. In sharp contrast, Noah stayed at home, waiting for others to come to him. He and his family were saved, while his generation perished.

The urgent issue is not personal salvation but the prevention of mankind's surrender to the demonic. The sanctuary has no walls; the opportunity to praise or to aid has no limits. When God is silent, man must speak in His place. When God is hiding His compassion, man must reveal this love in His name.

Words become stale, and faith is tired. Unless we labor in helping God to carry out His promise — to be a father to those who are forsaken, a light to those who despair in secret darkness — we may all be forsaken by Him. Man must be involved in redeeming the promise: Nation shall not lift up sword against nation, and there shall be no war any more.

From the Jewish point of view, any doctrine that downgrades the demands and merely proclaims the promise is a distortion. An influential Protestant theologian has said: "The key to the ethics in the New Testament is contained in the following passages: Romans 6, 7, and the beginning of Romans 8. Here, as nowhere else, we perceive in great clearness and detail the identity of the central points in dogmatics and in ethics. The Sermon on the Mount, on the other hand, although it is the necessary presupposition of Christian ethics, is not its foundation. Its relation to Romans 6 is that of the Law to the Gospel."[5] I cite this viewpoint because it is utterly alien to the Jewish mind.

---

[5]Emil Brunner, *The Divine Imperative* (Philadelphia, 1947), 586.

Messianic Expectation

I should like to offer a rather controversial — and perhaps heretical — idea: that Christians have become less and less messianic; there is very little waiting. I may be mistaken. I hope I am. In primitive Christianity, there was a waiting for the second coming. In the consciousness of the Christian today, there seems to be no such awareness, no such waiting. Where is the promise of redemption?

Perhaps I can illustrate my point with a story told by a Christian pilgrim in the great drama by Maxim Gorki. There was once a man who was very poor and very old, who lived in Siberia. Things went badly for him, so badly that soon nothing remained for him to do but to lie down and die. But still he did not lose courage. He often laughed and said to himself, "It makes no difference — I can bear it! A little longer yet will I wait, and then I will throw this life aside and go into the Land of Justice." It was his only pleasure, this Land of Justice. At that time there was brought to Siberia an exile, a man of learning, with books and maps of all sorts. And that poor old sick man said to this great sage: "Tell me, I implore you, where lies the Land of Justice? How can one succeed in getting there?" Then the learned man opened his books, spread out his maps, and searched and searched, but nowhere could he find the Land of Justice. Everything else was correct, all the countries were shown, only the Land of Justice was not to be found.

The old man would not believe him. "It must be there," he said. "Look more closely! For all your books and maps," said he, "are not worth a whistle if the Land of Justice is not shown on them." The learned man felt himself insulted. "My maps," said he, "are absolutely correct, and a Land of Justice nowhere exists." The other was furious. "What," he cried, "have I now lived and lived and lived, endured and endured, and always believed there was such a country. And according to your maps there is none! That is robbery! You good-for-nothing knave! You are a cheat and no sage." Then he gave him a sound blow over the skull, and still another. And then he went home and choked himself. "There must be a Land of Justice," he said, "there must be and will be an Age of Justice."[6]

I would like to conclude with one more point. We Jews have gone through an event in our history which is like biblical history continued. The Jewish people everywhere have entered a new era in history. Jerusalem, the City of David, has been restored to the State of Israel. It is an event of high significance in the history of redemption. It is therefore proper, I believe, for me to share a few remarks with you on the subject.

---

[6]Maxim Gorki, *A Night's Lodging* (or *Submerged*), Act III.

But first: How should a Christian view this event?

According to the Book of Acts, right at the very beginning, the disciples to whom Jesus presented himself alive after his passion, asked him: "Lord, will you at this time restore the kingdom to Israel?" And he said to them: "It is not for you to know times or seasons which the Father has fixed by his own authority" (Acts 1:6–7).

Now, what is the meaning of this question and this answer? It was a time when Jerusalem was taken away from the Jewish people, the holy temple was destroyed, Jews were sold into slavery. Pagan Rome ruled in the Holy Land.

But there was a hope, a hope of deliverance from the pagans, there was the promise offered by the prophets that Jerusalem would be returned to the kingdom of Israel. So, when the disciples saw Jesus for the first time in these extraordinary circumstances, it is understandable this was the first question they asked, their supreme concern: "will you at this time restore the kingdom?" In other words, they asked the question about the restoration.

Jesus' answer was that the time of the fulfillment of the divine promise was a matter which lay within the Father's sole authority. So, earlier, he had assured them that he himself did not know the day or the hour of his parousia. "But of that day or that hour no one knows, not even the angels in heaven, nor the Son, but only the Father" (Mark 13:32). A similar awareness is common in Rabbinic literature. "Nobody knows when the house of David will be restored."[7] According to Rabbi Simeon ben Laqish (c. 250), "I have revealed it to my heart, but not to the angels."[8] Jesus' answer is as characteristic of the Rabbinic mind of the age as is the question itself.

However, this passage is generally interpreted in a different way. Reflecting a dichotomy in early Christian thinking, the position of the Galilean disciples was different from that of the hellenistic Christians. The original hope of the disciples was that the kingdom was at hand in the apocalyptic sense, but the hellenistic Christians, who in the end conquered the Empire, preached the Gospel as having present importance of each individual apart from the eschatological kingdom.

Thus Augustine explains that the meaning of the question was that, after the resurrection, Jesus was visible only to his followers, and that they were asking whether he would now make himself visible to everyone.[9]

---

[7] *Mechilta*, to Exodus 16:32.

[8] *Sanhedrin* 99a.

[9] F. J. Foakes Jackson and Kirsopp Lake, *The Beginnings of Christianity*, part 1, *The Acts of the Apostles*, 4:8.

Calvin maintains that "there are as many errors in this question as there are words."[10] Modern commentators assert that the question reflects the spiritual ignorance and hardness of hearts of the disciples,[11] "the darkened utterance of carnal and uninspired minds,"[12] and that the answer of Jesus was a rebuke."[13]

However, the simple meaning of the entire passage has a perfect *Sitz im Leben,* and both question and answer read like a *midrash.* The apostles were Jews and evidently shared the hope of their people of seeing the kingdom of God realized in the restoration of Israel's national independence. So now, hearing their master speak of the new age, they asked if this was to be the occasion for restoring the kingdom to Israel. We can scarcely fail to realize or to understand the naturalness of their question. The expectation was burned into their very being by the tyranny of the Roman rule. The answer confirms the expectation that the kingdom will be restored to Israel — an expectation expressed again and again in ancient Jewish liturgy. It is at point in history at

---

[10]He points out that apostles were gathered together when this question was posed, "to show us that it was not raised through the foolishness of one or two but through the concern of all. Yet their blindness is remarkable, that when they had been so fully and carefully instructed over a period of three years, they betrayed no less ignorance than if they had never heard a word. There are as many errors in this question as there are words. They ask Him concerning the kingdom; but they dream of an earthly kingdom, dependent upon wealth, luxury, outward peace, and the blessings of this nature. And while they assign the present as the time for restoring this kingdom, they desire to enjoy the triumph before fighting the battle. Before setting hands to the work for which they are ordained they desire their wages: they also are mistaken in this, that they confine to Israel after the flesh the kingdom of Christ which is to be extended to the farthest parts of the world. The whole question is at fault in this, that they desire to know things which are not right for them to know. No doubt they were well aware of what the prophets had said about the restoration of the kingdom of David, for they had often heard Christ speaking of this, and it was a common saying that in the depths of the captivity of the people every man's spirit was revived by the hope of the kingdom to come. They hoped that this restoration would take place at the coming of the Messiah, and so the apostles, when they saw Christ raised from the dead, at once turned their thoughts to this. But in so doing they betrayed what poor progress they had made under so good a Master. Therefore Christ in His short reply briefly reprimands their errors one by one, as I shall presently indicate. To 'restore' in this passage means to set up again that which was broken down and disfigured by many ruins. For out of the dry stock of Jesse should spring a branch, and the tabernacle of David which was miserably laid waste should rise again" (*Calvin's Commentaries, The Acts of the Apostles* [Edinburgh, 1965], 29).

[11]"The hardness of the disciples' hearts is apparent here as in Mark's Gospel: they awaited a material kingdom, for the Spirit was not yet poured out on them to give them a more enlightened conception of it" (C. S. C. Williams, *A Commentary on the Acts of the Apostles* [London, 1964], 56).

[12]G. T. Stokes, *The Acts of the Apostles* (New York, 1903), 29.

[13]R. B. Rackham, *The Acts of the Apostles* [London, 1901], 7); A. W. F. Blunt, *The Acts of the Apostles* [Oxford, 1922], 132.

which that restoration will take place that remains the secret of the Father.[14]

It is very likely that, following Daniel and Esdras, calculations were made to predict the time of the coming of the restoration. However, most Rabbis disapproved such computations which deal with "a time, two times, and half a time" of Daniel 7:25. Jesus' answer is not a rebuke of the apostles' hope, it is rather a discouragement of messianic calculations (see Luke 17:20–21).

Jesus' expectation that Jerusalem would be restored to Israel is implied in his prediction that "Jerusalem will be trodden down by the Gentiles, until the times of the Gentiles are fulfilled" (Luke 21:24). Some commentators see in these words a prediction of "the re-establishment of Jerusalem as a capital of the Jewish nation." By "the times of the Gentiles" is probably meant "the period God has fixed for the punishment of the Jews."[15]

Several weeks ago I was privileged to be in Jerusalem, and upon my return I wrote my impressions of Jerusalem and particularly of what the Wall, the Western Wall means to us. In the following personal remarks, I shall attempt to show what Jerusalem means to my people....

You see Jerusalem only when you hear. She has been an ear when no one else heard, an ear open to the prophets' denunciations, to the prophets' consolations, to the lamentations of the ages, to the hopes of countless sages and saints, and to the prayers flowing from distant places. And she is more than an ear. Jerusalem is a *witness*, an echo of eternity. Stand still and listen. We know Isaiah's voice from hearsay; but these stones have heard what he said concerning Judah and Jerusalem:

> It shall come to pass in latter days...
> out of Zion shall go forth the law,
> and the word of the Lord from Jerusalem.
> He shall judge between the nations,
> and shall decide for many peoples;
> nation shall not lift up sword against nation,
> neither shall they learn war any more.
> (Isa. 2:3, 4).

Jerusalem was stopped in the middle of her speech. She is a voice interrupted. Let Jerusalem speak again to our people, to all people.

---

[14]F. F. Bruce, *Commentary on the Book of the Acts* (Grand Rapids, 1954), 38.

[15]William F. Howard, *St. Luke*, The Interpreter's Bible, 308; E. Earle Ellis, *The Gospel of Luke* (London, 1966), 245. Alfred Plummer, *Commentary on ... St. Luke*, International Critical Commentary (New York, 1896), 483, lists six possible meanings.

The words have gone out of here and have entered the pages of holy books. And yet Jerusalem has not given herself away. There is so much more in store. Jerusalem is never at the end of the road. She is the city where the expectation of God was born, where the anticipation of lasting peace came into being. Jerusalem is waiting for the prologue, for the new beginning.

What is the secret of Jerusalem? Her past is a prelude. Her power is in reviving. Her silence is prediction; the walls are in suspense. It may happen any moment: a shoot may come forth from the stump of Jesse; a branch may grow out of his roots (Isa. 11:1).

Bibliography

References included in this bibliography are mainly to books and articles dealing with the topic of this volume, Jewish perspectives on Christianity. The extensive literature on Jewish-Christian relations and mutual dialogue has only been considered where it significantly contributes to this subject. In the case of the five Jewish thinkers whose views are presented, I have tried to include their most significant works, even where they do not directly deal with Christianity, in order to provide the background out of which their views on Christianity developed. Where a definitive edition of an author's collected works exists (e.g., Buber, Rosenzweig), it is also included here.

For each of the five authors a selection of books and articles dealing with his views on Christianity is supplied. As a final section, I have added a number of books and articles by authors other than those represented in this volume, under the heading "Recent Writings on Christianity by Jewish Authors."

General

Agus, Jacob B., ed. *Judaism and Christianity: Selected Accounts, 1892–1962*. New York: Arno Press, 1973. "The essays ... illustrate ... how Jewish scholars in the past century regard the emergence of Christianity out of the Jewish faith."

Ben Chorin, Schalom. "Das Jesus-Bild im modernen Judentum." *Zeitschrift für Religions- und Geistesgeschichte* (Leiden-Cologne) 5, no. 3 (1953): 231–257. Reprinted (in expanded form) in the author's *Im jüdisch-christlichen Gespräch*. Berlin: Käthe Vogt Verlag, 1962.

Casper, Bernhard. *Das dialogische Denken. Eine Untersuchung der religions-philosophischen Bedeutung Franz Rosenzweigs, Ferdinand Ebners und Martin Bubers*. Freiburg: Herder, 1967.

Fleischmann, Jacob [Eugène]. *The Problem of Christianity in Modern Jewish Thought* [Heb.]. Jerusalem: Magnes Press, 1964.

Geis, R. R., and H.-J. Kraus, eds. *Versuche des Verstehens: Dokumente jüdisch-christlicher Begegnung aus den Jahren 1918–1933*. Munich: Chr. Kaiser Verlag, 1966.

Hagner, Donald A. *The Jewish Reclamation of Jesus: An Analysis and Critique of Modern Jewish Study of Jesus*. Grand Rapids: Academie Books–Zondervan, 1984. Contains bibliography, 313–321.

Henrix, Hans-Hermann, and Werner Licharz, eds. *Welches Judentum steht welchem Christentum gegenüber?* Arnoldshainer Texte, vol. 36. Frankfurt am Main: Haag und Herchen Verlag, 1985.

Hoenig, Sidney B. "A Survey of Jewish Scholarship through the Ages on Jesus and Christianity" In *Fifteen Years of Catholic-Jewish Dialogue 1970–1985: Selected Papers*, 87–102. Rome: Libreria Editrice Vaticana, Città del Vaticano, 1988.

Jacob, Walter. *Christianity through Jewish Eyes: The Quest for Common Ground*. [Cincinnati:] Hebrew Union College Press, 1974. Contains bibliography, 239–250.

Kremers, Heinz, and Julius H. Schoeps, eds. *Das jüdisch-christliche Religionsgespräch*. Stuttgart-Bonn: Burg Verlag, 1988.

Liebeschütz, Hans. *Von Georg Simmel zu Franz Rosenzweig*. Studien zum Jüdischen Denken im deutschen Kulturbereich (Leo Baeck Institut). Tübingen: J. C. B. Mohr, 1970. Chap. 2: Leo Baeck and Protestantism; chap. 3/2: Franz Rosenzweig.

Lindeskog, Gösta. *Die Jesusfrage im neuzeitlichen Judentum*. 2d ed. Darmstadt: Wissenschaftliche Buchgesellschaft, 1973. Reprint of Uppsala ed., 1938. Contains bibliography, 328–369.

Moore, George Foot. "Christian Writers on Judaism." *Harvard Theological Review* 14, no. 3 (July 1921): 197–254.

Rengstorf, Karl Heinrich, and Siegfried von Kortzfleisch, eds. *Kirche und Synagoge: Handbuch zur Geschichte von Christen und Juden*, vol. 2. Stuttgart: Ernst Klett Verlag, 1970. See in Index, s.v. Baeck, Buber, Rosenzweig.

Rosmarin, Trude Weiss, ed. *Jewish Expressions on Jesus: An Anthology*. New York: Ktav Publ. House, 1977.

Schoeps, Hans Joachim. *The Jewish Christian Argument: A History of Theologies in Conflict*. Translated by D. S. Green from the 1961 German ed. New York: Holt, Rinehart, and Winston, 1963.

————. *Jüdisch-christliches Religionsgespräch in neunzehn Jahrhunderten*. Afterword by Edna Brocke. 4th ed. Königstein im Taunus: Jüdischer Verlag Athenäum, 1984.

Shermis, Michael. *Jewish-Christian Relations: An Annotated Bibliography and Resource Guide*. Bloomington and Indianapolis: Indiana University Press, 1988. Contains a section "Jewish Perspectives of Christianity: Works in Which Jews Have Contemplated [*sic*] Christianity," 71–74 (17 items).

The Study of Judaism: Bibliographical Essays. Introduction by Jacob Neusner. New York: Ktav Publishing House and Anti-Defamation League of B'nai B'rith, 1972. Contains information on Leo Baeck (144f.), Franz Rosenzweig (145f.), and A. J. Heschel (154–156) by Fritz A. Rothschild, and on Martin Buber (146–149) and Will Herberg (156f.) by Seymour Siegel.

Talmage, Frank E., ed. *Disputation and Dialogue: Readings in the Jewish-Christian Encounter.* New York: Ktav Publishing House and Anti-Defamation League of B'nai B'rith, 1975.

Williams, Arthur Lukyn. *Adversus Judaeos.* Cambridge: Cambridge University Press, 1935.

Leo Baeck

Works by Leo Baeck

Baeck, Leo. "Harnack's Vorlesungen über das Wesen des Christenthums." *Monatsschrift für Geschichte und Wissenschaft des Judentums* 45 (N.F. 9) (1901): 97–120. Reprint: "Harnacks Vorlesungen über das Wesen des Christentums." 2d enl. ed. Breslau: Wilhelm Koebner, 1902. 31 pp.

———. *Das Wesen des Judentums.* 1st ed. Berlin, 1905; 2d rev. ed. Frankfurt am Main: J. Kauffmann Verlag, 1923; 4th ed., 1926; 6th ed. Frankfurt am Main, 1932. English translation: *The Essence of Judaism*, translated by Irving Howe based on the translation by V. Grubenwieser and L. Pearl (1936), rev. ed., New York: Schocken Books, 1948.

———. "Romantische Religion. Ein erster Abschnitt aus einem Werke über 'Klassische u. romantische Religion.' " In *Festschrift zum 50 jährigen Bestehen der Hochschule für die Wissenschaft des Judentums*, 1–48. Berlin, 1922.

———. "Judaism in the Church." *Hebrew Union College Annual* 2 (1925): 125–144.

———. "Geheimnis und Gebot." *Der Leuchter*, 1921/22, 137–153. Reprinted in *Wege im Judentum: Aufsätze und Reden*, 33–48. Berlin: Schocken Verlag, 1933.

———. "Theologie und Geschichte." *Lehranstalt* 49 (1932): 42–54. English translation: "Theology and History," translated by M. Meyer in *Judaism* (Summer 1964): 274–285.

———. *Wege im Judentum: Aufsätze und Reden.* Berlin: Schocken Verlag, 1933.

———. *The Pharisees and Other Essays.* New York: Schocken, 1947. The 2d ed. (1966) contains a critical introduction by Krister Stendahl (see esp. p. xvii).

———. "The Faith of Paul." *Journal of Jewish Studies* 3, no. 3 (1952): 93–110.

———. "Some Questions to the Christian Church from the Jewish Point of View." In *The Church and the Jewish People*, Göte Hedenquist, ed., 102–116. London: International Missionary Council, 1954.

———. *Aus drei Jahrtausenden: Wissenschaftliche Untersuchungen und Abhandlungen zur Geschichte des jüdischen Glaubens.* 2d ed. Introduction by Hans Liebeschütz. Tübingen: J. C. B. Mohr, 1958.

———. *Judaism and Christianity: Essays.* Translated with an introduction by Walter Kaufmann. Philadelphia: The Jewish Publication Society of America, 1958. Contains: "The Son of Man," "The Gospel as a Document of the History of Jewish Faith," "The Faith of Paul," "Mystery and Commandment," and "Romantic Religion" (the last version).

Writings on Leo Baeck

Baker, Leonard. *Days of Sorrow and Pain: Leo Baeck and the Berlin Jews*. New York: Macmillan, 1978.

Freier, Recha. "Who Are the Guilty?," *Jewish Quarterly* (London), Spring 1965.

Friedlander, Albert H. *Leo Baeck: Teacher of Theresienstadt*. New York: Holt, Rinehart and Winston, 1968. Contains a comprehensive bibliography of Baeck's writings, 277–288.

Harnack, Adolf. *What Is Christianity?* Translated by Thomas Baily Saunders. Introduction by Rudolf Bultmann. New York: Harper Torchbooks, 1957. English translation of *Das Wesen des Christentums*, 1900. First English ed., New York and London, 1901.

Mayer, Reinhold. *Christentum und Judentum in der Schau Leo Baecks*. Stuttgart: W. Kohlhammer, 1961.

Reichmann, Eva G., ed. *Worte des Gedenkens für Leo Baeck* (commissioned by the Council of Jews from Germany, London). Heidelberg: Lambert Schneider, 1959.

Sandmel, Samuel. *Leo Baeck on Christianity*. Leo Baeck Memorial Lecture 19. New York: Leo Baeck Institute, 1975. 21 pp.

Simon, Ernst. "Geheimnis und Gebot: Über Leo Baeck." In *Brücken*, 385–393. Heidelberg: Lambert Schneider, 1965.

Wolf, Arnold J. "Leo Baeck's Critique of Christianity." *Judaism* 12, no. 2 (Spring 1963): 190–194.

Martin Buber

Works by Martin Buber

Buber, Martin. *Werke*. Munich: Kösel Verlag, Heidelberg: Lambert Schneider. Vol. 1 (1962): *Schriften zur Philosophie*; vol. 2 (1964): *Schriften zur Bibel*; vol. 3 (1963): *Schriften zum Chassidismus*.

———. *Der Jude und sein Judentum: Gesammelte Aufsätze und Reden*. Introduction by Robert Weltsch. Cologne: Joseph Melzer, 1963.

———. *Israel and the World: Essays in a Time of Crisis*. 2d ed. New York: Schocken Books, 1963. Contains: "The Faith of Judaism" (1929), "The Two Foci of the Jewish Soul" (1930).

———. *Briefwechsel aus sieben Jahrzehnten*. With a biographical outline by Grete Schaeder (1, 19–141), 3 vols. Heidelberg: Lambert Schneider, 1972–1975.

———. *I and Thou*. A new translation with a prologue "I and You" and notes by Walter Kaufmann. New York: Charles Scribner's Sons, 1970.

———. "The Two Foci of the Jewish Soul." In *Israel and the World*, 2d ed., 28–40. New York: Schocken Books, 1948, 1963; reprinted in Will Herberg, ed., *The Writings of Martin Buber*, 266–276. New York: Meridian Books, 1956.

———. *Two Types of Faith.* Translated by N. P. Goldhawk. London: Routledge & Kegan Paul, Ltd., 1951.

Writings on Martin Buber

Balthasar, Hans Urs von. "Martin Buber and Christianity." In *The Philosophy of Martin Buber*, Paul Arthur Schilpp and Maurice Friedman, eds., 341–359. The Library of Living Philosophers, vol. 12. La Salle, Ill.: Open Court, 1967.

Ben-Chorin, Schalom. *Zwiesprache mit Martin Buber.* Munich: List Verlag, 1966, 82–98, 153–154, 179–185, 194–195.

Brod, Max. "Judaism and Christianity in the Work of Martin Buber." In *The Philosophy of Martin Buber*, Paul Arthur Schilpp and Maurice Friedman, eds., 319–340. The Library of Living Philosophers, vol. 12. La Salle, Ill.: Open Court, 1967.

Brunner, Emil. "Judaism and Christianity in Buber." In *The Philosophy of Martin Buber*, Paul Arthur Schilpp and Maurice Friedman, eds., 309–318. The Library of Living Philosophers, vol. 12. La Salle, Ill.: Open Court, 1967.

Diamond, Malcolm L. *Martin Buber: Jewish Existentialist.* New York: Oxford University Press, 1960 (chap. 7: "The Jewish Jesus and the Christ of Faith," 73–106).

Friedman, Maurice. *Martin Buber's Life and Work.* 3 vols. New York: E. P. Dutton, 1981–1983.

Hammerstein, Franz von. *Das Messiasproblem bei Martin Buber.* Studia Delitzschiana, vol. 1. Stuttgart: W. Kohlhammer Verlag, 1958.

Horwitz, Rivka. *Buber's Way to "I and Thou": The Development of Martin Buber's Thought and His "Religion as Presence" Lectures.* Philadelphia: The Jewish Publication Society, 1988.

Kraft, Werner. *Gespräche mit Martin Buber.* Munich: Kösel Verlag, 1966 (see esp. 20, 48, 91, 115–116, 145, 152).

Osten-Sacken, Peter von der. "Begegnung im Widerspruch. Text und Deutung des Zwiegesprächs zwischen Karl Ludwig Schmidt und Martin Buber im Jüdischen Lehrhaus in Stuttgart am 14. Januar 1933." In *Leben als Begegnung: Ein Jahrhundert Martin Buber (1878–1978)*, 116–144. Berlin: Institut Kirche und Judentum, no. 7 (1978). Includes the original texts of Karl Ludwig Schmidt's and Buber's addresses of January 14, 1933.

Schaeder, Grete. *The Hebrew Humanism of Martin Buber.* Detroit: Wayne University Press, 1973. "The Dialogue with Christianity," 388–410.

Schilpp, Paul Arthur, and Maurice Friedman, eds. *The Philosophy of Martin Buber.* The Library of Living Philosophers, vol. 12. La Salle, Ill.: Open Court, 1967. Extensive bibliography by Maurice Friedman, 747–786.

Scholem, Gershom. "An einem denkwürdigen Tage." *Judaica* [1]. Frankfurt am Main: Suhrkamp Verlag, 1963, 207–215. Speech at the celebration of the conclusion of Buber's Bible translation, February 1961.

Smith, Wilfred C. *The Meaning and End of Religion.* New York, 1962. Discussion of this book in *Harvard Theological Review* 58:437–451.

———. *Faith and Belief.* Princeton, 1979, 325–326 (n. 65).

Stegemann, Ekkehard W. "Auf dem Weg zu einer biblischen Freundschaft: Das Zwiegespräch zwischen Martin Buber und Karl Ludwig Schmidt." In *Das jüdisch-christliche Religionsgespräch*, Heinz Kremers and Julius H. Schoeps, eds., 131–149. Stuttgart-Bonn: Burg Verlag, 1988.

Werblowsky, R. J. Zwi. "Reflections on Martin Buber's Two Types of Faith." *Journal of Jewish Studies* 39, no. 1 (Spring 1988): 92–101.

Wyschogrod, Michael. "Buber's Evaluation of Christianity: A Jewish Perspective." In *Martin Buber: A Centenary Volume*, Haim Gordon and Jochanan Bloch, eds. 456–472. New York: Ktav Publishing Co. (for Ben Gurion University), 1984.

Kirchliches Jahrbuch für die evangelischen Landeskirchen Deutschlands 57 (1930): 257–259.

Franz Rosenzweig

Works by Franz Rosenzweig

Rosenzweig, Franz. *Der Mensch und sein Werk: Gesammelte Schriften*. The Hague and Dordrecht (Netherlands). Vols. 1/1 and 1/2: *Briefe und Tagebücher*, 1979; vol. 2: *Der Stern der Erlösung*, 1976; vol. 3: *Zweistromland: Kleinere Schriften zu Glauben und Denken*, 1982; vols. 4/1 and 4/2: *Sprachdenken*: 4/1 *Jehuda Halevi: 95 Hymnen und Gedichte*, German and Hebrew, 1983; 4/2: *Arbeitspapiere zur Verdeutschung der Schrift*, 1984.

————. *Der Stern der Erlösung*. Frankfurt am Main: J. Kauffmann Verlag, 1st ed., 1921, 2d ed., 1930, 3d ed., Heidelberg, 1954, 4th ed., with an added Introduction by Reinhold Mayer and additional notes and indices by Annemarie Mayer, in *Gesammelte Schriften* 2. The Hague: Martinus Nijhoff, 1976.

————. *The Star of Redemption*. Translated by William W. Hallo. New York: Holt, Rinehart and Winston, 1971; paperback ed., Notre Dame University Press.

Rosenstock-Huessy, ed. *Judaism Despite Christianity: The "Letters on Christianity and Judaism" between Eugen Rosenstock-Huessy and Franz Rosenzweig*. University, Ala.: University of Alabama Press, 1969. With an Introduction by Harold Stahmer and essays about the correspondence by Alexander Altmann and Dorothy M. Emmet (the translator of the letters).

Writings on Franz Rosenzweig

Bowler, Maurice G. "Rosenzweig on Judaism and Christianity: The Two Covenant Theory." *Judaism* 22, no. 4 (Fall 1973): 475–481.

Clawson, Dan. "Rosenzweig on Judaism and Christianity: A Critique." *Judaism* 19, no. 1 (Winter 1970): 91–98.

Fackenheim, Emil L. *To Mend the World: Foundations of Future Jewish Thought*. New York: Schocken Books, 1982, chap. 2, sec. 3, 58–101.

Fleischmann, Eugène. "Franz Rosenzweig." In *Le Christianisme 'mis a nu,'* 182–224. Paris: Plon, 1970.

Friedmann, Friedrich Georg. "Franz Rosenzweigs Neues Denken. Sein Beitrag zum jüdisch-christlichen Dialog." In *Der Philosoph Franz Rosenzweig (1886–*

1929): Internationaler Kongress–Kassel 1986, W. Schmied-Kowarzik, ed., 1: 399–411. Freiburg and Munich: Verlag Karl Alber, 1988.

Glatzer, Nahum N., ed. *Franz Rosenzweig: His Life and Thought.* New York: Schocken, 1953.

Görtz, Heinz-Jürgen. "Franz Rosenzweig und Hans Ehrenberg." In *Das jüdisch-christliche Religionsgespräch*, Heinz Kremers and Julius H. Schoeps, eds., 90–113. Stuttgart-Bonn: Burg Verlag, 1988.

Horwitz, Rivka. "Judaism Despite Christianity." *Judaism* 24, no. 3 (Summer 1975): 306–318.

Mayer, Reinhold. "Apologie und Polemik bei Franz Rosenzweig." In *Der Philosoph Franz Rosenzweig (1886–1929): Internationaler Kongress–Kassel 1986*, W. Schmied-Kowarzik, ed., 1:413–424. Freiburg and Munich: Verlag Karl Alber, 1988.

Mendes-Flohr, Paul, ed. *The Philosophy of Franz Rosenzweig.* Hanover, N.H.: University Press of New England, 1988. Contains eleven papers on Rosenzweig delivered at a 1986 symposium in Jerusalem.

Mosès, Stéphane. *System and Revelation: The Philosophy of Franz Rosenzweig.* Detroit: Wayne State University Press, 1992. Chaps. 8 and 9 deal with Christianity and Judaism. French original: Éditions du Seuil, 1982.

———. "Judentum und Christentum in der modernen Welt: Der Briefwechsel zwischen Franz Rosenzweig und Eugen Rosenstock von Mai bis Dezember 1916." In *Das jüdisch-christliche Religionsgespräch*, Heinz Kremers and Julius H. Schoeps, eds., 71–89. Stuttgart-Bonn: Burg Verlag, 1988.

Neher, André. "Une approche théologique et sociologique de la relation judéo-chrétienne: le dialogue de F. R.–Eugen Rosenstock." *Cahiers de l'Institut de science économique appliquée.* Série M. Recherches et dialogues philosophiques et économiques, no. 6 (December 1959): 5–36.

Schmied-Kowarzik, Wolfdietrich, ed. *Der Philosoph Franz Rosenzweig (1886–1929): Internationaler Kongress–Kassel 1986.* 2 vols. Freiburg and Munich: Karl Alber, 1988.

Schwarzschild, Steven S. "Rosenzweig on Judaism and Christianity." *Conservative Judaism* 10, no. 2 (Winter 1956): 41–48.

Talmon, Shemaryahu. "Das Verhältnis von Judentum und Christentum im Verständnis Franz Rosenzweigs." In *Offenbarung im Denken Rosenzweigs*, Richard Schaeffler, Bernhard Casper, Shemaryahu Talmon, and Yehoshua Amir, eds., 119–141. Essen: Ludgerus Verlag, 1979.

Taubes, Jacob. "The Issue between Judaism and Christianity: Facing up to the Unresolvable Difference." *Commentary* 16, no. 6 (December 1953): 525–533.

Will Herberg

Works by Will Herberg

Herberg, Will. "The Theology of Antisemitism" [a review article on A. Roy Eckardt, *Christianity and the Children of Israel* (1948)]. *The Menorah Journal* 37, no. 2 (1949): 272–279.

——. "Beyond Time and Eternity: Reflections on Passover and Easter." *Christianity and Crisis*, April 18, 1949. Reprinted in *Faith Enacted as History*, 66–71.

——. *Judaism and Modern Man: An Interpretation of Jewish Religion*. New York: Farrar Straus and Young, 1951.

——. "A Jew Looks at Catholics." *Commonweal*, May 22, 1953, 174–177.

——. "Judaism and Christianity: Their Unity and Difference." *The Journal of Bible and Religion* 21 (1953). Reprinted in *Faith Enacted as History*, 44–64.

——, ed. *Four Existentialist Theologians: A Reader from the Works of Jacques Maritain, Nicolas Berdyaev, Martin Buber, and Paul Tillich*. Garden City, N.Y.: Doubleday Anchor Books, 1958; Introduction, 1–24.

——. *Protestant-Catholic-Jew: An Essay in American Religious Sociology*. Rev. ed. Garden City, N.Y.: Anchor Books, 1960.

——. "The Council, the Ecumenical Movement and the Problem of *Aggiornamento*." Address at the Golden Jubilee National Newman Congress, September 3, 1965. 8 pp. Typescript in the Will Herberg Collection at Drew University Library, Madison, N.J.

——. "A Jew Looks at Jesus." In *The Finality of Christ*, Dow Kirkpatrick, ed. Nashville: Abingdon Press, 1966. Reprinted in *Faith Enacted as History*, 84–93.

——. *Faith Enacted as History: Essays in Biblical Theology*. Edited with an introduction by Bernhard W. Anderson. Philadelphia: Westminster Press, 1976.

——. *From Marxism to Judaism: The Collected [Selected (?)] Essays of Will Herberg*. Edited with an introduction by David G. Dalin. New York: Markus Wiener Publishing, 1989.

Writings on Will Herberg

Anderson, Bernhard W. "Will Herberg as Biblical Theologian." Introduction to *Faith Enacted as History*, 9–28.

——. "Herberg as Theologian of Christianity." *National Review* 29, no. 30 (August 5, 1977): 884f.

Ausmus, Harry J. *Will Herberg: From Right to Right*. Studies in Religion. Chapel Hill: University of North Carolina Press, 1987.

Diggins, John P. *Up from Communism: Conservative Odysseys in American Intellectual History*. New York: Harper & Row, 1975, chap. 3 (118–159), chap. 7 (269–302), and chap. 9 (360–370).

Rothschild, Fritz A. "Herberg as Jewish Theologian." *National Review* 29, no. 30 (August 5, 1977): 885f.

Siegel, Seymour. "Will Herberg (1902–1977): A Baᶜal Teshuvah [Returner] Who Became Theologian, Sociologist, Teacher." In *American Jewish Year Book*

1978, 529–537. New York: American Jewish Committee, and Philadelphia: Jewish Publication Society of America, 1977.

Abraham Joshua Heschel

Works by Abraham Joshua Heschel

Heschel, Abraham Joshua. *Die Prophetie* [German]. Mémoires de la Commission Orientaliste, no. 22. Cracow: The Polish Academy of Sciences, and Berlin: Erich Reiss Verlag, 1936.

———. *Man Is Not Alone: A Philosophy of Religion*. New York: Farrar, Straus, and Young, and Philadelphia: The Jewish Publication Society of America, 1951.

———. *Man's Quest for God: Studies in Prayer and Symbolism*. New York: Charles Scribner's Sons, 1954.

———. *God in Search of Man: A Philosophy of Judaism*. New York: Farrar, Straus and Cudahy, 1955, and Philadelphia: The Jewish Publication Society of America, 1956.

———. *The Prophets*. New York: Harper and Row, and Philadelphia: The Jewish Publication Society of America, 1962 (paperback edition in 2 vols.: New York: Harper Torchbooks, vol. 1, 1969; vol. 2, 1971).

———. "A Hebrew Evaluation of Reinhold Niebuhr." In *Reinhold Niebuhr: His Religious, Social, and Political Thought*. C. W. Kegley and R. W. Bretall, eds. Library of Living Theology, vol. 2, 391–410. New York: Macmillan Company, 1956.

———. "Protestant Renewal: A Jewish View." *The Christian Century* 80, no. 49 (December 4, 1963): 1501–1504.

———. "No Religion Is an Island." Inaugural lecture as Harry Emerson Fosdick Visiting Professor at Union Theological Seminary, New York. *Union Seminary Quarterly Review* 21, no. 2, part 1 (January 1966): 117–134.

———. *The Insecurity of Freedom: Essays on Human Existence*. New York: Farrar, Straus and Giroux, 1966.

———. Discussion on Second Vatican Council and the Jews. In *Vatican II: An Interfaith Appraisal*, John H. Miller, C.S.B., ed., 373–374. Notre Dame and London: Notre Dame University Press, 1966.

———. "The Jewish Notion of God and Christian Renewal." In *Renewal of Religious Thought: Proceedings of the Congress on the Theology of the Church Centenary of Canada, 1867–1967*, L. K. Shook, C.S.B., ed., 105–129. Montreal: Palm Publishers, and New York: Herder and Herder, 1968.

———. *Israel: An Echo of Eternity*. New York: Farrar, Straus and Giroux, 1969.

———. *A Passion for Truth*. New York: Farrar, Straus and Giroux, 1973. Chap. 2: "The Kotzker and Kierkegaard," 85–113.

———. *Between God and Man: An Interpretation of Judaism from the Writings of Abraham J. Heschel*. Selected, edited, and introduced by Fritz A. Rothschild. Rev. ed. New York: Free Press-Macmillan, London: Collier Macmillan, 1976. Contains expository essay on Heschel and comprehensive bibliography up to 1975.

Writings on Abraham Joshua Heschel

Fleischner, Eva. "Heschel's Significance for Jewish-Christian Relations." In *Abraham Joshua Heschel: Exploring His Life and Thought*, John C. Merkle, ed., 142–164. New York: Macmillan, London: Collier Macmillan, 1985.

Merkle, John C. *The Genesis of Faith: The Depth Theology of Abraham Joshua Heschel*. New York: Macmillan, 1985. Bibliography: 271–277.

———, ed. *Abraham Joshua Heschel: Exploring His Life and Thought*. New York: Macmillan, London: Collier Macmillan, 1985. Symposium on the Life and Thought of Heschel, St. Joseph, Minn., 1983.

Rothschild, Fritz A. "Abraham Joshua Heschel (1907–1972): Theologian and Scholar" (necrology). In *American Jewish Year Book 1974*, 533–544. New York: American Jewish Committee, and Philadelphia: The Jewish Publication Society of America, 1973. Contains biographical sketch.

———. "Abraham Joshua Heschels Beitrag zum jüdisch-christlichen Religionsgespräch." In *Das jüdisch-christliche Religionsgespräch*, Heinz Kremers and Julius H. Schoeps, eds., 168–180. Stuttgart-Bonn: Burg Verlag, 1988.

Sherman, Franklin. *The Promise of Heschel*. Philadelphia and New York: J. B. Lippincott Co., 1970. Chap. 6: "Encounter between Christianity and Judaism."

Sherwin, Byron L. *Abraham Joshua Heschel*. 44–46. Atlanta: John Knox Press, 1979.

Recent Writings on Christianity by Jewish Authors

Ben-Chorin, Shalom. "The Image of Jesus in Modern Judaism." *Journal of Ecumenical Studies* 11, no. 3 (Summer 1974): 401–430.

Berkovits, Eliezer. *Faith after the Holocaust*. New York: Ktav Publishing House, 1973. Chap. 3: "The Vanishing West," 37–66. Originally published in *Judaism* 15, no. 1 (Winter 1966): 74–84, and 20, no. 1 (Winter 1971): 75–86.

Borowitz, Eugene B. *Contemporary Christologies: A Jewish Response*. Ramsey, N.J.: Paulist Press, 1980.

Cohen, Arthur A. *The Myth of the Judeo-Christian Tradition*. New York: Harper & Row, 1969.

Fackenheim, Emil L. "A Jew Looks at Christianity and Secularist Liberalism." In *Quest for Past and Future: Essays in Jewish Theology*, chap. 17, 263–277. Bloomington and London: Indiana University Press, 1968.

———. *To Mend the World: Foundations of Future Jewish Thought*. New York: Schocken Books, 1982 (paperback). "Concerning Post-Holocaust Christianity": 278–294. Reprinted (with changes) in *The Jewish Thought of Emil Fackenheim: A Reader*. Michael L. Morgan, ed., 244–254. Detroit: Wayne University Press, 1987.

Flusser, David. "Thesen zur Entstehung des Christentums aus dem Judentum." *Bemerkungen eines Juden zur christlichen Theologie*. Abhandlungen zum christlich-jüdischen Dialog, vol. 16. Helmut Gollwitzer et al., eds. Munich, 1984.

———. "Christianity." In *Contemporary Jewish Religious Thought*, Arthur A. Cohen and Paul Mendes-Flohr, eds., 61–66. New York: Chas. Scribner's Sons, 1987; paperback ed., Free Press, 1988.

Greenberg, Irving. "The Relationship of Judaism and Christianity: Toward a New Organic Model." *Quarterly Review* 4 (1984): 4–22.

Harris, Monford. "The Bifurcated Life — A Jewish Critique of Christian Thinking." *Judaism* 8, no. 2 (Spring 1959): 99–111.

Kaufmann, Yehezkel. *Christianity and Judaism: Two Covenants*. Translated from the Heb. *Golah ve-nekhar* (Exile and alien land) by C. W. Efroymson. Jerusalem: The Magnes Press, 1989.

Klenicki, Leon, and Richard John Neuhaus. *Believing Today: Jew and Christian in Conversation*. Grand Rapids: Wm. B. Eerdmans, 1989.

McKain, David W., ed. *Christianity: Some Non-Christian Approaches*. New York: McGraw-Hill Book Co., 1964; reprint: Greenwood, in library binding.

Matt, Hershel. "How Shall a Believing Jew View Christianity?" *Judaism* 24, no. 4 (Fall 1975): 391–405.

Neusner, Jacob. "The Jewish-Christian Argument in the First Century: Different People Talking about Different Things to Different People." *Cross Currents* 35, no. 2 (Summer/Fall 1985): 148–158.

———. "Judaism and Christianity: Their Relationship Then, Their Relationship to Come." *Cross Currents* 39, no. 1 (Spring 1989): 10–20.

———. "Two Faiths Talking about Different Things." In *The World and I* 2, no. 1, 679–690. Washington: Washington Times Corp.

———. "The Absoluteness of Christianity and the Uniqueness of Judaism: Why Salvation Is Not of the Jews." *Interpretation* 43, no. 1 (January 1989): 18–31.

Novak, David. "Jewish Views of Christianity." *The New Catholic World* 228, no. 1367 (September–October 1985): 196–202.

———. *Jewish Christian Dialogue: A Jewish Justification*. New York and Oxford: Oxford University Press, 1989.

Petuchowski, Jakob J. "The Dialectics of Salvation History." In *Brothers in Hope*, John M. Oesterreicher, ed., The Bridge, 5, 9–78. New York: Herder and Herder, 1970.

———. "'Arbeiter in demselben Weinberg': Ansätze zu einer jüdischen Theologie des Christentums." In *Unter dem Bogen des Bundes*, Hans-Hermann Henrix, ed., 204–215. Aachen: Einhard Verlag, 1981.

———. "Zur Tagesordnung eines jüdisch-christlichen Gesprächs." *Orientierung* (Zürich), September 15, 1982, 190–192.

———. "'Der Gott der ganzen Bibel' — aus jüdischer Sicht." *Orientierung* (Zürich), January 31, 1983, 22–24.

———. "Toward a Jewish Theology of Christianity." In *Renewing the Judaeo-Christian Wellsprings*, Val Ambrose McInnes, ed., 41–52. New York: Crossroad, 1987.

———, ed. *When Jews and Christians Meet*. Albany: State University of New York Press, 1988.

————. "Looking Beyond the Scriptures." *Anglican Theological Review* 72, no. 1 (Winter 1990): 26–38.

————, and Clemens Thoma. *Lexikon der jüdisch-christlichen Begegnung*. Freiburg: Herder, 1989.

Rosmarin, Trude Weiss-. *Judaism and Christianity: The Differences*. New York: The Jewish Book Club, 1943. Reprint: paperback, New York: Jonathan David, 1965.

Sandmel, Samuel. *A Jewish Understanding of the New Testament*. Cincinnati: Hebrew Union College Press, 1957.

————. *We Jews and Jesus*. New York: Oxford University Press, 1965.

————. "A Jewish View of Jesus." Jewish Information Service (London), n.d. [197?].

Soloveitchik, Joseph B. "Confrontation." *Tradition* 6, no. 2 (1964): 5–29; reprinted in *A Treasury of "Tradition,"* N. Lamm and W. S. Wurzburger, eds., 55–78. New York: Hebrew Publishing Co., 1967; also in *Studies in Judaica*, L. D. Stitskin, ed., 45–68. New York: Ktav/Yeshiva University Press, 1974.

Wyschogrod, Michael. "Judaism and Evangelical Christianity." In *Evangelicals and Jews in Conversation*, Marc H. Tanenbaum, Marvin R. Wilson, and A. James Rudin, eds., 34–52. Grand Rapids: Baker, 1978.

————. "The Law, Jews and Gentiles: A Jewish Perspective." *Lutheran Quarterly* 21, no. 4 (November 1969): 405–415.

————. "A Jewish Perspective on Karl Barth." In *How Karl Barth Changed My Mind*, Donald M. McKim, ed., 156–161. Grand Rapids: Wm. B. Eerdmans, 1986.

Supplementary Bibliography for the Paperback Edition

General

Charlesworth, James H., et al., eds. *Jews and Christians: Exploring the Past, Present, and Future*. New York: Crossroad, 1990.

Engelhardt, Klaus. "Zu theologischen Neuorientierung im Verhältnis der Christen zum Judentum." *Freiburger Rundbrief*, Neue Folge, 2. Jg. (1995), 1:19–26.

McInnes, Val Ambrose, ed. *New Visions: Historical and Theological Perspectives on the Jewish-Christian Dialogue*. Tulane Judeo-Christian Studies Edition, vol. 3. New York: Crossroad, 1993.

Mittleman, Alan. "Christianity in the Mirror of Jewish Thought." *First Things* 25 (August–Sept. 1992): 14–21.

Thoma, Clemens. *Die theologischen Beziehungen zwischen Christentum und Judentum*. Grundzüge, Band 44. Darmstadt: Wissenschaftliche Buchgesellschaft, 1982.

Williamson, Clark. *A Mutual Witness: Toward Critical Solidarity between Jews and Christians*. St. Louis, Mo.: Chalice Press, 1992.

Zannoni, Arthur E., ed. *Jews and Christians Speak of Jesus*. Minneapolis: Fortress Press, 1994.

Writings on Leo Baeck

Homolka, Walter. *Jewish Identity in Modern Times: Leo Baeck and German Protestantism*. European Judaism, vol. 2. Providence: Berghahn Books, 1995.

Writings on Martin Buber

Novak, David. "Buber and Tillich" [philosophical exegesis of Ex. 3:14]. *Journal of Ecumenical Studies* 29 (Spring 1992): 159–174.

Writings on Franz Rosenzweig

Anckaert L., and B. Casper. *Franz Rosenzweig: A Primary and Secondary Bibliography*. Instrumenta Theologica 7. Leuven: Bibliotheek van de Faculteit der Godgeleerdheid van de K. U. Leuven, 1990.

Dober, Hans Martin. "Die Verhältnisbestimmung von Judentum und Christentum nach Franz Rosenzweig." In *Lernen in Jerusalem—Lernen mit Israel*, ed. Martin Stöhr, 371–90. Veröffentlichungen aus dem Institut Kirche und Judentum no. 20. Berlin: Institut Kirche und Judentum, 1993.

Haberman, Joshua O. "Salomon Ludwig Steinheim und Franz Rosenzweig. Der erste und der letzte deutsch-jüdische Theologe der Offenbarung in der Neuzeit." In *Philo des 19. Jahrhunderts*, ed. Julius Schoeps et al., 43–61. Haskala no. 4. Hildesheim: Georg Olms, 1993.

Hammerstein, Franz von. "From Franz Rosenzweig's New Thoughts on the Christian-Jewish Dialogue in Germany after the Holocaust (on the reception of Franz Rosenzweig in Germany." In *Remembering for the Future*, vol. 3., ed. Y. Bauer, Alice Eckhardt, and H. Littell, 2471–2477. Oxford: Pergamon Press, 1989.

Layman, David Wayne. "Revelation in the Praxis of the Liturgical Community: Jewish-Christian Dialogue with Special Reference to the Work of John Williamson Nevin and Franz Rosenzweig." PhD. thesis, Temple University, 1994.

Miller, Ronald H. *Dialogue and Disagreement: Franz Rosenzweig's Relevance to Contemporary Jewish-Christian Understanding*. Lanham, Md.: University Press of America, 1989.

Spiegler, Gerhard E. "Dialogue as Affirmation: Franz Rosenzweig's Contribution to Christian-Jewish Conversations." In *Religious Issues and Interreligious Dialogues*, ed. Charles Wei-Hsun Fu and Gerhard E. Spiegler, 427–435. Westport, Conn.: Greenwood Press, 1989.

Zak, Adam. *Vom reinen Denken zur Sprachvernunft: Über die Grundmo-*

tive der Offenbarungs-philosophie Franz Rosenzweigs. Münchener philosophische Studien 1. Stuttgart: Kohlhammer, 1987.

Writings on Will Herberg

Rice, Daniel F. "Will Herberg: Catholic Apologist in Partibus Infidelium." *Drew Gateway* (Drew University) 49, no. 3 (1979): 10–20.

Works by Abraham Joshua Heschel

Heschel, Abraham Joshua. *To Grow in Wisdom: An Anthology of Abraham Joshua Heschel,* ed. Jacob Neusner and Noam M.M. Neusner. Lanham, Md.: University Press of America, 1990.

———. *Moral Grandeur and Spiritual Audacity: Essays,* ed. Susannah Heschel. New York: Farrar, Straus, Giroux, 1996.

Writings on Abraham Joshua Heschel

Blumenthal, David R. "Abraham Joshua Heschel: The Inadequacy of the Ecumenical Perspective." *Journal of Ecumenical Studies* 29 (Spring 1992): 249–253.

Kaplan, Edward K. *Holiness in Words: Abraham Joshua Heschel's Poetics of Piety.* Albany, N.Y.: SUNY Press, 1996.

Kasimow, Harold, and Byron L. Sherwin, eds. *No Religion Is an Island: Abraham Joshua Heschel and Interreligious Dialogue.* Maryknoll, N.Y.: Orbis Books, 1991.

Moore, Donald J. *The Human and the Holy: The Spirituality of Abraham Joshua Heschel.* New York: Fordham University Press, 1989.

Perlman, Lawrence. *Abraham Heschel's Idea of Revelation.* Brown Judaic Studies no. 171. Atlanta, Ga.: Scholars Press, 1989.

Rothschild, Fritz A. "Leben zwischen Verzweiflung und Hoffnung: Abraham Heschel als Interpret des Chassidismus." In *Der Chassidismus: Leben zwischen Hoffnung und Verzweiflung,* ed. Klaus Nagorni and Ralf Stieber, 89–106. Herrenalber Forum, Bd. 15. Karlsruhe: Evangelischer Pressverband für Baden, 1996.

Stöhr, Martin. "Abraham Joshua Heschel. Ein Kritiker und eine Stechfliege des religiösen Status Quo." In *Lebendige Tradition: Hilfen für die Gegenwart,* ed. Volker Hochgrebe and Klaus Hofmeister, 131–140. Würzburg: Echter, 1994.

Recent Writings on Christianity by Jewish Authors and Some Christian Theologians

Ben-Chorin, Shalom. "Did God Make Anything Happen in Christianity?" *Christian Identity: Concilium* 192, no. 2 (1988): 61–70.

Fisher, Eugene J., ed. *Visions of the Other: Jewish and Christian Theologians Assess the Dialogue.* New York and Mahwah: Paulist Press, 1994.

Fisher, Eugene J., and Leon Klenicki, eds. *In Our Time: The Flowering of Jewish-Catholic Dialogue.* New York: Paulist Press, 1990.

Klenicki, Leon, ed. *Toward a Theological Encounter: Jewish understandings of Christianity.* New York and Mahwah: Paulist Press, 1991.

Klenicki, Leon, and Geoffrey Wigoder, eds. *A Dictionary of the Jewish-Christian Dialogue.* Expanded edition. New York and Mahwah: Paulist Press, 1995.

Neusner, Jacob, with Andrew M. Greeley. *The Bible and Us: A Priest and a Rabbi Read the Scriptures Together.* New York: Warner Books, 1990.

Neusner, Jacob. *Jews and Christians: The Myth of a Common Tradition.* London: SCM Press; Philadelphia: Trinity Press International, 1991.

————. *Death and Birth of Judaism: Judaism in the Matrix of Christianity, Secularism and the Holocaust.* 2nd printing with a new introduction. Atlanta: Scholars Press for South Florida Studies in the History of Judaism, 1993.

————. *Telling Tales: Making Sense of Christian and Judaic Nonsense: The Urgency and Basis for Judaeo-Christian Dialogue.* Louisville: Westminster John Knox Press, 1993.

————, ed. *Judaism in Cold War America: 1945–1990,* vol. 4, *Judaism and Christianity: The New Relationship.* New York: Garland Press, 1993.

————. *Children of the Flesh, Children of the Promise: An Argument with Paul about Judaism as an Ethnic Religion.* Cleveland: Pilgrim Press, 1995.

Neusner, Jacob, and Bruce D. Chilton. *Christianity and Judaism: The Formative Categories,* vols. 1–3. Philadelphia: Trinity Press International, 1995–1997.

Sources and Acknowledgments

Leo Baeck

"Harnack's Lectures on the Essence of Christianity": selections translated by Dr. Elizabeth Petuchowski, from Leo Bäck, "Harnack's Vorlesungen über das Wesen des Christentums," *Monatsschrift für Geschichte und Wissenschaft des Judentums* 45 (N.F. 9) (Breslau, 1901): 97–98, 117–120.

"Mystery and Commandment": Leo Baeck, *Judaism and Christianity: Essays*, translated with an introduction by Walter Kaufmann, 171–185. Copyright © 1958 by The Jewish Publication Society of America. Reprinted by permission of The Jewish Publication Society.

"Romantic Religion": selections from Leo Baeck, *Judaism and Christianity: Essays*, translated with an introduction by Walter Kaufmann, 189–208, 211, 212–213, 214, 218–219, 220, 221–224, 234–235, 236–237, 240–242, 243–244, 248–251, 260–264, 265–266, 270–275, 281–282, 284–292. Copyright © 1958 by The Jewish Publication Society of America. Reprinted by permission of The Jewish Publication Society.

"Judaism in the Church": originally published in *Hebrew Union College Annual* 2 (1925): 125–144. Copyright © 1925 by the Hebrew Union College, Cincinnati, Ohio. Reprinted by permission of the *Hebrew Union College Annual*.

Martin Buber

"The Two Foci of the Jewish Soul": from Martin Buber, *Israel and the World: Essays in a Time of Crisis*, 28–40. Copyright © 1948 by Schocken Books, Inc., New York. Reprinted by permission of the Estate of Martin Buber.

"Church, State, Nation, Jewry" from Martin Buber, *Der Jude und sein Judentum: Gesammelte Aufsätze und Reden*, 1. Auflage. Copyright © 1963 Joseph Melzer Verlag, Cologne. 2. Auflage. Heidelberg: Verlag Lambert Schneider, forthcoming. Reprinted by permission of Verlag Lambert Schneider/Lothar Stiehm Verlag and the translator, Professor William W. Hallo.

"Two Types of Faith": selections from Martin Buber, *Two Types of Faith*, translated by Norman P. Goldhawk, 51–55, 162–174. London: Routledge and Kegan Paul, Ltd., 1951. Copyright © 1951 by Martin Buber. Reprinted by permission of Routledge and Kegan Paul.

"On Concluding the Translation of the Bible": selection translated by Dr. Elizabeth Petuchowski, from Martin Buber, *Werke*, 2. Band (*Schriften zur Bibel*), 1181–1182. Copyright © 1964 by Kösel Verlag KG, Munich, and Verlag Lambert Schneider, GmbH, Heidelberg. Translated and published by permission of Verlag Lambert Schneider/Lothar Stiehm Verlag.

Franz Rosenzweig

"Selections from the Letters": translated by Dr. Robert Schine, from Franz Rosenzweig, *Der Mensch und sein Werk: Gesammelte Schriften*, 1. Abteilung, 1. Band: *Briefe und Tagebücher* (1900–1918), 133–137, 141–143, 401–402. Copyright © 1979 by Martinus Nijhoff Publishers, The Hague, The Netherlands. Translated and published by permission of Kluwer Academic Publishers B. V., Dordrecht.

Also from *Judaism Despite Christianity: The "Letters on Christianity and Judaism" between Eugen Rosenstock-Huessy and Franz Rosenzweig*, edited by Eugen Rosenstock-Huessy, 131–136. Copyright © by University of Alabama Press. Reprinted by permission of Dr. Hans R. Huessy, Jericho, Vermont.

"The Star of Redemption": selections from Franz Rosenzweig, *The Star of Redemption*, translated from the Second Edition of 1930 by William W. Hallo, 336–353, 395–417. Copyright © 1970, 1971, by Holt, Rinehart and Winston, Inc. Reprinted by permission of Holt, Rinehart and Winston, Inc., and the translator, Professor William W. Hallo.

"A Note on Anthropomorphism": selection, translated by Bernard Barsky, from Franz Rosenzweig, *Der Mensch und sein Werk: Gesammelte Schriften*, 3. Abteilung: *Zweistromland*, 739–741. Copyright © 1984 by Martinus Nijhoff Publishers, Dordrecht, The Netherlands. Translated and published by permission of Kluwer Academic Publishers B. V., Dordrecht.

"The Significance of the Bible in World History": selection from *Franz Rosenzweig: His Life and Thought*, presented by Nahum N. Glatzer, 271–275. Copyright © 1953 by Schocken Books, Inc., New York. Reprinted by permission of Schocken Books.

Will Herberg

"Judaism and Christianity": originally published in *The Journal of Bible and Religion* 21 (April 1953). Reprinted by permission of the *Journal of the American Academy of Religion*, Decatur, Georgia, and Professor Donald G. Jones, Executor of the Will Herberg Estate.

"A Jew Looks at Jesus": from *The Finality of Christ*, edited by Dow Kirkpatrick, 91–101. Copyright ©1966 by Abingdon Press, Nashville. Reprinted by permission of Abingdon Press, Nashville, and Professor Donald G. Jones, Executor of the Will Herberg Estate.

Abraham Joshua Heschel

"More Than Inwardness": selections from Abraham Joshua Heschel, *God in Search of Man: A Philosophy of Judaism*, 293–296, 299. New York: Farrar, Straus and Cudahy, 1955. Copyright © 1955 by Abraham Joshua Heschel. Reprinted by permission of Farrar, Straus and Giroux, Inc.

"A Hebrew Evaluation of Reinhold Niebuhr": from *Reinhold Niebuhr: His Religious, Social, and Political Thought*, edited by Charles W. Kegley and Robert W. Bretall, 391–410. Copyright © 1956 The Macmillan Company, New York. Reprinted by permission of Sylvia Heschel, Executrix of Abraham Joshua Heschel.

"Protestant Renewal: A Jewish View": from Abraham Joshua Heschel, *The Insecurity of Freedom*, 168–178. New York: Farrar, Straus and Giroux, 1966. Copyright ©1963, 1966 by Abraham Joshua Heschel. Reprinted by permission of Farrar, Straus and Giroux, Inc.

"No Religion Is an Island": originally published in *Union Seminary Quarterly Review* 21, no. 2, part 1 (January 1966): 117–134. Copyright © 1966 by *Union Seminary Quarterly Review*, New York. Reprinted by permission of Sylvia Heschel, Executrix of Abraham Joshua Heschel.

"The Jewish Notion of God and Christian Renewal": selections from *Renewal of Religious Thought: Proceedings of the Congress on the Theology of the Renewal of the Church*, edited by L. K. Shook. Volume 1, pp. 106–124, 125–126. Copyright © 1968 by the Pontifical Institute of Medieval Studies, Toronto. Reprinted by permission of the copyright holder, the Pontifical Institute of Medieval Studies, Toronto.

Christianity (cont.)
 and Israel, 133–34
 Judaism and, 95–97, 151–53, 237,
  252, 271–73, 316
 differences and similarities, 240–42,
  246–55, 260, 267
 separation from, 142, 267, 301–3
 law and, 214–15
 messianism in, 336
 mystery and history in, 305
 mystery and sacrament in, 64–65
 mysticism and, 221
 and Old Testament, 15, 95–97, 223
 priest in, 202
 renewal of, 328–31
 as romanticism, 56–57, 59–60,
  62–65
 Rosenzweig on, 159–60
 saint in, 202
 theology of, 164, 200–201
 and time, 188–91, 196
 uniqueness of, 136–37
 and verification, 224–26
 and world, 167, 178
 see also Eschatology
Christology, 135, 163. *See also* Christ;
 Jesus
Church, 173, 194–95
 and state, 203–4
Commandment, 46–51, 297
 and deed, 75–76
 Protestantism and, 80
 See also Ethics; *Mitzvah*
Communication, Jewish-Christian,
 314–17
Covenant, 237, 240–42, 276–77, 305
Creation, 51
Creator, 285
Cross, 198
Culture, and history, 68–70

Dogma, 73–74, 307–8

Eckardt, A. Roy, 251, 253, 254
Ehrenberg, Hans, 160

Ehrenberg, Rudolf, 160
 letters to, 169–74
Election, 179–80, 212–13
Emunah (Heb), 151–53, 242
Eschatology, Christian, 206–7, 220–22
Ethics
 Bible and, 99
 mysticism and, 48–49
 Paulinism and, 77–78
 romanticism and, 58, 76–78
 See also Commandment
Evil, 284–86, 289–90, 292, 297
Ezekiel, 290

Faith, 65–68, 123, 151–53, 242,
 326–27

Geiger, Abraham, 44
Genesis, Book of, 285
Gnosticism, 96, 99, 224. *See also*
 Marcion
God
 Brunner on, 147
 covenant and, 258
 elimination of, 307
 as Father, 177, 200–201
 immediacy of, 124
 of Jews, 211–12
 "notion" of, 325
 revelation of, 136
 as Son, 200–201
 spiritualized, 207–8
 uniting of, 219–20
 and world, 288
Good, mixed with evil, 289–90, 292,
 297
Gospel, 50, 79, 277
Greeks, 61–63, 171

Haggada. See Aggadah
Hasidism, 112, 115, 269, 293–94
Halakhah, 249–50
Harnack, Adolf, 3, 8, 24–27, 42–45
Hebrew Bible (Old Testament)
 Book of Jonah in, 129
 and Christianity, 15, 95–97, 223

Contributors

Bernhard W. Anderson, formerly Dean and Professor of Biblical Theology at the Theological School of Drew University, is Professor Emeritus of Old Testament of Princeton Theological Seminary and Adjunct Professor of Old Testament at the Theological School of Boston University.

His writings include the widely used textbook *Understanding the Old Testament, Creation versus Chaos, The Unfolding Drama of the Bible,* and *Out of the Depths: The Psalms Speak for Us Today.* He is also editor of the two-volume Scribner's reference work *The Books of the Bible.*

Bernhard Casper is Professor of Christian Philosophy of Religion at the University of Freiburg i. Br. His writings include *Das dialogische Denken* (1967), a book on the thought of Franz Rosenzweig, Ferdinand Ebner, and Martin Buber, and *Sprache und Theologie* (1975).

He is co-editor of Rosenzweig's Letters and Diaries (vols. 1/1 and 1/2 of his *Gesammelte Schriften*) and has published a number of scholarly articles on the philosophy of Émmanuel Lévinas and Franz Rosenzweig.

J. Louis Martyn was the Edward Robinson Professor of Biblical Theology at Union Theological Seminary in New York and Adjunct Professor at Columbia University prior to his retirement in 1987. He has lectured at the universities of Amsterdam, Groningen, Utrecht, and Leiden as well as at the Pope Adrian College in Louvain, the *Kirchliche Hochschule* in Bethel, and the Institute for Advanced Theological Study in Jerusalem.

Known primarily for his books on the Gospel of John and for essays on the letters of Paul, he is the author of the commentary on Paul's Letter to the Galatians for the Anchor Bible.

John C. Merkle is Professor of Theology at the College of St. Benedict in St. Joseph, Minnesota, and at St. John's University in Collegeville, Minnesota. He is the author of *The Genesis of Faith: The Depth Theol-*

ogy of Abraham Joshua Heschel and the editor of *Abraham Joshua Heschel: Exploring His Life and Thought* (1985). He has also published numerous articles in scholarly and popular journals in Europe, Latin America, and North America.

Fritz A. Rothschild is the Joseph J. and Dora Abbell Professor Emeritus of Jewish Philosophy at the Jewish Theological Seminary of America in New York, where he has taught since 1960. From 1982 to 1990 he was the chairman of the Department of Jewish Philosophy. He has also served as Visiting Professor at New York University and Drew University and as the Martin Buber-Stiftungsprofessor at the University of Frankfurt am Main. He is the author of *Between God and Man: An Interpretation of Judaism from the Writings of Abraham Joshua Heschel.*
He has contributed chapters and articles on Jewish thought, especially the theology of A. J. Heschel, to a number of books and journals. He has lectured to academic and lay audiences in North America, South Africa, and Europe.

Ekkehard W. Stegemann has been Professor of New Testament at the University of Basel since 1985. He has written a number of articles on the subject of Christianity and Judaism and has published (with Rolf Rendtorff) a volume, *Auschwitz: Krise der christlichen Theologie* (1980). He is co-editor of *Kirche und Israel* and the *Neukirchener Theologische Zeitschrift.*

362

Index

Agape, 249
Aggadah, 25
Anthropomorphism, 227–28
Anti-Semitism, 107, 177, 310
Apocalypticism, 35–38, 41, 128
Augustine of Hippo, 101, 180

Baeck, Leo, 8, 9, 16
  on Christian ethics, 39–40
  on Christianity, 23–24, 28–30
  education of, 21–22
  on Harnack, 24–27, 42–45
  on history, 30–32, 34–35
  on Pauline apocalypticism, 35–38,
    41
Baptist movement, and Judaism, 32
Belief, Christian, 193
Bible
  Book of Genesis, 285
  Buber's translation of, 154–55
  and Christianity, 175
  demand and promise in, 334
  desanctification of, 304–5
  ethics and, 99
  evil and, 284–86
  in world history, 229–32
  See also Gospels; Hebrew Bible (Old
    Testament); New Testament
Bifurcation, meaning of, 222–26
Brunner, Emil, 146–47
Buber, Martin, 9–11, 16
  on Christianity, 116–17
  and Christians, 114–16
  life of, 111–13
  Nazis and, 118
Bultmann, Rudolf, 303

Calvin, John (Calvinism), 32, 104
Castle, The (Kafka), 148, 150
Casuistry, 81–82
Catholic Church, 31, 100–102, 275
  ethics and, 99
  evangelical piety and, 80
  faith and, 66–67
  humanity and, 83
  Jewish relations to, 321
"Chariot, The Tale of the," 217
Christ, 170, 194–96, 261–63. *See also*
  Jesus
Christendom, 191–93
Christianity
  after year 313, 169
  anthropomorphism in, 228
  Baeck on, 23–24
  and belief, 193
  Bible and, 175
  birth and rebirth in, 206
  Buber and, 114–17
  and Christ, 135, 194–96, 261–63
  and Christendom, 191–93
  and Church, 193–94
  Church and state for, 203–4
  dangers for, 210–11
  and deity, 170
  essence of, 28–30, 43, 199–200
  ethics of, 39–40
  and first man, 185–86
  and Greeks, 171
  Harnack on, 42–45
  Hebrew Bible and, 15, 95–97
  Herberg on, 236
  history of, 30–32
  humanity and, 205–6, 299

Christianity (cont.)
and Israel, 133–34
Judaism and, 95–97, 151–53, 237, 252, 271–73, 316
differences and similarities, 240–42, 246–55, 260, 267
separation from, 142, 267, 301–3
law and, 214–15
messianism in, 336
mystery and history in, 305
mystery and sacrament in, 64–65
mysticism and, 221
and Old Testament, 15, 95–97, 223
priest in, 202
renewal of, 328–31
as romanticism, 56–57, 59–60, 62–65
Rosenzweig on, 159–60
saint in, 202
theology of, 164, 200–201
and time, 188–91, 196
uniqueness of, 136–37
and verification, 224–26
and world, 167, 178
see also Eschatology
Christology, 135, 163. *See also* Christ; Jesus
Church, 173, 194–95
and state, 203–4
Commandment, 46–51, 297
and deed, 75–76
Protestantism and, 80
See also Ethics; *Mitzvah*
Communication, Jewish-Christian, 314–17
Covenant, 237, 240–42, 276–77, 305
Creation, 51
Creator, 285
Cross, 198
Culture, and history, 68–70

Dogma, 73–74, 307–8

Eckardt, A. Roy, 251, 253, 254
Ehrenberg, Hans, 160

Ehrenberg, Rudolf, 160
letters to, 169–74
Election, 179–80, 212–13
Emunah (Heb), 151–53, 242
Eschatology, Christian, 206–7, 220–22
Ethics
Bible and, 99
mysticism and, 48–49
Paulinism and, 77–78
romanticism and, 58, 76–78
See also Commandment
Evil, 284–86, 289–90, 292, 297
Ezekiel, 290

Faith, 65–68, 123, 151–53, 242, 326–27

Geiger, Abraham, 44
Genesis, Book of, 285
Gnosticism, 96, 99, 224. *See also* Marcion
God
Brunner on, 147
covenant and, 258
elimination of, 307
as Father, 177, 200–201
immediacy of, 124
of Jews, 211–12
"notion" of, 325
revelation of, 136
as Son, 200–201
spiritualized, 207–8
uniting of, 219–20
and world, 288
Good, mixed with evil, 289–90, 292, 297
Gospel, 50, 79, 277
Greeks, 61–63, 171

Haggada. See Aggadah
Hasidism, 112, 115, 269, 293–94
Halakhah, 249–50
Harnack, Adolf, 3, 8, 24–27, 42–45
Hebrew Bible (Old Testament)
Book of Jonah in, 129
and Christianity, 15, 95–97, 223

Jewish existence and, 320
Marcion and, 154
natural law and, 98
and New Testament, 230–31, 303,
  329–30
Paul and, 94, 146
primacy of, 329–31
See also Bible; New Testament
Hebrew Humanism (Buber), 113
Heilsgeschichte, 247
Heine, Heinrich, 1
Herberg, Will, 11–12, 235–39
Heschel, Abraham Joshua, 1, 5,
  12–13, 16
career of, 268–69
as communicator, 268
and Jewish-Christian relations, 271
writings of, 269–70
History, 30–32, 68–70, 305–7

Interfaith, 315
Islam, 323
Israel (state)
church as, 15
covenant of, 258–59
God of, 327–28
Jewish restoration to, 337–39
Judaism and, 132–34
nature of, 137
opposition to, 139
as remnant, 214, 218
as revelation, 274
suffering of, 138
I and Thou (Buber), 113

Jesus
Buber on, 11, 116, 120
and divinity, 106, 107, 135, 163
Jews on, 261–63
and messianic idea, 164, 276
as moral teacher, 256
and Paul, 116
person and significance of, 15
as prophet, 257
See also Christ

Jews
dangers for, 215–17
election of, 179–80
as *enfant terrible*, 185–86
God of, 211–12
hatred of, 224
humanity and, 204–5
on Jesus, 261–63
life for, 211
protest of, 223
restored to Israel, 337–39
and state, 184
stubbornness of, 174, 176
and world, 217
Jonah, Book of, 129
Judah Halevi, 322
Judaism
after year 70, 169
anthropomorphism in, 228
apocalypticism in, 128
Catholicism on, 275
and Christian dogma, 174, 176
Christianity and, 95–97, 151–53,
  252, 271–73, 316
as classical religion, 56, 60
co-existence of Christianity and, 237
rs corrective, 260
and deity, 170
differences of Christianity and, 142,
  246–51
faith of, 123
from within, 183
God of, 124–26, 130
Greek Bible and, 230–31
and Israel, 132–34
law and, 214–15, 278–79, 281–82
mystery and commandment in,
  46–51
mysticism and ethics in, 48–49
nature of man in, 287
and New Testament, 161
and "notion" of God, 325
opposition to, 139
paradox and, 291
Paul on, 93

Judaism (cont.)
  Plato and, 92–93
  Protestantism and, 303
  and redemption, 127, 130, 300
  similarity of, to Christianity, 240–42,
    251–55
  and time, 197–98
  uniqueness of, 136–37
  and verification, 224–26
  and world, 288–89
  See also Jews

Kafka, Franz, 147, 148, 150

Lavater, Johann Caspar, 4–5
Law
  Buber on, 122
  Judaism and, 278–79, 281–82
  Paul and, 51, 143–46, 174, 279
  sacrament and, 75–76
  of verification, 222–26
  world of, 214–15
  See also Torah
Luther, Martin (Lutheranism), 32, 66,
  68, 102

Maimonides (Moses ben Maimon),
  322
Man, 208–9, 293–96, 332–33
Man Is Not Alone (Heschel), 268
Marcion (Marcionism), 31, 329
  danger of, 39
  Judaism and, 96, 97
  and Old Testament, 154
  Paul and, 149
  See also Gnosticism
Marxism, 235–36
Mediator, The (Brunner), 146–47
Mendelssohn, Moses, 4–5
Messianic idea, 187–88
  birth of, 176
  and Christianity, 336
  in Church history, 105
  election and, 179, 212–13
  and Jesus, 164

romanticism and, 86–91
state of Israel and, 140–41
as universal redemption, 275
works and faith and, 143–46
Mishnah, 173
Mitzvah (pl *mitzvot*), 13, 14, 294,
  297–99, 335
Monotheism, 227
Mystery, 46–51, 64–65, 305–7
Mysticism, 48–49, 221, 269, 289–91

Nahmanides (Moses ben Nahman),
  3–4
Natural law, 98
Nazis (National Socialists), 118,
  310
New Testament, 161, 230–31, 303,
  329–30
New Thinking, The (Rosenzweig),
  161–62
Niebuhr, Reinhold, 235–36, 268,
  284–86, 292, 296–97

Oppenheim, Gertrud, letter to,
  185–86

Paul
  apocalypticism of, 35–38, 41
  Buber on, 120
  as Christian founder, 30–31
  and Hebrew Bible, 94, 146
  and Israel, 134
  Jesus and, 116
  on Judaism, 93
  law and, 51, 141–46, 174, 279
  and Marcion, 149
  romanticism and, 34–35, 41, 62–65,
    75–76
  See also Paulinism
Paulinism, 31–32
  Baeck on, 33, 34–35, 41
  and Christian history, 146–50
  ethics and, 77–78
  and faith, 153
  humanity and, 84

Judaism and, 95–96
Luther and, 32
works and faith in, 100
See also Paul
Pelagius (Pelagianism), 101–2
Piety, 80
Pistis (Greek), 151–53, 242
Plato, 92–93
Priest, 202, 208
Prophets, 306, 334–35
Prophets, The (Heschel), 269
Protestantism, 80, 279–80, 303
Psychology, 204–6

Realism, 286–87
Reconciliation, 52
Redemption, Judaism and, 127, 130, 300
Reden über das Judentum (Buber), 115
Religious existence, 313
Religious isolation, 311–12
Religious uniformity, 318
Remnant, 213–14, 218
Revelation, Israel as, 274
Roman Catholic Church. *See* Catholic Church
Romanticism
    Baeck and, 28–30
    casuistry and, 81–82
    Christianity as, 56–57, 59–60, 62–65
    commandment and deed in, 75–76
    culture and history, 68–70
    dogma and, 73–74
    and ethics, 58, 76–78
    and faith, 65–68
    of Greeks, 61–63
    humanity and, 82–86
    messianic idea and, 86–91
    nature of, 56–60
    of Paul, 34–35, 41, 62–65, 75–76
    redemption and, 85–86
    sacrament and, 70–73
    sentimentalism and, 78–81

Rosenstock-Hussey, Eugen, 8
    letters to, 174–85
Rosenzweig, Franz, 8, 130, 159–60

Sabbath, 54
Sacrament, 50, 64–65, 70–73, 75–76
Sacrifice, 181–82
Saint, 202, 208
Salvation, divine economy of, 240–42
Schmidt, Karl Ludwig, 118, 132
Sentimentality, 78–81
Shekhinah (Divine Presence), 218
Sinai, 297
Sola fide, 31, 50, 66, 103
Son of Man, 209
Spirit, 204–6
Star of Redemption, The (Rosenzweig), 159–60, 161
State, Jews and, 184
Synagogue, 173, 182

Theology, verification in, 222–26
Tillich, Paul, 6, 260
Time, 188–91, 196–98
Torah, 277, 295, 306
    and law, 218
    meaning of, 173, 192
    Paul on, 94
    See also Law
Two Types of Faith (Buber), 9–10, 119

Verification, meaning of, 224–26
Vocation, 247–48, 250, 261, 275

Works and faith, 106, 306
    in Calvinism, 104
    in Catholicism, 100–102
    dichotomy of, 280–81
    Paulinism and, 100, 143–46
    polarity of, 15
    Protestantism and, 279
World, 167, 178, 209–10, 216

Zionism, 112, 140, 270